The *AMERICAN HERITAGE*
History of
THE AMERICAN
REVOLUTION

The AMERICAN
History
THE AMER
REV

American Heritage/Bonanza Books · New York

By the Editors of AMERICAN HERITAGE
The Magazine of History

Editor in Charge: RICHARD M. KETCHUM

Narrative by BRUCE LANCASTER
with a chapter by J. H. PLUMB

Introduction by BRUCE CATTON

HERITAGE
of
ICAN
OLUTION

Staff for this Book

EDITOR
Richard M. Ketchum

ASSISTANT EDITOR
Stephen W. Sears

EDITORIAL ASSISTANTS
Margaret Di Crocco
Mary Serman Parsons
Judith Shaw
Nathaniel Spear III

ART DIRECTOR
Irwin Glusker

ART ASSISTANT
Trudy Glucksberg

This 1984 edition published by Bonanza Books,
distributed by Crown Publishers, Inc., 225 Park
Avenue South, New York, New York 10003, by
arrangement with American Heritage, a division of
Forbes Inc.

Library of Congress Cataloging in Publication Data

Lancaster, Bruce, 1896-1963.
    The American heritage history of the
American Revolution.

    Originally published: The American heritage
book of the Revolution.   New York : American
Heritage Pub. Co., 1971.
    Includes index.
    1. United States—History—Revolution,
1775–1783.   I. Title.
[E208.L23   1984]   973.3   84-9350

ISBN: 0-517-447363

h g f e

Table of Contents

Introduction

We had our American Revolution nearly two centuries ago, and the years have done something to it. The legends remain, and the statues and the grassy earthworks and the great body of tradition, but a good deal of the reality has been filtered out. When we look back we see Washington crossing the Delaware on a cold winter night, or kneeling in prayer in the snow of Valley Forge; we see the Minuteman, or the lanky Virginia rifleman picturesque in fringed buckskin; but somehow it all seems to be out of a pageant, and neither Washington nor the men who followed him quite come alive for us.

This is a pity, because the central reality in this great act that brought a nation to its birth was the living, aspiring, struggling people who were immediately involved in it. A romantic haze has settled down over the whole affair, and when we look through it the facts tend to be a little blurred. And what is most worth remembering—the thing that so often escapes us—is the fact that like all of history's wars the war of the American Revolution was a hard, wearing, bloody, and tragic business—a struggle to the death that we came very close to losing.

It was a struggle, furthermore, that was fought out by people very much like ourselves; which is to say that they were often confused, usually divided in sentiment, and now and then rather badly discouraged about the possible outcome of the tremendous task they had undertaken. It comes as a shock to realize how many Americans in 1775 were actually opposed to independence and a break with King George III. A good many historians believe that no more than a third of the provincials were active patriots; and they estimate that another third were Loyalists, with the remaining third uncommitted. To continue with the arithmetic a little farther, it is clear that a good many of the people who believed in independence were not always eager to fight for it. When the war began the colonies contained about two and one-half million men, women, and children—a population which should have yielded some seven hundred thousand men capable of bearing arms. Yet in 1780, only one year before the crucial battle at Yorktown, the Continental Army and the state militia together contained no more than one-sixteenth of the country's available manpower.

But all of this says nothing more than that the people of the Revolutionary period were extremely human. Enough of them, in the end, were willing to fight and die for what they believed in to make the dream of independence and freedom come true, and we who look back at them owe them a debt whose size is almost beyond our comprehension. They did not have a very easy time of it, and if they got confused and discouraged now and then it is not to be wondered at.

For behind the great struggle with the professional armies of Great Britain there was the unending struggle between patriot and Loyalist, a civil war just as real and as bitter as the one which broke in 1861. And although the principal battles were decided along the eastern seaboard, the fighting on the frontiers, along the rim of American civilization, was, if anything, even more violent, and it continued in many areas long after the peace treaty with England was signed.

Furthermore, although the Revolution was a civil war it was also, after 1778, something very much like a world war as well. The fighting extended from the West Indies to India, and at times England itself was in as much danger of invasion as in the year of the Spanish Armada.

Sometimes it is hard to see how the Americans could have won if the Revolution had not turned into a world war—that is, if France had not intervened in the wake of the surrender of Burgoyne's army—and yet there was an unconquerable toughness at the core of the American effort. The farmers and shopkeepers of Massachusetts and Pennsylvania and South Carolina and the other colonies were hard men to beat, and they went quite a way on their own, without any help from anyone but themselves. They knew very little about European methods of warfare (and despite all of the tales about frontier riflemen fighting Indian-fashion from behind trees, most of the great Revolutionary battles *were* fought according to the European style) and they were poorly equipped, usually ill-fed, and almost constantly badly clothed; but fighting against the world's greatest power they managed not only to hold off disaster but usually to give a little better than they got.

Somewhere, in the course of more than six bitter years of warfare, those Americans worked something out. They began to see, amidst the monotony and discomfort and acute danger and suffering of constant campaigning, that they were somehow more than just the soldiers of the separate colonies. Somewhere, through their efforts—because of their efforts, because of what they learned while they were making the efforts—a nation was born. As South Carolina's Christopher Gadsden had urged before the fighting even started, they began to see that "There ought to be no more New England men, no New Yorkers . . . but all of us Americans!" That came, and finally independence came after it, as it had to come once the vision had truly taken hold.

This book is an attempt to give flesh and blood to the war that gave us our independence, to get back to the reality beneath the legend—not only in words, but also, as far as it is possible, through pictures drawn and painted by men who lived through those times. If it provides a clearer understanding of what was believed and done during the Revolution—if it breathes a little life into the legend of the men who provided us with our freedom—it will have served its purpose.

King George III in his coronation robes, painted by Allan Ramsay

THE WORLD
BEYOND AMERICA

"The temper and character which prevail in our Colonies

are, I am afraid, unalterable by any human art . . .

An Englishman is the unfittest person on earth to argue

another Englishman into slavery."

EDMUND BURKE—MARCH 22, 1775

FOR the farmers in the valleys, hills, and plains of America and the fishermen scattered down its endless coast, Europe in the eighteenth century had little meaning. Few realized that their lives were tangled in a web of forces—diplomatic, social, economic—that stretched from London to Moscow, or that their fate might be settled on the plains of India or amidst the isles of the Caribbean. But it was so. For nearly a century Britain had been locked in a struggle with France; on its outcome the fate of the world depended.

And there were more subtle ties than these. When Benjamin Franklin walked the streets of London and Paris, he saw and heard what was familiar to him in Boston or New York. The same lovely proportions of houses and furniture caught his eye, richer perhaps and more ostentatious in decoration, but recognizably similar. He heard voiced the same discontents and the same aspirations. Frenchmen and Britons talked to him of the tyranny of feudal privilege, of the glories of liberty, of the need for equality. He learned how they, too, felt their lives to be thwarted by kings, nobles, and ancient forms. He came to understand the strength of the age-old institutions governing European society. Above all, he came to know that the fate of America was entwined with Europe, and that forces unleashed there would help to mold its destiny.

When George III succeeded to the British throne in 1760, the whole nation had become drunk with victory. The previous year—"the year of miracles"—London church bells had rung out day after day to celebrate fresh triumphs over France. Wolfe had taken Quebec, and French colonies dropped like ripe plums into the hands of marauding English admirals. As the *Annual Register* for 1759 recorded of Great Britain, "In no one year since she was a nation has she been favored with so many successes, both by sea and by land, and in every quarter of the globe." Trade flourished, production soared. War, as William Pitt, London's hero, had forecast, brought wealth—wealth and empire as vast as his own wild dreams. This lean, hawk-eyed statesman, sick in body and mind, felt called by destiny to lead England to greatness. He believed that France had to be reduced to a second-rate power, Spain despoiled; his hero, Frederick of Prussia, could keep the rest of Europe in proper subjection. Two years later—though Pitt, at odds with his self-willed monarch, had been cast from the ministry—the dream was fulfilled. In America, Canada, the West Indies, Africa, and India, French power had been destroyed. In 1761 the Navy, taking advantage of Spain's belated alliance with France, captured Manila, and the next year, Havana. British ships swept the seas, and the world lay at England's feet.

Yet neither the King nor Pitt's successors could bring themselves to accept so fabulous a prize. They feared, perhaps rightly, the jealously of the defeated powers. And so by the time peace was finally signed at Paris in 1763, with Pitt out of the ministry, England's demands had been reduced. Nevertheless the gains proved enormous. Canada, Florida, and all lands east of the Mississippi were cleared of Frenchmen and Spaniards. In India and the West Indies the spoils were nearly as great. All this was sufficient to make the British Empire the greatest the world had known since the fall of Rome—sufficient, too, to arouse that envy and hatred which George III and his advisers feared.

If in the eyes of many American colonists England was feudal, tyrannical, reactionary, in the eyes of European monarchs the English were a wild, upstart race, notable for their revolutions and their almost pathological adherence to liberty; a people who kept its kings in subjection and rioted at the least provocation; a nation of hard-drinking, beef-eating shopkeepers with the instincts of pirates. Compared with the rigid European systems of government and law

William Pitt, Earl of Chatham,
attributed to Richard Brompton

Britain appeared unstable and anarchic. Yet no one could deny that she was rich, possessing an exceptionally buoyant financial system, growing trade, and technological superiority. As early as 1721 Montesquieu perceived in England "liberty rising ceaselessly from the fires of discord and sedition, a prince constantly trembling on an unshakable throne, a nation which is . . . wise in its very madness, and . . . mingles commerce with empire." And these things mattered more than the power of despots.

Many contemporaries, however, including Americans, thought otherwise; to them the great European powers were stronger, richer, more cultured, and more secure than Britain—absolute monarchies, blessed by God and stable to eternity. And the greatest of these was France, whose language had become the lingua franca of science, diplomacy, and the arts.

The Earl of Pembroke insisted that his son must have, cost what it might, the best fencing and dancing masters in Paris. Russian, Swedish, German, Austrian, even Spanish and Italian aristocrats shared his sentiments. The French knew how to live as no one else did. The nobility of Europe spoke French, wore French clothes, sat on French furniture, bought French pictures, collected French porcelain, read French books, and pretended to believe in French philosophy. No one was educated until he had lived in Paris, visited Versailles, and listened to the intellectual gossip of the famous *salons*. There they imbibed the ideas of Bayle, d'Alembert, Condorcet, Diderot, Quesnay, and, above all, of Voltaire, the archpriest of the fashionable cult of reason, who set forth the doctrine that "we must regard all men as our brothers." These philosophers vaunted man's capacity to control his universe; they insisted that law, government, and religion could only be respected insofar as their principles could be justified on intellectual grounds; they derided tradition, superstition, revelation, and mystery. They talked endlessly of justice, equality, and reason. But the heart, too, needed its prophet and found him in Jean Jacques Rousseau. This vagabond son of a watchmaker ran counter to almost every movement of his time. He detested privilege, injustice, inequality, and man's brutality to man. Nature was his panacea, the primitive his ideal, all wrapped in a golden haze of sentiment and hope. So duchesses built dairies, installed a cow in a rococo setting and, to universal applause, milked it into a Sèvres vase. Grottoes, gothick follies, and lonely hermitages became a necessity for a nobleman's park. After a refreshing draught of nature, the *salons* shone more brightly, the witticisms crackled, and the sharp laughter blotted out the future. Whether or not Louis XV ever said *"Après moi le déluge,"* the remark summarized perfectly the temper of the times. To the earnest middle class, to men of the stamp of Benjamin Franklin or Thomas Jefferson, the ideas of Voltaire and Rousseau were serious matters. The King was not amused when Caron de Beaumarchais said he owed "more livres than there have been minutes since the death of Christ"; but neither were the mass of French people.

Men who hated the feudal privileges that warped their lives listened to Voltaire and Rousseau and longed for a juster, freer world. And the smart, slick talk of Versailles and Fontainebleau became revolutionary fervor in Philadelphia and Boston. Everywhere there was a sense of a new, brighter, more hopeful world struggling to be born; even monarchs felt it. Frederick the Great, autocrat of Prussia, patronized both Voltaire and Rousseau. So did Catherine of Russia. Both saw the need for efficient government, both hated the church and its privileges; but both feared the liberating influence of the new philosophy. As with monarchs, so with aristocrats; they were attracted and repelled. These smart, fashionable ideas corrupted their faith in themselves and in the institu-

A breast bowl used in Marie Antoinette's dairy

11

tions upon which their power was based. Only an eccentric few—the Lafayettes—could swallow the consequences of the new ideas—a world in which all men were free, equal, and brothers. The welcome given to the American War of Independence by the French aristocracy was due to their hatred of England, not their love for equality.

France led the world not only in thought but in all that adorns the life of man. The Court of Louis XV and afterwards that of his grandson Louis XVI achieved a standard of luxury that Europe had not witnessed since the Augustan emperors. As if to complement the fantastically elaborate etiquette of the Court, populated by nobles whose only "industry and function is that of dressing gracefully and eating sumptuously," architects, craftsmen, and painters of superlative skill created a world of decadent beauty. The *fêtes champêtres* of Fragonard, the luxuriant nudes of Boucher, the soft sentiment of Greuze, and the harsh realism of Chardin dominated European painting. The *ébénistes* of Paris and Versailles produced masterpieces of cabinet-making that render much of the vaunted work of Chippendale and Sheraton heavy and provincial.

Nor was such excellence confined merely to Paris and the Court. France was alive to its own greatness; alive to the riches which lay in its soil and in the hands of its craftsmen. The government created the finest transport system in Europe, the best roads, the best canals. New ideas in industrial techniques were eagerly sought after and, if need be, stolen. Population, trade, industry grew with each passing year. In science, Buffon, Lavoisier, and Laplace were the masters of Europe. Beholding in all this achievement "something which awes and commands the imagination," Edmund Burke decided that England was "an artificial country; take away her commerce, and what has she?"

With such wealth, with such intellectual and artistic supremacy, the future, most Europeans felt, must belong to France in spite of her recent setbacks in the struggle with Britain for empire. No European country could rival her. Prussia, well-disciplined as she was, lacked the proper sinews of a great power—coal, steel, men, money. Russia lay like a spastic elephant across the threshold of Europe. The Austrian Empire, better governed and more closely knit under the rule of Maria Theresa and her son Joseph II, seemed greater than she was. Lacking trade, industry, and proper communications, the Empire had no future; the fabulous wealth enjoyed by the Court derived from the rich but recent conquest of the Turk, and was soon dissipated. Geography denied Austria greatness, and if Austria had no future, Italy and Germany had no present. A fantastic conglomeration of principalities, electorates, bishoprics, grand duchies and the like, some well, some badly governed; some homes of enlightenment, some archaic and feudal; all were too small to play any part in Europe's destinies except to provide cheap cannon fodder for the armies of their richer neighbors. Beyond the core of Europe, Spain and Portugal drifted along, sometimes energized by an active statesman, but usually content to follow in the wake of their senior allies. Portugal had tied herself to Britain; Spain to France, by a family compact between their Bourbon rulers, signed in 1761. Nor was there any rival of France to the north. The Dutch, rich and thrifty, lay moribund under an ossified system of federalism which bound their energies in chains, preventing those quick decisions and desperate gambles so necessary for success in a world of armed competitive states. Scandinavia and Poland lacked force, and became mere pawns in the diplomatic game; their aristocracies grew rich and corrupt on French, English, and Russian gold.

France was indisputably master of Europe, yet in her fight for empire France had failed. She had been dismissed from the wide plains of the Mississippi,

Formal gown of a French
Jeune Dame de Qualité

forced to yield Canada, and beaten in the race for the fabulous riches of India. Few expected France to remain content with humiliations such as these. She retained springboards in the mouth of the St. Lawrence, in the Caribbean, and within India, and the statesmen of Europe feared both her power and the renewal of the contest for empire. The British felt that their seven-year struggle with France, with its huge expenditure of blood and treasure, had saved the Thirteen Colonies from French tyranny. That success placed moral obligations on America. Britain expected that any prospect of a renewed contest with France would strengthen America's sense of dependence on the mother country. Ironically, when that final contest came, in the Napoleonic wars, America was free—at first neutral, then an ally of France. Yet even so England prevailed. France proved to be no match for its brash, rich neighbor, a land that could lose an empire and yet remain strong enough to withstand the mighty force of the French Revolution and Napoleon.

To American eyes Britain in the third quarter of the eighteenth century was a familiar mixture of privilege and liberty, elegance and filth, antiquated habits and new inventions. New and old were jostled uncomfortably together; fabulous riches mingled with dire poverty, and the wonders of the age belonged to the few. Placid countryside and sleepy market towns suddenly woke to rick-burnings, machine-smashings, hunger riots. In a period of twelve months, Benjamin Franklin witnessed "riots about corn, riots about elections, riots of colliers, riots of coal-heavers, riots of sawyers, riots of Wilkesites, riots of government chairmen, riots of smugglers." The starving poor were run down by the yeomanry, herded into jails, strung up on gibbets, transported to the colonies. No one cared. This was a part of life like the seasons, like the deep-drinking, meat-stuffing orgies of good times and bumper harvests. Life was cheap enough. Boys were urged to fight, dogs baited bulls and bears. Bare-fisted boxers fought the clock around and maimed each other for a few guineas. Sailors and soldiers knew the lash and the savagery of power-drunk officers. Each passing year saw the ferocity of the law grow greater. Death came so easily: a stolen penknife and a boy of ten was strung up at Norwich; a handkerchief, taken by a girl of fourteen, brought her the noose. Every six weeks London gave itself up to a raucous fete as men and women were dragged to Tyburn to meet their end at the hangman's hands. This rough, savage life has been immortalized by Hogarth, Rowlandson, and Gillray—so much truer to life than the delicate gentility of a Gainsborough or a Zoffany.

Above and below, scenes in an 18th-century prison for debtors in England

Vile slums in the overcrowded towns bred cruel epidemics, and the treatment of disease was as violent as the sickness itself. Children died like flies; most men got through two or three wives. Yet the British were as tough and as callous as they were aggressive. They took these things in stride as part of life's vast gamble. As Bunker Hill was to show, they knew how to die. Living so close to death, they grew to love risk. Betting provided an outlet. Raindrops running down a windowpane, the fertility of a Dean's wife, horse races, cricket matches, dogfights, dice and cards—all were fit subjects for a bet. Fortunes vanished overnight. When Lord Stavordale lost £12,000 in a single throw, he thanked God that he was not playing for high stakes. The Duchess of Devonshire ruined her marriage by losing a million at cards. The lower classes aped their betters—cock-fighting ruined farmers, cricket bankrupted yeomen, pitch and toss emptied the pockets of the laboring poor. And this gambler's attitude to life blinded Englishmen to their own terrible dangers when the colonists rose in revolt and linked their fortunes with the might of France and Spain.

Although life was hard and cruel, often violent, always shadowed by death, it could be full of light and laughter and wonder. Some found an emotional release in religion, in the violent and passionate calls to salvation of John Wesley and George Whitefield. New wealth brought hope to others, for riches, no matter how unevenly distributed, were pouring into Britain, creating new standards of elegance for an ever-widening middle class. Amid turbulence, anarchy, and privilege, there were groups of highly intelligent, strong-minded men and women who possessed faith in man's capacity to order his world. Believers in science, in education, in industry, in invention, in good roads, new canals, sanitation, better laws, pure administration, social discipline, good housing, and higher wages for better work, they were determined to create a richer, juster, more efficient society. They knew that the future belonged to Britain, and their faith was derived from the evidence of their own eyes.

To this world Americans were both strangers and brothers. They, too, experienced savage, hate-driven mobs; bad harvests and sudden dearths scarred their lives. They knew the scorn of privilege and the law's ferocity. Nor were they unfamiliar with the sweeter side of life, the sustaining strength of religion, the sense of growing prosperity, the touch of elegance which the wider world brought to their towns and seaports. And yet wherever they looked they realized their subordination. They were a remote people and, by comparison, poor. The teeming exuberance of British commerce and industry mocked their own puny efforts, and the ringing golden guineas shamed the debased paper currency upon which their economy depended. Envy and the hope of emulation stirred the colonist's heart when he thought of Britain.

"A vast change has taken place in English social life within two generations," wrote Arthur Young. "View the navigation, the roads, the harbours, and all other public works. Take notice of the spirit with which manufactures are carried on. . . . Move your eye which side you will, you behold nothing but great riches and yet greater resources." What he said was true. Brindley's canal, constructed in the 1760's for the Duke of Bridgewater, demonstrated the reduction of costs by water-transport, widening markets and cheapening raw materials—coal, iron, wool. Mile upon mile of new roads were being engineered, and along them sped "commercial travellers," carrying in their bags miniature samples of furniture, dresses, pottery, and silver, to show in every market town.

Nothing, however, demonstrated England's wealth so vigorously as her crowded seaports. London, Liverpool, and Glasgow resounded to the hammer blows of workmen building new docks to house a merchant fleet greater than any the world had ever known. On their quaysides lay the produce of the New World: tall, straight masts from New England forests, barrels of tobacco and molasses from the South, furs from Canada and the far Mississippi, sugar and mahogany from the Caribbean—all the raw materials of England's trade that she carried to the most distant seas. Even Ch'ien Lung, the Celestial Emperor in Peking, had heard of this strange race of red-headed barbarians who were foolish enough to barter silver for tea. Wherever they sailed, the British sought profit rather than empire, and great wealth poured back to fertilize the expanding Industrial Revolution. Across the Atlantic, the American merchant knew only too well how Britain dominated world trade, for he was caught in a tangle of regulations which subordinated his own growing commerce to that of the motherland; even worse than the regulations was the supremacy of sterling, of which his currency bought so little, and for which his need grew ever greater.

Navigation, roads, harbors, a world-dominant currency do not tell the whole story; change was just as visible in the way of life of the prospering classes. In

"... if [the Americans] do not smuggle manufactures from other countrys, they must take them from Britain, or go naked."
—Thomas Gage, 1768

Scene on a canal, circa 1770

villages, in market towns, above all in London and in the new fashionable spas, spacious Georgian houses were being built with a sense of elegant proportion that has given them a pre-eminence for beauty to this day. They were decorated with exceptional taste, for their architects were familiar with the finest work of Italy and France. Within, plasterwork, marble fireplaces, and gilded paneling displayed the same faultless taste. Furniture, provincial and very plain by French standards, reached a level never since excelled by English craftsmen.

Silverwork of the highest order adorned the tables of the rich, while the newly invented Sheffield plate enabled the middle class to copy the aristocrats' silver at half the cost. Porcelain and ornamental pottery, both novelties to the nation at large, became manias for all. The well-to-do bought the beautiful productions of Chelsea, Bow, Derby, Worcester, or Wedgwood; the thrifty poor indulged themselves with the crude chimney ornaments of Staffordshire potters. Clothes were as rich, as ornate, and as handsome as the houses and towns in which they were displayed. Balls, plays, and concerts, at which the new compositions of Bach, Haydn, and Mozart could be heard for the first time, took place in a setting as harmonious as the melodies themselves. Sadlers Wells and Islington Spa provided shopkeeper and artisan with all the delights that their superiors enjoyed in greater elegance at Ranelagh or Vauxhall.

The aristocracy was richer—far richer than it had ever been. Italy, France, and Germany were ransacked for treasures, pictures, sculpture, tapestries. Private orchestras played to the musical; zoos entertained the naturalists; gardens, for which rivers were diverted and the Himalayas pillaged, delighted the botanists; private laboratories, rare libraries, and hired philosophers nourished the intellectuals. Whatever they desired, they bought. From peer to pauper there was a gusto about life, a confidence, an ebullience, and a waste that argued a profound belief in their own destiny. Indeed it bred an overconfidence, leading many to belittle the troubles in America as trifles and to dismiss airily the early defeats, for how could a few ill-armed, ill-disciplined colonists challenge the greatest empire since Rome?

Certainly they felt gauche before French fashions; admittedly they respected French art and French literature profoundly. They did not believe themselves educated until they had spent some years on the grand tour in France and Italy. Nevertheless they knew their government and their church to be the best in the world—the most jealous of liberty, the most conducive to prosperity. Nor were they blind to their own achievements. They worshiped Shakespeare, revered Isaac Newton and John Locke, took pride in Gibbon, Hume, and Blackstone, and delighted in the novels of Fielding, Smollett, and Richardson and in the plays of Sheridan and Goldsmith. And they were as impressed by the pontifications of Dr. Johnson as by those of any Encyclopedist. They were pervaded not so much by a sense of inferiority as by a desire to learn. Yet the wonders of this new age, its greatness and its hope, belonged to the few, not to the many.

War, commerce, and invention—these were the factors primarily responsible for setting the social life of Britain in violent motion and complicating the problems of its empire. Britain had been more or less continuously at war, except for eighteen years under Sir Robert Walpole, for more than a century. As a young man, William Pitt, later Earl of Chatham, in a speech of fiery eloquence told the Commons: ". . . when trade is at stake, you must defend it or perish." When he died, the City of London raised a monument to him at the Guildhall, upon which these words of Edmund Burke were inscribed: "A statesman by whom commerce was united with and made to flourish by war."

A detail from the plan of an English country house, showing the main hallway

Dr. Samuel Johnson

15

It was true. Marlborough's wars had reaped victory's harvest in the West Indies and the Spanish trade; Clive had wrested Bengal, worth £2,000,000 a year, from the supine hands of the decadent Moguls; and Chatham's genius had won the greatest gains of all—Canada, India, and West Africa had witnessed his conquests and paid for them out of increased trade. Tobacco, sugar, rice, furs, timber, fish, silk, cotton, and tea poured into British ports—a torrent of liquid wealth that fertilized all that it touched. Yet war had won trade, not empire. Chatham himself spurned Clive's offer of Bengal to the nation. He preferred to leave such desperate problems of government to the East India Company. Chatham saw empire in trade, in the possession of ports and strategic points, and in the denial of advantages to France, not in the rule and subjugation of millions of his fellowmen. Nothing illustrates this better than his attitude toward Quebec. He regarded its possession as a strategic necessity for these reasons: it would secure the entire trade in fur and fish; the French would be prevented from supplying their West Indian islands with lumber, which would drive up the price of French sugar to the advantage of British sugar merchants; France would lose a market for manufactures; France would no longer be able to build ships in America or acquire masts and timber; and finally, expulsion of the French would give security to British North American colonies.

Robert Clive, by
Nathaniel Dance

Possession of the vast plains of Canada did not interest Chatham, nor did he wish to dominate the lives of his fellowmen. Trade and wealth monopolized by English-speaking people was his aim, so when the conflict came with America this great imperialist could sympathize with the colonists' tribulations and bring to their aid his magnificent eloquence.

War not only increased trade, but also freed money and multiplied it. Sterling became the hardest currency in the world, creating prosperity for English merchants but bringing hardship to Americans. Between Britain and her colonies there was an adverse balance of trade that had to be paid in guineas. The debts of planters and merchants grew; the shortage of currency became acute. To prevent wild inflation the British government forbade paper currency, and the plight of American farmers and artisans grew worse, underlining their subservience and increasing their feeling of resentment toward Britain.

In England cheap money stimulated speculation in new enterprises and inventions which in turn had a profound effect on the Industrial Revolution. Plentiful money created demand—for goods, for food, for those small personal luxuries that are the symbols of affluence. And, as is usual in times of prosperity, the population began to grow until, by 1780, Britain was rapidly becoming a nation dominated by youth.

Interior of a merchant's office

The need for labor had long been apparent and, at last, a conscious attempt to alleviate problems of disease and sanitation was made. The shortage of hands stimulated men's ingenuity in other ways. Employers began to provide incentives—better wages, better housing, facilities for education and religious worship. Industrialists began to pay great attention to methods of production. Division of labor became the slogan of efficiency. The factory system spread, leading to greater discipline and evenly flowing production. At first workers hated it, and manufacturers were forced to employ women and children, both amenable to regular hours and repetitive tasks.

These things increased production, but never fast enough. All the great entrepreneurs of eighteenth-century England were also preoccupied with invention. "Everything," wrote Josiah Wedgwood, "yields to experiment." Manufacturers joined the Royal Society—Wedgwood himself contributed a paper on the pyrometer—and cultivated scientists. Watt's introduction of the steam engine in 1769, and the development of an improved version with rotary motion in 1781, freed mankind for the first time from the natural sources of power, opening up limitless vistas for industrial society. Joseph Priestley, one of the outstanding men of his day—scientist, philosopher, reformer—numbered dozens of manufacturers among his close friends and admirers. In all manufacturing towns the spirit of inquiry dominated men's minds. The result was a remarkable spate of inventions. Arkwright's spinning frame (1769), Hargreaves' jenny (1770), and Crompton's mule (1779) revolutionized the production of yarn and turned the spinning wheel into an antique. The demand for iron, stimulated by war, led to the inventions and improvements of Smeaton, Cort, and the Cranages; smelting by coal, invented earlier in the century and kept a jealous secret, spread throughout the industry. The works of Carron in Scotland and Dowlais in Wales became the wonders of their age. To show his faith in iron John Wilkinson, the great ironmaster, built iron bridges, iron boats, iron chapels, and was buried in an iron coffin. Human ingenuity left no industrial art unimproved.

Arkwright's spinning frame

The same vigorous spirit spread throughout England's greatest industry—the land. Improvement in agriculture was already many generations old, but from 1750 the pace of change quickened; agriculture leaped into fashion. George III was nicknamed "Farmer George" because of his passion for agriculture. The huge, beef-eating, beer-drinking caricature of all Englishmen—John Bull—was a farmer. More mouths to feed and more money for food brought prosperity to the land and, ironically, strengthened those traditional forces that were most opposed to all change in politics and society—the country gentlemen.

A totally different breed were the "new men"—men who took delight in reform and improvement. Their willingness to experiment, to risk the new against the old, did not stop at industrial organization or agrarian management. The Arkwrights, Strutts, Wilkinsons, Wedgwoods, and Cokes applied the same principles to society. They lost patience with traditional muddle. Old broken-down roads with puddles the size of ponds, in which men and horses floundered and drowned, were useless to them. Slums, pullulating with disease, were an affront to their intelligence as well as their humanity. Good houses spelled healthy workers and a better output in the factory or on the land. Paved streets, like good roads, meant lower costs. A plentiful water supply eased industrial problems, provided better sanitation, and improved health. Both social discipline and social opportunity seemed utterly desirable to the great entrepreneurs—Wilkinson the ironmaster, Wedgwood the potter, Boulton the engineer. At Liverpool men of like mind laid out the first public gardens; at Newcastle upon Tyne they founded literary and philosophical societies. They were active in all societies, reforming the manners and habits of the working classes. These new men lived in the ethos of social reform, and an unquestioning belief in progress was part of the air they breathed.

Yet at every turn they met traditional obstacles. Often they lacked the social or political power to achieve the smallest reform. Like the Americans, these men were hamstrung by privilege and thwarted by tradition. Any body of manufacturers wishing to cut a canal had to solicit, often for years, the country gentlemen in whose hands effective power lay. England was still governed by a remarkable collection of ancient, unreformed institutions, which were the slow accretion of time and as strong as a coral reef. Sometimes these could be circumvented, but only by much effort. Since only a break with the past could give them the future, these new men became ardent apostles of reform. Their leaders—Adam Smith, Jeremy Bentham, Joseph Priestley, and Richard Price—

Ironmaster John Wilkinson, by Lemuel Francis Abbott

17

directed their attention to reform on a national as well as local scale. In their own work they had come to appreciate the value of a rational approach. It was easy for them to believe that reason would be equally effective if applied to human institutions. Liberty and equal rights became their watchwords, and democracy their aim. When they read these words of Richard Price—"Perhaps I do not go too far when I say that next to the introduction of Christianity among mankind, the American Revolution may prove the most important step in the progressive course of human improvement"—they did not smile; they agreed. To them it was a self-evident truth that nations had a right to self-government, that there could be no justice in taxation without representation. America became for them a symbol of that liberty for which they thirsted. They, too, needed to break with a past which pressed so heavily upon them.

At times their political impotence bred despair for the future. As one of these new men wrote to his son in the 1770's, "Through the folly and wickedness of the present, you of the rising generation have indeed a dark prospect before you. . . . Your best way will be to gather as fast as you can a good stock of the arts and sciences of this country; and if you find the night of despotism and wretchedness overwhelm this hemisphere, follow the course of the sun to that country [America] where freedom has already fixed her standard and is erecting her throne; where the sciences and arts, wealth and power will soon gather round her, and assist and strengthen her empire there."

This black mood fell time and time again across their spirits. They saw opportunity and the promise of a larger future, but they lacked power. Society still revolved about its old gods—monarchy, established church, nobility—and little oligarchies of reactionaries hogged political power in the countryside and corporate towns. Even Parliament, whose struggle for liberty against the Crown had made their ancestors' days heroic, had now become effete, unrepresentative, concerned only with its own privileges and indifferent to freedom and justice. So naturally their sympathies swelled to all who cried out against oppression and privilege—Dissenters, Catholics, Irishmen, Americans. Powerless, they watched their country's empire break to pieces. They protested, they petitioned, they cursed George III, Lord North, and the Constitution—but without avail, for the traditional forces were still too strong. Harbingers of a new world they might be, but the old still held them in thrall.

Here lies a significant contrast to America. The Adamses, Hancocks, Jeffersons, and Washingtons held much the same attitude toward life as the Prices, Wedgwoods, and Hollises, but their position in American society was both more secure and more powerful. The colonies possessed strong traditional forces, the place holders of the Crown—customs officers, Royal governors, and their aides and secretaries—who were rarely ardent for social change. Broadly speaking, however, such men were often transient visitors to America, and those that did root themselves in colonial society were far less powerful than their British counterparts. The great tidal sweep of immigration and expansion constantly sapped and weakened ancient ties and old ways of government in America, whereas in England they had acquired adamantine strength.

There can be no proper comprehension of England's difficulties unless the power of conservative forces in English society is understood. The Glorious Revolution of 1688 had been a revolt by the property-owning classes against interference by the Crown in their local rights of government or inherited beliefs. Consequently eighteenth-century Englishmen had an almost mystical reverence for the word "freehold." A freehold was not merely a tenure of land—it could mean a benefice, a commission in the army or navy, the possession of an obsolete

Interior of the House of Commons

18

office or ancient privilege. To advocate the abolition of such sinecures as the Tastership of the King's Wines in Dublin smacked of revolution, for these were some man's freehold. Also the Glorious Revolution had given to the landed classes and their dependents a chance to batten on the state. Church, army, navy, the Plantations, the Court, and the administration had become a vast racket that provided relief for needy younger sons or dependent cousins. The Earl of Pembroke bought his son a commission so that he could wear a decent uniform on his grand tour. He did not see his regiment for four years, but naturally he drew his pay and rose in rank. Any army or navy list in these years reads like a roll call of the aristocracy. The natural assumption was that ships or regiments were property—property that belonged by divine hereditary right to the ruling classes. All the fat offices of colonial government went the same way, and the same was true of parliamentary representation.

Lord Egremont bought the parliamentary borough of Midhurst for £40,000; the Duke of Bedford sold Camelford for £32,000. And, as Chatham said, these little towns that sent representatives to Westminster but could be bought or sold like a parcel of fields, were "the rotten parts of the Constitution"—yet even he would not hear of their destruction. The sanctity of the Constitution, blessed by the Glorious Revolution, could not be invaded.

At the same time men witnessed a growing arrogance on Parliament's part, a jealous sensitivity to its privileges. Since it was Parliament's privilege to decide the question of its own membership, John Wilkes, elected for the most populous constituency in the country, Middlesex, was declared—not once but four times —not to be a member of Parliament because he had crossed his King and been convicted on a trumped-up charge of libel. This brilliant lecher, immortalized in the savage cartoon of Hogarth with its devil's leer juxtaposed to the cap of liberty, proved a master of political tactics. He outwitted secretaries of state, infuriated the King, and reduced Parliament to near-hysteria, so that Chatham could denounce its actions as "little better than a mob." And in so doing he became a symbol to worthier men; the hero of all who loved liberty, as popular in Boston as in Liverpool. "Wilkes and Liberty" was a cry that echoed far beyond Middlesex, and his name is forever entwined with the cause of America in which he so ardently believed. Yet the struggle of Wilkes showed how tender Parliament was of its rights; a lesson the colonists quickly learned, for though Parliament might be prepared to abolish obnoxious taxes, its *right* to tax remained sacred and inviolable, even to a Chatham.

Many Englishmen, like Silas Neville, who were excluded from the magic circle of government, seized on the little acts of tyranny, the assumption of privileges, on the minor corruption that was obvious to all, and saw George III as a Stuart tyrant and Parliament as a complacent tool. Instead of to Parliament, Neville and his friends looked to the people of America, who "are much more virtuous and understand the nature of liberty better than the body of people here and have men capable of leading them." But in England there were two worlds, and for those who ruled the situation was infinitely more complex, a bewildering world of duty that pressed heavily on privilege and profit.

t is time to consider the strong conservative forces that were the heart and sinews of British life. Throughout the changing centuries Britain had been ruled by the owners of the land. They dominated her counties; they filled Parliament and all the professions. Landownership meant running a parish, providing constables, churchwardens, overseers of the highways and of the poor. Landowners kept order, collected taxes, shared out collective duties,

Hogarth's caricature of John Wilkes

Beer-drinking, beef-eating Britons, taken from Hogarth's "Beer Street"

Bribing electors, a detail from one of William Hogarth's satires

provided for the sick and the destitute. Often they were harsh; yet to their own kith and kin and to those whose roots in the parish went as deep as their own, they parceled out a rough justice and engendered some human warmth.

Most little oligarchies of village rulers were linked by ancient friendships with the great landowners—the nobility and country gentlemen of long standing; often they were bound by economic ties, by renting of land, or supplying of services or materials to the "great house." The real rulers of the county were to be found among the squires and aristocrats and their ecclesiastical dependents. They provided the justices of the peace and officered the militia. Their politics were patriarchal; their destiny was to govern. A dozen families or so in most counties acquired a certain pre-eminence through wealth or ability, or both.

Yet as the American revolt progressed, the rights and wrongs of it infused new life even into county politics. Voters became aware of the wider world; they no longer blindly followed traditional loyalties to a family, but approved or rejected candidates according to their political attitudes. Instead of ignoring the voters and contenting themselves with family deals, candidates began to address themselves to their electors, haranguing them on America, on reform, on all major political issues. In county after county, the American war revitalized English political life. Docile voters suddenly became argumentative men.

But in the 1760's parliamentary ancestry was more important than views about America. The families of the Knights of the Shire read like a roll call from Debrett. Cholmondeleys sat for Cheshire, Courtenays for Devon, Lambtons for Durham, Cokes for Norfolk, and the same ancient names were to be found representing the small country towns or seaports. Over the generations a family had established its patronage over a borough. Such men, like the Knights of the Shire, were self-electing, but neither bribery nor government influence got them into Parliament. The security of tenure bred in them an attitude of such independence that all ministries needed to win the support of the majority of them if they were to survive. It was to these men that the oratory of the parliamentary leaders was directed. Tradition, the Constitution as laid down in 1689, was their watchword, rather than liberty. They believed in monarchy, in the Established Church, in the subordination of Ireland and the Plantations. Most of them were suspicious of Wilkes, worried by Chatham, angry with America, and content with George III.

Although these men provided the background to politics, they did not fill it. There were corrupt boroughs, many belonging to borough patrons who detested George III. They brought in their henchmen. A successful merchant with political leanings could usually pick up a seat if he wanted one; so could lawyers. And some boroughs with tiny electorates—like the City of Bath—spurned patronage and worshiped furious independents. There were boroughs with enormous electorates—open to any demagogue with a purse large enough to provide the Gargantuan orgies of beer-drinking and beef-eating that all voters regarded as their rights. Naturally the Crown controlled many boroughs and found seats for its admirals, generals, civil servants, and court officials, but it would be quite wrong to think, as many Americans did and still do, that George III or his ministers controlled very much of the membership of Parliament. Indeed, it has been shown that royal influence at this time was steadily declining; that George III controlled less in 1780 than he had done in 1760; and that the winners, as might be expected, were either the *nouveaux riches* or the long-established parliamentary families.

In 1767 a disturbed Benjamin Franklin had observed that "Every man in England seems to consider himself as a piece of a sovereign over America; seems to jostle himself into the throne with the King, and talks of *our subjects in the colonies.*" Yet if Franklin thought "Parliament cannot well and wisely make laws suited to the colonies, without being properly and truly informed," he might have noted that Parliament itself was wildly unrepresentative. As Dean Tucker wrote in a pamphlet addressed to a fictitious nephew in America: "I say not only two millions, but six millions at least, of inhabitants of Great Britain, are still unrepresented in the British Parliament. . . . Yet we raise no commotions, we neither ring the alarm bell, nor sound the trumpet; but submit to be taxed without being represented, and taxed too, let me tell you, for your sakes."

There spoke the voice of traditional England—content with anomalies, satisfied that government should be in the hands of men of great estate whose ancestry and education had fitted them to rule, and totally ignorant of that other England for whom the voice of America was the voice of truth.

English society was growing both more complex and more divided. The long struggle with France, the social upheavals of the Industrial Revolution created problems enough, but these were complicated further by the difficulties of colonial government. Natural irritations of long standing festered until they proved mortal. And it was Britain's misfortune that the troubles in her American colonies grew acute during the first years of a young King's reign. His personality and the political instability that his accession to the throne created made an already complex situation worse. George III has emerged as the bogeyman of the American Revolution—a fate this sad, tragic King in no way deserves.

A silhouette of George III, by his daughter, Princess Elizabeth

He came to the throne at a very early age, but mentally he was younger still. He had developed very late—he could not read until he was ten. He lacked faith in his own abilities and dreaded the burdens which the Almighty had placed on his shoulders. Yet his sense of duty was as monolithic as his obstinacy. He would rule even though it drove him beyond the borders of sanity to that doubtful world of madness that haunted his existence and finally claimed him. Nothing could deflect him from his sacred trust, and a part of that trust was to pass on to his descendants the powers and privileges of monarchy undiminished. The authority of the Crown, the authority of Parliament—these things were immutable. For Americans to challenge them was treason. These were the fixed stars of faith in his cloudy firmament.

There were others. His grandfather's ministers were cheats, black traitors; so men experienced in the arts of government and diplomacy quickly found themselves out of office. The King loathed the war with France as a burden the nation could not afford. He insisted on peace; so the vast victories of Chatham brought the nation small rewards. During the first decade of his reign, the period when the troubles with America went from bad to worse, Britain lacked stable government. Constant changes and squabbling groups of ministers deprived the country of any settled policy. Indeed, politicians were too deeply involved in the struggle for personal power to give their undivided attention to the problems of empire. A young, incompetent King; intriguing cliques of courtiers; hand-to-mouth and contradictory actions—this is the immediate background of the drift into war with America. Beyond that was a nation divided against itself and, looming on the horizon, the titanic struggle with France—suspended but not settled.

Many of the difficulties between England and America were of long standing. The colonial assemblies had been at loggerheads with royal governors for generations. The Navigation Acts by which American trade was subordinated to British interests were as frequently flouted as obeyed. Smuggling was rife, to

An English cartoon contrasting the Privy Purse in 1753, under George II, and in 1773, under George III

21

An attack on the government's mismanagement of the colonial problem shows the map of North America afire

the detriment of British interests. Troops which the Americans had provided for the wars against France had been ill-armed, ill-disciplined, incompetent. The British had borne the burden in men, materials, and money, yet in New England American prosperity was everywhere evident. "You cannot well imagine," James Murray of Massachusetts wrote in 1760, "what a land of health, plenty and contentment this is among all ranks, vastly improved within the last ten years. The war on this continent has been equally a blessing to the English subjects and a calamity to the French, especially in the Northern Colonies." Not so for the British, for whom the war and its peace brought greater burdens. Canada spelled security to America at vast expense to England; the western lands that drew Americans like a magnet merely threatened new Indian wars to the British. Pontiac's rising brought an immediate decision. By Royal Proclamation George III closed the lands west of the Alleghenies to immigration. And finally the British government resolved to make a reality of taxation, which had been for so long a dead letter. For years publicists had pressed the virtues of a stamp act—so difficult to evade, so easy to collect. Although there were some forebodings when the Stamp Act was passed in 1765, few foresaw the uproar which it caused—Benjamin Franklin himself tried to get collectors' jobs for his friends.

The British argued again and again that the revenue to be derived from the Act—£60,000 a year—was only a trivial part of the cost of North American defense. They stressed with the same sweet reasonableness the justice of the Royal Proclamation. The Indians would be content with the wide central plains; so costly wars would be avoided. The days of sweet reasonableness, however, were past. There were too many signs of British tyranny. Beyond the Proclamation and the Stamp Act were the suppression of paper currency and the Sugar Act (even if easily avoided), all seeming to be part of a deliberate policy to curtail America's freedom and deny that liberty which was an essential right of mankind. America rioted, and British weakness was immediately apparent. The army was tiny, safe only in its forts, and distance forbade speedy reinforcements.

The tumult in America baffled the ministry, frightened the merchants, and encouraged the parliamentary opposition. They placed the blame on Grenville, the minister responsible for taxing America. He possessed an excellent head for figures, no imagination, and extreme conceit. The king disliked him, and he lasted only until 1765—and in came another group of Whigs, led by Lord Rockingham who had vigorously condemned Grenville's foolhardiness in imposing the Stamp Act. They repealed it, but now they were courtiers and King's men, and repeal was not enough for George III. The Americans, he believed—and here most men of authority were with him—needed to be taught a lesson and put in their place. Already British politicians were disturbed by darker fears—if America successfully asserted its right to reject British taxation, what might not happen in Ireland? Its disgruntled, rebellious people might rise up and open their doors to the French. Throughout the tragic story of Anglo-American conflict the fear of what Ireland might do exerted its baleful influence, for the specter of a breakup of Great Britain haunted the King's mind, jeopardized his sanity, and increased his resolve never to give in to American demands. Much to his relief, for he had deep forebodings about the wisdom of repealing the Stamp Act, the Rockinghams passed the Declaratory Act in which Britain's inalienable right to tax the colonies was asserted.

The repeal of the Stamp Act sent a wave of joy through the colonies, and Chatham said he "never had greater satisfaction." There were banquets, festivities, and sermons without end. Fine, flowery sentiments were the order of the day: "Let the past, like the falling out of lovers, prove only the renewal of love."

But it was the moment for a great statesman. America had displayed her temper and bared her grievances. Nothing irreparable, however, had been done on either side. Difficulties abounded, yet they were difficulties which both sides had lived with for generations. Nothing could have been more propitious at this time than the action of George III in dismissing Rockingham and calling Chatham to lead the nation. Chatham's lofty mind was dominated by high ideals. He reverenced liberty and sympathized with America's tenderness on the subject of taxation. France was so real a danger to him that all rights had to be suspended if the loyalty of America was likely to be jeopardized by their assertion. As he himself said, "America must be embraced with the arms of affection." So long as Chatham held the reins of power, there was hope; yet no sooner were they in his hands than he went mad, hopelessly and completely. This tragedy was darkened by the King's obstinacy; day after day, month after month, he waited for Chatham's recovery. When it came, it was too late. Not only was Chatham too weak to govern—his ministry was in ruins, and all hopes of reconciliation with America gone. He found the British nation more terribly divided than it had been since the days of the Stuarts.

A caricature of Charles Fox's sympathies, half-radical, half-royalist

Charles Townshend, a brilliant, unstable politician, had gambled an empire for the sake of popularity. As Chatham's Chancellor of the Exchequer he knew how deeply the repeal of the Stamp Act had been resented by the country squires as well as by the King. Many Americans, expressing their aversion to internal taxes such as the Stamp Act, had admitted the validity of Britain's right to impose external taxes. Townshend seized on this bogus distinction to impose duties on glass, lead, paint, paper, and tea. This was the beginning of the end.

Riots, boycotts, and savage attacks on governors and customs men gave the Townshend duties a warm reception in the colonies. So great was the outcry, so deep the passions aroused that the American problem exacerbated political feeling in Britain as well as the colonies. Men linked the problems of liberty raised by Wilkes with the demands for liberty by America; in the suppression of one and denial of the other they recognized the clear imprint of the King's tyrannical nature. The massive attacks of Junius, that brilliant anonymous propagandist—like Wilkes, a friend of America—hammered home this theme in unforgettable invective. Never before had a government or a king been subjected to such furious criticism in the press. At the same time Burke added the majestic voice of his rhetoric to America's cause: "The people of the colonies are descendants of Englishmen. England, Sir, is a nation which still I hope respects, and formerly adored, her freedom. The colonists emigrated from you when this part of your character was most predominant, and they took this bias and direction the moment they parted from your hands. They are therefore not only devoted to liberty, but liberty according to English ideas, and on English principles. The temper and character which prevail in our colonies are, I am afraid, unalterable by any human art. We cannot, I fear, falsify the pedigree of this fierce people, and persuade them that they are not sprung from a nation in whose veins the blood of freedom circulates."

Edmund Burke delivering an oration in Commons

Although everyone realized the folly of Townshend's measures, the ministers who succeeded him were doubtful about repealing them. When at last Lord North rose to pre-eminence in the ministry, he decided on partial repeal. Nothing more was possible. Public opinion was hardening, with a minority for, but a majority against, America. The King was adamant. The duty on tea must be kept as a symbol of America's subjection.

The drift to war could not be stopped. The ostentatious American support of

A caricature of Lord North

". . . the famous quarrel between America and England, which will soon divide the world . . . imposes on each power the necessity of examining closely to see how the coming of this separation will influence it for good or ill."
—Beaumarchais to Louis XVI, 1776

Wilkes and the flouting of the Crown's authority in the *Gaspee* affair alienated many Englishmen who had scarcely given a thought to American problems before. The boycott of British goods, particularly tea, threatened the livelihood of many English merchants. More and more, sympathy for America was confined to those narrow circles of forward-looking men or to professional politicians in opposition. But it was the Boston Tea Party which finally outraged the massive traditional forces of British society. For a time George III and Lord North became popular, and the Coercive Acts were powerfully supported not only in Parliament, but also in the nation at large. It seemed easy enough to teach Americans a final lesson and reduce them to obedience. After all, the colonies hated each other almost as much as they hated the mother country; if they made trouble, they could be crushed one by one. Nor was much resistance expected. Although British troops were few, they were tough, disciplined, well-armed professionals, more than a match for rioters and amateur militiamen. If worse came to worst, the colonists could be starved into subjection. The British navy ruled the seas. Those few who knew the temper of America and the eager hopes of France raised their voices in vain.

Once the moment of anger had passed and the havoc wreaked by the Coercive Acts had been made all too painfully apparent, sympathy for America reasserted itself, giving fresh courage to American agents in Britain and sowing fresh doubts in the minds of the ministry and its supporters. Both the sympathy and the doubts redoubled as the vista of war opened. Vast distances, lack of troops, the drain of money, fear of France and Spain, and anxiety about Ireland sapped Lord North's courage and made him falter. George III, however, knew his duty. The Americans must be made to obey, for it was his sacred trust to pass on his empire unchanged and undivided to his heirs. So his policy was simple—suppress the revolt, use force, do not negotiate. North, an adroit politician, fine debater, and skillful administrator, but a prey to anxiety, lacked this simplicity of approach. He was a warm-hearted man, naturally timid, deeply loyal; above all, loyal to his King. He hated the war; indeed, he longed to give up a position for which he felt he lacked the abilities. He constantly hoped something would turn up—victory, a chance of compromise, a change of heart. What he could not do was give all his energy to waging a ruthless war. And his choice of subordinates proved disastrous: Sandwich at the Admiralty and Germain at the War Office mark the nadir of British military competence. As the sick and dying Chatham had long ago forecast, France and Spain seized their opportunity for revenge, for they knew that America was a part of a wider world. So from the height of greatness Britain plunged to defeat.

In the final analysis that defeat would be due not only to time and space and the difficulties of waging war three thousand miles away, nor even to the revolutionary valor of the Americans, but to the complexity of British society itself. From defeat would spring unexpected victories. Indeed, out of this tragic combat, both sides gained. In England, the failure of the Crown and of aristocratic society was so complete that they never recovered their old powers. Defeat so destroyed their own faith in themselves that the abdication of their power to the middle class, to the new men of the Midlands and the North who had acclaimed America's victories, became merely a matter of time. America acquired freedom; Britain moved toward a less privileged society. Furthermore, for the first time, she was made to realize that empire was more than trade and riches—that it was a complex problem of duties as well as rights. And, strangely, for America there proved after all to be no separate destiny, only the leadership of the English-speaking world.

J. H. PLUMB

The crucial battle of Quiberon Bay broke French naval strength in 1759. Attempting to lure a pursuing British fleet into shoal water in a raging November gale, French Admiral Conflans was outmaneuvered and defeated.

Britannia Rules the Waves

Long before the Seven Years' War, Englishmen had discovered that "wooden walls are the best walls of this kingdom," and by 1760 the Royal Navy's control of the sea had spelled the difference between success and failure. While Britain's ally Frederick the Great of Prussia took charge of fighting on the Continent, the British fleet had harassed French commerce and colonies from India to America—a strategy which paid off handsomely in 1759.

In September of that year, young General James Wolfe led an army onto the Plains of Abraham above Quebec and gained a victory which ended the century-long struggle between England and France for domination of North America. While Wolfe was besieging Quebec, a French invasion fleet was routed by the British under Admiral Edward Boscawen, and the only remaining menace to England's security was the Brest fleet. In a November gale, Admiral Sir Edward Hawke drove this French flotilla on the rocks at Quiberon Bay.

With France's naval power broken, final British victory in the Seven Years' War was only a matter of time. Yet, curiously enough, that success led to the loss of Great Britain's prized American colonies. Confident that England had attained the heights of glory, penny-wise politicians neglected their great navy, while, across the Channel, a thirst for revenge spurred French shipyards to feverish activity. A fine new navy was built upon the ruins of the old one, and beautifully designed ships slid down the ways to join France's growing squadrons. Two decades after the battle at Quiberon Bay the French navy was superior to the British—a superiority which lasted just long enough for the French and American armies to isolate General Charles Cornwallis at Yorktown, Virginia, in the fall of 1781.

Europe's Monarchs
Seek Revenge

Under Frederick the Great, Prussia became a real power in Europe.

The men and women who ruled Europe in 1763 were a remarkably disparate and colorful group of autocrats. There was Catherine the Great of Russia, who considered herself a "true gentleman," and Frederick of Prussia, who decided quite frankly that he and Catherine were "a pair of brigands." Charles III of Spain would earn a reputation as one of the better Bourbons, while his cousin, Louis XV of France, would go down as one of the worst. Although France was still the greatest power on the Continent, the misrule of Louis and his mistresses had brought it perilously close to disaster.

If these monarchs had one quality in common, it was their dislike of England—a feeling that ranged from distrust to unconcealed hatred. Humiliated by the Peace of Paris in 1763, they awaited the opportunity for revenge, and perceived it in England's mounting colonial troubles.

By abandoning its alliance with Prussia, Britain lost even the friendship of Frederick the Great, and in 1779 the Earl of Sandwich wrote that "we have no one friend or ally . . . all those who ought to be our allies except Portugal act against us."

Ironically, European royalty fostered the American Revolution. Not through any love of liberty, but out of self-interest and a desire for revenge, these rulers assured the success of the revolt against their fellow sovereign, George III.

Undaunted by her sixteen children, Maria Theresa ruled Austria.

Louis XV (opposite) reigned from 1715 until 1774, when his death occasioned this rueful epitaph: "Here lies Louis the Fifteenth, Second of the name of Well-Beloved; God preserve us from the third." The decision of his grandson, Louis XVI, to ally his country with the United States made final American victory possible; but it so overburdened the precarious French economy that it led to revolt in France and to the well-meaning King's overthrow.

This 1769 cartoon shows Frederick the Great of Prussia, Maria Theresa of Austria, Louis XV of France, and Charles III of Spain plotting to divide the British Empire among themselves.

The Enlightenment's intellectual curiosity led men to expand their physical horizons, too. Captain James Cook had explored the southern hemisphere and Alaskan waters before he was killed in Hawaii (above) in 1779.

The Century of Enlightenment

In Beaumarchais' *The Barber of Seville*, Dr. Bartholo grumbled about the eighteenth century: "What has it ever produced to make us praise it? Foolishness of all sorts: freedom of thought, the law of gravitation, electricity, toleration, inoculation against smallpox, the *Encyclopedia* . . ."

His complaint was a concise if incomplete summary of that great intellectual flowering, the Enlightenment, which transformed Europe in the 1700's. A combination of increased wealth and insatiable curiosity resulted in a ferment of questioning. The scientific attitude made more strides than it had in centuries; in the *salons*, idle conversation became an art form glittering with ideas, against a background of music by Gluck, Haydn, and Mozart; and writers set forth moral, economic,

and political arguments which would alter the future course of civilization.

Four French intellectuals were the era's guiding lights. Voltaire, the "Universal Man," was both source and symbol of much of the concern for political and religious liberty which animated the times. Montesquieu's *The Spirit of Laws* not only "turned the heads of the whole French people," but influenced men across the Atlantic, who used it to justify their disputes with British authority. Diderot's *Encyclopedia*, designed "to assemble the knowledge scattered over the face of the earth," also transmitted challenging ideas disguised as mere definitions. In a class by himself was Jean Jacques Rousseau, who, in his *Social Contract*, passionately questioned why man, born free, should be enslaved.

Montesquieu

Voltaire

Diderot

Rousseau

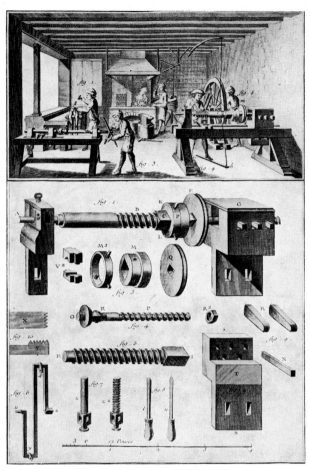

A typical plate from Diderot's great Encyclopedia *has detailed drawings of the tools used in a press-screw factory.*

One of the prodigies of the age was Wolfgang Amadeus Mozart, whose genius was apparent from childhood. Virtuoso as well as composer, he is shown playing the harpsichord.

New Men and New Ideas

If, in the early years of the eighteenth century, Frenchmen had stood in awe of John Locke's political theories and Newton's science, by the middle decades France had seized the philosophical initiative. Now luggers and packets pitching across the Channel toward England carried contagious ideas of the Enlightenment which would, before many years had passed, transform the world.

Soon the voice of Reason echoed in the writings of Blackstone, Gibbon, and Lord Chesterfield; reform cried out from the drawings of Hogarth and Rowlandson. And in the British colonies across the Atlantic, men like Thomas Jefferson and John Adams read long into the night, poring over the works of Montesquieu, Rousseau, and Voltaire.

In 1765 Edmund Burke predicted that "new men will come in, and not improbably with new ideas..." Come in they did, and although it took years for a majority of the population to feel the effects, the practical English lent reality to French theory.

Lady Mary Wortley Montagu introduced inoculation from Turkey to curb the ravages of smallpox. From Scotland came teachings of the Hunters in surgery, of Smellie in midwifery, of Pringle in personal hygiene, each adding a little time to the precious span of human life. Roads were paved and canals built. Robert Bakewell began raising woollier sheep and fatter cattle. "Turnip" Townshend's new farming methods increased the land's productivity. Inventors like Arkwright, Hargreaves, and Crompton revolutionized the production of textiles; Wilkinson proved what could be done with iron. It was as if a great light had appeared after centuries of darkness, and men, suddenly seeing a world of opportunity spread out before them, would change everything before they were through.

In William Hogarth's "Marriage à la Mode," a newly rich citizen (center) negotiates with a gouty nobleman. By marrying his daughter to the peer's son, he will gain prestige, his lordship money.

Opened in 1761, this aqueduct on the Duke of Bridgewater's canal was a marvel of the age. The canal sped coal from the Duke's mines to Manchester. Although roads were being improved, stagecoach passengers (below) were still jostled over what Arthur Young called in 1770 "a cursèd string of hills and holes."

Methodist George Whitefield's gospel of reform alarmed conservatives on both sides of the Atlantic. In America his fiery sermons led to the religious upheaval known as the "Great Awakening."

A Nation
of Shopkeepers

The eighteenth-century London coffeehouse served also as information center and newsroom. It was a place where Tories and Whigs, merchants and politicians, scholars and wits discussed candidly the turbulent events on the local and international scene.

Morland's aptly titled "Fruits of Early Industry and Economy" idealizes the prosperous merchant. Seated by a window overlooking the busy water front, the entrepreneur receives an accounting from a clerk. His handsome family and a Negro servant hover nearby, and on the wall is a painting, presumably of his country house.

While the face of England was being changed, its foreign commerce ushered in a new generation of men whose ambitions, attitudes, and bursting prosperity began to affect the entire structure of eighteenth-century society. Merchants who had foreseen America's economic importance reaped a rich harvest when the Navigation Acts gave them a virtual monopoly of colonial traffic, and other men were quick to follow their lead. In 1756 Rolt's *New Dictionary of Trade and Commerce* described the phenomenon: "The merchant is now invited to every port, manufactures are established in all cities, and princes who just can view the sea from some single corner of their dominions are enlarging harbours, erecting mercantile companies, and preparing to traffick in the remotest countries."

Nor was material wealth the only by-product of England's bustling wharves. With his new affluence the merchant acquired social mobility, through purchase of a seat in Parliament or a place in society. Slowly, almost imperceptibly, he began to crack the traditional barriers of privilege. And when the uproar from America threatened to upset the commercial *status quo*, the voice of the British merchant was heard more often, and with increasing weight, in the houses of Parliament.

The Custom House Quay on the Thames was a scene of constant activity, where trading vessels from east and west discharged their exotic cargoes. When the Stamp Act abruptly checked the flow of raw materials from the American colonies, British merchants sided with the colonists in a determined effort to protect their trade.

In 1780 George Stubbs painted Wedgwood and his family in a grove near their estate. The successful manufacturer is shown with a piece of the popular black basalt ware at his elbow.

A jasper-ware teapot made by Wedgwood

Views of Britain ornament the Wedgwood service designed for Catherine the Great.

The Rise of Industrialism

As Britain's expanding foreign trade created a demand for increased production, a new generation of entrepreneurs began transforming the English landscape. Small market towns mushroomed into manufacturing centers like Birmingham, Leeds, Manchester, and Sheffield. To factory and foundry came men of all classes, eager to offer their brains and hands in return for financial gain. Hard work, thrift, and a keen business sense were the keys to success. "Happily for this country," said a member of Parliament in 1764, "the commercial interests of Great Britain are now preferred to every other consideration." Prototype of this new merchant class was Josiah Wedgwood, who within a few years revolutionized the entire pottery industry. He made use of new materials, precision tools, assembly lines, and advertising methods; and even promoted the building of canals to speed his wares to Liverpool for export. To his business partner he wrote in 1766: "What do you think of sending Mr. Pitt upon crockery ware to America. A Quantity might certainly be sold there now & some advantage made of the American prejudice in favour of that great man." Other businessmen were just as mindful of the necessity of American trade to their livelihood. Two months before hostilities flared at Lexington, the merchants of Birmingham petitioned Edmund Burke to remedy the evils arising "from a continual Stagnation of so important a branch of our Commerce as that with North America."

An astonished resident of Birmingham (above) described it as "A Street of Houses in the Autumn, where he saw his horse at Grass in the Spring." By 1781 what had been a "pitiful Market Town" was a bustling industrial city of 50,000 inhabitants, iron and steel foundries, the Turner brassworks (background, right), and producers of buttons, buckles, thread, and enameled snuffboxes. The famous Boulton & Watt steam-engine factory was in nearby Soho.

By 1788 the banks of the Severn at Broseley (below) were withered and the sky almost obscured by sooty fumes from the blast furnaces of John Wilkinson's iron foundry and boring mill. The valley echoed with the roar from the huge bellows, where cannon and precision-made cylinders for Boulton & Watt's steam-engine factory were produced. Wilkinson floated the first iron barge on this same river, over which he also constructed the world's first iron bridge.

The Rotunda in Ranelagh Gardens was a favorite rendezvous of many fashionable Londoners from 1742 until the end of the eighteenth century.

London Town

At the hub of Great Britain lay London, its harbor crowded with riches from the high seas. Like a huge magnet, it attracted a hodgepodge of people comprising about one-tenth of England's growing population. To men of an older school the city was an evil "overgrown monster" which would surely destroy its inhabitants. To reformers clamoring for better government it was less the seat of Parliament than a throne of high finance from which the merchant princes ruled. But to the average Englishman it was an exciting, pulsating metropolis, best described by Samuel Johnson's dictum: "When a man is tired of London he is tired of life."

Along its narrow cobblestone streets vendors hawked their wares, and shopkeepers did a brisk business with aristocrats and *nouveaux riches* who ran "from one taylor to another, for the newest cut." At theaters and in the pleasure gardens that ringed the city of London, the nobility now found themselves jostled by the new middle class. Small houses were going up in the very shadows of great Georgian mansions, commercial traffic grew denser over London Bridge and on the Thames, and the air was heavy with coal smoke. Times were changing, and London mirrored the bustle of a vigorous nation.

From the Duke of Richmond's house the Venetian painter Canaletto captured the beauty of London's harbor. Elegant gentry idle on the Duke's terrace, boats glide by, and St. Paul's great dome rises across the river.

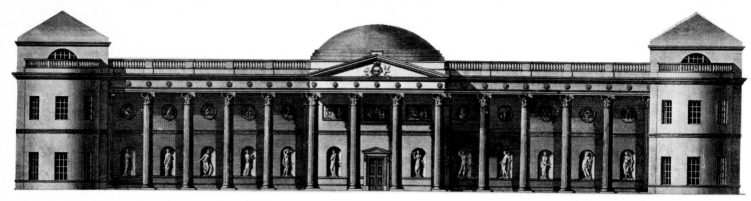

The classic façade of the Earl of Bute's Luton Park House was over 240 feet long. It was designed by the famous architect Robert Adam.

The Great Age of the Landed Gentry

The adroit, handsome Earl of Bute, an early favorite of George III, was descended from a natural son of one of the Stuart kings.

Since the beginning of the eighteenth century the size of England's country estates had grown larger, and the wealth of the great landowners had increased by leaps and bounds. Every county had a few families, usually aristocratic, whose riches and way of life set them apart politically as well as economically and socially. Not only did the landed gentry control local politics, they also dominated Parliament; and their natural conservatism was at the root of many difficulties which divided England and America.

The center of life of these agrarian millionaires was a rural palace on which no expense had been spared. Designed by master architects such as the brothers Adam, James Gibb, and William Kent, they were filled with furniture by Chippendale and Sheraton, paintings by Gainsborough, Romney, Sir Joshua Reynolds, and Ramsay, not to mention treasures brought back from the continent of Europe. The elegance and proportions of these mansions and their exquisite grounds reflected a good deal more than mere wealth. They bespoke a profound confidence in a way of life which inspired men to build not just for their own time, but for their grandchildren's.

Yet for those who would heed them there were signs that this settled, well-ordered world could not continue indefinitely. England itself was growing too large and too complex for the constitution which this landowning class had created; and in those irritating colonies beyond the Atlantic, and across the Channel in France, the tides of economic and social life were shifting rapidly, eating away at the edges of this golden era.

In eighteenth-century England, society revolved around the great country houses. Here, on their enormous landholdings, the gentry and nobility spent much of their time. Frequently, to break the pleasant monotony of their lives, they traveled, with their retinue of servants, to a friend's estate, where they might spend several weeks. The conversation piece at right was painted by William Hogarth and depicts an afternoon party, or assembly, at the lush countryseat of Sir Richard Child.

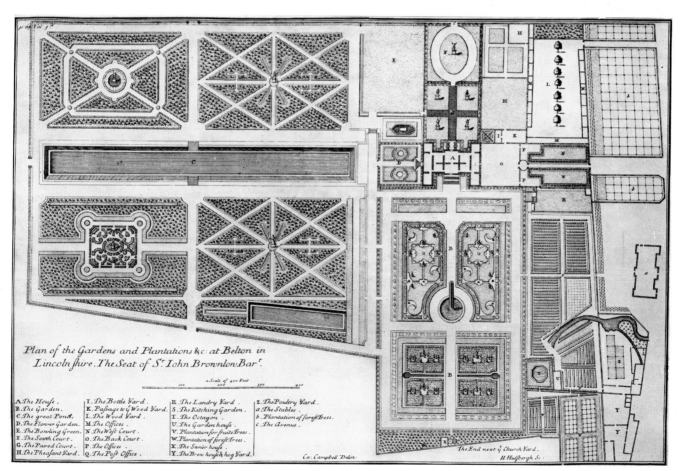

Plan of the Gardens and Plantations &c: at Belton in Lincolnshire. The Seat of S.ʳ John Brownlow Bar.ᵗ

a Scale of 400 Feet

A. The House .
B. The Garden.
C. The great Pond.
D. The Flower Garden .
E. The Bowling Green.
F. The South Court .
G. The Paved Court .
H. The Pheasant Yard.

I. The Bottle Yard .
K. Passage to ẏ Wood Yard.
L. The Wood Yard .
M. The Offices .
N. The West Court .
O. The Back Court .
P. The Offices .
Q. The Post Office .

R. The Landry Yard .
S. The Kitching Garden .
T. The Octagon .
U. The Garden house .
V. Plantation for fruite Trees .
W. Plantation of forest Trees .
X. The Somer house .
Y. The Brew house & hog Yard .

z. The Poultry Yard .
a. The Stables .
b. Plantation of forest Trees .
c. The Avenue .

Ca: Campbell Delin   The End next ẏ Church Yard .

H. Hulsbergh Sc :

This formal garden, one-third of a mile wide, included a bowling green, elaborate outbuildings, decorative fruit trees, and a pheasant yard. The house (A, right center) overlooked the long narrow "great Pond" at left.

The Bartholomew Fair, an annual trade festival which lasted from three days to a fortnight, provided amusement for all ranks of society. Thomas Rowlandson, from whose water colors this and the two engravings at right were made, was one of the greatest illustrators of this period.

London aristocrats and rabble alike flocked to nates convicted of minor offenses against society. pillory, are being abused by a mob, which some-

"The Soldier's Return" is the title of this water color painted in 1770 by the Swiss artist Grimm. A peglegged veteran comes home after years of service abroad to find his wife remarried and his own children relegated to the workhouse (right).

Itinerant laborers tilled wheat fields but reaped precious little of what they sowed.

Charing Cross to revile and hurl refuse at unfortu-
Here two men, their heads and hands locked in a
times even stoned the hapless criminals to death.

In the center of a small amphitheater two cocks fight a life-and-death battle to the delight of a
noisy, gambling audience. A visitor to England in 1753 noted: "The people, whether of high
or low rank, behave like madmen, betting higher and higher up to 20 or more guineas."

*If this beggar woman became a burden
to the local parish, she was driven out.*

Poverty Amid Plenty

Beneath the surface prosperity, obscured by the domes of Wren's churches and the palatial homes of the rich, was the grinding, poverty-stricken existence of underprivileged England. The lower classes huddled together in crumbling, infested tenements, soured with the stench of dead animals and excrement that rose from filthy alleys and open sewers. For the masses, wages were low and working hours long. Starvation was common, punishments for petty crimes cruelly harsh, and life so cheap that the hangings at Tyburn were a welcome amusement for thousands.

Such people were not unknown to America. These unfortunates manned England's army and navy, and most emigrants came from the middle or lower classes. As Crèvecoeur wrote, "The rich stay in Europe; it is only the middling and the poor that emigrate." Possibly 40,000 British convicts were shipped to America in the eighteenth century, prompting Dr. Johnson's remark: "Sir, they are a parcel of convicts, and if they get anything short of hanging they ought to be content." Benjamin Franklin playfully offered American rattlesnakes to the motherland in return for the criminals, but the practice of dumping "the excrescence of England" in the colonies was a real source of grievance.

G R

To generations of Americans, George III has overshadowed eighteenth-century England, looming as the very model of a tyrant. Yet not until the Revolution was well under way did their ancestors lose their deep respect for this tragic man. Only 22 years old when he succeeded his grandfather, George III was mentally and emotionally little more than a boy. Lonely and uncertain, he nevertheless had a strong sense of morality and a determination to rule as well as to reign. With obstinate devotion to what he saw as his duty, the King refused to show the slightest leniency toward the colonists, believing that they must be forced into absolute obedience.

The burdens of office and constant wrangles over the American problem contributed to his periodic fits of insanity, and his frequent changes of ministries from 1763 to 1770 created the illusion that George III was actually the dominant figure in British politics. Gradually he became the "tyrant" to the colonists, and was attacked as such by Americans and the opposition in Parliament.

As events in America approached their tragic climax, the King was unable to find a minister who could cope with the situation. And by 1775 his knack of making perfectly legitimate royal powers seem despotic when he exercised them had thoroughly alienated the colonists, creating among them a frail unity which would have been unthinkable ten years earlier.

To many Britons war in America spelled doom. In this 1775 cartoon the King, eyes shut, is drawn by obstinacy and pride into a chasm. While America burns, the Constitution and Magna Charta are trampled, and national credit vanishes.

This impressive portrait of George III, Queen Charlotte, and six of their fifteen children was painted in 1771 by John Zoffany. Only 33 years old at the time, the lonely, conscientious King had already shown signs of the insanity which was to darken his life. Bitterly attacked in the early, turbulent years of his reign, he was caricatured as a despot, a spendthrift, or as "Farmer George" (below, left, with the Queen) for his agricultural interests. Long after the American Revolution, when the French began to subject their royal family to insult, and when George III's own children had betrayed him, Englishmen began to appreciate his natural virtues. Gradually his simple dignity, his intensely moral private life, and his unusual frugality brought him popularity and the tardy respect of his people.

43

Lord George Germain

George Grenville

Charles Townshend

Lord North

Placemen and the Opposition

North, Fox, and Burke do a Coalition Dance about a masked bust of "King Wisdom 3d," who had opposed this "desperate Faction."

Idiots and dying men stuff the ballot box in Hogarth's bitter 1758 engraving of corrupt voting methods prevalent during this period.

When George III ascended the throne in 1760, it was his sincere belief that his grandfather's advisers had led the country near to ruin. At once he set out to depose the powerful Whig faction which had dominated George II's reign and chose, to replace William Pitt as chief adviser, the "pompous, slow, and sententious" Earl of Bute. Within a year Bute's influence over the King declined, and by 1763 he had been replaced with George Grenville.

A man "great in daring, and little in views," it was Grenville who began to put teeth into George III's policy that "the Colonies are not to be emancipated from their dependence on the supremacy of England." His solutions, such as the Stamp Act, met stiff opposition in America and in Parliament, especially from men like Pitt, Fox, and Burke, who identified the colonists' struggle to preserve "home rule" with their own fight against an autocratic king.

As the rumbling tide of American resistance heightened, George cast about from one minister to another for a man of ability. Grenville was followed, in 1765, by the short-lived "lutestring ministry, fit only for the summer" of Lord Rockingham; and Rockingham's departure brought in the Duke of Grafton, whose Chancellor of the Exchequer, Charles Townshend, considered the whole colonial uproar over taxes "perfect nonsense." In a final disastrous move, George III picked, in 1770, the man who would bring his country's fortunes to the lowest point in modern history—Lord North. This short-sighted statesman, whose "wide mouth, thick lips, and inflated visage gave him the air of a blind

At left are shown four of the ill-chosen ministers who advised George III and tried to carry out his suppressive colonial policy. At right and below are the principal opposition figures, who were frequent champions of the colonists' cause.

Charles James Fox

Edmund Burke

John Wilkes

trumpeter," had neither strength nor inclination to alter the course of events.

If the King's ministers stood for compliance, the opposition symbolized independence in thought and action. There was the brilliant dandy, Charles James Fox, dismissed from North's cabinet because of his speeches against tyranny. There was the eloquent Edmund Burke, staunch defender of Amer-

ican rights. And, sharpest of all thorns in George's side, there was the ugly, vain, ambitious John Wilkes, who became a focus for discontent in England and America. The rallying cry "Wilkes and Liberty!" echoed through the streets of London and Boston alike as "that devil Wilkes" undermined confidence in the King, creating a crisis such as Britain had not witnessed for generations.

In 1778 the colonists lost an ally when William Pitt, then Earl of Chatham, was stricken in the House of Lords. His dramatic collapse occurred as he was delivering a fiery attack on the government's American policies.

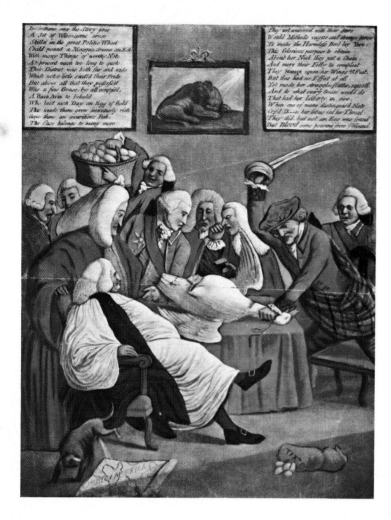

The 1776 Whig cartoon at left shows Tory ministers about to kill the goose that laid the golden eggs, symbolizing the American colonies. At right, colonial agent Benjamin Franklin is arraigned by the Privy Council in 1774 for his release of certain private letters written by Thomas Hutchinson, the Royal Governor of Massachusetts. Without Franklin's knowledge, parts of these letters, suggesting "an abridgment of . . . English liberties" in America, were circulated by propagandist Samuel Adams to incite rebellion.

Hopes for a Reconciliation Fade

In the tense decade before 1775 the King and his ministers drew up measure after measure designed to bind American colonists to the motherland, only to see the rift widen. In 1766 William Pitt warned: "Will you sheathe your sword in the bowels of your brothers, the Americans? You may coerce and conquer, but when they fall, they will fall like the strong man embracing the pillars of this Constitution, and bury it in ruin with them."

Less and less often the voice of reason was heard, and even patient Benjamin Franklin began to lose hope for appeasement. Country gentlemen, appalled by mounting taxes brought on by the French wars, demanded that the colonies carry their share of the debt burden; bungling politicians turned the screws

of economic and political control tighter and tighter; and when Americans reacted by boycotting English goods, the merchant's powerful voice was added to the din.

Americans, not comprehending the British point of view, found it unreasonable and oppressive; Englishmen thought the colonists' attitude outrageous. As early as 1765 Thomas Pownall had foreseen what might happen. "The particular danger," he said, "is that of furnishing [the Americans] with a principle of union. . . . If ever the colonies revolt, and set up an empire in America, here begins the history of it . . ." Indeed, transplanted Englishmen began to sense this as each dispute with their motherland brought Virginia closer to Massachu-

setts, and Pennsylvania to South Carolina.

Some Britons protested when Grenville put through that "most pernicious" revenue plan, the Stamp Act. Lord Chesterfield said "it has given such terror to the Americans that our trade with them will not be, for some years, what it used to be . . ." But to Americans this was not just a matter of trade—it was a final act of tyranny. After 1765 there were retreats on both sides, to be sure, but there would be no reconciliation. And when news of Boston's destructive Tea Party reached England early in 1774 it was the ultimate offense to all men of substance, regardless of their politics. The fuse had been lit. When it would reach the powder keg of revolution only time would tell.

In 1767 Franklin designed and sent this cartoon to friends. It prophesies the sad plight of Britannia stripped of her colonies.

Samuel Adams points to the Massachusetts Charter in this portrait by Copley

THE EVE
OF REVOLT

"The Revolution was effected before the war commenced.

The Revolution was in the minds and hearts of the

people. . . . This radical change in the principles,

opinions, sentiments, and affections of the people was the

real American Revolution."

JOHN ADAMS—1818

ON THE morning of September 13, 1759, gray-black clouds rolling down the valley of the St. Lawrence lowered over the Plains of Abraham and the rock-citadel of Quebec, high above the river. The fields once owned by the pilot Abraham Martin were masked by a gray-yellow blanket of smoke, through which long lines of men in scarlet and white were driving east toward the city. Before them stumbled broken masses of troops in mud-spattered white, heading for the gates of Quebec and fancied safety.

Veteran British troops were driving veteran French in utter rout from the fields of pilot Abraham, while in the rear the British commander, General James Wolfe, lay dying on the sodden, bushy turf. Through the yawning Porte St. Louis rode the French leader, the Marquis de Montcalm. Swaying in the saddle from mortal wounds, his fading senses brought him the echoes of wild cheering as kilted men fell on Canadian militia and French regulars with the broadswords of the Scottish glens.

It was a small engagement, probably involving few more than 5,000 men on a side, a miniature battle fought in the heart of nowhere. Yet its repercussions were infinitely beyond the comprehension of those men who saw the British colors flutter up the flagstaff on Cape Diamond in place of the Bourbon lilies.

The effects of Wolfe's victory were everywhere slow in making themselves apparent. At times the halyards of the British flag seemed frayed and thin above the jutting Cape. But day after day, month after month, that flag still flew, and its continued presence bore a message to thoughtful ministers of state far overseas in Europe.

Governmental processes trundled along on the slow wheels of the eighteenth century until, at last, in the city of Paris, quill pens were sharpened, parchments spread out, candles lit for the thick red sticks of wax as great seals were produced. Weary-eyed clerks entered the date, February 10, 1763, while bowing ministers of Great Britain and France signed documents proclaiming that from this day all Canada was to be British, not French. And with Canada went the city of Quebec on its high rock, the City and the Rock that were the key to the vast St. Lawrence. In a single stroke, the shadow of that Rock (and all that its possession by a hostile foreign power implied) was lifted from the thirteen British colonies, profoundly influencing what was said and thought and done by the colonists.

James Wolfe, mortally wounded in the attack on Quebec, 1759

The scrape of quill pens and the rustle of parchment that confirmed the transfer of this enormous northern land mass to British keeping were a low-pitched prelude to a great stirring and awakening that was to swell slowly, almost imperceptibly, through the provinces south of Canada. Of utmost significance to America and Americans was the lowering forever of the French flag throughout that wild domain.

The Treaty of Paris ushered in a brief span of time upon which British North Americans would look back a few years later as a sort of Golden Age. No hostile power threatened. The whole Atlantic coast line and its shallow, thinly settled hinterland belonged to England and to the thousands of transplanted Europeans, mostly from the British Isles, who had flocked to the New World since the dawn of the previous century. The prospect was dazzling, and men such as the Reverend Jonathan Mayhew of Boston preached lyrically of a "vast Anglo-American Empire," hastily adding, "I do not mean an Independent one!"

The solidarity that Mayhew and others after him invoked was, however, geographical rather than political and cultural, and hence a little unreal. Groups of Europeans had come to America at widely varying times and for even more widely varying reasons—profit, adventure, greater opportunity, freedom from political and religious oppression, real or fancied. They had brought up against the coast, struggled ashore, clotted at their landing places, and then begun a slow, inevitable inland drift. None of these groups remained static after arrival, but went through a steady process of change as they met and reacted to the innumerable forces at work in the vast new land.

From Maine's shadowy northern border down to the southernmost fringes of Pennsylvania, the unit of life was the farm—the relatively small holding that could be developed by the landowner, his immediate family, and such help as might be available locally. Such a farm was, in principle, self-sufficient for one family, its relatives and dependents. And this implied a wide diversification of products rather than reliance on one staple crop, if the family was to survive. A farmer might raise cattle for the market as well as for himself, but he would also put land under corn and rye and wheat. Given water, he set up a gristmill and then a sawmill. Bog iron on his land would lead to a forge and to a smithy capable of manufacturing nails or anchors. If the region about him were well developed he might turn most of his time to making flour or ironware, confident that his output would be enough to sell or barter for the necessities or luxuries that he no longer produced. Even then he would keep enough productive fields and herds to be safe, just in case.

A nexus of such holdings led to a settlement which grew into a village, and then into a town big enough to support churches, schools, local government, and the products and services of the artisan. Over roads and navigable waterways traveled an increasing flow of news, through the medium of travelers, letters, and the infant but lusty American press. Thousands of people living on the utmost fringes of the colonial world became ever more aware of a horizon far wider than their own immediate milieu, and awaited eagerly the arrival of news from remote places. This receptivity was to be of the utmost importance in the years to come.

Such a society was in theory and often in practice a leveling one, denying the existence of "the squire in the big house on the hill" with humbler folk touching respectful forelock to him. It put a premium on labor, for who would hire out when he could stand as his own master on his own land? It also made it almost impossible to create a labor pool of any size or stability.

Vast holdings did exist, of course, particularly in New York, where earlier Dutch grants had been confirmed by the British, and there virtual wilderness principalities had been claimed. But through most of the northern colonies, the transplanted European had the bright star of opportunity always before him— the lure of ownership of the land.

The South was less a geographic term than it was a different way of life, although settled largely by men of the same origins and backgrounds as those farther north. This was a land of large holdings, of small population centers, of fierce concentration on one crop—tobacco—which was to set its seal on eighteenth-century southern life as deeply as would cotton in the nineteenth. And essential to tobacco production was Negro slavery. Tobacco was the sure cash crop, the equivalent of a man's skill in tanning leather or working iron or shaping silver. Acreage had to be large to produce a worthwhile return, and this one fact made slavery inevitable. The plant quickly exhausted the land, so a substantial planter had to count his acres by the thousands rather than by the score. The ideal of extensive holdings throttled off the growth of centers of population. People scattered over the face of the land, tried to turn their holdings into self-contained units with selected slaves performing those services re-

An 18th-century engraving of a "new cleared" American farm

An English traveler's impression of an American stage wagon

51

English trade-card advertisement for Virginia tobacco

quiring artisan skills. This tendency necessarily limited the field of endeavor of white newcomers, whatever their gifts, and drove them to new land where, with a little luck, a man could rise to the planter class.

Tobacco cultivation extended down into North Carolina, where the one-crop standard was somewhat diluted by the great stands of pine and the naval stores they produced. In South Carolina tobacco was replaced by the double staples of rice and indigo, the latter enjoying a Crown subsidy. But the Maryland-Virginia norm held in these colonies, too—a life based on slave labor and an avoidance of urban centers, with the one glittering exception of gem-like Charleston. Georgia, a Crown colony only since 1752, was shaping itself in the same pattern.

This dispersion of population greatly hampered the growth of schools and roads. The most prosperous sent their sons to England to be educated, while the less favored depended on itinerant teachers or did without. The network of coastal rivers and streams sufficed, for the most part, to float staple crops to the sea for shipment abroad. Newspapers could hardly flourish on any important scale, and churches had small congregations.

There were some exceptions to the southern pattern. Maryland and Virginia exported pig iron and milled wheat. North Carolina had its naval stores and South Carolina was making great strides in cattle raising. In the western reaches of all these colonies, the smallholder with few, if any, slaves often prospered lustily. Many of these settlers had worked west from the coast, but an increasing flood was moving steadily down the north-south valleys from Pennsylvania and New Jersey. Soon they began to edge east, and a conflict of two separate ways of life threatened, particularly in the Carolinas.

This sharp cleavage in the development of North and South seemed to predicate two alien worlds taking firm root on the same continent and with no natural boundary between them. Yet a good many identical forces were playing on people without regard for their way of life or for geography. From Maine to Georgia, the land dominated people's thinking. First it must be broken if a man was to survive, then it had to be owned to ensure permanence of that survival. In the changing life of the New World land was immutable. Land was the magical commodity upon which prosperity was based, which determined the owner's scale of living and his position in society.

Another factor which influenced American life and thought was that the colonists could not afford *not* to waste. The tree line must be pushed back whether the clearing was for a few acres of New Hampshire corn or a hundred acres of Maryland tobacco. When farms and plantations and towns lay at last in open country, then the old forest-enemy became an asset, but the habit of waste was so ingrained that a century and more would pass before that change was generally realized.

A frontier log cabin, engraved in France by Victor Collot

From the Georgia swamps to the pine ridges of Maine, all sections suffered from a perennial shortage of coined money, and what did circulate was maddeningly lacking in uniformity. The very first settlers in any region brought little cash with them. Later comers were apt to be backed by credit in England rather than supplied with actual currency. The bulk that did circulate must have come from trade with forbidden areas, a practice at which many Royal officials did not even bother to wink. Coins of all nations circulated freely, if not lavishly, and the average man had to be, in a rudimentary way, an exchange broker. The notebook of the dead pirate captain in *Treasure Island* with its "table for reducing French, English and Spanish moneys to a common value" could have been no novelty to the colonist. Paper money had been issued from time to time by various legislatures, usually unsecured and subject to repudiation, devaluation, and revaluation. Accounts were often settled partly in mixed currencies and paper, partly in goods and services. The journals of Matthew Patten of Souhegan East, New Hampshire, are full of such entries. "I got 1½ bushell of Indian corn from Geo. Hadley. He owed me 3 £ Old Tenor . . . If corn is sold at 2 pistareens a bushell, then I am to pay him half a pistareen and if the price is 15 s/ a bushell, then I have got my just due . . . I got 2½ doz. Mohair Coat buttons from james Vose which cleared all he owed me . . . He paid me 79 £ Old Tenor and 8 johannas equal to 64 Dollars and 2 Crowns and 2 Dollars and 2 Quarters of a dollar and 5 pistareens, the whole amounting to 82 Dollars and 40/ Bay Old Tenor." In other areas, standard values were set for such items as beaver pelts, "Merchantable rice" or "heavy drest deerskins."

Yankee mariner, from *A Book of Trades, or Library of Useful Arts*

Along with North and South, the seacoast itself, especially in New England, could almost be viewed as a unique and separate division, driven by many forces which did not apply inland. A great Massachusetts fishing industry absorbed the thought and energy of thousands and shipped its products up and down the seaboard, to the West Indies, to England. From Maine to Georgia, trading ships worked out to sea, bound for other American ports, for the West Indies, or for such European harbors as British law allowed or, often, did not allow. These phases of coastal life were tied tightly to the shore line and possibly could have existed without the colonization of the interior.

At deep water the only real cities of British North America had arisen, a mere four in number, marked by a concentration of wealth and by the appearance of a powerful merchant class. Here, too, flourished the budding American press, whose sheets were carried by land and water to spots far from the place of publication. Pennsylvania farmers and Carolina planters could find, in addition to their own sheets, the Boston *Independent Advertiser* or the New York *Weekly Post Boy* in a tavern or city coffeehouse. New Englanders and New Yorkers could read the Pennsylvania *Gazette* or the South Carolina *Gazette*, brought by coastal traders. The cities also offered an active field for artisans of all types, men who would have been hard put to find sufficient outlets for their skills in the hinterland. Unskilled labor was apt to flock to the cities and form growing labor pools for the peculiar life of a metropolis. And these pools injected another factor into colonial life. When hard times came, whether transitory or protracted, idle men became a hot core of discontent, easily shaped by hands that knew how to mold it.

The four cities, in particular, had reached a stage of physical development that rarely failed to surprise visitors from Europe. There was Boston, perched on its polliwog peninsula within the sheltering arms of Massachusetts Bay. As early as 1720 one Daniel West had been staggered by the town, observing that from the number and quality of the buildings, the scale of living, and the caliber of conversation, "a gentleman from London would almost think himself at home." By 1750, another traveler noted over 3,000 houses, a third of them brick "and Pretty well Ornamented having Yards and Gardens adjoyning Also." New York clustered at the south tip of Manhattan Island, while Philadelphia, true metropolis of the New World, lay on the Delaware River looking down toward the calm, deep waters of Delaware Bay. Beyond Philadelphia there was nothing urban until Charleston was reached, a city spreading over the broad triangle between the Cooper and Ashley rivers, its influence dominating South Carolina and, to a certain extent, North Carolina and

". . . nothing but a high price will induce men to labour at all, and at the same time it presently puts a conclusion to it by so soon enabling them to take a piece of waste land."
—*American Husbandry, 1775*

Georgia. Uniquely, Charleston was a symbol of the South, far more than was Boston of New England or Philadelphia of Pennsylvania.

In the beginning the colonies had been individually linked to England through charters that displayed a bewildering lack of uniformity. Granted under successive reigns for widely differing motives to still more widely differing groups, they created a tangle of conflicting rights, claims, and restrictions. There were constant squabbles between the Crown and the various colonial governments, which had led on the one hand to threats of charter revocation or cancellation; on the other, the colonies answered with an opposition that ranged from surly acquiescence to flatfooted defiance.

By 1763 a fair degree of uniformity in local government had been reached and three distinct classes of colonies had emerged—Crown, Proprietary, and Corporate. Massachusetts, Rhode Island, and Connecticut belonged generally in the last group; Maryland, Delaware, and Pennsylvania in the second; and the rest in the first. The differences are not particularly important, save in a detailed study of colonial development, but it may be noted that all operated under a governor appointed or approved by the Crown, except in Rhode Island and Connecticut where the office was elective. The governor was supported by a council, also Crown-appointed save in Massachusetts, Rhode Island, and Connecticut. All colonies had a legislature elected by qualified freemen.

A Royal governor had wide, sweeping powers under Crown directives, and on paper his position was strong. Actually, those powers had to be exercised over a locally elected group, the legislature, which could make his position easy or downright untenable. Given colonial bodies that were touchy concerning their own rights and privileges, clashes between them and arrogant, often ignorant Royal appointees were bound to follow, were bound to worsen with the years. An exceptionally able man could have managed these legislatures or assemblies to the mutual benefit of England and the colony; but few Royal governors were even second-raters. Often political hacks rewarded for work done in England, they came here utter strangers to the country and its people, and rarely took the trouble to learn. Except in the case of New England, they were able to pack their councils, which acted as upper house to the legislatures, with creatures both malleable and ductile.

Despite many striking differences in government, in development, in modes of life, and in thought and aim, enough vital similarities existed so that, unconsciously, the Thirteen Colonies were undergoing manifestations of common experience which were transforming a mass of humanity into a nation. So far the colonists and the parent country were blandly unaware of this, as they were of a still more startling fact. The 2,000,000-odd souls who swarmed along the eastern seaboard and flowed gradually inland had ceased to be British colonists. Through the alchemy of environment, they had become Americans.

The inhabitants of these Thirteen Colonies, who, in the words of Stephen Vincent Benét, had eaten "the white corn-kernels, parched in the sun" and who, unknowingly, would "not be English again," moved briskly into their Golden Age. But already the gold had begun to tarnish and the first dull streaks came overseas from the east. England had just emerged from a long and costly struggle, a World War in terms of the eighteenth century, a war in which the conquest of Canada was merely a phase. In London, men whose views had to span a far wider range than just the Thirteen Colonies were totting up the cost of that struggle, wondering how it was to be met and how to keep their growing empire in balance.

Franklin's famous cartoon first appeared in 1754 in his Pennsylvania *Gazette*

The men who had these matters in mind were probably not the ablest group that Britain could have assembled. There were wasters and hacks and trimmers and place-seekers among them. There were also sound, wise men, far-seeing, calm-minded, who were able to set off what ought to be done against what could be done. Whatever their merits, their task was to solidify all parts of the new empire and not to prop up one at the expense of another.

Blundering humanly, acting with sometimes the best of intent and sometimes with the worst, the men who ruled England in the name of George III wrestled with a vast problem. The colonists contributed their own share of blunders, stupidities, and chicaneries. If there was failure in London to understand just what the American world was, that world was often blind to the problems of London.

Behind most of the decisions made by Britain's statesmen in this period was the nagging, omnipresent question of paying for an exhausting war that had left a national debt of some 130 million pounds sterling. And another question was linked to the first—who was to pay for the 10,000 British regulars thought necessary to garrison North America to keep the beaten French from turning speculative eyes on their lost possessions?

Not illogically, the ministry of George Grenville asked itself who would benefit most from such a garrison. Obviously, the colonists—so let them contribute to the upkeep of the great victory won for them by British arms. What the ministers' logic overlooked was the fact that New York and Massachusetts had, in great part, financed the last decisive campaign of General Jeffery Amherst and that Pennsylvania, too, had disbursed heavily in the cause of empire. The ministers also lost sight of the fact that none of this had been repaid.

It was suggested that an appeal be made to the several colonial legislatures to contribute. But the ministry, while knowing very little about American affairs, was dolefully aware that in the past such appeals had been more productive of protestations of loyalty than of money. Outright levies on the colonies were obviously in order, and positive steps were taken.

Soon colonial merchants were in an angry turmoil as rulings from overseas threatened to upset the commercial routine that had been evolved over the years. The collection of Royal customs, long an amiable joke, was to be tightened stringently, and the collectors, usually appointees from England, were ordered to get to work. Royal governors and the Royal Navy were to help, the latter body apparently being turned into a glorified customs patrol. The ancient and largely forgotten Acts of Trade and Navigation were dug out of the archives, and searchers found long lists of items that ought to produce revenue.

For example, highly profitable trade had flourished unchecked and unrebuked with Portuguese Madeira, whose wines were paid for with huge quantities of American barrel staves for wine casks. Now the colonists must buy Madeira wine through British shippers at a far higher cost, at the same time losing the lucrative Madeira market for barrel staves. Other rulings decreed that American exports to the European continent must first clear through British ports, an added step that swelled costs above any hope of profit.

Paradoxically, the worst blow came not through a raising of rates but a lowering of them. For years an import tax of sixpence per gallon had stood on the books against non-English West Indian molasses, but affable collectors had been satisfied with a far lower rate. A steady stream of ships beat their way down to the French and Spanish Indies laden with dried fish, lumber, naval stores, and horses, and brought back molasses which was then processed

Contemporary engraving of a merchant's counting house

"Men of war, cutters, marines with their bayonets fixed, judges of admiralty, collectors, comptrollers, searchers, tide waiters, land waiters, with a whole catalogue of pimps, are sent hither not to protect our trade, but to distress it."
—*A New England merchant*

into rum. The local consumption of this item was enormous, but even so it lagged behind production. By 1750, Massachusetts alone was exporting more than 2,000,000 gallons a year.

Now the official rate was pegged at threepence per gallon, cutting the levy in half, on paper. Actually it doubled it, since there was unwelcome evidence that the Crown really meant business, and intended to collect the full amount. In effect, the new Acts limited the source of molasses to the British West Indies, an area that could neither meet the demands of the distilleries nor absorb the export cargoes from the colonies. Up went the cost of molasses to the importers; down came the price that the island buyers would pay. The export-flow slowed, became stagnant. Cash reserves melted and local paper money dropped dizzily.

The cumulative effect of all these measures brought a gale of protest from everyone affected. In Massachusetts, the legislature claimed they "violated the right of levying taxes conferred by the Charter" on that body. Then, as though emboldened by this protest, it appointed a Committee to correspond with other colonial bodies. Down in Rhode Island, hollow-eyed merchants figured that even if they could afford to pay the new duty on molasses, the entire output of the British West Indies could supply barely a fifth of what the thirty-odd distilleries about Narragansett Bay required. New York was as hard hit, and Pennsylvania, badly shaken, added its voice to the tumult. The colonies farther south, being less affected, were understandably silent.

The combined outcry reached London in full force, but the new regulations stood unchanged, and the first common cause for a group of the colonies crystallized out of the waste syrups of far-distant sugar mills. Now all the measures became known as the Sugar Act, although the word "sugar" was barely mentioned in them.

Word had drifted west over the Atlantic of still another step which the ministry planned to put into effect in the next year, 1765. A direct tax was to be laid on all sorts of licenses, publications, and legal papers, and since compliance was to be attested by the use of special stamped paper, this measure was called the Stamp Act. In the past, one colony had often been silent while another voiced a protest. Now, without exception, all legislatures rose in astounding unison. From north to south a deep-throated roar of dissent welled up.

In Charleston the Assembly announced that "it is inseparably essential to the freedom of a people and the undoubted rights of Englishmen that no taxes be imposed upon them but by their own consent." Virginia unconsciously paraphrased South Carolina, while the northern colonies, already in fine voice from their unruly din over the Sugar Act, redoubled their volume. Actually, the whole matter had gone beyond protest. By jibbing first at the Sugar Act and now at the Stamp Act the colonies seemed to be challenging the authority of Parliament. The temper of England changed, and old friends of the colonies now backed the ministry. The matter of revenue became lost to sight and instead there loomed a far graver question: just what were the rights of Parliament and what were the rights of the colonists? This vital point had never been defined in the past. How would the present and future meet it?

In the meantime, measures for collecting existing duties, as well as those imposed by the Sugar Act, were running into heavy going. What constituted violation was subject to widely varying interpretations. Merchants were infuriated when it was decreed that all violations, real or suspected, be tried by the admiralty court in distant Halifax. Since admiralty courts did not allow trial by

Warning inspired by the Stamp Act, from the Pennsylvania *Journal*, 1765

jury, a very uneasy feeling arose that all trial by jury in all courts was to be abolished. Smuggling cases in local courts were almost sure to be settled for the defendant. But a man tried in Halifax could be quite certain of a verdict against him, since the prosecuting officer had only to satisfy the judge of the probability of guilt, with no possible redress for false arrest.

Further to alarm the whole country, the new year 1765 brought in a flood of failures and bankruptcies. Most of these were due to a general postwar slump, but the new Acts made fine targets for those most pressed or merely seeking a convenient focal point for blame. Traders and shippers made fumbling attempts at a boycott on British goods. New York also set up WPA-like projects to teach manufacturing skills to the unemployed. Boston, very hard hit, urged its people to adopt a rigid standard of austerity. In England, colonial agents appealed to British merchants who, like their American counterparts, were feeling the depression and were keenly aware that the bulk of their revenue came from America. The Englishmen were alarmed, but as the Massachusetts Agent, Jasper Mauduit, wrote home, they "talked much but there was no bringing them to action."

Ratified, signed, and sealed, the Stamp Act was sent winging through the spring gales of 1765 to each of the Thirteen Colonies. Trans-Atlantic passage in those days was unpredictable, and His Majesty's ships bearing the official decrees made their landfalls up and down the coast at widely differing times. And what those ships brought began a series of detonations up and down the coast like bombs equipped with delayed-action fuses.

In Williamsburg—lovely, sun-drenched capital of Virginia—a session of the House of Burgesses was nearing its close. Members drifted out of the triple-arched doorway past the twin semicircular bays with their *poivrière* roofs. A visitor, like young lawyer Thomas Jefferson, could probably have named them all —George Wythe, George Fairfax of Fairfax County, a Randolph or two from Henrico County, George Mason of magnificent Gunston Hall up the Potomac, his militia Colonel neighbor from Mount Vernon, George Washington, Benjamin Harrison of Charles City, a Lee, another Lee . . .

The members were probably discussing the speech that Patrick Henry of Hanover County had made, a speech that shook the slender spire of the capitol. Cautious men muttered that Henry had come close to treason in his defiant speech against the new Act; but all agreed that there had been a good deal in Henry's words, and they gathered at the Raleigh Tavern to probe into them. Out of discussion and wrangling came the Virginia Resolutions or Resolves, the first colonial answer to the Stamp Act, stating firmly that only Virginians could tax Virginians. Much that was highly inflammatory had to be cut out of the final version of the Resolves, but what did pass was strong enough to shock Joseph Royle, ultra-Royalist editor of the Virginia *Gazette,* to the point of suppressing any mention of what had actually been agreed upon. He would have done far better to have marked the whole passage "stet."

High-explosive paragraphs had been killed off in the House of Burgesses, but the backers of those items had copies of the full proceedings struck off, saying nothing about their final elimination. Then the copies were sent far and wide. The Newport *Mercury* published the text in full, and soon the Rhode Island Assembly, roaring its approval of what it thought Virginia had done, adopted the Resolves almost *in toto.* Most other colonies endorsed Virginia's supposed action in greater or lesser degree, and all joined in formal declaration that they should not be taxed by Parliament so long as they were not represented.

The·TIMES are Dreadful, Dismal Doleful Dolorous, and DOLLAR-LESS.

The Pennsylvania *Journal*'s bitter comment on the colonists' plight

A romanticized interpretation of Patrick Henry's speech to the House of Burgesses

It is hard to tell how violent the repercussions would have been had the tight-minded Mr. Royle allowed the rather mild actions of the Burgesses to be printed. It can only be said that most people accepted the highly radical un-adopted measures in good faith, since no correction of them appeared in the staid, prim Virginia *Gazette.*

Out of the approving roar that greeted Virginia's supposed action there emerged one definite step, logical enough in retrospect but superbly daring as seen from the year 1765. The Great and General Court of Massachusetts, to give that legislature its full title, sent out a ringing call for a Congress of all the colonies to meet in New York to consider unified action. The response was staggering—Virginia, North Carolina, and Georgia alone abstaining solely because of the interference of their respective Royal governors. New Hampshire was not represented, but registered its approval of the meeting.

Wall Street in New York had been a busy place since the old Dutch times, but no scene out of its past could have matched that of the October days of 1765. There were gold- and silver-laced hats, plain country hats, crimson and sky-blue and mulberry velvet coats, sober broadcloth and homespun swarming down the street's easy slope from Trinity Church. Delegates arrived on foot, on pad saddles, in glittering coaches, and they spoke in the accents of nine widely separated regions. One by one they turned into the Town Hall. There was Timothy Ruggles of Massachusetts, devoted to the ideal of the King above everything. Radical James Otis was with him, eyeing New Yorkers like the landed Livingstons or a Lispenard as the latter eyed Henry Ward of Rhode Island or Edward Tilghman of Maryland. The South Carolinians were there, Thomas Lynch, John Rutledge, and brilliant Christopher Gadsden. Surveying the whole throng, Delaware's Caesar Rodney thought this Congress "an Assembly of the Greatest Ability I ever Yet saw."

Timothy Ruggles was voted into the chair, perhaps as a gesture of courtesy to the colony that had sent out the call. Opposition to Ruggles would have been bitter had men known that he came armed with secret instructions from his Governor, Francis Bernard, to bring about a quick vote of submission to all Parliamentary Acts; but these instructions were in vain. Delegates whose thoughts were a world apart from Ruggles' swung into action. At first the debate was noisy rather than effective as men struggled to find their mental balance. Then Christopher Gadsden's voice rose above the muddled tumult, crying that the delegates must close ranks, must "stand on the broad and common ground of natural and inherent rights . . . as men and descendants of Englishmen!" His words swept on, spelling out a thought that had only been waiting for expression: *"There ought to be no more New England men, no New Yorkers . . . but all of us Americans!"*

Thus rallied, the Congress finally produced a Declaration of Rights and Grievances, stating firmly though respectfully that only the colonies themselves could levy taxes on colonists. This was a moderate enough statement, but it boldly defined what it held to be American rights. Pro and con, the American press carried the words of the Congress far and wide. By road and ship, Americans wrote to distant friends, keeping the issue alive. One Englishman, resident in America, wrote home to contrast "the remarkably pliant and submissive disposition of the inhabitants of Bengal" with that of the cantankerous colonies. His view was narrow, yet, by including distant India, this writer was thinking in terms of empire, something that few Americans would or could bring themselves to do. The prevalent colonial temper blinked the

From the Adams Papers

BOSTON, APRIL 9, 1773.

SIR,

THE Committee of Correspondence of this Town have received the following Intelligence, communicated to them by a Person of Character in this Place. We congratulate you upon the Acquisition of such respectable Aid as the ancient and patriotic Province of *Virginia,* the earliest Resolvers against the detestable Stamp-Act, in Opposition to the unconstitutional Measures of the present Administration. The Authenticity of this Advice you may depend upon, as it was immediately received from one of the Honorable Gentlemen appointed to communicate with the other Colonies. We are,

Your Friends and humble Servants,

Signed by Direction of the Committee for Correspondence in *Boston,*

} *Town-Clerk.*

To the Town-Clerk of   , to be immediately
delivered to the Committee of Correspondence for your Town,
if such a Committee is chosen, otherwise to the Gentlemen the
Selectmen, to be communicated to the Town.

A covering form letter for copies of the Virginia Resolves, distributed by Boston's Committee of Correspondence

fact that North America was merely one unit in a vast and growing entity, all of whose parts a British Parliament had to consider.

Another element emerged—the city mobs. Some evolved out of the heat of the times, others existed full-fledged, like that in Boston which had developed from the old "Pope's Day" brawls between the North and South Enders. Palsied, Harvard-bred Samuel Adams had earlier conceived the idea of uniting these rather uninhibited groups as a weapon for underscoring some strong popular wish, and had somehow managed to make them one. They were by no means composed of unemployable riffraff, but included men of high intellectual and economic status who turned out disguised as silversmiths, flax-teasers, or ropewalk men.

"Pope's Day" carriage in Boston, from a 1769 broadside

The Stamp Act was to take effect November 1, 1765, and in the interim the machinery of enforcement had to be assembled. With the appointment of the first stamp officer, the colonial kettle boiled over. Mobs went into action at once. In Boston matters got out of hand for the first and only time. Stamp officers were manhandled, the mansion of Massachusetts-born Lieutenant Governor Thomas Hutchinson was virtually taken to pieces, and his superb library, along with his priceless manuscript history of Massachusetts, was dumped into the street. New York, after a slow start, went even further than Boston, laying siege to the little Royal Artillery garrison at the Battery, burning the official coach of able Lieutenant Governor Cadwallader Colden, and wrecking the house of one Major James, commandant of the New York troops. The pattern was repeated elsewhere with varying degrees of intensity. In Charleston, South Carolina, the stamp officer recognized thinly disguised friends, relatives, and business associates in the mob. Up and down the country, men who had scrambled for the position of stamp officer now hastily and fearfully resigned. So the mobs came into being, and were soon distinguished by a common name that would outlast their organizations and the need for them. Colonel Isaac Barré, wounded at Quebec and long a friend of the colonists, speaking in Parliament, had wrapped them all in the title "Sons of Liberty."

All these actions had the effect of drawing a line through the colonies. It was not a line that separated those who opposed the Stamp and Sugar Acts from their supporters, for the latter were relatively few. Rather, the cleavage showed between those who opposed the Acts but felt in duty bound to obey them, and those who vowed that they should not be put into effect. Let it be officially admitted just once that Parliament had the right to tax, the latter group said, and any British government could extend its rule logically into every phase of life.

As 1765 died the Stamp Act was a matter of law, but rarely did a local government dare to bring out the stamped papers. Since these instruments were essential for the legal execution of a hundred phases of life from birth certificates to ships' manifests, all sorts of shaky, unsatisfactory makeshifts were devised, and affairs went on at an uneasy, nervous tempo. The earlier fumblings toward a trade boycott were revived, and some 900 merchants agreed to import nothing from England until the Stamp and Sugar Acts were repealed. British merchants took fright, and much of their alarm reached Parliament and the Rockingham ministry which had succeeded that of Grenville. In the spring of 1766, news of the repeal of the Stamp Act reached the New World.

There was little American rejoicing, however, for with repeal came a frightening pronouncement to the effect that the *right* to tax the colonies had always existed, and would exist for all time. Late summer brought on the fall of the Rockingham ministry, which was succeeded by one under the great William

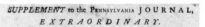

This Pennsylvania *Journal* supplement announced repeal of the Stamp Act

The aged Pitt speaking in Commons

Pitt, long friend of America. But Pitt was aging, ill, and failing mentally. Under him the official tax on molasses was dropped to a mere penny a gallon, and distillers were happy once more; but their joy was offset by other rulings that channeled all colonial exports, whatever their destination, through British ports, thereby whittling profits to a razor-thinness. All dreams of a renewed Golden Age under Pitt, now Earl of Chatham, vanished.

New York was the next colony to erupt. Governor Moore, who succeeded Cadwallader Colden, snouted out an old law known as the Mutiny Act under which New York could be made to pay for the upkeep of the small British garrison there. Fuming and spluttering, the Assembly was called on for several thousand pounds for this purpose. The Act was probably applicable, but New Yorkers claimed that they were being made to pay for the entire cost of a force that was supposed to protect all the colonies. Also it seemed to them a tax levied without colonial assent. If they submitted, the sum could be increased year after year until they and their fellows could be made to carry Britain's whole army budget. If the army, why not the navy, too? The Assembly merely sat on its hands, or "stood bluff" in the language of the day, and let Moore's demand go by unanswered.

Across in England, the helm had slid from Pitt's failing grasp into the hands of Charles Townshend—from the hands of a statesman into those of a glib, trimming politician—and the slope down which Anglo-American relations had been skidding grew slicker and steeper, with the Townshend Acts hovering just over the frosty rim of the new year of 1767.

Townshend's first step was to fight off a violent faction in his own party that clamored for the full use of the army and navy to bring New York to its senses. Instead, he got through a measure suspending that Assembly until such time as it might see fit to produce the funds in question. Then he turned to the matter of over-all revenue. Since the colonists objected to internal taxes, he assumed that *external* levies would be acceptable, and produced a set of rates on a list of imports from England, a schedule of innocent items like paper and lead and glass and paint and tea.

There was little American outcry at first. As for the New York Assembly, it out-slicked Townshend himself, voting a sum of money for the troops, but wording the grant so deftly that it seemed to come from spontaneous, open-hearted generosity rather than as a highly grudging answer to a demand from the mother country.

Before long, however, the colonists discovered that there was more to the Townshend Acts than a mere levying of duty. The so-called Writs of Assistance were virtually blank search warrants. An American board of customs commissioners, directly answerable to the Royal Treasury, was set up in Boston. Although the new duties were ostensibly for the defense of the colonies, the elastic phraseology stated that they would defray "the Charge of the Administration of Justice, and the Support of Civil Government." In other words, all fiscal control of local government and of the courts was to pass out of the hands of the electorate and into the control of men paid by the Crown. It was obvious that these men would not look to the governed for support, but to the hand that paid them. In a few years all American affairs would be run by a few influential families and their allies. The "squire in the big house on the hill" was clearly foreshadowed by these phases of the Townshend measures —a squirearchy, a government by landed gentry, and probably hereditary at that. If such fears seem farfetched today, one need only look back at what developed in Upper Canada during the first quarter and more of the nine-

"A very small office in the customs in America has raised a man a fortune sooner than a government."
— James Otis

teenth century, when the Robinsons, Boltons, Hagermans, Strachans, and others, most of them able, well-intentioned men, fought to make a private preserve of their own from the Ottawa River on to Toronto and the west.

Yet 1767 rolled away down its course of months with less friction than might have been expected. Ominous mutterings could be heard, however, from the west, increasingly audible along the Carolina coast. For more than a decade, an element alien to the planter-culture had been filtering south into the inner highlands. Settlers, hardy though poverty-stricken, had come from Virginia and Pennsylvania and Maryland, fearing that their original holdings lay open to Indian attacks after Braddock's defeat in 1755. The ways and thoughts of these uplanders did not fit those of the lowlanders. Trouble was brewing and soon would ripen into violence.

Up in Pennsylvania, John Dickinson, trained in London's Middle Temple, had been pondering on that first Congress of the colonies. Late in 1767 the Pennsylvania *Chronicle* began to publish the fruits of those ponderings, in a series of essays entitled *Letters from a Farmer in Pennsylvania to the Inhabitants of the British Colonies*. These *Letters* were printed in other papers, erupted in pamphlet form, covered all the colonies, and crossed over to England. Dickinson was presenting little that was new, but he had linked together the causes of a score of earlier outbursts and stated them reasonably and concisely. "Farmer John's" thesis was simple enough: Parliament had no power to tax for revenue; the Townshend Acts violated all known rights; the suspension of the New York Assembly set a precedent that could strangle any elected colonial body. The least-lettered man could understand and repeat what Dickinson had said, could begin to feel that common experience which all were sharing.

Dickinson had expressed the thoughts of just one citizen; but up in Boston burning, untrammeled Samuel Adams was busy along broader lines. His thoughts flowed with Dickinson's, but he was organizing them for action by the Massachusetts legislature in February, 1768. As a result, that body denounced the Townshend Acts as establishing taxation without representation, stated that colonial representation in England was impossible, and declared that the very idea of making colonial judges and governors independent of the electorate was utterly intolerable. These pronouncements, which entered history as the Massachusetts Circular Letter, were sent to the other twelve colonial bodies with a demand for united action.

Action came quickly enough, but not from the Assemblies. Across the water, Lord Hillsborough, successor to Townshend, fairly exploded. The Massachusetts men had conspired to "promote unwarrantable combinations, and to excite an unjustifiable opposition to the constitutional authority of Parliament." The governors of the other colonies must order their Assemblies to ignore the Circular Letter on pain of instant dissolution. As for Massachusetts, its Assembly was dissolved until it had recorded its "disapprobation of that rash and hasty proceeding."

Hillsborough's rhodomontade brought forth a universal roar of wrath. Up and down the country, Assembly after Assembly was dissolved. From Virginia, a soldier who had fought loyally against the French and Indians wrote in anger that he, for one, was ready to take up arms to defend colonial liberties. He signed himself George Washington. Lord Hillsborough, most unwittingly, had assisted John Dickinson and Samuel Adams in putting solid ground under colonial feet.

In the face of all this the Townshend Acts took effect in the worst possible

John Dickinson, painted by Peale

"The cause of liberty is a cause of too much dignity, to be sullied by turbulence and tumult."
—*John Dickinson, "Letters from a Farmer in Pennsylvania," 1768*

61

manner. Port collectors up and down the coast were chosen from men who had basked in the entourage of the Royal governors, and such appointments robbed the Crown of the one element which might have made the whole plan work— popular support. What this lack cost became quickly apparent, notably in a case involving young John Hancock, who, from his mansion on Beacon Hill, was calmly managing the fortune left him by his uncle Thomas.

British troops landing in Boston, from Remick's 1768 water color

The Hancock ship *Liberty* was seized in Boston Harbor by customs officials whose grounds for seizure were indisputable. But the port of Boston rallied to the Hancock cause. Officials were handled roughly, the cargo landed. The Royal Navy intervened, not too successfully. Then the denizens of Boston's port turned on the house of the Comptroller of the Customs, Benjamin Hallowell, smashed his windows, drove him to the shelter of Castle William, and, as a final touch, dragged the Customs Collector's official barge ashore, trundled it through the streets, and burned it joyously on the Common in front of Hancock's house.

This was bad enough; but when word came from England that young Hancock was to be fined £100,000, the case dragged on and on through the Boston courts until, in 1769, Attorney General Sewall published a frustrated, despairing statement, "Our Sovereign Lord the King will prosecute no further hereon."

The *Liberty* incident served unmistakable warning that no Crown officer could prevail against John Hancock and the popular backing that he received. It was obvious, too, that the ports of Philadelphia or Wilmington or Charleston would have reacted much the same under similar circumstances.

In the waning days of September, 1768, a great flotilla worked in among the low, green islands of Boston Harbor, decks bright with the scarlet of the British army. Anchors splashed, longboats took the water, and, platoon by platoon, His Majesty's troops were oared to Long Wharf, their coats showing the pale buff facings of the 14th West Yorkshires, the yellow of the 29th Worcestershires, the purple of the 59th East Lancashires, with Royal Artillery in blue and red scrambling after them.

Faneuil Hall in Boston, from the *Massachusetts Magazine*

The city had seen Royal troops often enough in the past, assembling to take the field against the French and Indians. But these soldiers were to act as a police force, to protect Royal officials in their efforts to carry out orders. Sons of Liberty were aghast at the very pointed garrisoning of their city. There was a meeting at the house of Will Molineaux, who held firm control over the wilder elements of the Boston mob and who seems to have clamored for instant physical action. Luckily, wiser counsel prevailed, and out of the thoughts of John and Samuel Adams, James Otis, Josiah Quincy, Jr., and Dr. Joseph Warren, a program of passive disobedience was adopted.

Its immediate results were less explosive than Molineaux had urged, but they still produced quick, hot friction. A hated measure known as the Quartering Act called upon any colony to house British troops. Now Boston announced frostily that no quarters were available. Only one regiment had tents, so Colonel Dalrymple of the 29th, senior officer ashore, forced entry into hallowed Faneuil Hall, billeted his men there, and later moved a number of them into the State House itself.

So the Boston garrison settled itself in its new post. With the best will on both sides, the situation would have been awkward. But even mild good will was absent, and the troops lay in the city like a hard substance against an aching tooth. Certainly Bostonians did nothing to relieve the pressure. The badly paid, badly fed troops were induced to desert and in the first fortnight a good thirty of them went over the hill. Others hired themselves out for all sorts of unskilled labor at the barest of wages, and at once the touchy workers of Boston began to fume, with fights breaking out between civilians and soldiers. It is not the British way to face such matters passively and Dalrymple's command soon found ways of striking back. If Dr. Joseph Warren spent an evening at the Bunch of Grapes, he was liable to be challenged on his way home by unsympathetic sentries, and forced to identify or account for himself. Young officers found they could raise Boston temperatures by whanging and tootling away with massed drums and fifes outside churches during meeting time.

General Thomas Gage, commander of all British forces in North America, came up from New York and managed to bring an uneasy sort of peace over the city. The Sons of Liberty remained sensibly quiet, even in the face of the arrival of the 64th Staffordshires and the 65th York and Lancs.

All this, as the year 1768 drew to its close, was amply disturbing. Yet a man of the times could, with surface logic, draw a pencil line along the coast and reason that trouble touched only the ports and those who drew a living from them. A closer look would show that inland life was profoundly affected. Port taxes and restrictions were looked upon as denials of basic colonial rights and such denials could be extended to reach the deepest settlements or farms. This point was underscored again and again by the spoken, written, and particularly the printed word. Editorially there was a massive unanimity in the press, for the Sons of Liberty were more than reluctant to allow much liberty to opposition sheets. Mr. Royle of the Virginia *Gazette,* the man who suppressed all mention of the Virginia Resolves, was hustled out of the way and his paper taken over by local Sons. In Boston, John Mein closed his *Chronicle* and fled to England.

A colonial printing press developed by Benjamin Franklin

The patriot press, with the field to itself and often bolstered by a stern, unbending disregard for the truth, bombarded inlanders with blood-chilling warnings. If a tax on merchandise went through unchallenged, who was foolish enough to think that a killing land tax was impossible? If Parliament could seize John Rowe's wharf or John Hancock's ships, it could just as easily move in on fields, barns, livestock, harvests, future crops, houses. Such thoughts, verbal, written, or printed, may seem like the most clumsy rabble-rousing. Yet many Americans of those days could cite, either from hearsay or from personal experience in another land, taxes on windows and on hearths as well as on land, crops, and livestock. A settler from Ireland could remember a land bled white by taxes, by rents equal to the yield of a given tract, and by strangling commercial restrictions, rigidly enforced. Who was bold enough to say "It can't happen here!" as long as England clung to its right to tax?

During the spring session of 1769, Colonel George Washington was given the floor in the Virginia House of Burgesses. Reading the text of a set of Resolves in his usual restrained voice, Washington restated the claim that only Virginians could tax Virginians. Then the scope of his speech widened, denouncing the ministry for its harshness in dealing with the Massachusetts Circular Letter. After this came a clear, sharp warning against threats from England that a 200-year-old Act would be whistled up under which the Crown could bring malcontents to England for trial. There was a quick lifting of powdered heads. Any man present could easily compile a list of Americans liable to be touched by such an Act.

Colonel Washington resumed his seat while the Speaker probably hoped for some reply from the floor to tone down or kill off the Resolves. The Burgesses sat silent and the chair reluctantly called for a vote. Then the delegates rose,

A blacklist of merchants who ignored the nonimportation agreement, printed in the *North American Almanac*, 1770

unanimously backing the Colonel's words with a response that was more important than the not too inflammatory tone of the Resolves. Still more important was the choice of the man to present those Resolves. The shadows of the future were beginning to take shape. The next day Lord Botetourt, Royal Governor, somewhat tactlessly dissolved the House, and the members filtered out of the capitol to gather in the Raleigh Tavern in informal but earnest session. Out of this and other meetings came a solid vote to join Massachusetts in a strict nonimportation agreement and to notify the other colonies of the decisions. There was a quick closing of ranks throughout the country, only Pennsylvania and, surprisingly, ever-cantankerous New Hampshire abstaining.

A strange, nervous quiet settled over the colonies, broken only by heat-lightning flickerings of coming trouble throughout the Carolinas. But this was domestic, not overseas trouble. The uplanders wanted courts such as they had known in other sections in premigration days, and their tone became harsh when they found such avenues to progress blocked. Absence of law led the uplanders to take it into their own hands with results that were often ill-considered and unfortunate. Such self-appointed legal bodies called themselves Regulators, and it was not long before the coastal planters began to look upon these men as even more threatening to their own particular rights than Parliament itself.

Across in England, merchants and those who looked to them for political support began totting up figures as 1769 waned. The nonimportation agreement was hurting badly. British merchants began to breathe more easily when, with the coming of 1770, the Townshend Acts died, and their death broke the great nonimportation log jam. One by one local and colonial associations broke up in relief, overlooking the fact that repeal had not been complete. A little, insignificant tax on tea remained, and by its very presence reaffirmed the Crown's doggedly held right to tax.

Other friction points began to throw off sparks to threaten the deceptive calm. In the city of New York, ill-feeling between Sons of Liberty and the Crown garrison cracked out in an ugly brawl. This clash, the "Battle of Golden Hill," was an omen. No one had been killed, no shots had been fired; but New York might flare up again. And in Boston, nerves were stretched thin as the apprehensive garrison glowered at a surly town. The British War Office had made an unfathomable move, shifting the 64th and 65th regiments up to Halifax; so there remained in Boston little save the 14th West Yorks and the 29th Worcesters, a force too small to be effective, yet strong enough to be a decided irritant.

On the evening of March 5, 1770, a crowd of rowdies flung sticks and snowballs at the forlorn British sentry near the Custom House. A squad of duty-troops swarmed out to support the bedeviled guard, but the mob pressed closer. Captain Preston of the 29th raced over to the post, shoved down muskets, pushed aside bayonets, shouting to his men not to fire . . . not to Fire . . . not to FIRE! It may be that this last word tightened a finger on a British trigger, but whatever the cause, a musket flared orange in the dark, followed by another and another, and dead and wounded port toughs lay dark against the slush of King Street. In the distance, boots pounded and drums rolled, telling of more troops coming. As the mob shrank back, Captain Preston acted with cool courage to get his men in hand. Then the mob was gathering again and the bells of Boston tolled ominously. The next rush could bring on a massacre.

Somehow Lieutenant Governor Thomas Hutchinson beat his way to the

State House and appeared on the east balcony. The moon was rising as he stood there, a calm, unmoving target hated by many a radical. As he spoke, quiet came slowly into the melting March night. The mob carried off its casualties and the troops were herded back into barracks. By dawn it was known from Copps' Hill to the Battery March that, under Hutchinson's orders, Captain Preston and eight men were to be tried for the murder of civilians.

John Adams and Josiah Quincy, Jr., undertook the defense of the troops and, in the face of hot demands from press and pulpit for conviction, forced through an acquittal of all save two, who were lightly punished. Such, in very general outline, was the celebrated "Boston Massacre" and its immediate results. No one came out of it very well, except for Hutchinson, Preston, Adams, and Quincy. The whole affair was local and might have been buried except for one man—Samuel Adams, the shabby, intense master-propagandist.

First of all, Adams forced the removal of the 14th and the 29th from the city to Castle William in the harbor, and the two units became known as "Sam Adams' Regiments." Then he turned the dead port toughs into martyrs, orating and thundering how they had been shot down in cold blood by hireling troops. Broadsides and ballads followed until March 5 became a hallowed anniversary, marked by solemn and often grisly ceremonies.

Samuel Adams clung to this event the more tightly since, with the cooling of men's minds by the repeal of the Townshend Acts, he had become that most pathetic of figures—a fanatic with no vivid, popular issues to embrace. There was plenty of trouble about, but everything conspired to turn men's thoughts away from British rule, to focus attention inland. Connecticut settlers in Pennsylvania's lovely Wyoming Valley clashed violently with Pennsylvanians over claims to the land. In the wilderness between New Hampshire and New York known as the Hampshire Grants men from Massachusetts and New Hampshire, from upper New York and New York's Dutchess County were quarreling, sometimes physically, over possession of the land. The mainspring of opposition to the Crown seemed to have gone slack. Milder patriots had grown both alarmed and disgusted with the potential power of the city mobs, whether in New York or Charleston. John Adams, weary of public life, planned to retire to his Braintree farm. John Hancock, remote and elegant in his Beacon Hill house, was markedly cool to Samuel Adams. Down in Philadelphia, John Dickinson had grown more cautious, and no further Farmer's Letters came from his pen. In Maryland, Daniel Dulany was found to be championing the cause of the Royal Governor, and from now on took his place as a Crown supporter. Where could a man like Sam Adams turn for support?

Worse was to come, diverting more attention from Sam Adams' cause. In North Carolina the uplanders took the field against the lowlanders as 1771 flowered. Upland leader Harmon (or Herman) Husbands had been arrested and jailed at New Bern, North Carolina, where grim Governor Tryon was building a wilderness palace for himself and his successors. So the uplanders, the Regulators, took matters into their own hands and marched on New Bern with the amiable double intent of freeing Husbands and burning the town. To the amazement of the generally unpopular Tryon, his old enemies the planters, stormy opponents of the Crown and its officials, rallied to his side.

Tryon and his allies met the Regulators along the Alamance and utterly smashed them. Many leaders were hanged and the survivors could only wait in seething anger for their next chance. To look ahead a little, that chance did not come until war was raging between England and the colonies. Then

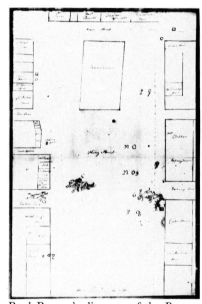

Paul Revere's diagram of the Boston Massacre, used at the trial of the British soldiers in 1770, was much more accurate than his engraving of the action reproduced on page 92

many of the Regulators, whose economic and political position seemed to mark them as friends of the most violent Sons of Liberty, thought only of striking against the lowlanders who were in revolt against the Crown.

The attitude of the whole country, north to south, looked hopeless to those who longed for a showdown between England and the colonies. Extremists could only bide their time, waiting for England to blunder, to fan the cooling ashes of discontent and light the blaze again. The months rolled on down the channel of the year and the mother country most maddeningly steered a course that was reasonably inoffensive even to radicals. Yet the calm was deceptive. In June, 1772, the armed schooner H.M.S. *Gaspee,* virtuously pursuing smugglers through the night waters of Narragansett Bay, ran aground. It suddenly found itself the hunted, not the hunter, and was boarded, captured, and burned to the water's edge. Many moderate Americans, as well as the ultra-Loyalists, added their voices to the howl of rage that went up from Royal officials, and the first answering rumble from London sent Crown sympathizers capering in joyous anticipation. A Commission of Inquiry was set up in Rhode Island to gather in all those suspected of violence against a Royal ship and send them for trial—to England. But the investigation soon lost all headway, blanketed by what seemed to be a total loss of memory on the part of Rhode Islanders. At last, in apoplectic frustration, the Commissioners reported that they could find no suspects, and hence could forward no prisoners for trial—and probable hanging—in London. This was a body blow to the Crown and its adherents. Many men had worked hard and honestly to enforce the King's law, but now the starch went out of them. The Collector of Customs for Rhode Island mourned, "There's an end to collecting a revenue and enforcing the acts of trade."

An 18th-century post rider

The temperature of 1772 rose higher and ardent Sons of Liberty began to stir everywhere. Before the end of the year more fuel was given them. In Massachusetts, Governor Thomas Hutchinson announced that, as of 1773, his salary and those of all Massachusetts judges would be paid by the Crown. It would have been hard to dream up a step more fatal to the British cause. The instant colonial officials looked to England for pay and support, they slipped completely out of local control. They would be most careful, from the very nature of things, to follow English instructions, to report what England wanted to hear, leaving the colonists mute. It is possible that the British government hoped to use Massachusetts as a control guinea pig before extending the new policy to other colonies. What the announcement actually did was to hand Samuel Adams and like-minded men a glittering propaganda weapon. Adams sprang into action at once, toiling to revive and greatly expand those Committees of Correspondence that earlier troubles had called into being. A Boston Committee was set up, its 21 members empowered to communicate with other Massachusetts towns. Then, as though intoxicated by this success, the Committee's field was widened to take in all colonies and, in a final wild gesture, "the World!"

The formation of similar bodies in other towns and colonies was urged, and a flood of political writings poured out of Boston. This output proved immensely successful, and the continent-long chain of Committees that sprang into being through it endured as an invaluable asset to the American cause. Selected riders carried the writings of the members deep into the Berkshire hills, to the green shores of Rhode Island, down through the rolling Connecticut fields, far over the New Hampshire border. No horseman was busier than silversmith Paul Revere, who might have a mass of pamphlets or letters or only a scrap of paper bearing the single line: "Mr. Revere will give you all the news. J. Adams."

As such ripples spread wide from Boston, they met counterripples lapping up from the south, west, and north. Virginia formed its own Committee, then South Carolina and New Hampshire, until almost every colony was linked in a network over which flowed expressions of solidarity, promises of help, protests, fresh ideas.

Across in England, where ministries had been rising and falling regularly, the luckless Lord North had taken the Prime Ministerial reins which he would hold for more than ten years. One of his acts in 1773 was to concoct in all innocence a startling new issue for the flourishing Committees of Correspondence. The East India Company was in financial straits, and its stock had dropped on the London Exchange from £280 to £160. So the company was given a tea monopoly in the American colonies, prices being carefully framed so as to undersell even the rather freely smuggled article. There were flaws in an otherwise not too unsound plan. Colonists of all shades of opinion were not inclined to smile on monopolies, particularly when such matters were to be in the hands of gubernatorial favorites who would reap a golden harvest.

This well-meant boost for the East India Company repeated nearly all the stupidities and ineptitudes of the Stamp Act. Even clear-thinking Thomas Hutchinson stumbled badly. His brother-in-law had been named to fatten on the Stamp Act perquisites; now he named two sons as lucky managers of the tea. Up and down the country, action was followed by predictable reaction. As soon as the tea appointees became known delegations called on them, demanding their instant resignations. Memories of the woes of the Stamp Act officials usually produced eager compliance. Bitter, hidebound Tories joined Sons of Liberty in such demonstrations.

The new tea grievance doubled Samuel Adams' work and he, in turn, redoubled his efforts. Meanwhile, a still vaster windfall was about to fall into his palsied but able hands. In England, a genuine colossus of the colonies had been working calmly and devotedly toward a solution of the troubles that plagued America and England. To this man, Benjamin Franklin, Deputy Postmaster General for the colonies and Agent for Massachusetts, came, through devious channels, a packet of letters. They were written by Thomas Hutchinson and his brother-in-law, Andrew Oliver, Province Secretary, to one Thomas Whately, a man deeply concerned with the Stamp Act. The pages showed Franklin that a good many Parliamentary blunders were due to the fact that only one side of many colony questions—that of the squirearchy—was reaching that body.

Franklin forwarded these letters to Boston, asking that they be treated as confidential material. Eventually, despite the warning, copies found their way into the hands of the Boston Committee of Correspondence, which broadcast them to other bodies. Since these letters had been privately written to a man in England who felt much as Hutchinson and Oliver did, and hence differed widely from what the writers had given out for home consumption, Sons of Liberty read the text as plotting against the rights of the colony. Samuel Adams, who had been instrumental in securing distribution of the letters, was delighted with the feelings they aroused and presently succeeded in prodding the Massachusetts lower house into taking a drastic step. His Most Gracious Majesty George III was humbly and respectfully petitioned by the House

Samuel Adams, engraved by Revere

Contemporary wash drawing by
Ramberg of the Boston Tea Party

Handbill announcing arrival of a
tea ship, probably in Philadelphia

of Representatives to remove Messrs. Hutchinson and Oliver from office.

Sam Adams was riding a glorious wave crest that rose as he thought of the tea ships heading for Boston, New York, Philadelphia, and Charleston. He had a pretty clear idea of what their reception would be. He knew, for one thing, that the Sons in New York had been swamping Manhattan with handbills stating just what dangers any merchant would run in trying to handle the tea known to be somewhere at sea in the ship *Nancy*.

Well before that craft arrived off Staten Island, a courier from the northeast cantered down the Post Road and into New York, the tireless Mr. Paul Revere, to "give you all the news." This time he brought a very full budget, and uneasy doubts left the New Yorkers as they learned of the precedent that Boston had set. The tea had duly arrived in three ships. A number of Bostonians in Indian garb, their faces blackened, had boarded those ships and, with the surprising assistance of the crews, had spilled overboard a grand total of 342 chests of tea. There had been no violence of any sort, but a rather firm answer had been made to Lord North and to Governor Hutchinson.

Paul Revere returned to Boston, and soon Samuel Adams was writing to James Warren, brother of Dr. Joseph, "Before the arrival . . . of the news from Boston, the Citizens of New York had got to be divided . . . But immediately they became united and determined that [the tea] should not be landed . . . The Ministry could not have devised a more effectual measure to unite the Colonies. Old Jealousies are removed and perfect Harmony subsists between them." The orderly, if rankly illegal, action of Boston's Long Wharf did much to rehabilitate the reputation of the Sons of Liberty in the colonies. Soon they found moderates siding with them, and not only in Boston. New Yorkers dumped their tea into the East River. Philadelphia allowed the chests to be landed and then left them to rot in warehouses. Charleston, too, received the tea in bond, and there it remained until the outbreak of hostilities when, in a gloriously imaginative gesture, it was sold at public auction and the proceeds funneled into the South Carolina war chest.

Trans-Atlantic reaction came swift and hot. May of 1774 saw riders fanning out of Boston to shout their news, to toss handbills marked with skull and crossbones, with mourning wreaths, and with liberty caps into spots where men were likely to gather. The news dealt with the Boston Port Bill and its shattering implications. The port of Boston was closed, even to the shortest ferry-run, and the city could be supplied only across the narrow neck that linked it to the mainland. The Royal Government was leaving Boston for Salem and the Customs were being shifted to Marblehead. To make sure that this tight cloture be enforced, additional regiments of infantry were to reinforce the 14th and the 29th, backed by the Royal Navy in the harbor. This state of affairs was to endure until such time as the Bostonians had paid for the jettisoned tea, plus the duty which would have accrued to His Majesty's Customs had that cargo been landed.

Other cities and centers throughout the country were in a position to contemplate the plight of Boston with academic detachment, since Boston alone was touched by it. With the prosperous trade of that Massachusetts port at an end, could not New York, Philadelphia, Newport, and Charleston merchants reach out for a big slice of Boston's commerce? Paul Revere, who had ridden clear to Philadelphia with the details of the Port Bill, had a burning story to bring back to the Boston Sons of Liberty. New York and Philadelphia, far from being academic, promised Boston full support. Before long, other centers farther south showed themselves unanimously blind to the plausible Crown reasoning that the Bill touched Boston alone. Charleston, Wilmington, and Baltimore all echoed New York and Philadelphia.

Support was more than moral. Charleston sent money and rice—the latter to be used as food or sold for the benefit of the city of Boston. New York guaranteed Boston a ten-year supply of food and, in earnest of the pledge, more than 100 sheep wound across Long Island meadows, headed for the Sound and Massachusetts. Out of Connecticut came another bleating convoy, driven by a veteran of the old French wars, Israel Putnam of Pomfret. In large scale or small, the other colonies were ranging themselves solidly behind Massachusetts. No one seems to have come forward with the idea that it would have been simpler all around if Boston had obediently paid what the Crown demanded.

An English satire, "The Bostonians in Distress," inspired by the Port Bill

London was by no means through. A fresh Act stipulated that any Crown official charged with a capital offense in putting down a riot or collecting revenue should be sent to England for trial, a reasonable enough provision in view of the known hostility of colonial bench and bar. But, as acquittal before a British court might be taken for granted, this measure seemed to give the Crown officers a free hand to use violence without colonial reprisal. This was followed by still another Act aimed at "better regulating the government of Massachusetts Bay and purging their constitution of all its crudities."

As men in Delaware and New York and Virginia and Georgia studied this last step it was all too clear to them that the sacred Charter of Massachusetts had been virtually canceled, leaving only vestigial traces of self-government. The governor's council was to be Crown-appointed and responsible only to the Crown. The attorney general, judges, sheriffs, and justices of the peace were to be named by the governor, and even juries were to be selected by a Crown-appointed sheriff. The town meeting, mainspring of Massachusetts life, could still be held, but only when the governor gave his written consent. Even then the agenda had to be approved by him. These measures, along with the Port Bill, became known as the "Intolerable Acts" and shook all the colonies, although their specified target was fractious Massachusetts alone.

Soon afterward North's ministry announced a measure that sent hot, nervous tremors running up and down the country. This was the Quebec Act, setting Canadian affairs in order. By this, the French Canadians had most of their ancient rights and customs confirmed, with the Roman Catholic Church guaranteed against any interference. The boundaries of Quebec were extended as far south as the Ohio River, and the Act would apply in that vast territory beyond the Alleghenies.

Wise as these measures were, with the possible exception of the boundary extension, they sent up a united clamoring from the colonies. The protection of Catholicism was a sore point. Many read into it an implication of union between Church and State, a notion abhorrent to vast numbers of colonials. More directly controversial was the boundary question. Great stretches of those western lands had been marked down for veterans of old wars. Some colonies laid claim to huge stretches by virtue of ancient, ill-defined Charter grants. And soon another measure forbade emigration beyond the Alleghenies.

A bishop unable to land in America, an English comment on the Quebec Act

The forge-heat of these events led many otherwise moderate men into dangerous channels of thought. If protests to the Crown went unheeded, then resistance must follow or all rights as Englishmen were lost forever. If the Crown persisted in its errors, the ultimate answer could only be—Independence.

In the spring of 1774, that word—Independence—had been spoken by implication in the uneasy hush of Williamsburg in Virginia. The Burgesses made

Nomination of New York delegates to the Continental Congress in 1774

"I wish for a permanent union with the mother country, but only on the terms of liberty and truth. No advantage that can accrue to America from such a union, can compensate for the loss of liberty."
— Samuel Adams, 1774

public a resolution stating that "A Congress should be appointed . . . from all the Colonies to concert a general and uniform plan for the defense and preservation of our common rights . . ." The tone of the resolution became deeper, more ominous. The Congress ought, it went on, to issue "humble, dutiful remonstrance to the King, who was to be conjured and besought to reflect that from our Sovereign there can be but one appeal." And what could that appeal be except force?

This message met with immediate response. All the other colonies except Georgia agreed that such a Congress should and would be held in Philadelphia in September, 1774.

Meanwhile, in Massachusetts, Thomas Hutchinson was turning over the highest office in the colony not to another civilian appointee, but to General Thomas Gage, who assumed the titles of Vice-Admiral, Captain-General, and Governor-in-Chief. Boston, and the lands stretching inland from it, were to all intents and purposes passing from civil rule to military occupation. Other colonies took silent note of the change, wondered if similar changes would take place in their capitals, and wondered if Massachusetts, hedged by British muskets, would dare send delegates to that Congress in September.

Under the August sun, James Bowdoin's coach with its four matched bays, liveried coachman and grooms, and armed servants, turned south down Boston's Tremont Street, accompanied by more than 100 citizens in plainer carriages or on horseback. The route skirted the edge of the Common, swarming with the reinforced garrison, and a word from General Gage could have thrown a wall of bayonets across the street, blocking the whole procession. In the Bowdoin coach rode the Massachusetts delegates, John and Samuel Adams, Thomas Cushing, and Robert Treat Paine.

Gage stayed his hand, the cavalcade passed on, and the delegates, friends, and well-wishers wound across narrow Boston Neck while onlookers wondered at the sudden splendor of Samuel Adams in his fine claret-colored suit. The man who could plan effectively for everyone but himself was always in debt, and his new outfit had been anonymously supplied by craftsmen of the Sons of Liberty, whose emblem was embossed on his new gold canetop and gold buttons. John Adams, looking ahead to the Congress and its responsibilities, wrote in his diary, "There is a new and grand scene open before me," then added humbly, "I feel myself unequal to this business."

Drawn like iron filings to a magnet, delegates from every colony moved on Philadelphia, and the bells of the city's churches tolled out in resonant greeting. This awe-inspiring metropolis of more than 30,000 souls was a new and startling experience to many of the guests. Men from Congregational Connecticut or Church of England Virginia wrote home in amazement that they found Quakers, Church of Englanders, Presbyterians, Mennonites, "Saturday and Sunday Anabaptists," Schwenkfelders, Zinzendorfers, Roman Catholics, Reformed, Lutherans, Dunkards, all pursuing their workaday and Sabbath lives in at least outward tranquility.

The mercantile-minded wandered among the bowsprits that jutted over the wharves, through the countinghouses down by the river, and made note of methods strange to them. They learned to cock their heads each Tuesday night as Christ Church chimed out the "Butter Bells" that told of tomorrow and market day, when they could sally forth at dawn to see produce-laden country carts jolt into the metropolis.

Brilliant, conservative Joseph Galloway, an uneasy dissident against Crown acts, had marked down for this, the First Continental Congress, the sweeping Georgian splendor of the State House, later known as Independence Hall. To his dismay, local factions managed to switch the setting to lovely Carpenters' Hall, built by master craftsmen for master craftsmen. In vain Galloway pointed out that this Hall was much smaller than the State House; but he seems to have overlooked the psychology of the choice. Here there would be no Royal Arms, nothing to suggest the restraining hand of a distant government. And by moving into the seat of the powerful Carpenters' Company, tacit notice was served that the business of Congress touched those who worked with their hands as well as those who tended business or estates.

Some forty strong, with other delegates still on the way, Congress met and elected Peyton Randolph of Virginia as presiding officer. Thomas Lynch of Charleston nominated as secretary "A gentleman of Family, Fortune and Character," Charles Thomson of Philadelphia. Thomson was duly confirmed despite mutterings that he was "confoundedly Headstrong."

These preliminary steps allowed the delegates to orient themselves, to stare at fellow-Americans from distant colonies. Big, dark John Sullivan, lawyer and militia Major from New Hampshire, could soon pick out Roger Sherman of Connecticut and Matthew Tilghman of Maryland, George Read of Delaware and Christopher Gadsden of South Carolina. Gray old Stephen Hopkins of Rhode Island, veteran of that first, feeble Congress at Albany in 1754, sat near the dais, listening to John Dickinson of Pennsylvania and Caesar Rodney of Delaware.

To John Sullivan fell the honor of speaking first in the mellow, bright room with its fine carving. He reported that his fellow New Hampshiremen had instructed him and Colonel Folsom "to devise, consult, and adopt measures to secure and perpetuate their rights, and to restore that peace, harmony and mutual confidence which once subsisted between the parent country and her colonies."

Other speakers showed a uniformity of purpose that must have lifted the hearts of Robert Paine and the Adamses. Thomas McKean of Delaware ripped out against "taking away the property of the Colonists . . . new-modelling the government of the Massachusetts Bay . . ." Edward Rutledge of South Carolina boldly spelled out what most were thinking: "That the Acts and Bills of Parliament in regard to Massachusetts Bay affect the whole Continent of America." Through all this, Massachusetts sat strangely passive. In the broad corridor of Carpenters' Hall men whispered that for all their earlier big talk the Bostonians were milksops compared to the southern planters.

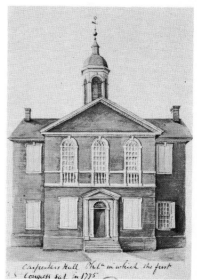

Sketch of Carpenters' Hall in Philadelphia, where the Congress met

There were countless questions to settle. Tempers rose and members shook their fists in angry debate. The matter of representation burned at white heat. How many votes should a given colony have? Should the basis be per capita or property? Patrick Henry was on his feet shouting, "Let freemen be represented by numbers alone . . . The distinctions between Virginians, Pennsylvanians, New Yorkers, New Englanders are no more. I am not a Virginian, but an American!" At last a measure framed by young John Jay of New York was approved, giving one vote to each colony.

More splits and rifts began to show, merchant against farmer, great landowner against small, conservative against radical. In fact, matters were drifting away from that radical Samuel Adams, who began to fear that conservative pressure would produce some water-toast document that would be smilingly tabled by the ministry in London. Then a bombshell as welcome and as useful to him as the Boston Massacre had been was whisked into town in the saddlebags of that indefatigable post rider, Paul Revere.

There had been a meeting of Massachusetts men in Suffolk County and out of it had come a statement known as the "Suffolk Resolves." Peyton Randolph read out the document to the Congress, and when he had done any member could easily summarize the Suffolk blast. All the Coercive Acts were declared unconstitutional and hence not to be obeyed. The people of Massachusetts were urged to form a government of their own to collect taxes and withhold them from the Royal authorities until the Acts had been repealed. They were advised to gather arms and form their own militia. Heavy economic sanctions were recommended in terms that neither Charles Thomson nor Samuel Adams could have bettered.

The hall exploded when Randolph had done reading. Men swarmed to the Massachusetts delegation cheering and shouting. Emotion swept higher, and Congress finally adopted the Suffolk Resolves without a comma changed. From that point, Congressional action was predictable, and went almost as far as the radicals dared hope, although it was apparent that the time was not yet ripe for their ultimate aim. (One afternoon Colonel George Washington, Richard Henry Lee, and Dr. Shippen of Philadelphia called on the Massachusetts men. Robert Paine nodded approval of John Adams' quick reply to a pointed question: "There is no man among us that would not be happy to see accommodation with Britain." Paine added, "Independence? A hundred times no!" Samuel Adams seems to have said nothing.) Even so, the Coercive Acts were bitterly denounced, along with various revenue measures that dated back a decade and more. In a set of resolutions, colonial rights were set forth bluntly —the rights to life, liberty, and property, the rights of Assemblies to exclusive powers of taxation and internal policy. Some thirteen Acts of Parliament were declared illegal, with the rider that economic sanctions were to be applied until they were repealed.

To implement all this, a Continental Association was formed, based on measures first framed at Williamsburg, Virginia. As of December 1, 1774, all imports from England were to cease. A committee was to be elected in every city, town, and county to enforce the decrees of the Association. Such a closing of ranks had surely been beyond the dreams of any member as he arrived in Philadelphia. Ultraconservative Joseph Galloway, nearly helpless with rage and frustration, nonetheless signed the document with the others. He and his fellow-ultras must have been stunned by the power of the response. From Delaware north, the colonies could do fairly well without England. But to the south, British trade did not merely mean prosperity—it was the very taproot of existence.

On October 20 there was a farewell dinner at the City Tavern on Walnut Street, with Colonel Washington magnificent in gold braid and blue. Thomas McKean wore deep maroon velvet, and Samuel Adams managed to freshen up the Boston mechanics' gift-suit of claret-color. Cousin John appeared in blue and canary with a fine wig, and danced a quadrille with Mrs. Thomas Lynch of Charleston.

With this triumphant celebration the delegates prepared to leave Philadelphia. They had thrown out a bold and momentous defiance. And, of almost equal significance, the Congress had not belonged to Peyton Randolph or Caesar Rodney or Samuel Adams or to any one man. It had spoken as a body, prompted by what a Massachusetts jurist more than a century later was to call "the felt necessities of the times."

"When a certain great king,
whose initial is G,
Shall force stamps upon paper,
and folks to drink tea;
When these folks burn his tea
and stamp paper, like stubble,
You may guess that this king
is then coming to trouble."
—Philip Freneau, 1783

72

The Fall
of New France

To young James Wolfe, victory on the Plains of Abraham overlooking Quebec brought death and immortality. While Great Britain rejoiced and went wild with victory, across the Channel there was a curious mixture of despair and relief. Even the thoughtful Voltaire gave thanks for France's delivery "from a vast stretch of frozen country," and Louis XV's mistress Madame de Pompadour said simply, "Now the King can sleep." Whether Louis knew it or not, this 1759 battle decided the fate of North America.

The results of England's victory at Quebec were not recognized officially by statesmen until the Treaty of Paris in 1763, but citizens of Britain's colonies in America knew that the defeat of Montcalm's army meant the end of New France. From this moment on, the Union Jack would wave undisturbed along the Atlantic seaboard from Hudson Bay to the Florida Keys; and as far west as the Mississippi, tiny frontier outposts were free from the threat of French attack.

The colonists now began to realize that they were Americans, separated by an infinity of time from a distant motherland. The French wars had helped bind them together, creating dependence of a sort one upon the other, and when the struggle was over, the habit stuck. In 1759 England's triumph seemed to be a climax to bloodshed and strife. In reality, it was but a prelude to more of the same; for the end of the French threat released tensions which had been accumulating in the colonies for years, and Americans now began to focus their grievances against what they considered to be British tyranny.

General James Wolfe's "utmost desire" was to "look steadily upon danger." This detail from Benjamin West's heroic painting shows him "expiring in the arms of victory" on the Plains of Abraham outside Quebec in 1759. His foe, the Marquis de Montcalm, also fell in this battle, which marked the end of France's North American empire and paved the way for colonial revolt.

Land for the Taking Up

The engraving above was based on Governor Thomas Pownall's description of how an American farm evolved. After the land was cleared, a cabin was built, water power put to use, and a more permanent house constructed (right). In 1763 George III's decree that Americans were not to settle beyond the headwaters of rivers emptying into the Atlantic met with angry protest. Then land-hungry pioneers simply brushed aside the edict and headed for the forbidden ground, following Daniel Boone's trail through Cumberland Gap (right). The thought occurred to one prophetic governor of Virginia that these restless "movers" acquired "no attachment to Place; But wandering about Seems engrafted in their nature."

74

As long as anyone could remember, men in England's colonies had waited for the day when the French would be driven out of America, making available those limitless lands that stretched beyond the Alleghenies. In Europe, no matter where a man had lived, land had been tightly held for generations, and what might be bought was at a price few could afford. The deep-seated hunger for property had driven many a family over thousands of perilous miles to America, where even the poorest might eventually claim their own piece of ground.

Cheap land in the back country was the way to wealth and prestige, and after 1763 its supply seemed limited only by the distant horizon. All a man needed was courage, enterprise, and a strong back; and between 1765 and 1768 nearly 30,000 of them headed west, pouring over the Appalachians' crest in search of the future.

When John Finlay and his followers plunged into the "Dark and Bloody Ground" of modern Kentucky, the news created greater excitement among the people of Carolina, one historian noted, than the report of Columbus' discovery had aroused at the Court of Spain. In Finlay's footsteps came Daniel Boone, and behind him, waves of new settlers from Maryland and Virginia. From the Watauga River in North Carolina to the upper Ohio, the woodsman's axe was hewing a new kind of society where opportunity, as well as land, was there for all who would seek it.

"Scarcely a shoemaker, a joiner, or silversmith but quits his trade," Governor John Wentworth of New Hampshire wrote in 1768, "as soon as he can get able to buy a little tract of land and build a cottage in the wilderness." Every colony's economy rested on an agrarian base, and eight out of ten men made their living from the soil. Even those whose livelihood came from other pursuits made part-time use of the soil, or speculated in the "wild lands" of the West. Before the Revolution only five cities numbered over 8,000 people, and these centers contained less than five per cent of the entire population. Land was wealth, but it was more, as Hector St. John de Crèvecoeur observed. Land "has established all our rights; on it is founded our rank, our freedom, our power as citizens."

An ever-increasing number of emigrants moved along the "Great Philadelphia Wagon Road" and other trails leading west, filling the Appalachian slopes and turning arable wilds into prosperous farms like the one at right, painted about 1845 by Edward Hicks. But not for generations would travel and communications catch up with the settlements, because of the poor interior roads. The sketch above, by Benjamin Latrobe, shows an accepted mode of travel in the colonial era.

New England's Flourishing Merchant Class

Merchant John Amory made a fortune in Boston. He took the side of the Crown, however, and left America after hostilities began.

Land was one key to the fluidity and wealth of American society, but no one could overlook the Atlantic as a source of prosperity. Particularly along the New England coast, where fishing and trade occupied the time and energies of thousands, the sea had given rise to a powerful merchant class.

Whenever they opposed the Crown's restrictive policies toward America, British merchants were supporting what they considered their own, and England's, best interests in the field of trade. But it became gradually apparent even to them that these perverse New Englanders were going far beyond the proper bounds of the mercantile system. Instead of producing raw materials for the mother country, they were engaged in manufacturing on their own. They were acting as middlemen between the other colonists and England's businessmen; and what was far worse, their energetic pursuit of that "coy mistress, trade," was driving British ships from colonial waters. Each time Parliament attempted to rectify this situation by tightening imperial restrictions on manufactures and trade, it brought forth loud howls of protest from these prosperous, influential Yankees. And the result was downright evasion of the law through smuggling or other means, or a stiffening resistance to government itself.

The water color above shows School Street in Salem about 1765. Nearly 90 ships sailed from the port then, and a few years later a Salem merchant became America's first millionaire. So many different kinds of money circulated in the colonies that elaborate exchange tables like the one at right were almost essential. Appropriately, the artist decorated this one with drawings symbolizing the lure of the counting house and sea (top).

One of New Hampshire's first settlements, Portsmouth (left) developed into an important New England shipbuilding center. In 1778, when Pierre Ozanne painted this view, more than 100 privateers were operating out of the harbor.

The Versatile Colonial Craftsman

Revere made this famous punch bowl for Sons of Liberty in 1768.

In some ways, Paul Revere serves as an example of the typical colonial craftsman. Yet few artisans of his time were as versatile, and fewer still were involved so thoroughly in the turbulent events which preceded the American Revolution.

Primarily a silversmith, and an acknowledged master in his field, this remarkable man was also a bellmaker, volunteer militiaman, dentist, engraver, goldsmith, inventor, the first man to roll sheet copper in the United States, and—most important to the Revolution—a trusted express rider for Boston's Sons of Liberty.

Generally speaking, the ten years prior to 1775 were prosperous ones in New England, and although patriot propaganda made much of economic grievances, Paul Revere's business was good. What was important to him and to others like him was the manner in which rights and privileges were being whittled away by politicians in London. Revere

would certainly have agreed with the Bostonian who wrote: "A colonist cannot make a button, horseshoe, nor a hob-nail, but some sooty ironmonger or respectable button-maker of Britain shall bawl and squal that his honors worship is most egregiously maltreated, injured, cheated and robb'd by the rascally American republicans." It was becoming painfully obvious to men of this kind that Parliament planned to "crush their native talents and to keep them in a constant state of inferiority."

Irritated by measures which cramped initiative, confined trade, and restricted their liberties, Americans met in clubs and taverns and assemblies. In ever-widening arcs the words of discontent and resistance spread through correspondence, through pamphlets and newspapers, or were carried by express riders like Revere from one colony to another until the impossible had happened, and the colonies were united against the mother country.

About 1765 Copley painted the Boston silversmith at his bench.

In spite of British efforts to halt American manufacturing, this 1766 drawing indicates that many small industries were thriving. In 1767 Paul Revere engraved "A Westerly View of the Colledges in Cambridge New England" (left), a charming picture showing Harvard, the first institute of higher learning in the colonies.

Economic Problems Trouble the South

The prosperous city of Charleston (top) was the South's leading port. In its harbor, vessels were loaded with cash crops from inland rice fields or indigo plantations (above). While the planters and their families escaped each summer to Charleston's more benign climate, and made the city a center of wealth and culture, the slaves on whom the economy depended labored in the miasmal lowcountry fields. In the water color (left), by an unknown artist, Negroes dance during a respite in the day's work.

Nowhere did British mercantile theories apply so neatly as in the southern colonies. These rich agricultural provinces supplied the mother country with staples like rice, tobacco, cotton, and indigo, while, lacking local industries, they bought virtually all their manufactured goods from England.

By 1765, however, the planters of Virginia and Maryland, in particular, were being squeezed dry by the system. To acquire cash or credit, many of them had pledged future crops to British businessmen, and their economic status depended not only upon the price a London merchant set for their tobacco, but also on what that same merchant charged them for manufactured items. Heavy debts, the Governor of Virginia observed, were making the planters "uneasy, peevish, and ready to murmur at every Occurrence."

Meanwhile, beyond the Tidewater plantations, less fortunate, land-hungry settlers moved into the Appalachian plateau. Ever-resentful of the influential planters and their privileges, they created a more democratic society which conflicted, almost inevitably, with the older aristocracy. The most dramatic example of this struggle occurred in the Carolinas, where determined upcountry men, lacking a voice in local government affairs, took the law into their own hands. Ironically, when the Revolution broke out, some of these "Regulators" sided with the Crown, largely because most of the planters had given their support to the patriot cause.

On Sundays, Virginia's widely separated planters met at churches like Bruton Parish in Williamsburg (above) to worship and talk business and politics. The 1784 drawing below shows a wharf where tobacco was loaded for shipment. Their one-crop system put southern planters at the mercy of London merchants.

The Thriving Middle Colonies

That area which lay roughly between Albany and Baltimore contained the best-balanced economy of the Thirteen Colonies. While the soil, climate, and topography were generally suited to farming, travelers also noted a keen interest in manufacturing. The Pennsylvanians, one man said, "make almost everything in such quantity and perfection, that in a short time this province will want very little from *England*, its mother country."

The soil was still uppermost in colonial thinking, however, even in the bustling city of Philadelphia, where a native son claimed in 1768 that "Every great fortune made here within these fifty years has been by land." The rich earth along the Delaware, the Schuylkill, and the Susquehanna was becoming the breadbasket of the colonies. In New York, which few considered "ripe for manufactures," the Hudson was a vital artery for the bountiful natural resources, and vessels of sixty and seventy tons were hauling everything from beeswax to barrel staves to Manhattan Island's "commodious keys and warehouses." Enterprising merchants ranged far afield in search of clients, although one New Yorker considered "⅞ of the people in New England" so guilty of "d—d ungrateful cheating" that he was "afraid to trust any Connecticut man." Nevertheless, self-interest usually prevailed, building ties between one region and another. When the war finally came, the balanced economy of these thriving middle colonies would serve the cause well.

Exactly two blocks from the State House (opposite page), cabinet-maker Benjamin Randolph was busy fashioning furniture "in the Chinese and Modern Tastes" for wealthy Philadelphians during the 1760's and '70's. His trade card (above), engraved by James Smithers, reflects the shift in buyers' tastes from the chinoiserie *of Chippendale to Gothic and rococo styles.*

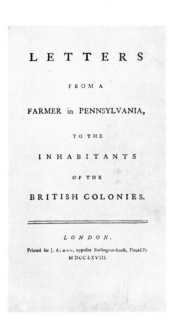

In 1768, John Dickinson's Letters from a Farmer in Pennsylvania *reflected the moderation of colonial opposition to Great Britain. Although the conservative Dickinson sacrificed his popularity to oppose independence, he enlisted as a Continental soldier.*

This wash drawing of the Pennsylvania State House is from a 1778 sketch by Charles Willson Peale. Planned by Andrew Hamilton and Edmund Woolley, the building was constructed in the 1730's as a meeting place for the Province's Assembly. Here George Washington was given command of the Continental Army, the Declaration of Independence was signed, and the Constitution framed. In the 1820's people began to call the building Independence Hall.

One of the earliest views of Baltimore (left), after a sketch made in 1752 by John Moale, shows it as a village of some 200 inhabitants and less than 50 houses. Only a few years elapsed from the time when fishermen dragged their nets in the Basin and a Union Jack fluttered from a solitary brig, until American ships clogged the harbor of "the most Increasing Town in the Province." By 1776 Baltimore ranked ninth in size among colonial cities.

New York Harbor

About 1757, when this lovely view of New York was painted by an unknown artist, the city had only "2 or 3,000 houses and 16 or 17,000 inhabitants." In the foreground of the picture are nine British

ships, probably privateers, at anchor in the East River. At the extreme left is a French vessel, captured by the English during the Seven Years' War. On the shore a straggling militia company parades below the steeple of Trinity Church (center), and behind the wharves and boatslips are gabled houses built during the period of Dutch ownership. At far left a British flag flies over Fort George.

85

Patrick Henry

Thomas Paine

John Hancock

James Otis

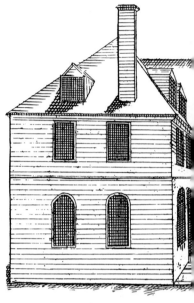

In Williamsburg's capitol (above)

Colony vs.

By 1765 there were three general types of governments operating in the Thirteen Colonies. Seven of the provinces—New Hampshire, New York, New Jersey, Virginia, North and South Carolina, and Georgia—were Crown colonies, with royally appointed governors. Maryland, Delaware, and Pennsylvania were Proprietary colonies, where families like the Baltimores or Penns named the governor, subject to the King's approval. Three others—Massachusetts, Rhode Island, and Connecticut—were Corporate colonies in which, as a Tory wrote, "The people . . . chuse their Governors, Judges, Assemblymen, Counsellors, and all the rest of their Officers; and the King and Parliament have

Disputes between colonial Whigs and Tories over government policies often came to a boil at local town meetings (left).

Lt. Gov. Colden, New York

...ginia House of Burgesses held many stormy sessions.

Gov. Hutchinson, Massachusetts

Gov. Dunmore, Virginia

Crown

Paul Revere engraved the "Join Or Die" device reproduced at left for the masthead of the patriot newspaper, the Massachusetts Spy. *The snake, composed of the united colonies, and based on an earlier design by Benjamin Franklin, menaces a crouching British griffin.*

as much influence there as in the wilds of Tartary."

While there were a few able Royal governors, most of them were second-rate political hacks with little or no knowledge of the people or places they were sent to rule. Because the governor was the key official in every colony, this inevitably led to trouble, especially with legislative Assemblies determined to maintain whatever degree of independent action they had so far achieved. It is worth remembering, too, that the Royal officials were often hopelessly outclassed by their American opponents. They were up against the best the colonies had to offer—men like Sam Adams, George Mason, Patrick Henry, John Dickinson—whose voices were raised with increasing importance in legislature and town meeting, in newspaper column and pamphlet, in coffeehouse and tavern.

Superimposed on the whole colonial structure was a complex network of officials and committees in London, engaged in overseeing the colonies. The resultant official apathy and over-organization, combined with the difficulty of communication and colonial obstinacy, created a situation in which the Americans achieved considerable self-government without actually having willed it.

With remarkable ineptness, Great Britain managed, during the decade prior to 1775, to unite the most articulate and important groups in colonial society—the planters, lawyers, merchants, and printers, in particular. George III and his ministers backed the Americans into a corner where they could do little else but agree with Christopher Gadsden's statement that "nothing will save us but acting together."

To enforce the Sugar Act, Parliament ruled that colonial merchants accused of smuggling were to be tried in admiralty courts at Halifax (above). New Englanders naturally feared the outcome of trials held so far from home.

Birth and Death of the Stamp Act

Before the actual war of the Revolution could begin, there had to be a revolution "in the minds and hearts of the people," as John Adams put it. One of the most important factors in this change of heart was an innocent-looking document which received the assent of George III "by commission" on March 22, 1765. It was to be known as the Stamp Act. That it was also to be a piece of political dynamite was soon evident.

Already, colonial merchants had been exposed to what they considered the rank injustice of having violations of the Sugar Act tried far from home and friendly jurors, in admiralty courts at Halifax. Now other important groups, outraged by the Stamp Act, joined the merchants in violent protest. "The people, even to the lowest ranks," John Adams wrote in 1766, "have become more attentive to their liberties, more inquisitive about them, and more determined to defend them . . ."

It is well to remember that these people were still Englishmen, demanding justice in the tradition that "it is the peculiar Right of Englishmen to complain when injured." But the bonds of loyalty were weakened by each wave of protest against the Stamp Act, by sermon, pamphlet, and mob violence, by the call that went out for a Congress of all the colonies, by nonimportation agreements that finally caused British merchants to petition Parliament for the measure's repeal.

William Pitt expressed the relief of many Britons when he said he "never had greater satisfaction than in the repeal of this Act," but in America the damage had gone too deep. From this time on, the colonies would move steadily toward independence.

Resistance to the Stamp Act was often violent. The woodcut above shows a New Hampshire stamp agent hanged in effigy. At right, an engraving from Trumbull's popular M'Fingal depicts a Tory strung up on a liberty pole. The source of this uproar was the stamp at left, which was to be affixed to all licenses, publications, and legal papers. Opposition to the Act brought many phases of colonial life to a standstill.

This British print, published two weeks after the Stamp Act's repeal, shows George Grenville cradling his dead "child." In the background, three ships await "goods NOW ship'd for America," as proclaimed on the warehouse at right.

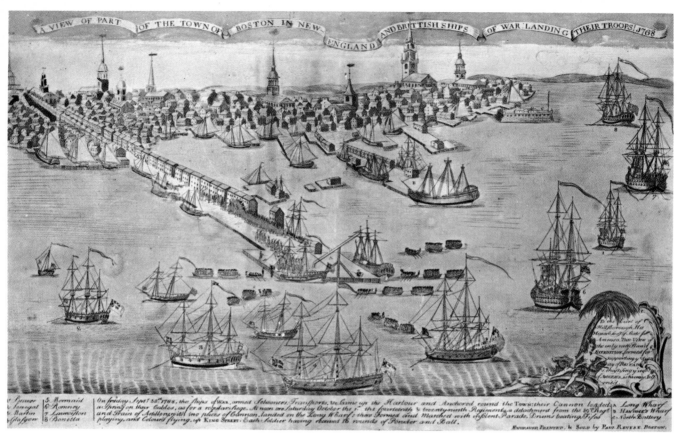

A VIEW OF PART OF THE TOWN OF BOSTON IN NEW ENGLAND AND BRITTISH SHIPS OF WAR LANDING THEIR TROOPS! 1768

The British in Boston

On September 30, 1768, a British fleet anchored in Boston Harbor "as for a regular Seige." The next day soldiers of the 14th and 29th regiments debarked at Long Wharf and "marched with insolent Parade" up King Street, as shown in Paul Revere's engraving (above). Troops of the 29th, unable to secure lodgings in town, pitched tents on the Common. The engraving at left, after Christian Remick, shows them in front of John Hancock's handsome Beacon Hill mansion.

Although the view (right) of Boston's State Street was painted after the Revolution, the area had changed but little. The Boston Massacre took place in front of the Old State House (center). At right, behind the carriage, is the British Coffee House, a favorite of English officers who were quartered in town before the war.

The British government was understandably nettled by Boston's "Treasonable and desperate Resolves" against the Crown. Smuggling was rife, Sons of Liberty were making life unbearable for customs officials, and the Massachusetts Assembly was behaving "in the Stile of a ruling and Sovereign Nation, who acknowledges no Dependence."

To protect Royal officials in the execution of their duties, 4,000 redcoats arrived in Boston Harbor during the fall of 1768. Even under normal circumstances the presence of General Thomas Gage's troops (nearly one for every four inhabitants) would have led to trouble. Now, the imposition of an occupation force on a city already torn with strife made bloodshed a foregone conclusion.

When Bostonians refused to house the soldiers, British officers commandeered public and private billets. Frequently the ill-fed, ill-paid men hired themselves out for menial jobs at low wages, incurring the bitter wrath of Boston's unemployed. Street fights flared, mobs taunted the troops with cries of "bloody backs," and all the while Samuel Adams and his Sons maneuvered in the background, fanning the flames of revolt.

General Thomas Gage had served with Braddock in 1755. From 1763 until 1775 he was commander of Britain's forces in America.

The BLOODY MASSACRE perpetrated in King———Street BOSTON on March 5ᵗʰ 1770 by a party of the 29ᵗʰ REGᵗ

BUTCHER'S HALL

Engrav'd Printed & Sold by PAUL REVERE BOSTON

UnhappyBoston! fee thy Sons deplore,
Thy hallow'd Walks befmear'd with guiltlefs Gore:
While faithlefs P—n and his favageBands,
With murd'rous Rancour ftretch their bloodyHands;
Like fierce Barbarians grinning o'er their Prey,
Approve the Carnage,and enjoy the Day.

If fcalding drops fromRage fromAnguifhWrung,
If fpeechlefs Sorrows lab'ring for a Tongue,
Or if a weeping World can ought appeafe
The plaintive Ghofts of Victims fuch as thefe;
ThePatriot's copiousTears for each are fhed,
A glorious Tribute which embalms the Dead.

But know,Fate fummons to that awful Goal,
WhereJUSTICE ftrips the Murd'rer of his Soul:
Should venalC—ts the fcandal of theLand,
Snatch the relentlefsVillain from her Hand,
KeenExecrations on this Plate infcrib'd,
Shall reach aJUDGE who never can be brib'd.

The unhappy Sufferers were Meſsʳˢ SAMᴸ GRAY SAMᴸ MAVERICK, JAMˢ CALDWELL, CRISPUS ATTUCKS & PATᴷ CARR
Killed. Six wounded; two of them (CHRISTᴿ MONK & JOHN CLARK) Mortally

Paul Revere's engraving of the Boston Massacre was a potent piece of Whig propaganda. Five men were killed, not seven, as the legend states, and the rioters in front of the State House (center) were scarcely as docile as Revere shows them. The "5 Coffings for Massacre" (right), also by Revere, appeared on broadsides during 1770.

Outbreaks of Violence

Early in the 1770's two acts of violence made it plain that the period of passive resistance, as exemplified by nonimportation agreements among merchants, was coming to an end. Conservative Americans and Britons suddenly realized that politicians and mobs were gaining the upper hand.

The first incident occurred on the night of March 5, 1770, when a crowd of Boston toughs provoked troops from the weakened British garrison into firing on them. This "Massacre," in which five Bostonians died, was grist for Sam Adams' propaganda mill, but undoubtedly cost the patriot movement the support of many conservatives and fence-sitters. The second outburst took place two years later in Narragansett Bay. The armed schooner *Gaspee* ran aground while chasing a smuggler and was boarded by Providence patriots, who burned her to the water's edge. It was another victory for the extremists.

Abraham Whipple (right) was one of the Providence merchants who destroyed the British schooner Gaspee *in 1772 (below). During the Revolution, he made a large profit from privateering, and once captured ten British merchant ships on ten successive nights.*

The Colonial Period Ends

The Boston Tea Party shocked England, antagonizing even the colonies' best friends.

To rescue the near-bankrupt East India Company, Parliament in 1773 passed the Tea Act. By allowing the company to sell tea directly to America without first putting it on public sale in England, the British middleman was eliminated, and tea could be sold at ten shillings the pound—half its former price, and less even than American smugglers charged for it. So far as the colonists were concerned, however, tea still carried a hated tax, and they were alarmed by the threat of British monopoly implied in the Act. "Do not suffer yourself to sip the accursed, duttied STUFF," one American warned. "For if you do, the devil will immediately enter into you, and you will instantly become a traitor to your country."

On December 16, 1773, 150 thinly disguised Boston patriots boarded English ships and dumped 342 chests of tea into the harbor. In colony after colony, variations of this tea party were repeated until, under patriotic pressure, the "obnoxious Drug" virtually disappeared from use. Boston's action produced an "electrical Shock" of giant proportions in England. Nothing the colonists had done thus far so united British public opinion against them, one Englishman stating flatly that this was "the most wanton and unprovoked insult offered to the civil power that is recorded in history." From this moment on, relations between colonies and mother country were all downhill. What Americans called the "Intolerable Acts" were followed by the Quebec Act, and in the fall of 1774 delegates from the several colonies headed toward Philadelphia, "to concert a general and uniform plan for the defense and preservation of our common rights." The end of one era and the beginning of another were just over the horizon.

This scene, at the intersection of Second and High

streets in Philadelphia, was familiar to delegates to the First Continental Congress in 1774. At left center is the spire of Christ Church.

Patriots pulling down the statue of George III in New York, 1776

THE WAR BEGINS

"I cannot but lament . . . the impending Calamities Britain and her Colonies are about to suffer, from great Imprudencies on both Sides—Passion governs, and she never governs wisely—Anxiety begins to disturb my Rest . . ."

BENJAMIN FRANKLIN—FEBRUARY 5, 1775

WHILE the First Continental Congress was assembling, debating, resolving, and finally adjourning, Boston, the focal point of colonial resistance and of ministerial retaliation, simmered under the heavy lid that had been clapped over it. All through the spring, summer, and fall, British troops poured ashore, and the fleet, now under fussy, pettish Admiral Samuel Graves, R.N., thickened the harbor with its masts.

Cold weather came on and there could be no more camps on the Common. Instead, under the revised Quartering Act, a billeting officer could knock on the door of any warehouse, shop, or private home to demand lodging for the King's troops. Such measures, necessary as they were if the garrison were not to freeze, added to local tension, which needed no further tautening.

Thomas Gage made honest efforts to solve at least part of this problem by having quarters erected for some units. But, strangely, he found a sudden dearth of labor in a city that should have answered his every need. Wages were raised, bonuses offered, but the Boston artisans remained untempted. What work was carried out suffered inexplicable defects. Bostonians may not have known the word "sabotage," but they seem to have been adept at it.

The city began to bulge. Hundreds, possibly thousands of men had been thrown out of work by the Port Bill, and many flocked into Boston chasing the will-o'-the-wisp of employment and forming a tinder-dry element in an already smoldering place. Other refugees began to appear, by no means in sympathy with the rebels. Prominent figures and insignificant ones began to find that Congressionally appointed committees were attempting to impose a regime under which they were not willing to live. Families, rich and poor, split —Tory or Loyalist members flocking naturally enough to the shelter of the King's regiments and men-of-war.

In the ever-growing flickers of heat-lightning that might turn to actual bolts at any moment, the Boston Sons of Liberty continued their accustomed activities. Joseph and James Warren, Molineaux, Revere, and the rest held their meetings, prepared their broadsides, kept the presses of Messrs. Edes and Gill smoking. Through all this, General Gage remained surprisingly passive. There is a chance, of course, that he counted on the Port Bill to choke and starve the city into submission without the use of violence; but he could hardly have been more wrong, if he really entertained this idea. The waterways were closed; but overland came long strings of provision-carts from north, west, and south—"Lord North's Coasters"—whose cargoes were smuggled in after dark. The nearby ports of Salem and Marblehead, supposed to replace Boston as trade and customs centers, behaved most illogically, refusing to benefit by Boston's misfortunes. Newport, New York, and Philadelphia merchants and traders made no move to crowd in for their share of the prize.

Yet there were pleasanter, lighter sides to the Boston picture. Francis Shaw complained to his neighbor, silversmith Paul Revere, that that damnable Quartering Act had shoved a full-fledged Major of Royal Marines into his house. Yet that Major, John Pitcairn, an amazingly gentle and understanding man, quickly overcame Shaw's bitter prejudice, and in the few months of life that were left to him won solid trust and affection from Sons of Liberty in all walks of life. And young Lord Percy, of the bearskinned 5th Northumberland Fusiliers camped along the edge of high Beacon Street, soon became a popular figure in the house and at the table of John Hancock.

But such palliatives, individual and collective, could not affect the boiling emotional kettle that was Boston. General Gage, properly concerned with the health and morale of his command, began sending troops on mild route

A

BILL,

INTITULED

An Act for the better providing suitable Quarters for Officers and Soldiers in His Majesty's Service in *North America.*

WHEREAS Doubts have been entertained, whether Troops can be quartered otherwise than in Barracks, in case Barracks have been provided sufficient for the quartering of all the Officers and Soldiers within any Town, Township, City, District, or Place, within His Majesty's Dominions in *North America:*

And whereas it may frequently happen, from the Situation of such Barracks, that if Troops should be quartered therein, they would not be stationed where their Presence may be necessary and required : Be it therefore enacted by the King's most Excellent Majesty, by and with the Advice and Consent of the Lords Spiritual and Temporal, and Commons, in this present Parliament assembled, and by the Authority of the same, That, in such Cases, it shall and may be lawful for the Persons who now are, or may be hereafter, authorised by Law, in any of the Provinces within His Majesty's Dominions in *North America* ; and they are

The Quartering Act, 1765

marches that took them across the narrow Neck and into the interior. Flippant young officers, pushing on to Waltham or Dedham, were amused to see rustics drilling in the fields, but more sober-minded seniors were impressed with the unity and purpose in these formations.

Without warning, one such march turned out to be more than mere practice. A few scarlet-coated companies swung over the Charles into Cambridge, and seized powder and arms belonging to the Province. Then they passed on to Charlestown, nobbled up more Province supplies and returned, rejoicing, to Boston. Militarily Gage's move was sound. Psychologically it was an error, since the rather hurried maneuver could be read as showing fear. More than that, his act sent an alarm winging through the clear September air and provided the Massachusetts militia with an excellent dress rehearsal. Luckily there was no collision with the regulars, and the alarm which reached high above the Merrimack and far down by the Connecticut border showed how improvement could be made for future calls.

Province House in Boston

The Provincial Congress of Massachusetts, meeting illegally but regularly in Cambridge within sight of Gage's sentries across the Charles, set up a body called the Committee of Safety. Headed by John Hancock, it was given power to call out the entire militia of the colony when in the Committee's judgment such an appeal seemed necessary. To back up such a call, special groups were formed within the various militia units—men who could be counted on to answer at once, under arms. These had to have some special designation, and since they were subject to instant call, someone labeled them Minutemen, and as such they entered history.

Through spies, informers, Tory sympathizers, Thomas Gage knew pretty well what military measures were being taken outside of Boston. He certainly was not prepared, as winter came on, for the swift and highly successful action of some Whig "miscreants" who boldly snapped up the militia fieldpieces of the colony, supposedly closely guarded in the gun-shed "that stands directly opposite the encampment of the 4th Regiment and in the middle of the Street near the large Elm tree." Now the British commander could reflect sourly that the Rebels, in addition to unguessed numbers of armed militiamen, had suddenly acquired several highly serviceable pieces of artillery.

Other news came into the high rooms of Province House. New Hampshire patriots, led by Major John Sullivan, lately returned from the First Continental Congress, swept down on Fort William and Mary at Portsmouth, overpowered the token guard, and made off with a really important store of ammunition.

John Hancock

In such an atmosphere 1774 dragged to its chill end, with Boston more crowded than ever. People began to wonder about supplies, particularly when they learned that the Royal Navy alone had contracted for "a Tun weight of Mutton every day." What would be left for civilians?

The winter of 1774–75 was providentially mild for New England, but affairs of men met no tempering influences. The Committee of Safety voted that "all kinds of warlike stores be purchased sufficient for an army of fifteen thousand men," and selected the village of Concord as a suitable depot, far from the reach of Gage's raids. And the Provincial Congress, working hard to transform city, town, and village militia companies into a Massachusetts army, even appointed five generals to command it—Jedediah Preble, Artemas Ward, Seth Pomeroy, John Thomas, and William Heath. They were nearly all "retreads," the service of some of them dating back to Louisbourg in '45, but they had seen action and commanded public confidence.

In a February thaw, Colonel Thomas Leslie took his 64th North Staffordshires to Salem by sea, to seize Province supplies. Leslie, known to Bostonians as "an Amiable & good man . . . distinghused . . . by his humanity and affability," ran into verbal opposition from the Salem fathers and sensibly re-embarked his troops, mission unaccomplished, where a more headstrong man might have brought on bloodshed. News of the attempted coup set Minute Companies assembling as far north as Amesbury, well above the Merrimack.

As though to show that the civil arm of England was as active as the military, news reached Massachusetts of a fresh Act, whose manifest unwisdom must have sent hundreds of men shifting from Tory allegiance to Whig. Not merely Massachusetts but *all* the New England colonies were forbidden to trade anywhere save in England or the British West Indies. Worse, the entire New England fishing fleet was barred from the North Atlantic fisheries.

While the Provincial Congress, discreetly shifted to Concord in order to be out of Gage's reach, was considering the Fisheries Bill and its component parts, military problems were abruptly thrust upon it. Not a few companies this time, but an entire brigade had been led out of Boston by Lord Percy on a practice march that swung through Watertown and Cambridge. Probably unwillingly, even a little fearfully, the Congress at Concord resolved that whenever troops "to the Number of Five Hundred shall march out of Boston . . . it ought to be deemed a design to carry into execution by Force the late Acts of Parliament . . . and therefore the Military Forces of the Province ought to be assembled and an Army of Observation immediately formed, to act *solely on the defensive* so long as it can be justified on the Principles of Reason and Self-Preservation and *no longer.*"

Thomas Gage was in an increasingly awkward position. He had his mission—enforcement of the Acts of Parliament and pacification of Massachusetts. If, in Parliamentary minds, he had ample military means to carry out what was ordered, each proposed course of action must have brought into Gage's mind the increasingly swift massing of armed militia which had followed every show of force. Yet something had to be done or awkward questions would be asked in London.

All this his opponents knew, and the Whig observers in Boston looked and listened and estimated. On April 15, 1775, Gage's orders to his troops may have been discussed at the Green Dragon or the Bunch of Grapes taverns—orders detaching the grenadier and light infantry companies, the elite, specially trained and equipped units of each regiment, for extra maneuvers and instruction. Why? What were these picked troops going to do? All in all, they would tot up to over 700 men, a task force that could strike swift and hard.

Warren sent word by Paul Revere to Lexington, where Sam Adams and John Hancock were lodging with the Reverend Jonas Clarke, close to the Congress in Concord. Gage might have arrests in mind, and who were better subjects than Adams and Hancock? Lexington passed the word to Concord, and at once the village labored night and day, packing stores and shipping them west to Worcester. Seven hundred men might have the seizure of Province military supplies as objective.

Someone brought word of work being done to the longboats and barges of the fleet. Again, why? To float redcoats across the Charles for a quick landing on the Cambridge side, where roads led north to Lexington and Concord? Or would grenadiers and light infantry march over the Neck and onto the mainland instead, with a whole continent opening before them—not just two Massachusetts villages? On the night of the eighteenth, Paul Revere was wakened at his house on North Square, spirited by friendly hands past guardposts, and

"The war is actually begun! The next gale that sweeps from the north will bring to our ears the clash of resounding arms! Our brethren are already in the field!"
—Patrick Henry, March, 1775

Boston's Green Dragon Tavern

sculled across the Charles under the slow-turning stern of H.M.S. *Somerset*. Back in Boston, two lanterns glowed in the spire of the Old North Church in prearranged signal that the British were out and would move by water, not across the Neck.

There was a horse waiting on the Cambridge shore, and Revere rode inland, spreading the word of the night move but keeping his primary mission firmly in mind—to warn Sam Adams and John Hancock in the Lexington parsonage. This accomplished, he pushed on toward Concord, still atingle with his news. Halfway there, near the Hartwell farm, he was snapped up by mounted British officers, part of a thin screen that Gage had thrown out to the north of Boston to intercept just such people on just such errands. Revere was soon released; but his mission had been accomplished, and the word that he had brought "to every Middlesex village and farm" had gone on ahead of him.

On through the dead, dark hours that follow midnight, the British column pushed north. In command was fat, slow-witted Colonel Francis Smith of the 10th Lincolnshires. Next in seniority was Paul Revere's North Square neighbor, Major John Pitcairn of the Royal Marines. The choice of Pitcairn for this detail was an odd one, militarily speaking, since there were no marines present, but from a practical standpoint his selection was excellent. Recognized as a fine soldier, he was also respected by colonists of all shades of opinion. If there were a parley with opponents of the Crown, who could be more acceptable as a spokesman than Pitcairn?

The troops who marched with this pair were probably in a very uncertain mood. They had been routed from their quarters long after tattoo, the equivalent of our modern "taps," had been beaten. They had been most uncomfortably boated across the Charles, forced to disembark in knee-deep water, and then been kept standing about for two mortal, cold hours. After fording a waist-deep backwater, they pushed deeper and deeper into Massachusetts, past the town of Menotomy, where they heard the sounds of distant guns, ringing bells, and hoofbeats drumming on hidden roads. As they drew nearer to Lexington they caught dim glimpses of armed men hurrying over the dark fields to the right and left. Smith and Pitcairn saw and heard all this, and mounted officers came galloping up to report a thickening concentration in and about Lexington. Smith, possibly at Pitcairn's prompting, sent a courier back to Boston for reinforcements.

Day was just breaking, clear and unseasonably warm, with premature appleblossoms shimmering in roadside orchards, as Pitcairn and his men wound down the curving hill that leads past Munroe's Tavern into Lexington. They could hardly have been surprised to see two companies (the Minute and the Alarm) in battle order on the near end of the Green, nor the slanting shadows of many men moving through nearby woods or fields.

Lexington's Captain John Parker on the Green, and Major John Pitcairn on the road estimated the situation, and each took appropriate action. Parker, heavily outnumbered, ordered his two companies to disperse. The Marine, under instructions to disarm quietly any militia encountered, swung his men from column into line, trying to oblique beyond Parker's left flank, ordering his men "on no account to Fire or even attempt it without orders."

Someone did fire. Just whose finger tightened on the trigger will probably never be known, although Pitcairn's own report to Gage strongly suggests that the shot came from an American straggler near the edge of the Green. Several British volleys crashed out, and smoke coiled heavily about Buckman's Tavern and the Harrington house, over the Green itself. For a moment, the troops

One of the lanterns hung in the Old North Church

A German drawing of the clash at Lexington Green

101

Israel Putnam's sword

Flag of the Bedford Minutemen

got out of hand, broke ranks, rushed toward houses from which they swore shots were coming. Pitcairn and his officers shoved and bullied their men back into formation, firing ceased, and the militia scattered as Colonel Smith came on with the grenadiers. The column reformed and, in a long, thick rope of scarlet and white, pushed doggedly west toward Concord, whose stores were the true objective. Pitcairn had no casualties to report, save a slight wound to his own horse and a still slighter one to a man of the Lincolnshires. As to the eight American dead—well, they should have known better than to fire on the King's troops.

Over in Concord, men waited through the dark hours, knowing only that a British column was headed north out of Boston, with their own town its probable objective. Toward dawn Reuben Brown, the local saddler, volunteered to ride toward Lexington for fresher news, and he brought tidings that most men dreaded to hear—there had been fighting on Lexington Green. The saddler had seen the bright uniforms, the smoke against the grass, had heard the volleys. Beyond that he could tell nothing.

Concord might have been lacking in military dash, but it had that cold courage which enables men to march out into the unknown, to pick up coolly whatever cards fate has thrown face down. So the local companies, joined by men from nearby Lincoln, formed and set out along the road that led toward Lexington, fifes and drums at their head. Those not in column climbed to the prow-like nose of the ridge that looks east along the road. A mile or so out of Concord, the militia caught the sudden sheen of scarlet, the wink of cap-plates and bayonet points, and trained eyes among them correctly estimated the force as far greater than their own hundred-odd. In very good order the militia countermarched and headed decorously back to town, almost as an escort of honor for the massive column a hundred rods behind them.

First came the militia—drab, orderly, unhurried. Then a blaze of moving color—black coats, white coats, dark blue and sky-blue coats, orange and buff and yellow coats of the musicians, all laced and arabesqued and chevroned. Long afterward, Minuteman Amos Barrett remembered this pageant-approach to the town of Concord: "we . . . march[d] before them with our Droms and fifes agoing and also the B[ritish]. we had grand musick."

Pageant shifted to reality. The militia fell back, crossed the Concord River by the North Bridge, and headed for the old Muster Field on the high ground beyond. Smith and Pitcairn occupied the town and set their men searching for stores. Some companies were sent out to hold the South Bridge. Seven companies of light infantry were ordered to the North Bridge on the heels of the retreating militia. Three of the seven were to hold the bridge while the others pushed on, following up a rumor that arms were hidden on Colonel Barrett's farm, a mile or so away.

On the Muster Field the Concord and Lincoln companies found other units arriving from more distant towns like Chelmsford, Carlisle, and Acton. For a while they waited, observing the British companies by the North Bridge. Then someone saw smoke rising from among the trees that masked the town, and an obvious, if incorrect, conclusion was drawn—Concord was being put to the torch. In double file, all the companies started down the hill toward the bridge, headed by Captain Isaac Davis, the gunsmith, and his Acton company.

This time there was no question about who fired first. The British light infantry formed as though for street fighting and loosed a succession of ragged volleys, one of the first balls killing Isaac Davis. The militia fanned out, returned the fire accurately, and all at once and utterly inexplicably, the British broke and fled back to Concord. These were fine troops, probably as good as there were in the world of 1775. The panic must be laid to their Boston conditioning, to their harrowing night march, and, perhaps most important, to the fact that few if any of their own officers were with them.

The militia made no attempt to follow up the rout, but pushed on to a hill overlooking the town and waited—and wondered. So far, their luck had been more than good. The British musketry was very bad, as Amos Barrett noted: "It is straing their warnt no more killed, but they fird to high." But a single awesome thought must have occurred to every militiaman—"We've fired on the King's troops!"—a far more serious matter than making inflammatory speeches, writing seditious letters, or dumping tea at Griffin's Wharf.

Meanwhile, the four British companies that had gone on to Barrett's returned, grew panicky as they saw traces of the fight at the bridge, and raced into town under the very muzzles of the militia muskets which, luckily for them, stayed silent. Some time after noon Colonel Smith assembled his command and started it back east along the Lexington road. After some hesitation the militia followed rather cautiously, keeping to the north.

The Colonel of the Lincolnshires had delayed too long. As he cleared the town, he and every grenadier and light infantryman could see fields to the north and south abristle with fresh militia companies coming on from more distant towns. For a brief moment nothing happened. Then at a little bridge close by the junction of the Bedford and Lexington roads, near the Meriam house, the last files of Smith's command wheeled about, very likely without orders, and fired a farewell volley. This was the opening of the real fight of the nineteenth of April, 1775.

From path and road and field the militia closed in on the column, firing from behind stone walls, from behind houses and woodpiles and sheds. Men ran out of ammunition and went home. Men were killed as the light infantry swept the flanks of the attackers. Men were frightened by bullets that, in the words of one participant, "Whisled well," and gave up the fight. But always more men and more companies were arriving, so that the British column marched through "a Veritable Furnass of Musquetry." A stand was attempted, but Smith was wounded and Pitcairn lost his horse and pistols, and the retreat became a rout, with redcoated veterans of unquestioned courage and discipline throwing away arms and equipment as they ran.

Suddenly Lexington Green was in front of them, with the militia, who would not stand up in formal fight, closing tighter and tighter. A debacle loomed. Then, with melodramatic timing, clouds of scarlet and white showed on the hill across the Green by Munroe's Tavern. Lord Percy had brought out the bulk of the Boston garrison in answer to Colonel Smith's early morning plea for reinforcements.

It was only a breathing spell. The retreat was soon resumed and the column, now some 2,000 strong, was hounded and harried on and on by an enemy with which it was unable to come to grips. Through Menotomy, toward Cambridge, through present Somerville the British staggered until, gasping and spent, the whole command flung itself to the ground on the little hills above Charlestown known as Breed's and Bunker's. Close inshore lay ships of the Royal Navy, gunports open. The expedition that had waded across the backwater of the Charles the night before was safe, along with the column sent to relieve it.

Actually British casualties had been staggeringly light in relation to the volume of fire to which the combined commands had been subjected. Gage's official report lists no more than 72 killed out of more than 2,000. From the militia standpoint this showed shockingly bad marksmanship, yet there was no reason

A cartoon of British looting on the retreat from Concord

"Is life so dear, or peace so sweet, as to be purchased at the price of chains and slavery? Forbid it, Almighty God! I know not what course others may take; but as for me, give me liberty, or give me death!"
—Patrick Henry, March, 1775

103

why these men should have been good shots. They were townsmen, professional men, farmers—not frontiersmen or long hunters. What mattered was that a call had been sent out, and men by the thousands, from all walks of life, had answered it. That answering marked not merely a day on a calendar but a turning point in the life of a whole continent. An old order died on the nineteenth of April, 1775, simply because so many ordinary citizens believed so deeply in what underlay that call.

As night crept in from the sea, weary men began tramping home with the night. But hundreds stayed, guided by the vaguest of orders, guided more by an uneasy sense that their time of service was not yet up. A homing militiaman, topping the heights of Menotomy, could look back over a vast, darkening bowl and feel a sudden, inexplicable tightening of the throat. An immense, glowing horseshoe of scattered lights was closing in an arc about Charlestown and Boston, an arc thickened by the fires of companies from the central and western parts of the Province, still arriving in response to that call.

Those fires, flaring and ebbing and flaring, burned on through the changing seasons of 1775 and 1776. They saw the British fleet carry away the troops who had drawn triggers at the little bridge near Concord. Then they sank into the silver gray of their ashes, only to spring up again, not merely the fires of a Provincial army but of an American army—on Long Island, in the Jerseys, below Quebec, in Pennsylvania, down in the Carolinas and Georgia, and, at last, before Cornwallis' lines between the York and the James rivers in Virginia.

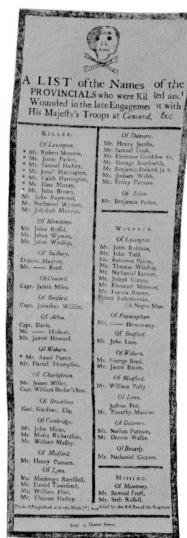

List of American casualties on April 19, published in Boston

One member of the Committee of Safety grasped immediately the significance of Lexington and Concord. Colonel Joseph Palmer of Braintree, riding into Watertown on the morning of the nineteenth, somehow received word of the haphazard musketry on Lexington Green, and hurriedly wrote out a bulletin. "To all friends of American Liberty . . . a Brigade . . . Marched to Lexington . . . they fired without any Provocation, and killed 6 Men and wounded 4 Others. . . . The bearer Israel Bissel is charged to alarm the Country quite to Connecticutt, and all persons are desired to furnish him with fresh Horses, as they may be needed."

Israel Bissel was a veteran postrider and, realizing the importance of the hasty scrawl that he carried, was not content with riding "quite to Connecticutt." He pushed on down to the Sound, then west along its sandy borders, showing what he bore to all Committeemen, shouting his news on greens and in taverns. The twenty-third, Sabbath or no Sabbath, found him pelting into New York, where people clawed at his stirrups, demanding news and more news. Then he was off again, across the Hudson, across the Jersey flats. On the twenty-fifth, Germantown and Philadelphia rose slowly over the horizon.

From Philadelphia sure hands sent his message south, as Paul Revere's had been sent earlier. Scrawls on copies of Palmer's letter tell their own tense story. "Forwarded to Col. Thomas Couch . . . he to forward to Tobias Randulph, head of Elk, Maryland." "For God's sake send the man on without the least delay." "For the good of our Country, and the welfare of our lives and liberties, and fortunes, you will not lose a moment's time."

There was trouble in Virginia and the militia companies were out, buzzing furiously over the seizure of Virginia powder and stores by Lord Dunmore, Royal Governor. By sundown of the twenty-eighth, news of what had happened in Massachusetts on the nineteenth spread along the Potomac and its affluents, and men knew that the trouble was national, not local. Under the advice of Peyton Randolph and Colonel George Washington the militia sullenly dispersed, since violence might "produce effects which God alone knows the effects of." But before breaking up, they passed a resolution. "We do now pledge ourselves to each other to be in readiness, at a moment's warning, to reassemble, and by force of arms, to defend the law, the liberty and rights of this *or any sister Colony,* from unjust and wicked invasion." The southern militiamen were closing ranks with the Minutemen of Massachusetts.

On May 8, the brigantine *Industry* brought the news of April 19 to Charleston. South Carolina had little to gain and a great deal to lose by anything more than a sympathetic nod toward the far northeast; but such logic overlooked the colony's earlier spontaneous dispatch of supplies and credit on receipt of news of the Boston Port Bill. Now the timid, the ultraconservative, the Crown-above-all men crept or were elbowed into the background, and the Assembly voted to raise two infantry regiments of 750 men each and a squadron of 450 mounted rangers. Then, as if to stress the fact that this was no mere gesture, one million pounds were appropriated to back up this and other measures. In the years to come, no colony would be more torn by war; no colony would stand more unflinchingly to the end.

Artemas Ward, senior General of the Massachusetts army, aging, heavy, "sick of the stone," with understandable reluctance took command of the great arc about Boston. Companies that had swarmed along the battle-road were massed confusedly across the northern and western approaches to the city, with officers trying to give orders to men from a dozen different villages or towns. There was more coherence to the southwest and south, since many of the units stationed there had arrived too late for the fight and had not undergone the disintegration of battle.

Artemas Ward, by Peale

Ward, devoted and hard-working, did what he could with what he had. Taking the northern sector under his own immediate charge, he assigned the southern to General John Thomas of Plymouth County, a highly respected man who had turned from doctor to soldier during the French and Indian War. Somehow, a new army was formed, under the very guns of a powerful, well-organized, and finely equipped British force in Boston.

There were vast problems concerning rations, rank, and pay, and an intense, sometimes bitter spirit of localism that defied the best efforts of Ward, Thomas, the Provincial Congress, and the Committee of Safety. A company from Sturbridge might march beside one from Barre, but each unit regarded the other as a dubious ally rather than a group of comrades. This spirit prevailed, at the start, in all the colonies, yet regiments were formed to serve to the end of the year, thus earning the title of the "Eight-Months Army."

Almost from the start, the men who manned the lines about Boston were undergoing a subtle change, turning from a Massachusetts army into something more far-reaching. New Hampshire sent men south at the first hint of the alarm of April 18 and 19—rangy men who made a remarkable march under a seasoned Indian fighter, Colonel John Stark. Israel Putnam, another old Ranger, brought in 3,000 men from Connecticut, including the Governor's Foot Guards commanded by Benedict Arnold. May found a column from Rhode Island on the march, a column complete with tents, wagons, supplies, and even a train of artillery. Patriotic merchants—Providence Gentiles and Newport Jews—had outfitted and equipped this force. Its commander was a tall, handsome young man who limped slightly and had a marked asthmatic wheeze. Nathanael Greene's quiet star was in the ascendant as he reported to General John Thomas at Roxbury, and it never set until his task was done and he had the last British army of the south pinned fast in Charleston in the far Carolinas. These three

"The Yankey's return from Camp," from a 1775 broadside

A British satire on the Rebel
soldiers in camps near Boston

PLAN OF THE TOWN OF BOSTON WITH THE
ATTACK on BUNKERS HILL in the Peninsula of CHARLESTOWN,
the 17th of June 1775.

A British plan of Boston
and Charlestown Peninsula

"foreign" armies placed themselves under Massachusetts command, and the force that had taken the field through the dark hours of April 18–19 became a New England army. And all the while, Gage sat passive in Boston, allowing the slow transformation to take place without interference.

Ruinous Fort Ticonderoga, slumbering at the narrow south end of Lake Champlain, was garrisoned by a few files of the 26th Cameronians under Captain De la Place. In the early hours of May 10, 1775, the torpid guard at the main gate was overwhelmed by a wild, yelling rush of men who poured up the bank from the waters. De la Place and his command were bundled off as prisoners of war, and the Royal colors were hauled down.

The whole swift action was an odd one. The attacking force was led by Ethan Allen, born in Connecticut but lately a resident of the Hampshire Grants, now Vermont. His authority for the coup came from the Province of Connecticut, though most of his men were Green Mountain Boys. In unwilling association with Allen was Colonel Benedict Arnold of Connecticut, who had come west with some troops sponsored by the Provincial Congress of Massachusetts. Now they had taken a British fort in the territory of a colony, New York, which so far had not been involved in any of the current hostilities. To whom did the fort now belong? To New York? To Massachusetts or Connecticut? Or to the amorphous Hampshire Grants? This question was to cause grave headshaking in the Second Continental Congress, where some earnest souls were even to suggest that Ticonderoga be returned to the Crown.

The fort itself was of little value in its present state of dilapidation. Captain John Montresor, Royal Engineers, reported that explosions, fires, and neglect had transformed de Lotbinière's works into "an amazing Useless Mass of Earth." Whatever its value, Ticonderoga was in colonial hands, difficult as it might be to say which colony could lay claim to it. Such considerations do not seem to have bothered either Allen or Arnold. The latter, his ego still smarting over being elbowed aside by the gigantic, declamatory Allen, gathered up men and small craft, drove north a few miles down the lake, seized Crown Point, pushed on to occupy briefly the British post at St. John's on the Richelieu River, and then sailed south in triumph to Ticonderoga. As to that most dubious "Gibraltar of the New World," its future now lay in the hands of the Continental Congress, while within its shattered walls lay untouched a wealth of artillery.

Back in the Boston area the New England army took shape slowly. In his headquarters in present Wadsworth House at the edge of Harvard Yard, Artemas Ward and his advisers came to a decision which, though sound in intent, led to a series of spectacularly wrong steps. Two masses of high ground commanded Boston—the heights of Dorchester and Roxbury just to the southwest, and those of Charlestown across the Charles River. To have fortified Dorchester Heights would have been logical, since they commanded the narrow Neck that led to the mainland and if furnished with artillery could have made much of the water front untenable. Having considered all this, the American high command gravely selected Charlestown with its low twin hills, where Messrs. Breed and Bunker grazed their cattle.

Charlestown Peninsula was shaped much like Boston, a fat polliwog swelling out into the water and tied to the shore by a long, narrow tail that was often overflowed by the Mystic River on one side and the Charles on the other. A garrison there could be neatly cut off by landing parties from the King's ships which stood ready to hand for just such purposes.

Nonetheless, on the evening of June 16 a detail of men was sent out from

Cambridge to dig, and with them, unseen but ominous, marched three serious headquarters omissions. No steps had been taken for their relief; no food or water was sent out; and worst of all, there was no ammunition reserve in case the British decided to interfere.

Once on the peninsula, an error of commission occurred. Ward's orders had been to fortify Bunker's Hill, the higher peak, but misunderstanding or stupidity set the diggers to work on Breed's, which was closer to the water, to the guns of the Royal Navy and the Boston batteries, and also to the beaches where hostile troops might be landed. As for the long Neck in the rear, no one seems to have thought of that. All night long the detail dug, and by dawn Breed's was crested by a redoubt, its weak left flank partially protected by earthworks and a rail fence that ran clear down to the Mystic shore.

Sunrise of the seventeenth brought first incredulity, then sheer amazement to the British in Boston. The night before, Charlestown peninsula had been a green, unpeopled knob. Now it swarmed with men, and fresh-turned earth showed brown on crest and slope. Fortifications had been thrown up in a shockingly short time, and a lesson was stamped, perhaps too indelibly, into the consciousness of British commanders: never give the Yankees time to dig.

The Battle of Breed's Hill,
June 17, 1775

Thomas Gage reacted with a celerity that was unusual for him and may have been due to the presence of a group of three newly landed generals—Sir William Howe, Henry Clinton, and handsome, purple-prosed John Burgoyne. Swift orders went out from Province House, and soon British ships and land batteries began to blast, and round shot went whining over the Charles to dart and skitter among the still-laboring men above Charlestown.

There is nothing more demoralizing to green troops than artillery fire, and all logic shouted that the very first salvos from Boston should have sent the weary, unfed, unwatered, and unsupported diggers racing for the mainland in panic. Instead, the greater part of them somehow managed to keep on with their work under the eyes of the four senior officers present—Colonels William Prescott, Richard Gridley, Israel Putnam, and Thomas Knowlton.

The perfection of a June morning wore on; then there was a moving blaze of color along the Boston water front, as barges and longboats filled with scarlet-clad regulars. Men in the blue and red of the Royal Regiment of Artillery trundled fieldpieces into heavier craft. Drums pounded, fifes cut shrill into the warm air, and a floating pageant lurched out across the Charles to the silver splash of oars. H.M.S. *Lively* and *Falcon* increased their rate of fire. Barge by barge, the flotilla scraped ashore, disgorging troops on the northern and eastern beaches of the Charlestown knob.

Sir William Howe, commanding the landing force, had a fine view of the slope ahead of him and noted its tangle of rail fences, clumps of blackberry and blueberry bushes, and, at the crest, the bristle of the main American redoubt which kept strangely and disturbingly quiet. Estimating the situation, he sent back for reinforcements, which reached him promptly. They included Royal Marines under Major John Pitcairn, who was undertaking what was to be his last assignment.

Miniature of Major John Pitcairn

The forces on the beaches shifted, reshuffled, and the assault started—long scarlet and white lines, three-deep, climbing like a slow surf toward the redoubt or over the northeast beaches. On they went under the June sun, each man carrying a load reckoned at 120 pounds and including three days' rations and blankets. This was a frontal attack against an entrenched force of unknown strength, despite the fact that Howe, under cover of the omnipresent fleet, could have landed his men at the base of the Neck and clamped a strangle hold about

Dr. Joseph Warren, by Copley

the American garrison. But custom, eighteenth-century military honor, and possibly a not too farfetched belief that the defenders could not stand against such a disciplined mass, decreed the head-on smash.

As the slow, purposeful scarlet and white lines moved closer, the Breed's Hill defenders must have felt a crushing sense of isolation. William Prescott and Dr. Joseph Warren were at the redoubt, calmly inspiring. Thomas Knowlton and John Stark were with their Connecticut and New Hampshire men, prolonging the left down to the Mystic. But no one man was in command on the Charlestown bulge. Nearby Bunker's Hill was black with troops who had come on during the morning, but there they stayed, largely because there was no one to tell them where to go or what to do when they got there.

By logic and precedent, the Americans should have loosed one ragged, scattered volley, and then fled. Something inexplicable, the true miracle of June 17, kept them steady. In the redoubt a gray-haired farmer prayed aloud, "I thank thee, O Lord, for sparing me to fight this day. Blessed be the name of the Lord." And he and his fellows waited, incredibly patient, fighting back hot terror as the redcoats came on, closer, closer, until faces could be distinguished, little details like the brass matchboxes that the grenadiers wore fastened to their chests.

No one knows who gave the order to fire, or if the trigger-discipline of this day was spontaneous. British sources agree that the first ripping volley was delivered when the bayonet points, sharp in the sun, were less than fifteen paces from the lines. Bearskin caps flew in the air; bright uniforms were strewn over the trampled green of the grass. Then powder-blackened eyes in the redoubt, along earthwork and rail fence, looked out incredulously as the disordered wreckage of the attack went pounding back in angry flight to the beaches and the waiting boats.

By late afternoon, the slopes of Breed's Hill were red with a litter of scarlet and white, thickened by the failure of a second attack that had been smashed as utterly as the first. Eyes in Boston, eyes behind the defenses, watched the shredded companies re-form and wondered if any troops could rally after two such murderous smashings. The answer came quickly.

Drums beat once more, and limping officers, some with bandaged heads or arms in rude slings, were giving orders, grimly blotting out the stark fact that "Some had only eight or nine men a Company left; some only three, four or five." Men in the defenses watched them form, start up those ghastly slopes once more, and, watching, slipped shaky fingers into cartridge pouches. Four rounds left? No, only two. Perhaps none. As before, they waited, clutching bayonetless muskets.

The British came on through the smoky dusk, faces set, breath sobbing in their chests, dreading the resumption of that inexplicably controlled fire that withheld its stab until the last possible moment. There was one, perhaps a second, blast that shook the attackers, then silence from the works. Grenadiers, light infantry, line companies—bayonets eager—were among the defenders, and massacre seemed inevitable. But, as miraculous as the impromptu American fire control, spent troops with useless muskets managed somehow to bring off an orderly retreat to the mainland.

So General William Howe had won for General Thomas Gage an utterly useless peninsula, and at horrible cost. Colonel James Abercromby of the Grenadiers was dead, and so was Major John Pitcairn of the Marines. The total casualty list showed 1,054 dead and wounded out of some 2,200 who had gone in through the smoke and flying lead of the three attacks. And

The battle for the Breed's Hill redoubt, from a German drawing

something intangible died in the British command on that June afternoon. No officer who witnessed the slaughter could ever get the memory of it out of his mind. Where drive and initiative were displayed by the British high command during the rest of the war, they usually came from someone who had neither toiled up the slopes that led from the beaches to Breed's Hill nor watched others on that ghastly ascent.

As for Artemas Ward's men, they fell back to Prospect Hill on the mainland. Their losses had been relatively light, the best estimates showing some 500 killed and wounded, most of them probably in that last wild rush. It was then that Dr. Joseph Warren had vanished in a murky cloud of smoke and death. June 17, 1775, had been an important day for both sides. But, still unknown to them, an even bigger day had just been marked in faraway Philadelphia, where the Second Continental Congress was assembled.

The Second Congress, sitting in the Georgian splendor of the Pennsylvania State House, had been considering in committee a most disturbing letter brought from the Boston lines by bland, smiling Dr. Benjamin Church. Stripped to its essentials, this letter was an appeal from the Massachusetts Committee of Safety asking, even begging the Congress to adopt the New England army now blockading Boston as an *American* army and to set up a civil government to administer all matters colonial.

Soon John Adams arose, to sketch out his idea of a "Grand American Army" made up from all the colonies, since what had happened in Boston could happen in New York or Charleston or in any spot to which the minds of his listeners might turn. And to command such an army? Here the delegates leaned forward in a sudden hush. Most were prepared for—and many favored—the nomination of a New Englander, perhaps General Artemas Ward, now commanding the only army *in esse*. But Adams went on. He had, he said, just the man in mind, "a gentleman whose skill as an officer, whose independent fortune, great talents and universal character would command the respect of America and unite the full exertions of the Colonies better than any other person alive." John Adams paused, letting his colleagues speculate. Then he went on. "A gentleman from *Virginia* who is among us here and well known to all of us . . ."

The member from Fairfax County, Virginia, at this point slipped out of the hall as inconspicuously as a man six foot two could in an age when a mere six-footer was a rarity. Adams went on with his nomination of Colonel George Washington, and the session was thrown open for debate.

Discussion went on for two more days. Then, on June 16, 1775, John Hancock of Massachusetts, presiding in place of the absent Peyton Randolph of Virginia, stated that he had "the order of Congress to inform George Washington, Esq., of the unanimous vote in choosing him to be General and Commander-in-Chief of the forces raised and to be raised in defence of American Liberty. The Congress hopes the gentleman will accept."

Standing before the members of Congress in the scarlet and blue uniform of Colonel of Virginia Militia, George Washington drew out a sheet of paper and read a statement: "Mr. President: Tho' I am truly sensible of the high Honour done me in this Appointment, yet I feel great distress from a consciousness that my abilities and Military experience may not be equal to the extensive and important Trust . . . As to pay, Sir, I beg leave to Assure the Congress that as no pecuniary consideration could have tempted me to have accepted this Arduous employment . . . I do not wish to make any proffit from it."

Connecticut broadside offering a bounty to gunsmiths in 1775

"Here Anarchy before the gaping crowd Proclaims the people's majesty aloud . . . Legions of senators infest the land, And mushroom generals thick as mushrooms stand."
—*Jonathan Odell, Loyalist Poet*

It had rained heavily throughout the morning of July 2, 1775, and General Artemas Ward at Cambridge canceled whatever plans he had made for the formal reception of the new commander in chief, who had been supposed to ride in from Watertown. When, in clearing weather, General George Washington rode into the rain-soaked college town by the Charles, he found it dozing through a Sunday afternoon, and one James Stevens, a soldier on duty in Cambridge, made a single, bored notation for July 2, 1775: "Nothing heppeng extroderly."

After naming the commander in chief, Congress had appointed four major generals to serve under him: Charles Lee, a fantastically ugly Englishman, late of His Majesty's forces and claiming to hold a General's commission from the King of Poland; Artemas Ward; Philip Schuyler, a Hudson River patroon of vast holdings and influence; and, somewhat surprisingly, the gnarled, scarred old Indian fighter, Israel Putnam of Connecticut. Brigadier generalcies followed these appointments, selection being based sometimes on political influence, sometimes on past military service, and occasionally on hope of future development in the field.

A woodcut shows Washington taking command of the army at Cambridge

Chain of command—mainspring of any army—was finally brought into reasonably manageable shape, largely through the quiet impact of Washington's personality and by the common knowledge of the vast sacrifices that he himself was making in the common cause. Out on the American left, Charles Lee maintained his headquarters in the beautiful Royall mansion, which soon became known, in not improbable tribute to the then occupant, as Hobgoblin Hall. Under Lee as brigadiers were dark, hot-tempered John Sullivan of New Hampshire and handsome young Nathanael Greene of Rhode Island. In the center, about Cambridge and under Washington's eye, Israel Putnam and William Heath were in command; while the far right, out by Roxbury, came under the care of Artemas Ward, seconded by John Thomas of Massachusetts and Joseph Spencer of Connecticut.

There were other people here in this strange New England milieu for the Virginian to note. On a ride of inspection with Charles Lee the two generals met a fat young civilian, whose left hand was carefully muffled in white silk. That evening the fat young man wrote excitedly to his wife, Lucy, "I met the Generals . . . when they had viewed the works they expressed the greatest pleasure and surprize." Henry Knox must have spent many profitable hours over the writings of Vauban back there at his Boston bookstore, for while Washington's eye for fieldworks was amateur, Charles Lee was the hard-bitten professional from whom praise had to be earned.

There were units, too, that must have lodged in the mind of the commander in chief on his endless rides and inspections. There was the whole Rhode Island Brigade, complete with tents and artillery, well uniformed and disciplined, and taking solid form under young Greene's increasingly skilled hand. There was John Glover's 21st Massachusetts Regiment from Marblehead, with its cocked hats and short blue jackets of good sea-cloth and loose, nautical white trousers. Virtually born at sea, they could handle anything that floated, and there was a great bitterness in their hearts, for the Fisheries Act had spelled ruin for them and their town. Discipline came easily to them, for each understood that a crew must work together, that a command must be instantly obeyed. In the months and years to come, the commander in chief was to reach out for the 21st and its peculiar skills, and it would always answer. It was to snatch a whole army and oar it away from deepest catastrophe. Again, John Glover's men were to ferry what was left of that same army to lightning attack across

Washington's headquarters, Cambridge

a stormy, ice-choked river that was, militarily, impassable. And later still, its sure, silent boats would carry General John Sullivan's men, outnumbered but not outfought, beyond the reach of deadly enemy attack.

As the first American army took shape slowly under Washington's hand, Gage and his British remained oddly passive in Boston. There may have been some hope on the part of Gage and then Howe, who succeeded him in October, that the blockading army would fall to pieces of its own weight. The powerful British striking force of some 10,000 limited itself to cannonading the American lines and to futile little raids and skirmishes. And the British command also passed up one source of strength that could have been important. In Boston there were some 6,500 civilians, a good third of them avowed Tories, either residents of the city or refugees from the hinterland. The men among them, headed by the same Timothy Ruggles who had presided at that first Stamp Act Congress, were in a hot, angry mood—more than eager to fight for the Crown. But they were snubbed, put off for one reason or another, and what could have been a valuable Crown asset withered away, useless.

As fall came on, lights burned late in the commander in chief's headquarters. Problem after problem was spread out across Washington's desk. By the end of the year, the so-called Eight-Months Army would be no more. In fact some units, which insisted on their own reckoning of time in the field and jeered at the army's count, would leave well before that date. How could a new army be recruited in the face of the poised British might? How could it be armed, when virtually all of its muskets were the personal property of those men so soon to go home? But somehow, the great change-over was accomplished. When men could not be persuaded to re-enlist, short-term militia were called up to man the lines while recruiting officers beat their drums in distant towns and hamlets. A surprising number did stay, however, due in no small part to the slowly growing influence on the New Englanders of the tall Virginian. He was not a man whom troops ran after, cheering and tossing their hats. But when he passed through post or camp, men were apt to stand a little straighter, grip their muskets a little tighter, and compose stilted letters home explaining just why it seemed fitting that they should stay on, after all.

A severe blow in the form of treachery fell on the commander in chief's shoulders. Letters intercepted by quick-witted Nathanael Greene, and acted upon by dynamic Israel Putnam, proved that Dr. Benjamin Church, long-time member of the Committee of Safety and recently appointed head of all the military hospitals of the army, had been in steady communication with British headquarters in Boston. Luckily, no lasting harm had been done; but the thought must have been in many minds that if there could be one Church, why not another?

As though to ease the unbearable strain on the commander in chief, and indirectly on all his army, early December brought Martha Custis Washington to Cambridge, all the way from Mount Vernon in Virginia. The presence of the one great confidante of his life must have been a godsend to the harassed commander in chief. With her he could share deep-biting anxieties that he might not voice to his officers. To her he could spell out his perplexities over enlistments, or he could speculate on what his position would be if only he had a few heavy guns to mount on Dorchester Heights, that land mass so far neglected by both sides.

Whether or not the heavy guns were to take their place along the arc of the siege lay squarely on the shoulders of Henry Knox, whose field fortifica-

This American leaflet urged the British troops to desert during the Boston siege

"Father and I went down to camp,
Along with Captain Gooding,
And there we see the men and boys,
As thick as hasty pudding.

Yankee Doodle, keep it up,
Yankee Doodle, dandy,
Mind the music and the step,
And with the girls be handy."
—From the Song, 1775

tions Washington and Charles Lee had admired. Many men had cast longing thoughts toward the ordnance that slumbered in de Lotbinière's star-shaped fort at Ticonderoga. Now ex-bookseller Knox had gone west to do something about it. Virtually alone, he faced the problem of shifting this mass of artillery, in the dead of winter, from the west bank of Champlain over a nearly roadless wilderness to western Massachusetts, and thence over killing ridges to the blockade of Boston.

At Ticonderoga Knox had valuable help from General Philip Schuyler, the area commander, but soon he was on his own. Teamsters and oxen had to be hired, sledges rented or, in some cases, built on the spot. Once under way, the long column sought out what roads there were. Day by slow day, through heavy snows, through maddening thaws, the Ticonderoga guns lurched east, across the Taconics, along the very eaves of the Berkshire Hills into Great Barrington in Massachusetts From dawn till sunset, day in and day out, hoofs churned and runners hissed over the snow until, at Framingham, Knox was able to write to the commander in chief that 59 pieces of ordnance of all calibers, large and small—a "noble train of artillery"—were ready to be turned over to the American army. It had been a stupendous feat, and it is largely a forgotten one. When the last sledge came to a halt at its destination, the fate of Boston, its garrison, and its Loyalists was settled.

Throughout the night of March 4, guns thundered all along the American lines. From Boston, artillery answered in rather bored routine, but the British command seems to have paid little attention to this sudden activity. Then, early on March 5, a sleepy British sentry blinked through the dawn mists, staring in disbelief at Dorchester Heights. The crests, bare at sundown, were now crowned with works, fully manned, and heavy guns covered the rear of the Roxbury lines, a good part of Boston, Castle Island, and great stretches of the fleet anchorage. The whole British position was clearly untenable.

Yet military honor and tradition demanded that Sir William Howe attempt a breakout, and he massed his men for an attack on the heights, an attack which could only have ended in a far bloodier Breed's Hill without even the token capture of ground as the prize. Luckily for him and his cause, a terrific storm, described locally as a "Hurrycane," swept north up the bay, swamping or dispersing his landing craft before his men could embark.

Howe abandoned his plans for attack, and fleet and transports sailed for Halifax, laden with the Boston garrison and with most of the Tory families who had sought refuge under His Majesty's colors. On March 17, John Sullivan led his men into the abandoned Charlestown lines. Israel Putnam plunged into Boston itself, to find a city whose desolation was offset, militarily, by the discovery of great caches of Royal stores, most oddly abandoned.

On the eighteenth, the commander in chief quietly entered Boston. Characteristically, he made no dramatic speech or gesture in taking over the city. When he attended divine worship, the first to be held here under the new flag of the Colonies—thirteen red and white stripes with the Union Jack in the canton—he asked Dr. Eliot, dean of the Boston clergy, to preach a sermon of devout thanksgiving, not of war. Dr. Eliot found his text in Isaiah, and George Washington of Virginia bowed his head to the words, "Look upon Zion, the city of our solemnities: Thine eyes shall see Jerusalem a quiet habitation, a tabernacle that shall not be taken down."

But even while looking upon Zion, a man at prayer must have thought about Howe's great flotilla, still hanging off Nantasket Roads, and wondered from what point of land its sails would next be sighted.

"... the Tories were thunder-struck when orders were issued for evacuating the town ... Many of them, it is said, considered themselves as undone, and seemed, at times, inclined to throw themselves at the mercy of their offended country, rather than leave it."
—An Eyewitness Account, 1776

The Shot Heard Round the World

General Thomas Gage, His Majesty's commander in chief in America, had less than 4,000 troops in Boston with which to enforce the Port Bill in the seething Bay Colony. "To keep quiet in the Town of Boston only," Gage decided, "will not terminate Affairs; the Troops must March into the Country." But each of his practice marches provoked larger, swifter mobilizations of colonial "minnit men." On April 19, 1775, the inevitable explosions occurred at Lexington and Concord. The contemporary map below shows Gage's troops in red, who started "by sea" from Boston toward Concord. In their wake, the first colonial dead lie on Lexington Green (left center), and they trade volleys with the militia, in blue, at Concord's North Bridge (left). News of the British march brings streams of Minutemen (mistakenly shown in red, top) to harry the English withdrawal to the peninsula north of Boston. Also shown are the principal Rebel camps which immediately ringed Gage and his men in Boston. When the King's subjects fired on the King's troops, the American Revolution had begun.

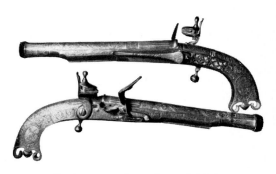

In the retreat from Concord Major Pitcairn, Royal Marines, lost these pistols, which American General Israel Putnam used during the war.

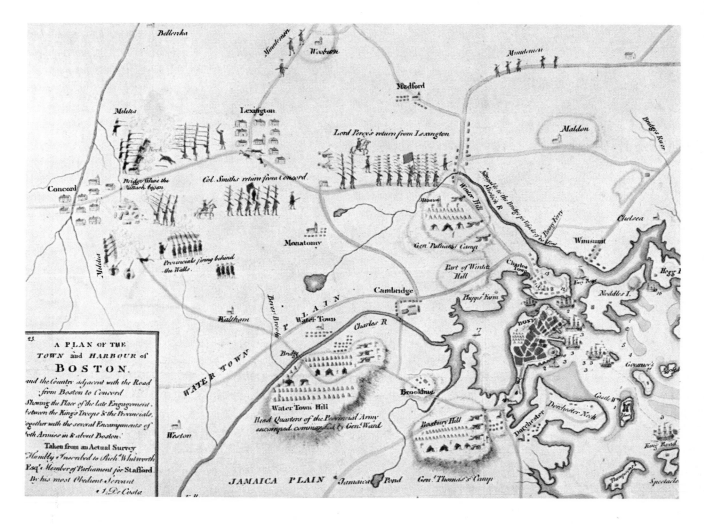

The Fighting Begins:

Lexington and Concord

These engravings by Amos Doolittle, a Connecticut militiaman who arrived soon after April 19, 1775, capture crudely but accurately the battles of Lexington and Concord. *Above, left:* The Lexington militia disperses after a volley from Major John Pitcairn's advance guard. Probably a nervous militiaman fired first, then the British charged with bayonets and Pitcairn re-formed them with difficulty. Marching to Concord, the redcoats were joined by the main force under Lieutenant Colonel

Francis Smith. *Above, right:* Smith and Pitcairn reconnoiter from Concord cemetery while their regiments march into town. *Below, left:* After their repulse at North Bridge, beyond Concord, Smith and his 700-man force begin a nightmare withdrawal to Lexington. One soldier recalled that "a grait many Lay dead and the Road was bloddy." *Below, right:* Temporarily rescued by a relief column from Boston under Lord Percy, the British soon resume their retreat. Describing it, one man said,

"We were fired on from Houses and behind Trees . . . the Country was . . . full of Hills, Woods, stone Walls . . . which the Rebels did not fail to take advantage of . . ." Not until dusk, after marching and fighting continuously for twenty hours, did the exhausted redcoats reach Charlestown Peninsula and safety. Gage listed 73 killed, 174 wounded (only one of each 300 American bullets found a target), the Rebels 49 and 41, in what a British survivor called an "ill plan'd and ill executed" expedition.

Big Guns for Boston

An amateur soldier who became one of Washington's most trusted lieutenants, Henry Knox had carefully studied the volumes on artillery usage in his London Book Store in Boston before the war. This portrait is by Stuart.

Three weeks before war began, one of Sam Adams' agents wrote from Montreal that "the Fort at Tyconderogo must be seised as soon as possible should hostilities be committed by the kings Troops. The people on N. Hampshire Grants have ingaged to do this Business . . ." The strategic value of Fort Ticonderoga and nearby Crown Point —ruinous as both works were—was also seen by a Connecticut Colonel named Benedict Arnold. Commanding the portage that connected Lake Champlain with Lake George, Ticonderoga was the key to the historic invasion route between Canada and the colonies. So at dawn on May 10, Green Moun-

tain Boys from the "N. Hampshire Grants," led jointly and quarrelsomely by Ethan Allen and Arnold, took the tiny garrison at Ticonderoga by surprise, Allen bellowing to its sleeping commander, "Come out, you old rat!" After the battle of Breed's Hill (following page) Washington regarded the need for the fort's cannon as so great that "no Trouble or Expence must be spared to obtain them." The task of bringing them to Boston fell to Henry Knox, former bookseller who became commander of artillery. This feat he achieved, said Knox, only "after having climbed mountains from which we might almost have seen all the Kingdoms of the Earth."

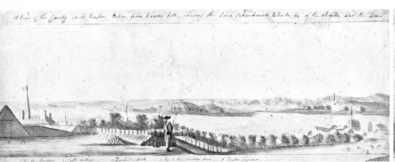

This view of the Rebel lines encircling Boston was made from Beacon Hill by a British officer. Dorchester Heights is visible in the first

Henry Knox selected 59 of Fort Ticonderoga's guns for the wintry, 300-mile trip to Boston. Hauled by sledge, his "noble train of artillery" was dogged by one mishap after another, including a "cruel thaw."

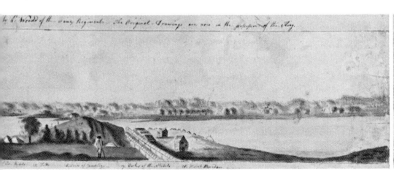

segment (left); the large house in the second section is John Hancock's. Bunker's and Breed's hills are to the right of the steeple in the fourth panel.

Dr. Joseph Warren, a leading patriot, was a major casualty when the third British charge finally carried the Breed's Hill redoubt. John Trumbull's painting also shows the mortally wounded Major Pitcairn (center) being carried from the field.

In June, 1775, American troops were ordered to fortify Bunker's Hill on Charlestown Peninsula. Amid the general confusion of the night move, however, the works were actually begun on Breed's Hill, closer to Boston. Gage could easily have trumped this foolhardy move by landing troops on narrow Charlestown Neck and cutting off the entire Rebel force. Instead, with utter disdain for the raw colonials, the British made a frontal assault. At the staggering cost of 1,054 casualties out of 2,200 engaged, they gained a narrow victory in the first real battle of the war. But the lesson was plain: the entrenched Rebel was a formidable opponent.

Two weeks later George Washington took command, and in October William Howe relieved Gage. Washington's greatest problem, as the siege of Boston wore on, was to keep an army in the field.

At dawn on March 5, 1776, the astonished English gaped at Dorchester Heights, overlooking Boston. "With an expedition equal to that of the genii belonging to Aladdin's wonderful lamp," Knox's cannon had been emplanted and works built in one night of prodigious effort. Outmaneuvered, Howe embarked his troops for Halifax, and American patrols found Bunker's Hill guarded by dummy sentries labeled, "Welcome Brother Jonathan."

The Battle for Breed's Hill

In the contemporary engraving above of the Breed's Hill battle, Boston is seen at right. Charlestown, afire from the British cannonade, burns at center; and at left the too-formal Rebel line breaks an enemy thrust. An English print (below, left) satirizes the British "victory" as well as outsized coiffures of the day. Although Howe's evacuation of Boston (below) was delayed by adverse sailing weather, he bought himself a peaceful departure by threatening to burn the town if attacked.

119

A detail from Trumbull's painting of the death of Montgomery at Quebec

FIRST CAMPAIGNS, NORTH AND SOUTH

"The Sun never shined on a cause of greater worth. 'Tis

not the affair of a City, a County, a Province, or a King-

dom; but of a Continent—of at least one eighth part of

the habitable Globe."

THOMAS PAINE, *Common Sense*—JANUARY, 1776

As the military situation around Boston lapsed into a stalemate, the first stirrings of the colonies' united military efforts began to be heard. The Canadian land mass, a beckoning treasure, seems to have cast a spell over the Continental Congress in 1775. There was, of course, the militarily sensible premise of seizing the enemy's northern staging points and thus protecting the colonies' upper periphery. But beyond this, there was the simple desire to bring Canada and its inhabitants into the fold. Already New Englanders had won Fort Ticonderoga and control of Lake Champlain, and the priceless water route that pointed like a sword at the heart of Canada must have looked like a God-given highway to sudden, glorious conquest. So the invasion of Canada got under way [*see* map, page 131]

From the Congress a simple but splendid message went out to General Philip Schuyler. A strangely worded half-order, half-suggestion, it told the area commander that "if [he] finds it practicable, and that it will not be disagreeable to the Canadians," he should at once seize St. John's, Montreal, and any other parts of Canada that it might occur to him to take. Another impulse had helped trigger this drive northward. It had been a warning sent from the depths of the wilderness by an astute American woodsman who had been consorting with Indian tribes and habitants. He was no buckskinned Natty Bumppo, but a Yale graduate, a lawyer, and, in calmer times, King's Attorney for the Province of New York. His name was John Brown, and he wrote urgently to Ticonderoga that General Sir Guy Carleton, British commander in Canada, had been building some good-sized craft that "can easily sweep the lake. I therefore humbly beseech that some effectual measures may be immediately entered into to keep the command of this lake."

Brown's letter had arrived during Schuyler's absence, but his second-in-command acted at once. This was General Richard Montgomery, son of a baronet, onetime member of Parliament, more lately member of the Provincial Congress, and former British officer. It was obvious to him that Carleton's ships must be destroyed.

Sunset of August 28, 1775, saw a strange flotilla, cobbled together out of almost no proper materials, but with a great deal of energy and hope, pushing north down Champlain from the shaky American base at Ticonderoga. Aboard the schooner *Liberty,* the sloop *Enterprise,* and a lesser flock of row galleys, bateaux, and canoes, were Waterbury's 5th Connecticut, Ritzema's 4th New York, and a few gunners, shoving off toward the mysterious immensity of Canada, with the Green Mountains dusk-cloaked on their right and the Adirondacks catching the last flecks of sunset gold on their left.

Before long, General Schuyler caught up with the expedition and assumed command. A landing was made along the Richelieu River, water-exit from Champlain. The improvised, ill-equipped force was assembled somehow and began its slow, slogging march north toward St. John's, dragging its little artillery train and supply wagons through unbroken country, through swamps, across ledges. Schuyler's health, always a question mark despite a deceptively brisk and robust appearance, broke down, and the command fell again into the hands of General Richard Montgomery.

There was an infinity of matters to go wrong, and most of them did. Sickness ravaged the token army. Supplies ran short. Torrential rains fell. Montgomery's subordinates insisted on arguing and debating every order that he gave. And the British had erected a fort at St. John's, manned by detachments of the 7th Royal Fusiliers and the 26th Cameronians, backed by an artillery detail and Canadian militia. It was not much of a fort and not a

The water route between Canada and Albany

very strong garrison, but it was too much for Montgomery's raw, ill-supplied, sick troops to handle by assault; so the commander settled down to siege operations. It had been hoped that the post would fall in five days. Instead, British Major Preston hung on doggedly. Swamps, bad weather, and internal dissensions blunted every stroke that Montgomery planned, and it was not until November 2, 1775, that Preston, aware that no help could come to him from Sir Guy Carleton, and menaced by a battery that Montgomery had finally succeeded in planting on high ground overlooking the fort, surrendered after a two-month siege.

The remnants of the 7th (which included a young British officer named John André) and the 26th filed off as prisoners of war. Montgomery could write "Mission accomplished" as far as John Brown's warning about the St. John's ships was concerned, but there remained the rather carefree Congressional directive about seizing "Montreal and any other parts of the country." So he re-equipped his men out of captured supplies, and on November 5, under a snowy sky, his command took the ragged corduroy road that led to the St. Lawrence and the island city. As a man in the weary column remembered, "Under our Feet was Snow and Ice and Water, over our Heads Clouds Snow and rain, before us the mountains appeared all white with Snow and Ice," as they pressed on "to new Sieges and new Conquests."

November 13 saw the American occupation of Montreal, the capture of its little garrison and fleet of eleven vessels; but the biggest prize was missed. Sir Guy Carleton, mainspring of all British activity in Canada, escaped and dropped downriver to Quebec, virtually alone. Nonetheless, the water road to the city on its cliffs, high above the river, lay open to Montgomery.

At the same time that Montgomery and Schuyler were heading off toward Canada, other American eyes turned to Quebec. It had occurred to Washington, sifting and sorting through the myriad problems that beset him in the big house on Brattle Street, that weak as Carleton was supposed to be, the Schuyler-Montgomery expedition might be markedly speeded up if British attention could be drawn away from it by a diversion. This diversion looked feasible on a map. A force of about 1,000 men could land in Maine, ascend the Kennebec in bateaux, negotiate a hard portage to Dead River, pole on to the Height of Land on the shadowy Canadian border, and thence erupt down the Chaudière to its mouth, nearly opposite Quebec. But plans, maps, and surveys glossed over heavy waterfalls, long, boiling rapids, killing portages up steep ridges, plus the normal run of accidents that a few men traveling light by canoe might avoid, but which would surely fall upon a large body chained to heavy bateaux and forced to carry supplies with them. Nor was the climate of a waning year taken sufficiently into account.

Once decided upon, command of the diversionary expedition was handed over to that stormiest of stormy petrels—the restless, impetuous Colonel Benedict Arnold. This was a task that appealed to his undoubted energy, talents, and courage, and he threw himself headlong into it. In a short time, over a thousand volunteers had gathered in and about Cambridge. Spearheaded by three companies of riflemen from Pennsylvania and Virginia, the force was backed by some ten companies of men from the New England colonies.

The column had left Cambridge by the dangerously late date of September 13, and in its ranks were men whose names would far outlast the Revolution. There was intense Benedict Arnold himself, slim, girlishly handsome Aaron Burr, and huge Captain Daniel Morgan with his riflemen. Lieutenant Colonel Christopher Greene, cousin to General Nathanael, led the detach-

General Richard Montgomery

"Early this morning weighed anchor with a pleasant gale, our colors flying and fifes a-playing, and the hills all around covered with pretty girls weeping for their departing swains."
—*Private Joseph Ware, 1775*

ment that followed Morgan's men, and after him came Major Return Jonathan Meigs and Captain Henry Dearborn. Christian Febiger, a Danish soldier, kept pace with the rest as Arnold's adjutant, striking out along the road to Newburyport and the waiting ships that were to take the whole command to the mouth of the Kennebec.

As long as good weather held along the sapphire blue of that Maine river, things did not go too badly, in spite of dissensions in the command, the alarmingly slow passage of miles, and the frailness of the bateaux, whipped up out of green wood and marred by necessarily hurried workmanship. Bateaux with their precious supplies were overturned in rapids, were battered to pieces in long hauls up waterfalls. Then the weather broke and the rains came. More and more supplies were ruined. Arnold checked his bearings, and found that he had spent double the time he had allowed for the whole trip and had used up half of his provisions. Men began boiling rawhide and eating it. Captain Dearborn's huge black dog disappeared into a cook-pot. At Dead River, on October 15, Colonel Greene's command supped on candles, stewed into a sort of water-gruel. Then Colonel Roger Enos of Connecticut decided to turn back with his whole division and was branded a coward, although his defection was well reasoned and actually saved the whole expedition, since it diminished the number of mouths to be fed.

Arnold's march to Quebec

There was snow at the Great Carrying Place over the Height of Land, and starving men died as they staggered on under the load of the few remaining bateaux. Private George Morison of the Pennsylvania Rifles wrote afterward that men fell from sheer exhaustion. If a man tried to help a fallen comrade, he himself lost his footing. "At length the wretches raise themselves up . . . wade through the mire to the foot of the next steep and gaze up at its summit, contemplating what they must suffer before they reach it.—They attempt it, catching at every twig and shrub they can lay hold of—their feet fly from them—they fall down—to rise no more."

Then on November 8, through bitter, snowy weather, the skeletons that made up the column pushed down the last stretches of the sinister Chaudière, and Private James Melvin somehow found energy enough to note briefly in his diary, "Marched six miles and came to point Levi, on the River St. Lawrence, opposite Quebec."

It had been an epic feat, that struggle against hunger and weather and terrain. Few men then alive on the continent could have carried it off as had Benedict Arnold, and yet it was far from a one-man exploit. As Arnold stood on the south bank of the St. Lawrence under the towering, reddish cliffs of Levis, with the vast rock of Quebec looming across the winter flood, he knew his force was far too weak to attempt a move against the great natural citadel. What was the next step to be?

Quebec's Upper Town (right) and Lower Town, *circa* 1777

As November died, word came out of the west to Arnold and his men. Montgomery was moving to join them, and on December 2, 1775, the two forces met at Pointe aux Trembles above Quebec. Together they would attack the cliff city, and as soon as possible, since most enlistments ran out with the old year. The combined command was small, Arnold having something over 650 men left and Montgomery less than 400, all that he had dared bring down from Montreal.

The bold plan depended for success on the supposed weakness of the Quebec defenders and on surprise. Before dawn on the given day, the attack was to be launched over terrain that has changed very little with the years.

Montgomery's command would strike from the west, close along the river, following the road that still runs at the base of the towering cliffs. Arnold was to come in from the east at a point known as Sault au Matelot. Meeting in the heart of the Lower Town, the two bodies were to combine and drive up the killing, twisting slope into the core of the Upper Town.

The night of December 30 brought on a whirling, driving storm that lasted well into the early hours of the next day. In the narrow street Près de Ville at the west end of the Lower Town a barricade had been erected, protected by the river on one side and by the looming sweep of the cliff on the other. Behind it was a blockhouse, manned by a mixed guard of some fifty Canadian and British militiamen, including a few British sailors from ice-bound vessels, to handle the little battery of three-pounders, one gun of which was kept ready-loaded with grapeshot.

In the early, snow-swirled hours of December 31, British Sergeant Hugh McQuarters detected movement along the track that led east from Wolfe's Cove. The movement became clearer, resolved itself into a body of men in formation pushing cautiously on. McQuarters, in charge of the loaded piece, held his fire. Some fifty yards from the blockhouse, the shadowy mass halted in the blinding snow. One man detached himself, came on slowly, followed by two or three others, apparently trying to make out the nature of the obstacle ahead. Then McQuarters dropped his linstock to the breech of the piece that suddenly flamed out in stunning explosion, sending a rain of grapeshot down the funnel-like approach to the blockhouse. The smoke cleared, and McQuarters saw that the little advance party had been wiped out. More, the half-seen mass behind them was falling back in panic, leaving the cluster of bodies lying dead in the snow. The British had no way of knowing at the time, but that one shot marked the beginning and end of Montgomery's attack. He had been the leading figure of that first and only reconnaissance, and his death shattered the morale of the men who followed him.

The attack on the east fared no better. Caught in a tangle of twisting streets under the sheer cliffs, fired on from houses and unseen barricades, with Arnold, like Montgomery, wounded and out of action in the opening moments, the Americans were shot down or captured; and the remnants fell back, taking Arnold with them. Daniel Morgan was a prisoner, as were Henry Dearborn, Christian Febiger, Christopher Greene, and many others.

The pathetically optimistic attempt to seize Canada, "if . . . it will not be disagreeable to the Canadians," died in the snow-blasts of December 31, 1775. Its aftermath was a long record of slow retreat west up the St. Lawrence, of blunders, of devastating epidemics, of fresh troops from Pennsylvania and from Washington's command about Boston being sent north to waste away in futility.

The wreck of the original force, infecting newcomers with the bitter virus of defeat, was back at the Richelieu, at St. John's, at Ile aux Noix, and finally at the ruinous works of Crown Point and Ticonderoga. But there was little time to take stock of the reasons for defeat, to recoup, or to rally strength.

Spring thaws had ended Carleton's problems. English ships crowded the St. Lawrence, their decks bright with the scarlet and white of the British army and, as a new and ominous touch, the dark blue coats of regiments hired by the Crown from the Duchy of Brunswick in central Germany.

It took time to group, organize, and fit out such a force, but eventually Carleton began to move slowly west along the St. Lawrence and up the Richelieu, where he embarked his command—all British except for some

Monument to Montgomery commissioned by the Second Continental Congress in 1776

Hesse-Hanau gunners under tough old Georg Pausch—in a fleet partly built on the spot and partly dragged overland. Then, in early October, he swept south up the lake toward Crown Point and Ticonderoga.

To counter his blow, there was nothing except the most makeshift of fleets, with even more hastily improvised crews. Commanded by and indeed largely the creation of Benedict Arnold, this scratch collection lay in wait behind Valcour Island, up the west shore of Champlain. Arnold's only hope was to sally from his shelter and catch the British flotilla in the flank or rear. But adverse winds and clumsy crews negated his leadership and unquenchable combativeness. And besides, the British fleet was largely in the hands of the Royal Navy, guaranteeing expert management. In a two-day fight that began on October 11, 1776, the American flotilla was smashed down to the last bateau and canoe, Arnold and a few men managing somehow to get ashore and reach Ticonderoga, leaving the lake and its forts open to Carleton.

Then, strangely, Carleton drew back down the lake without the least gesture toward Ticonderoga and its shaky garrison, pleading the approach of winter as his excuse. North he went, and peace settled over Champlain and the lands toward which its waterway led.

The *Royal Savage,* the flagship of Arnold's fleet at Valcour Island

With the beginning of the year 1776, hot bubbles of unrest were rising and bursting along the perimeter of the Thirteen Colonies. In North Carolina it was February, and the clans were astir, marching out from dozens of settlements with pipes, kilts, bonnets, and claymores, as in bygone times they had marched to Glencoe and Prestonpans and Culloden.

Most of these Highlanders were men who had cast their lot with the Stuarts in 1745 and had fought against King George II. But now, by some peculiar logic or emotion of their own, they marched under the once-hated Royal standard, aiming to make contact with the King's troops, who were expected to land on the North Carolina coast. On their way they confidently planned to smash a Rebel force believed to be moving northwest toward them.

The march went on—McDonalds and MacRaes and Camerons and Mc-Kenzies and MacLeods—some 1,500 of them following one Donald McDonald, until they came near Moore's Creek that joined South River. The Rebels, about 1,000 strong under Colonels Richard Caswell and John Alexander Lillington, had already reached the creek and had gouged shallow trenches among the myrtles on the bank which was closest to the advancing Scots. Then someone realized that it is not sound military practice to site a position with a body of water at your back, and the whole mass retired to the other side where more works were thrown up.

On a soft February day, between dawn and sunrise, McDonald's advance hit the abandoned works on the creek bank, and by most faulty reasoning concluded that deserted trenches on one side meant deserted country on the other. Claymores out, muskets primed, and pipes skirling, the Highlanders rushed the bridge only to stumble into withering fire from Caswell's and Lillington's men. Smoothly improvising, the Rebels launched a counterattack; the climbing sun lit up knots of kilted men in flight and somberly touched ghastly heaps of kilted dead, exposing the complete failure of McDonald's coup and the hopeless shattering of his force.

Small as the action was, it had vital importance. The rising of the clans had failed utterly, and for months to come North Carolina's Tories were to be a negligible factor. More important, their failure took the spirit out of their fellows in Virginia and South Carolina, and as a result, the

"The insurgents retreated with the greatest precipitation . . . Many of them fell into the creek and were drowned. . . . This, we think, will effectually put a stop to Toryism in North Carolina."
—*Unknown Rebel, 1776*

Rebel cause in each of these areas was strengthened immeasurably.

Perhaps a good deal of history might have been changed had the Highlanders delayed their push to the coast, for as March came on, a small British flotilla under General Henry Clinton dropped anchor off the Carolina coast. Someone in government circles had reasoned that a show of force would attract powerful support from Carolinians loyal to the King, and Clinton's expedition had been sent off with that idea in mind. Fortunately for the Rebels, the fleet under Admiral Sir Peter Parker, carrying the bulk of the red-coated army, did not rendezvous with Clinton until mid-April, and by that time the Loyalists were scattered beyond hope of recall.

For several weeks the British fleet hung off the Carolina coast, largely because Clinton and Parker had no clear idea of what to do. Back in London, news of the Moore's Creek disaster prompted the Cabinet to issue orders calling off the whole expedition, but by the time these instructions reached Clinton it was too late. The fleet had headed south through the bright days and soft nights of May, masts sweeping invisible arcs against the wide dome of the sky. Out of sight to the west lay the coast, sheltered by an endless chain of islands. More than halfway down this coast was the flotilla's objective—the city of Charleston, which lay on the flattish tongue of land between the Cooper and Ashley rivers.

So far, South Carolina and Charleston had engaged in no overt hostility toward the Crown, had sent no troops north against the Royal forces there, and might conceivably have been swung to the side of the Crown or at least confined to an ineffectual, if benevolent, neutrality toward their fellows. The selection of colony and city as points of attack suggests muddled thinking on the part of Clinton and Parker, since such an act could only result in bringing the Carolinians solidly and irrevocably into the war against England.

By June 4, 1776, ten British warships and some thirty transports dropped anchor off Charleston Bar, while Clinton and the military and naval brass of the great flotilla went into deep and prolonged conferences that dragged on for a full week. In Charleston men climbed the soaring, white spire of St. Michael's Church on Meeting Street to stare out through the high, round windows at their harbor and the distant menace of the British fleet. Their feeling seems to have been one of grim confidence. Word of the flotilla had reached them long before the sails had been sighted off the bar, and reaction had been swift. Dwellings and warehouses that might have masked a field of fire along the water front had been ruthlessly torn down. Forts had been built and manned on two long, sandy islands—Sullivan's and James—that shut off the last approaches to the inner harbor and the city itself.

Charlestonians rarely counted pennies or pounds, whether they were betting on horse races, sending thousands of guineas' worth of supplies to far-off Boston, or demolishing a whole water front in time of crisis. And they had not stinted their regiments. The 1st, now holding James Island, and the 2nd, on Sullivan's, were smartly uniformed, well equipped, and well drilled, though a Northern equalitarian might have been shocked by a stipulation that they be "Officered by Gentlemen, with hired Soldiers in the ranks."

The very names on the rolls at James and Sullivan's were heartening, nearly all of them Charlestonians. In command of the 1st was Colonel Christopher Gadsden, who had shucked his Congressional garb for a uniform, with Charles Cotesworth Pinckney and William Cattell under him. The 2nd was led by Colonel William Moultrie, as familiar to the citizens as St. Michael's spire, and he was backed by Isaac Motte—another known, respected, and trusted

"The sight of these vessels alarmed us very much . . . Traverses were made in the principal streets, flèches thrown up at every place where troops could land, military works going on everywhere, the lead taken from the windows of the churches and dwelling houses to cast into musket balls . . ."
—Colonel William Moultrie

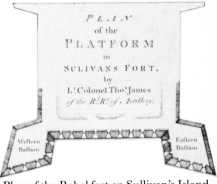

Plan of the Rebel fort on Sullivan's Island

quantity. It was not quite the same with the Major of the 2nd. Not a Charlestonian, he came from a little plantation up the Santee, not far from Eutaw Springs. Small, almost frail, swarthy and wizened, he rarely spoke, and then in monosyllables. Yet Charlestonians were more and more drawn to the little Huguenot, Francis Marion.

And South Carolina was not standing alone. General Robert Howe brought a fine contingent of North Carolina infantry. Down the long road from the north came the 8th Virginia, marching behind its Colonel, the Reverend Peter Muhlenberg, who had almost literally stepped from his Shenandoah pulpit to take his place at the head of the regiment. Ending a killing ride from Cambridge, ugly, splinter-thin General Charles Lee burst into the city, objected to whatever had been done and to whatever was planned, and in general acted as an arrogant, disrupting influence. Despite him, rather than because of him, work went on—largely due to the tact, wisdom, and devotion of John Rutledge, President of the Council.

General Clinton and Admiral Parker managed somehow to work out a plan of attack. Parker's ships were to close on the south tip of Sullivan's Island and smother the palmetto-walled fort with their fire, while a ponderous string of barges landed the 28th Gloucesters and the 15th East Yorkshires on Long Island, a virtual prolongation of Sullivan's, separated from it by a narrow gut.

On June 28 the attack was launched, and from the very start everything went wrong for the British. The infantry, supposed to sweep down from Long Island onto Sullivan's and the fort, found that the narrow gut was utterly unfordable—something which Clinton's reconnaissance had overlooked. Carolinians under Colonel William Thompson shot to bits the few attempts that were made. The ships fared even worse in their sweep past the south end. They ran aground, fouled one another's range, and blundered into the wrong channels. When they were able to fire, the spongy palmetto logs of Fort Sullivan absorbed the heavy shot easily.

Inside the blind, sweltering casemates of the fort, raw gunners faced the awesome swoop and plunge of the attacking ships as coolly as the men on the crest of Breed's Hill had met the weight of Howe's battalions. They served the guns steadily, refused to panic when powder ran low, and kept up unhurried fire until fresh supplies were rushed over from the mainland. Few shots were wasted. Out in the slow-moving procession of ships, hulls showed ragged gaps; masts splintered and crashed overboard. Decks were swept by cannon balls and small-arms fire; gun crews and their officers were struck down at their posts. "No slaughterhouse could present so bad a sight with blood and entrails lying about, as did our ship," an officer of H.M.S. *Bristol* wrote. As for Admiral Sir Peter Parker, facing the stinging fire alongside his lowest ratings, he suffered the supreme humiliation of a splinter-wound that, said an eyewitness, "ruined his Britches . . . quite torn off, his backside laid bare, his thigh and knee wounded."

As the sun dropped below Charleston, watchers from a hundred points noted that the swirls of cannon-smoke were drifting back, back from Sullivan's. Soon it was obvious that each tack of Parker's ships was taking them slowly out of range, until they lay, still under sail, out of reach of the battered fort's clanging guns. A few days passed, but the attack was not renewed. At last Parker's anchors went up, and his sails stood off to the northeast— bound for New York through the soft sea-shimmer that masked the horizon. The war had left the South, and years were to pass before the low Carolina coasts were to hear once more the thud of hostile guns.

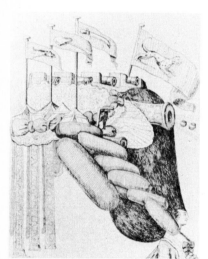

"Miss Carolina Sulivan," a satire on the British defeat at Sullivan's Island

"The behaviour of the garrison, both men and officers, with Colonel Moultrie at their head, I confess astonished me. It was brave to the last degree. I had no idea that so much coolness and intrepidity could be displayed by a collection of raw recruits."
—General Charles Lee

128

Arnold began his drive on Quebec with 1,100 men. About half of them, sick and nearly starved, conquered the boiling rapids and brutal portages, the flooded swamps and numbing cold. The 350-mile march took six weeks.

The March on Canada

In September, 1775, about 1,100 Americans left Boston on the first leg of what was to be one of the most terrible marches in military history. Many Americans had looked north toward Canada that summer, eyeing its bases for Indian raids, seeing the potential staging areas for any British attempt to invade or isolate New England. Acting under orders from Congress, a force commanded by Richard Montgomery was already heading north down Lake Champlain toward Montreal. So, partly because the map made it appear to be simple, partly because it would force the enemy to fight on two fronts, George Washington now directed Benedict Arnold north, via Maine, against Quebec. But the difficulties in moving a heavily laden force through the trackless wilderness of Maine in late autumn had been tragically underestimated. Only Arnold's leadership and raw courage sustained the "thin and meager" survivors who finally reached Quebec; while Montgomery was in frequent trouble before taking Montreal. Not until the last, bitterly cold days of 1775 did the two little armies meet outside Quebec.

Sir Guy Carleton, Governor of Quebec

This 1758 print of Quebec shows the government buildings and churches of the Upper Town and, clinging to the slopes below, the Lower Town. The latter was the focus of the American attack. In the foreground is Point Levis.

Failure Before Quebec

The fortress city of Quebec had cast its shadow over generations of American colonists, who knew it as the key to that land from which such devastation had been sent against their borders. The city occupied a bold promontory above the juncture of the St. Lawrence and St. Charles rivers, and was protected on the land side by a thirty-foot wall. In 1759 Montcalm had fought outside the city and had lost the battle; in 1775 Carleton decided to fight from within it. Opposing his 1,300 troops were about 1,000 Americans, virtually without artillery, whom Carleton regarded correctly as too weak to sustain siege operations. On the last day of 1775, in a raging blizzard, Arnold and Montgomery launched surprise attacks against two sides of the Lower Town. The initial penetrations were successful, and for a moment the desperate gamble held promise of victory; but when Montgomery was killed and Arnold wounded, Carleton's counterattack on the leaderless American forces turned the tide. Throughout the bitter winter Arnold clung to his lines around the city, but spring brought heavy reinforcements of British regulars and German mercenaries to Carleton and ended all American hopes for a great northern victory.

While its central action is romanticized, the contemporary print (right) does indicate the precipitous trail around Cape Diamond that Montgomery's men used. The head of the column surmounted one barricade, but a blast of fire from a blockhouse killed Montgomery and most of his officers. The subsequent retreat left unsupported Arnold's simultaneous attack on the other end of the Lower Town.

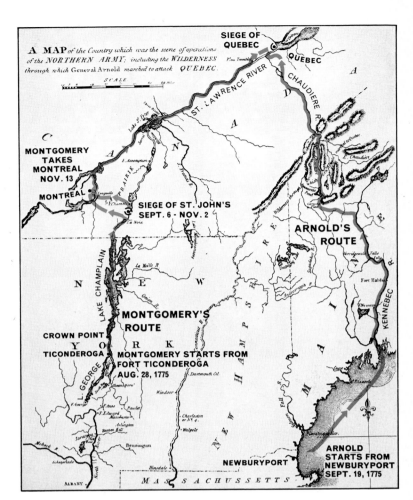

The American attack was cloaked by a "thick small snow" driven by "outrageous" winds (above); but rockets signaling the assault alerted the British garrison. The map at right shows the routes of the two American invasion forces that converged on Quebec late in 1775.

On the map:

A MAP of the Country which was the scene of operations of the NORTHERN ARMY; including the WILDERNESS through which General Arnold marched to attack QUEBEC.

SIEGE OF QUEBEC

QUEBEC

ST. LAWRENCE RIVER

CHAUDIERE R.

MONTGOMERY TAKES MONTREAL NOV. 13

MONTREAL

SIEGE OF ST. JOHN'S SEPT. 6 - NOV. 2

ARNOLD'S ROUTE

LAKE CHAMPLAIN

MONTGOMERY'S ROUTE

CROWN POINT

TICONDEROGA

MONTGOMERY STARTS FROM FORT TICONDEROGA AUG. 28, 1775

KENNEBEC R.

NEW HAMPSHIRE

MAINE

NEWBURYPORT

MASSACHUSSETTS

ALBANY

ARNOLD STARTS FROM NEWBURYPORT SEPT. 19, 1775

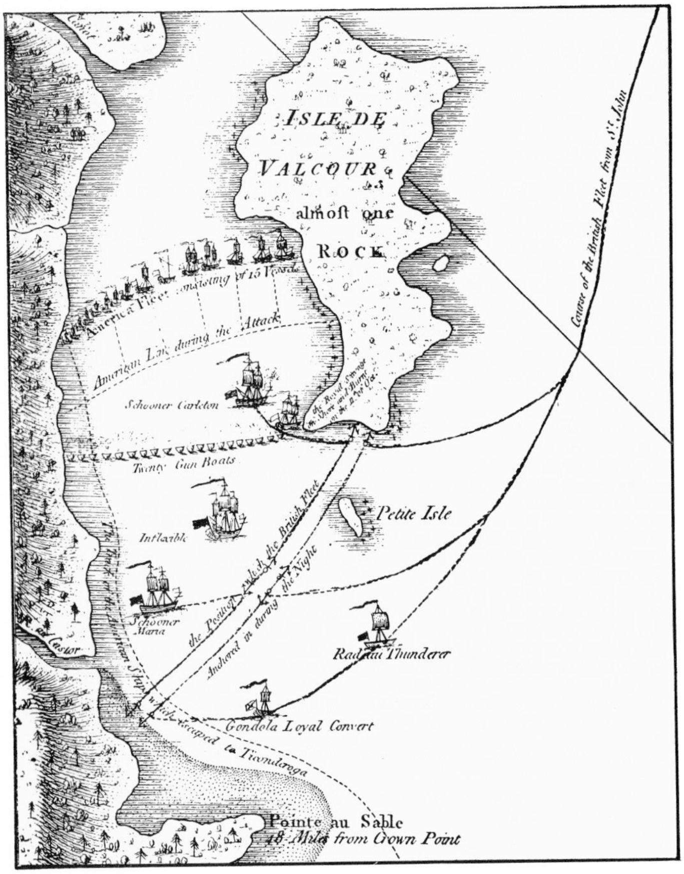
ISLE DE
VALCOUR
almost one
ROCK
Schooner Carleton
Twenty Gun Boats
Petite Isle
Inflexible
Schooner Maria
Radeau Thunderer
Gondola Loyal Convert
Pointe au Sable
48 Miles from Crown Point

This map details the positions and tactics of the two fleets during the engagement also pictured in the contemporary painting below.

Valcour Island

For nearly a century the attention of military men had focused on the natural invasion route provided by the combination of Lake Champlain, Lake George, and the Hudson River. Richard Montgomery had followed it north to Canada in 1775; now, in 1776, Sir Guy Carleton would head south, attempting to cut off New England from the other colonies. Between him and a possible juncture with Howe in New York stood only Benedict Arnold and remnants of the badly beaten Canadian invasion force. Somehow Arnold had cobbled together a tiny squadron of vessels, and on October 11, 1776, he met the British at Valcour Island in Lake Champlain. The battle ended with the destruction of Arnold's hopelessly outgunned "fleet," but Carleton inexplicably failed to continue south. Although Arnold and his gallant landlubbers had barely hindered his advance, the approach of winter made the British commander decide to go back to Canada again. The next English move out of the north would await 1777 and John Burgoyne.

Arnold anchored in the channel between Valcour Island and the mainland (below, left) forcing the British to beat upwind with difficulty to reach him.

f
g
h
i
k
l

The line of small craft across the channel mouth are British gunboats. (*The Royal Collection, Windsor Castle; Crown copyright reserved.*)

"*Commander Arnold*" *had few seasoned sailors to man his ships pictured in the water color above, and few competent gunners.*

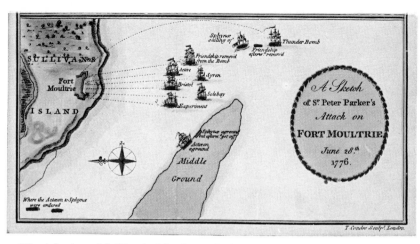

The defenders of Sullivan's Island were in luck when three British frigates, attempting to flank the fort, swung wide and were stranded on the Middle Ground.

A Strike at Charleston

At the same time that American survivors of the invasion of Canada were trickling back to Fort Ticonderoga, the British Admiralty dispatched an expedition against the southern colonies. Hoping to capitalize on Loyalist sympathy in the South, Admiral Sir Peter Parker had an impressive force of ten fighting ships, plus transports for Sir Henry Clinton's 2,500 troops. The first blow to British plans came when North Carolina Tories, heading for a rendezvous with the fleet, were mauled by Rebels at Moore's Creek. Then Parker and Clinton decided to attack Charleston, the South's leading port. Guarding the channel into that harbor was a log and earth fort on Sullivan's Island, commanded by Colonel William Moultrie. Clinton landed troops to take it from the rear, but they got nowhere. Then on June 28, 1776, the great ships closed in to unleash a "furious and incessant cannonade." The fort's palmetto logs and sandy earthworks, which simply absorbed shot and shell, made this almost totally ineffectual, while the slow but decisive fire from Moultrie's guns gave Parker's ships a fearful pounding. His flagship *Bristol* was hulled seventy times, and one of its officers wrote, "No slaughterhouse could present so bad a sight . . . as our ship." That night—after suffering a painful wound as a result of being struck by a sharp shell fragment—Admiral Sir Peter Parker withdrew. A great American defensive victory had gained two years of peace for the South.

John Blake White's painting shows the fort's interior at the height of battle. The 7,000 cannon balls fired at them caused only 36 American casualties.

134

General Sir Henry Clinton

Colonel William Moultrie

Admiral Sir Peter Parker

The drafting committee submits the Declaration of Independence to Congress

136

THE DAY
OF FREEDOM

"We hold these truths to be self-evident, that all men are

created equal, that they are endowed by their Creator

with certain unalienable Rights, that among these are

Life, Liberty, and the pursuit of Happiness."

THE DECLARATION OF INDEPENDENCE

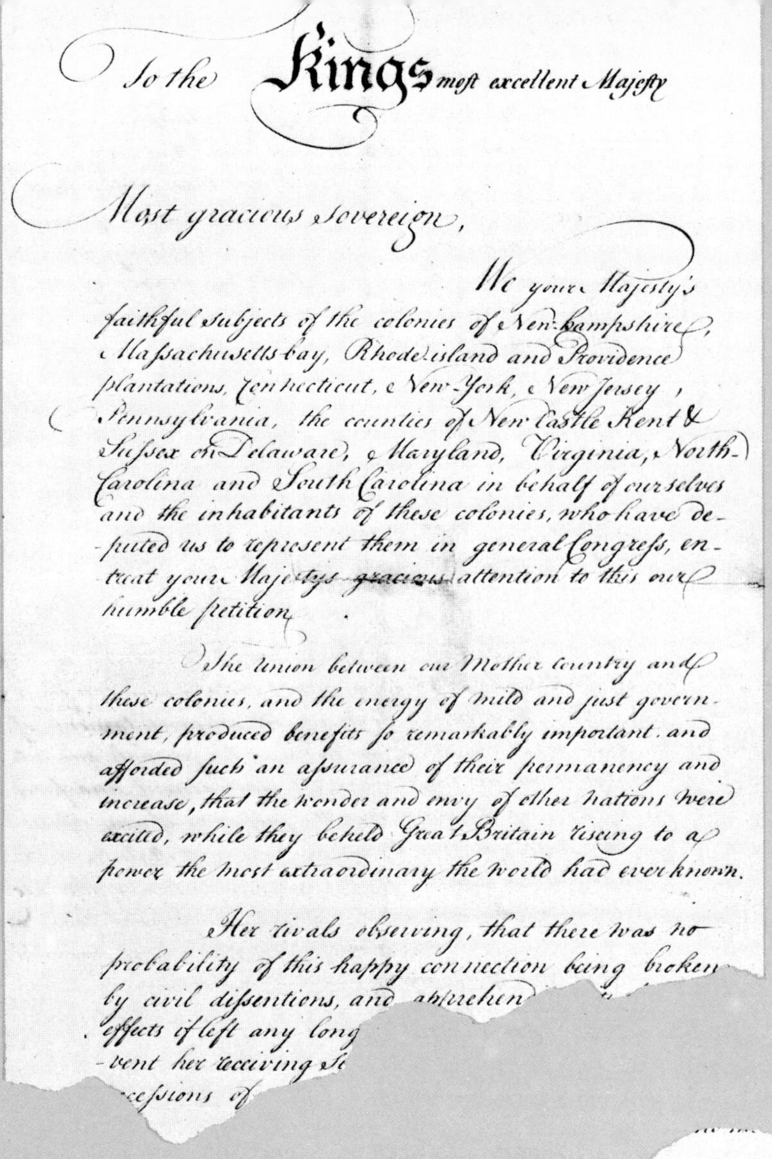

The Olive Branch Petition

To the Kings most excellent Majesty

Most gracious sovereign,

We your Majesty's faithful subjects of the colonies of New-hampshire, Massachusetts bay, Rhode island and Providence plantations, Connecticut, New-York, New Jersey, Pennsylvania, the counties of New Castle Kent & Sussex on Delaware, Maryland, Virginia, North Carolina and South Carolina in behalf of ourselves and the inhabitants of these colonies, who have deputed us to represent them in general Congress, entreat your Majesty's gracious attention to this our humble petition.

The union between our Mother country and these colonies, and the energy of mild and just government, produced benefits so remarkably important, and afforded such an assurance of their permanency and increase, that the wonder and envy of other nations were excited, while they beheld Great Britain rising to a power the most extraordinary the world had ever known.

Her rivals observing, that there was no probability of this happy connection being broken by civil dissentions, and apprehen[ding] ... effects if left any long... ...vent her receiving ... ...essions of...

... opportunity would be restored ... ...cerity of their professions by eve... ...n becoming the most dutiful subjects ... ...tionate colonists.

That your Majesty may enjoy a long & prosperous reign, and that your descendants may govern your dominions with honor to themselves and happiness to their subjects is our sincere and fervent prayer.

John Hancock

Colony of New-hampshire
John Langdon

Massachusetts-bay
Thomas Cushing
Sam Adams
John Adams
Robt Treat Paine

Rhode island & Providence plantations
Step Hopkins
Sam: Ward

Connecticut
Elipht Dyer
Roger Sherman
Silas Deane

New York
Phil. Livingston
Jas Duane
John Alsop
John Jay

New Jersey
Wil Livingston
John De Hart
Richd Smith

Pennsylvania
B Franklin
Geo: Ross
James Wilson
Edw: Biddle
Wm Dickinson

Newcastle Kent & Sussex on delaware
Cesar Rodney
Tho M:Kean
Geo Read

Maryland
Mat. Tilghman

This historic document was the colonists' final effort to settle their differences with England amicably. The "Olive Branch," as John Adams named it, was signed in July, 1775 — after Lexington, Concord, and Breed's Hill. It was a calculated risk on the part of independence men in the Second Continental Congress, who gambled that Britain's refusal to accept it would swing the conciliatory minority into favoring separation from the mother country. For the sake of unanimity it was signed by all members of Congress, except a few like George Washington who were on active duty. A model of placative, obsequious language, the petition was carried to England by William Penn's grandson Richard. When George III refused to see him, the way was made clear for the Declaration of Independence, which twenty-five of the same men signed just one year later.

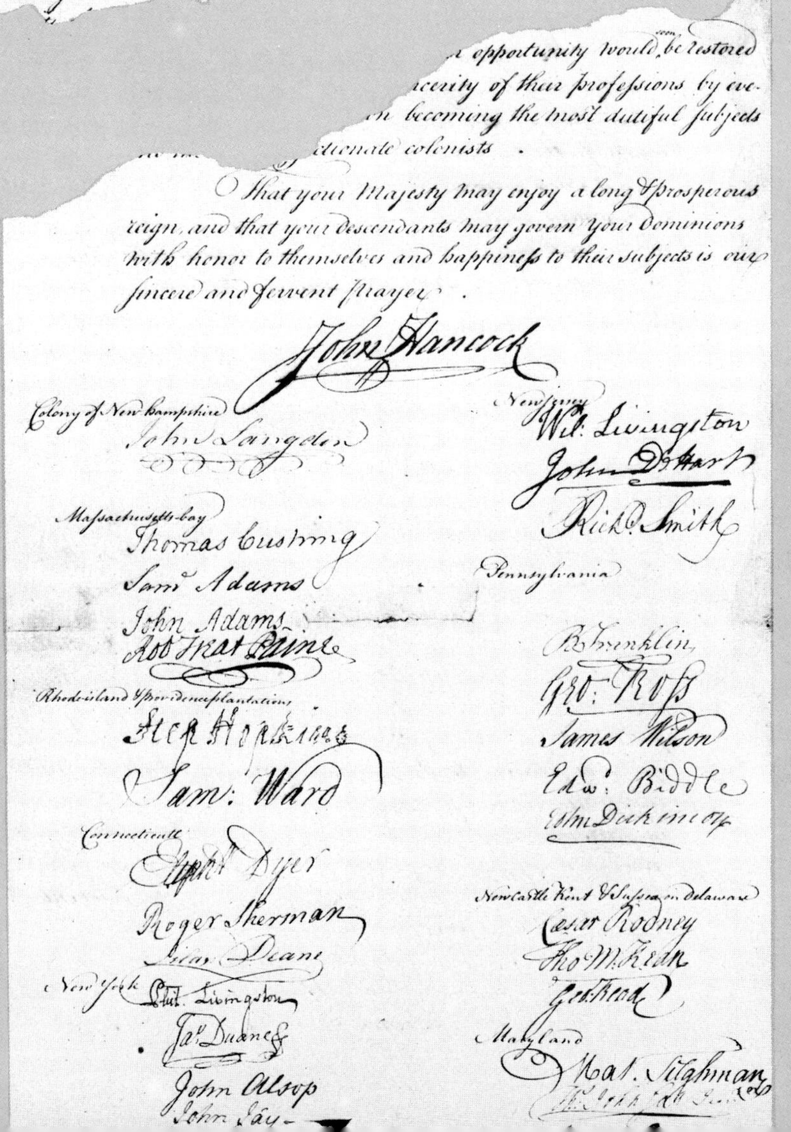

WHILE the blockade of Boston dragged along its uncertain course, while Richard Montgomery and Benedict Arnold battered on in their shoestring invasion of Canada, winter lay bland on Philadelphia where the Continental Congress was in session. In the State House chamber twin fireplaces threw out a muted crackle as obbligato to the endless debates over which John Hancock presided. Tense delegates clamored for the floor, rising with objections or passing hastily scrawled notes from row to row. During recesses they paced the wide central corridor, arguing, pleading, storming at one another. They slipped in and out of each other's lodgings, walked hurriedly, still debating, along Market Street, oblivious to the flow of city life about them. Broadcloth elbow and homespun, gold-laced beaver and austere felt hat rubbed and bobbed along side by side as these men felt their way, stage by stage, toward a rational form of living that had to be evolved for the Thirteen Colonies which some were beginning to call states.

James Wilson, by an unknown artist

The roads that their thoughts followed lay steeply uphill, with no markers or guideposts of precedent to direct them, and not even the most opinionated man could be quite sure of the right trail to the peak. Divisions in the Congress grew sharper and sharper. It was no longer a question of Whig against Tory, but rather what was the natural relationship between the colonies and the mother country.

John Dickinson, James Wilson, and Robert Morris of Pennsylvania, with James Duane of New York, were beginning to stand out as spokesmen for those who felt that while the position of the Crown was unquestionably wrong and should be resisted, the true aim lay in the resumption of amicable relations with England—as soon as the just American grievances had been settled.

Drifting further and further from such a trend were those who held that reconciliation was a glittering ideal, but one that was beyond the haziest fringes of the imagination. Here stood John Adams, backed by Christopher Gadsden and Virginia's George Wythe, Richard Henry Lee, and Francis Lightfoot Lee.

As the days went on, one word was whispered more and more, cropping up in debates to the sincere anguish of the conservatives—the word "Independence." One of its earliest appearances was in a resolution from the South Carolina Assembly, instructing its delegates to the Continental Congress. When John Rutledge, President of the Assembly, first saw that resolution, he was shaken to the point of uncontrollable tears, as was his fellow Carolinian, Henry Laurens. Yet the resolution was certainly mild enough, merely empowering the delegates to use their own judgment in voting should the question arise; North Carolina, much more uncompromising, instructed its delegates to "apply to Mr. John Adams of Massachusetts for his views on the form of Government they should assume—if Independence be declared."

Henry Laurens, by Charles Willson Peale

The conservatives exploded. Independent, the colonies could not possibly survive, and the very thought of separation from England was national suicide. Besides, the radicals were confusing the issue. Parliament and the ministries were the villains, not the King, from whose predecessors all charters had stemmed. From Boston, General George Washington had written that he could not bring himself to think of Howe's force as the "King's Troops." He called that body the "Ministerial Army." As for that damnable word "Independence," one agonized delegate shouted that he felt "like a child being thrust violently out of his father's house."

Through conservative threat and protest John Adams moved steadily on. In his own mind he knew exactly the course to be followed if the colonies were to emerge into a future of calm waters. Over and over he stated his case. "Nothing can save us but discipline in the army, governments in every Colony and a confederation of the whole." Many of his points were shaky, could be hammered down in debate by his opponents; but after each rebuttal he was always on his feet again, driving home his credo: "A Union and a confederation of Thirteen States, independent of Parliament, of Minister and of King!" And in all this he was playing no lone hand, but merely expressing the unleashed dynamism of America. He was the effect, not the cause, stating "the felt necessities of the times." Then, unexpectedly, his words and thoughts were caught up, underscored again and again, strengthened, and sent broadcast over the country.

An Englishman, sponsored by Benjamin Franklin, had come to the colonies and had somehow found the knack of putting in laymen's terms what Adams and his fellows had been saying in the Congress. A man or woman did not have to be law-trained or skilled in political economy to follow the message of Thomas Paine's little 47-page pamphlet, *Common Sense.*

Many of Paine's attacks on the British government, on the King himself, and on the very institution of royalty were so high-pitched that even the most radical Americans shied away from parts of his text like frightened horses. But there was much more than mere hot tirade in *Common Sense,* and stark phrases drummed and echoed in people's memories as they read them or listened to them being read. " 'Tis not the affair of a city, a county, a province or a kingdom, but of a continent . . . Now is the seed-time of continental union, faith and honor. . . . Time hath found us. Time hath found us! O! ye that love mankind, stand forth. . . . Ye that dare oppose not only the tyranny but the tyrant, stand forth! O! receive the fugitive, and prepare . . . an asylum for mankind."

The model country that Paine outlined was far removed, utterly alien to Americans. But his basic words and thoughts rolled out in a clamorous swing and sweep, creating a harmony of their own. And the final page of *Common Sense* carried a single line of stark black letters that spelled out with uncompromising daring: THE FREE AND INDEPENDENT STATES OF AMERICA.

The question of the future course of the colonies and the nature of their relationship to the mother country and the rest of the world loomed large enough to fill every last second of available time. But news from that mother country and the outside world beat, blizzard-like, into debate, demanding action or at least serious notice.

George III's October message to Parliament reached America during January of 1776, terrifying the fearful, swinging many conservatives away from their dream of reconciliation, and stiffening the already taut spines of the radicals. The Royal address ripped out at disturbances in the colonies as a "desperate conspiracy" fomented to establish "an independent Empire." Royal patience was completely worn out, and drastic steps were in order. The army and navy were to be enlarged, and since recruiting officers found a disgusting apathy on the part of the people, Royal agents had concluded treaties with various petty German rulers to hire portions of their ever-standing armies to serve in America under the British flag. As to the prosecution of repressive measures across the Atlantic, detailed plans were in the hands of Lord George Germain, Secretary of State for the American Colonies (a rather puzzling choice, since that same gentleman, then known as Lord George Sackville, had been cashiered for cowardice at Minden in 1759 and read out of the service as "unfit to serve His Majesty in any Military Capacity whatever").

As a partial offset to the thought of the empire's massed might, poised for a blow at the colonies, reports from the European mainland began trickling in, opening up golden vistas to the harassed delegates. Charles Gravier, Comte de

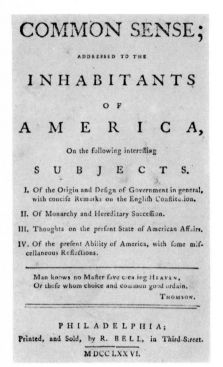

Title page of Paine's pamphlet

Vergennes, Foreign Minister for Louis XVI of France, had put his astute and experienced mind to a study of British difficulties. Was this a chance to avenge the French defeats that had culminated in the Treaty of Paris in 1763? Vergennes sent the many-talented if somewhat equivocal Caron de Beaumarchais, author of the immortal *Le Barbier de Séville,* to England to sniff out the atmosphere there. Encouraged by Beaumarchais' reports, Vergennes then tactfully opened up negotiations with Grimaldi, Foreign Minister for Charles III of Spain, a country which had also suffered heavily under that Treaty of 1763. Perhaps the time was ripe for the resumption of activities, overt or covert, against England.

It is highly doubtful if any member of the Congress looked upon developments that might come from these rumored negotiations as being in the nature of a helping hand stretched out to further American ideals. They knew that both powers had heavy colonial holdings themselves and hence could scarcely view with complacency the sight of any revolt against royalty. Nor would those powers be anxious to aid in setting up an independent nation that was largely Protestant. The idea was to nibble away at England while the chance presented itself and take care of any awkward by-products later.

By May of 1776, Vergennes and Grimaldi agreed to set up a dummy trading concern under the innocuous name of Hortalez et Cie and without (they claimed) the faintest of governmental connections, directed by private citizen Beaumarchais. What could the governments of France and Spain do if this drab, workaday company insisted on selling warlike supplies to men who just happened to have American leanings?

To cast ahead a little, so fully did this innocent bud blossom that a good eighty per cent of the powder used by American troops for the next two years is estimated to have come from the bountiful stores of Hortalez et Cie. As a technical note, most of this powder was the product of the great scientist Antoine Laurent Lavoisier, who was producing probably the finest explosive then known to man.

F ar more urgent than the threat of gathering British strength or the quick hope of material aid from continental powers was the never-ending flood of immediate local military decisions and plans for the future that swept into Philadelphia. Few of these could be side-stepped. From the very start, the whole united colonial organization had been dedicated to the subordination of the military man to the civilian. That first urgent appeal from the Massachusetts Committee of Safety in 1775 had specified that Congress adopt the New England army as the American army, that it appoint a commander in chief who, from the very nature of things, would be subordinate to Congress. The Massachusetts plea was quite in tune with the thinking of the larger Congress. Such an arrangement went far to avoid the possibility of a military dictator suddenly imposing his single will on the Thirteen Colonies. It also brought about, through the entire course of the war, a dispersion of effort. While George Washington was unquestionably commander in chief of the main American army—that strange body that grew out of the hurried rush of Minutemen on April 19, 1775—Congress, through boards and committees, had little compunction about interfering with his authority in matters administrative, strategic, and tactical. Washington himself, while often disputing Congressional measures in practice, seems always to have accepted his subordination to that body in principle. Important expeditions, important appointments to command, diversions of strength —all were ordered by Congress, quite apart from what the main army might be doing or planning. The system as it evolved was awkward, dangerous, and

"All sensible people in England are convinced that the English colonies are lost to the mother country, and this is my opinion too."
—*Beaumarchais, 1775*

An American soldier's hat, taken from a German print

141

very nearly fatal; yet it is hard to see how any other course could have been followed, given the entire framework within which that development occurred.

There was the question of Canada, an increasingly ominous one as the new weeks and months of 1776 brought reports back to Philadelphia. Montgomery's expedition, begun by General Philip Schuyler on orders of Congress, and Arnold's campaign, sent out by Washington to bolster the Congressional effort, had collapsed, and the wreck of the combined forces was drifting sullenly west along the St. Lawrence in complete defeat.

This might have been the time to cut losses, to withdraw what was left of those invasion troops far out of British reach, to recruit and regroup them for some stroke that offered better chances of success. But the will-o'-the-wisp of conquest still danced before Congressional eyes. In February, 1776, a highly select Committee was chosen to venture into Canada on an exploratory mission. Its objective—to swing the Canadians, particularly the leaders, over to the side of the colonies.

The most important member of the Committee was Benjamin Franklin. In addition to being uncannily wise and astute, he possessed certainly the most universally developed mind of the New World, if not of the entire western world. *"Philosophe, physicien, Rimeur, savant, musicien, Et voyageur aérien,"* to paraphrase Rostand. With him went Samuel Chase of Maryland, "deeply impressed with a sense of the Importance . . . of Canada, very active, eloquent, Spirited and capable." Another Marylander, not yet a member of Congress, Charles Carroll of Carrollton, was also one of the group. John Adams had met Carroll and wrote James Warren that he "was much pleased with his Conversation. He has a Fortune . . . computed to be worth Two Hundred Thousand Pounds Sterling . . . a liberal Education in France and is well acquainted with the french Nation." Far outweighing this was the fact that Carroll was a Catholic and would be accompanied by his cousin John Carroll, a Jesuit priest.

The Quebec Act of 1774, with its enlightened protection of the Roman Catholic Church in Canada, had been greeted in the colonies with hysterical invective, sharp and vicious and aimed in large part at that very protection. The invading American troops, most of them Protestants, had often displayed a bigotry hardly calculated to endear them to habitant or seigneur, further alienating a people who had been well aware of earlier attacks on their faith. It was hoped that Franklin, his natural wisdom ripened by residence abroad, and the Carrolls might be able to cancel out the harm already done.

The mission which the seventy-year-old Franklin led out in late March ended in predictable failure. Franklin, Chase, and the Carrolls found that the habitants, politely receptive in the early days of invasion, had grown more and more difficult and were understandably reluctant to furnish supplies in exchange for ragged paper currency, which could not conceivably be exchanged for honest gold or silver pieces. The Canadian clergy, naturally resentful of every slur against them, every insult to their faith, could hardly have been expected to rally their colleagues and parishioners to the support of a Protestant army. As for the seigneurs, the great landholders established in feudal state, the Quebec Act had confirmed beyond any question most of their sweeping rights and privileges, much as the Dutch patroons along the Hudson had been left alone when British colors replaced those of the Netherlands in New York. What possible talking point did a commissioner from the Continental Congress have to sway them from the new regime?

And even if habitant, bishop, and seigneur had been inclined toward the American cause, there was still the St. Lawrence and Quebec. No amount of

Benjamin Franklin, detail from an engraving of the Congress voting independence

"That the late act of Parliament for establishing the Roman Catholic religion and the French laws in that extensive country now called Canada, is dangerous to an extreme degree to the protestant religion and to the civil rights and liberties of all America."
—Suffolk County Resolves,
September 6, 1774

142

skilled argument could cancel out the fact that the Royal Navy controlled the great waterway or that the British flag still flew from Cape Diamond at Quebec.

Despite every setback, military and political, Congress clung to the Canadian dream, and orders were issued, sending regiments like Colonel Enoch Poor's 2nd New Hampshire or Colonel Elias Dayton's 3rd New Jersey out on the road that led to the fort at the south end of Champlain. Higher rank was sought to bolster that base from which any stroke north had to be launched. Horatio Gates, Washington's adjutant at Cambridge, and now a Major General, was sent up there to take command. At once he became embroiled with General Philip Schuyler, politely and with much exquisite military punctilio, over who was in charge of what. Red-haired, unlucky Colonel Arthur St. Clair, like Montgomery and Gates a former British officer, appeared at Ticonderoga. The whole northern theater was becoming what Spain and Portugal were to be for Napoleon, what Gallipoli became for the Allies in 1915 and 1916—an endlessly bleeding wound that drained strength away from the main effort.

A 1777 engraving of the Philadelphia State House

The news of the British evacuation of Boston brought another flood of problems, along with highly justifiable rejoicing, into the State House at Philadelphia, for the very freeing of the Massachusetts city posed the question of where the main American effort should be or could be exerted. Few in Congress seem to have realized that the answer lay not in their hands nor in those of Washington. Rather, it was shrouded in the dank Nova Scotian mists, as the British fleet and the British army which it had taken from Boston received more and more ships of the line, frigates and sloops, fresh scarlet regiments with varicolored facings. George III and his ministers were showing that they had been greatly in earnest in their talk of dealing with that "desperate conspiracy" overseas. General William Howe and his Admiral brother, Black Dick Howe, not only possessed ample military and naval resources, but also held the trump card of war —mobility. They and their successors would always have that card as long as they controlled the seas, and where was any American navy to challenge that hold seriously?

What the main American army under Washington was to do would depend on where, when, and how the two brothers played their trump. Would Boston again sight great flotillas of warships and transports? Would the British masts break the horizon off Sandy Hook? Or would the blow fall on rich Philadelphia, where the Congress, along with its other problems, still battled over the exact nature and extent of the rebellion?

This one overriding debate still rolled on, but its nature began to change as spring crept down over the Schuylkill and couriers from distant Provincial Congresses rode up, mud-spattered, with carefully worded resolutions to present to the Continental Congress.

These communications could hardly be tossed en masse into the Congress sitting as a whole, nor was it good parliamentary practice to dissect them one by one. To reduce to proper legal form, to set forth in coherent terms the separate resolutions of the Thirteen Colonies, a Committee was appointed, although some members felt that such consideration was beyond propriety. One by one the appointees went along the quiet Philadelphia sidewalks, through air soft with the first touch of early summer, to the new house of Graff, the bricklayer, at Seventh and Market streets. There, in his second-floor living room, their host and fellow committeeman, tall, redheaded, rawboned Thomas Jefferson of Virginia, greeted them.

There was the always urbane, always unruffled Benjamin Franklin, spectacles

Thomas Jefferson, by Peale

Roger Sherman, by Ralph Earl

pushed up onto his forehead. John Adams came, happy to be a guest of the man to whom he felt the closest intellectual kinship of anyone in America. Connecticut's Roger Sherman climbed the stairs to the second floor, quietly rejoicing that voices from all over the country had dispelled his last doubts. And Robert Livingston appeared, a New York patrician as yet uncommitted, but a little bewitched by the pleasing thought that if he followed the lead of the others, he would goad the equally patrician and ultra-Loyalist De Lancey family into a most gratifying outburst of shrill, hysterical fury.

These five men faced the vast task of shaping words and building them into sentences, of smoothing and fitting and dovetailing their raw material into a giant, soaring structure whose classic splendor would catch the marveling eyes of men in far corners of the world. It was at once obvious that too many hands would bring forth a product as tangled as a cat's cradle made by an idiot.

Perhaps the idea first occurred to Benjamin Franklin, still weary from his futile expedition into Canada, for the eyes behind those often tilted spectacles had a way of probing surely and deeply into men. Or it might have come spontaneously from two or more of the Committee in those very first talks. Whoever made the choice, the essentials of the work in hand were placed in the care of Thomas Jefferson. The Virginian objected at first. It is possible that his mind was on Monticello, where no less than 34 whites and 83 Negro slaves depended on him for a livelihood. He was also deeply concerned with the doings at Williamsburg, where a convention was assembling to draw up a workable constitution for his state. He protested further that his seniors, Messrs. Franklin, Sherman, and Adams, were far better suited to the work than a man of only 33.

John Adams waved aside the objections of his young Virginia friend. The issue was so delicate that Adams, as one of the New England radicals ("The Wise Men from the East," Robert Morris had dubbed them) felt he should keep well in the background. And besides, Thomas Jefferson wrote ten times better than any other man present.

The man from Monticello was left alone at his task, and as he paced the sitting room in the Graff house, or roamed down to the water front past the jutting sprits of moored ships or out into the country toward Germantown and its solid stone houses, the structure took slow form in his mind. His thoughts chipped away at awkward proportions here, sketched out an entablature there, rejected a classic order, softened the angles of a pediment. His colleagues often walked with him, climbed the stairs to his room on Seventh Street, surveyed the plans that were slowly evolving, suggesting an easement, hinting that a gentler approach might meet with greater favor when the capstone had been placed.

The word-structure grew. "When in the course of human events it becomes necessary . . ." Now a colleague might interpolate softly, "You have here 'to advance from that subordination in which they have hitherto remained.' How about that? There are implications—currents of thought in admitting that subordination. Couldn't we say 'to dissolve the political bands which have connected them with another'? Something along those lines." Benjamin Franklin, peering through his small-lensed spectacles, was struck by one phrase. "Here— on this line—'We hold these truths to be sacred and undeniable.' It appears to me to be still stronger if we say that we hold them to be 'self-evident.'" Thomas Jefferson could always listen to advice, and these corrections, along with others, stood. But the structure as a whole remained Jeffersonian.

The first day of July, 1776, found the tall windows of the chamber where the Congress met wide open to the warm breezes that flowed out of the west. A full

CONTINUED ON PAGE 149

Ink stand used at the signing of the Declaration of Independence

Jefferson preserved his original draft of the Declaration (next four pages), which includes marginal comments made by Adams and Franklin

A Declaration by the Representatives of the UNITED STATES
OF AMERICA, in General Congress assembled.

When in the course of human events it becomes necessary for ~~a~~ one people to
dissolve the political bands which have connected them with another, and to ~~assume~~ as
-sume among the powers of the earth the separate and equal ~~station~~ station to
which the laws of nature & of nature's god entitle them, a decent respect
to the opinions of mankind requires that they should declare the causes
which impel them to the ~~change~~ separation.

We hold these truths to be self-evident; that all men are
created equal & independent; that ~~from that equal creation they derive~~ they are endowed by their creator with ~~equal~~
~~rights, some of which are~~ inherent & inalienable, rights; that among these are
life & liberty, & the pursuit of happiness; that to secure these rights, governments are instituted among men, deriving their just powers from
the consent of the governed; that whenever any form of government
shall becomes destructive of these ends, it is the right of the people to alter
or to abolish it, & to institute new government, laying it's foundation on
such principles & organising it's powers in such form, as to them shall
seem most likely to effect their safety & happiness. prudence indeed
will dictate that governments long established should not be changed for
light & transient causes: and accordingly all experience hath shewn that
mankind are more disposed to suffer while evils are sufferable, than to
right themselves by abolishing the forms to which they are accustomed. but
when a long train of abuses & usurpations [begun at a distinguished period,
&] pursuing invariably the same object, evinces a design to ~~subject~~ reduce
them under absolute Despotism, it is their right, it is their duty, to throw off such
~~government~~ & to provide new guards for their future security. such has
been the patient sufferance of these colonies; & such is now the necessity
which constrains them to ~~expunge~~ their former systems of government.
the history of the present king of Great Britain is a history of unremitting injuries and
usurpations, [among which appears no solitary fact ~~to contra-~~ to contra-
dict the uniform tenor of the rest but all have] in direct object the
establishment of an absolute tyranny over these states. to prove this, let facts be
submitted to a candid world, [for the truth of which we pledge a faith
yet unsullied by falsehood.]

he has refused his assent to laws the most wholesome and necessary for the pub-
-lic good:

he has forbidden his governors to pass laws of immediate & pressing importance,
unless suspended in their operation till his assent should be obtained;
and when so suspended, he has utterly neglected ~~utterly~~ to attend to them.

he has refused to pass other laws for the accomodation of large districts of people
unless those people would relinquish the right of representation in the legislature, a right
inestimable to them, & formidable to ~~tyrants~~ its only:

~~dissolved Repre..-~~ ~~..tive houses repeatedly & ..ually~~
~~manly firmness~~ his invasions on the rights of the people:
~~..mixed..~~, he has refused for a long ~~space of time~~ time after such dissolutions to cause others to be elected, ✗ mr Adams
~~whereby the~~ legislative powers, incapable of annihilation, have ~~returned~~ to
the people at large for their exercise, the state remaining in the mean time
exposed to all the dangers of invasion from without, & convulsions within:

has endeavored to prevent the population of these states, for that purpose
obstructing the laws for naturalization of foreigners; refusing to pass others
to encourage their migrations hither, & raising the conditions of new ap-
-propriations of lands:

he ~~..st suffered~~ the administration of justice totally to cease in some of ~~these~~
~~states~~ refusing his assent to laws for establishing judiciary powers:

he has made [our] judges dependant on his will alone, for the tenure of their offices,
the + & payment
and amount of their salaries: + Dr Franklin

he has erected a multitude of new offices [by a self-assumed power,] & sent hi-
-ther swarms of officers to harrass our people & eat out their substance:
~~.. .. ..~~
he has kept among us in times of peace standing armies [& ships of war:] without the consent of our legislature

he has affected to render the military independant of & superior to the civil power:

~~he has combined with others to subject us to a jurisdiction foreign to our constitu~~-
-tions and unacknoleged by our laws; giving his assent to their pretended acts of ~~acts~~
of legislation, for quartering large bodies of armed troops among us;

  for protecting them by a mock-trial from punishment for any murders
  which
  ~~they~~ should commit on the inhabitants of these states;

  for cutting off our trade with all parts of the world;

  for imposing taxes on us without our consent;

  for depriving us in many cases of the benefits of trial by jury;

  for transporting us beyond seas to be tried for pretended offences:
  for abolishing the free system of English laws in a neighboring province, establishing therein an arbitrary government,
  and enlarging it's boundaries so as to render it at once an example & fit instrument for introducing the same absolute rule ..

abolishing our most valuable ~~important~~ laws

for taking away our charters & altering fundamentally the forms of our governments,

for suspending our own legislatures & declaring themselves invested with power to

legislate for us in all cases whatsoever

he has abdicated government here, [withdrawing his governors, & declaring us out

of his allegiance & protection:] by declaring us out of his protection & waging war against us

he has plundered our seas, ravaged our coasts, burnt our towns & destroyed the

lives of our people:

he is at this time transporting large armies of foreign mercenaries to compleat scarce paralleled in the most barbarous ages & other

the works of death, desolation & tyranny already begun with circumstances

of cruelty & perfidy unworthy the head of a civilized nation: totally

he has endeavored to bring on the inhabitants of our frontiers the merciless Indian

savages, whose known rule of warfare is an undistinguished destruction of

all ages, sexes, & conditions [of existence:]

[he has incited treasonable insurrections of our fellow-citizens, with the

allurements of forfeiture & confiscation of our property

he has waged cruel war against human nature itself, violating it's most sa-

-cred rights of life & liberty in the persons of a distant people who never of-

fended him, captivating & carrying them into slavery in another hemi-

-sphere, or to incur miserable death in their transportation thither. this

piratical warfare, the opprobrium of infidel powers, is the warfare of the

Christian king of Great Britain. determined to keep open a market

where MEN should be bought & sold he has prostituted his negative

for suppressing every legislative attempt to prohibit or to restrain this

determining to keep open a market where MEN should be bought & sold.

execrable commerce: and that this assemblage of horrors might want no fact

of distinguished die, he is now exciting those very people to rise in arms

among us, and to purchase that liberty of which he has deprived them,

by murdering the people upon whom he also obtruded them: thus paying

off former crimes committed against the liberties of one people, with crimes

which he urges them to commit against the lives of another.]

in every stage of these oppressions we have petitioned for redress in the most humble
only
terms; our repeated petitions have been answered by repeated injuries. a prince

whose character is thus marked by every act which may define a tyrant, is unfit
free
to be the ruler of a people who mean to be free. future ages will scarce believe

that the hardiness of one man, adventured within the short compass of twelve years
to lay
only a foundation so broad & undisguised for tyranny

over a people fostered & fixed in principles

of liberty: freedom]

Nor have we been wanting in attentions to our British brethren. we have
warned them from time to time of attempts by their legislature to extend a juris-
-diction over [these our states] we have reminded them of the circumstances of
our emigration & settlement here. [no one of which could warrant so strange a
pretension: that these were effected at the expence of our own blood & treasure,
unassisted by the wealth or the strength of Great Britain: that in constituting
indeed our several forms of government, we had adopted one common king, thereby
laying a foundation for perpetual league & amity with them: but that submission to their

credited: and we appealed to their native justice & magnanimity, [as well as to] the ties
of our common kindred to disavow these usurpations which [were likely to] interrupt
our connection & correspondence. they too have been deaf to the voice of justice &
of consanguinity, [& when occasions have been given them by the regular course of
their laws, of removing from their councils the disturbers of our harmony, they
have by their free election re-established them in power. at this very time too they
are permitting their chief magistrate to send over not only soldiers of our common
blood, but Scotch & foreign mercenaries to invade & destroy us. these facts
have given the last stab to agonizing affection, and manly spirit bids us to
renounce for ever these unfeeling brethren. we must endeavor to forget our former
love for them, and to hold them as we hold the rest of mankind, enemies in war,
in peace friends. we might have been a free & a great people together; but a communication of grandeur & of freedom it seems is below their dignity. be it so, since they
will have it: the road to happiness & to glory is open to us too, we will tread it
apart from them, and acquiesce in the necessity which denounces our
eternal separation!

We therefore the representatives of the United States of America in General Congress assembled, do, in the name & by authority of the good people of these states,
reject & renounce all allegiance & subjection to the kings of Great Britain
& all others who may hereafter claim by, through, or under them; & utterly
dissolve all political connection which may have heretofore subs-
-sisted between us & the people or parliament of Great Britain; and finally
we do assert and declare these colonies to be free and independant states,
and that as free & independant states they shall have full power to levy
war, conclude peace, contract alliances, establish commerce, & to do all other
acts and things which independant states may of right do. and for the
support of this declaration we mutually pledge to each other our lives, our
fortunes, & our sacred honour.

session was in progress, members poised in their seats, as the underlying reason for all the work of Thomas Jefferson and his associates was presented for debate. There was Farmer John Dickinson of Pennsylvania, looked upon not so long ago as a rather dangerous radical on account of his famous *Letters,* on his feet in fervent protest. "My conduct this day I expect will give the finishing blow to my . . . popularity," he shouted. "Yet I had rather forfeit popularity forever, than vote away the blood and happiness of my countrymen." So spoke Dickinson in anguished sincerity, as other members of Congresses then undreamed-of were to speak against trends of their times with which they could not agree, to which they would not conform.

On he went, dealing out hard, powerful strokes that shook the convictions of even the most radical there in the Pennsylvania State House. Independence! What else could it mean but an all-out commitment to a war for which the states were utterly unprepared—militarily, economically, and politically—and to which England had pledged the whole of its resources. Independence! What was sure to follow on its proclamation was, cried Dickinson, "like destroying our house in winter . . . before we have got another shelter." England had barely flexed its muscles as yet. Now Americans could expect the utter destruction of their cities. Indians would be turned loose along the frontiers, and those frontiers would inevitably shrink, draw closer to the sea, until scalping parties would whoop along New York's Wall Street or Philadelphia's Market Street. And suppose, just suppose, that England found the task of subduing the states a long and difficult one. The cost of that in lives and treasure could smash the British Empire, and then France and Spain could sweep back, asserting old claims to lands where English colonists had dwelt for generations—and who could stem such a sweep? Logic and reason backed John Dickinson's forecasts; what he predicted *should* have happened, and in some instances did. No man in his senses could have guessed the actual course of the years to come, but history is seldom sensible in the routes that it follows.

John Dickinson, by Peale

Dickinson had estimated correctly when he guessed that this position would cost him his popularity. Yet if this was an affair of the conscience, so was his belief in America. He enlisted in the Continental Army as a private, declaring his dedication to "the defence and happiness of those unkind Countrymen whom I cannot forbear to esteem as fellow Citizens amidst their Fury against me."

Heavy black clouds rode the air currents down the valley of the Schuylkill and the Delaware; thunder boomed and lightning flashed and flickered over Philadelphia as John Adams rose, by common consent, to answer the Pennsylvanian. Against the thunder-smashes that volleyed away outside as though at the sinister command of an unseen stage manager, against the surfbeat that rose in the hall from voices of the opposition, the little lawyer from Braintree hammered out his case.

The text of his speech is lost, and Adams himself thought disparagingly of an effort which to him must have been a weary repetition of dozens of other speeches he had made, or of private arguments with individual members. In retrospect he called it an "idle mispence of time," but his Virginia friend, Thomas Jefferson, recorded that Adams "came out with a power of thought and expression that moved us from our seats."

When the last delegate had spoken, John Hancock, wishing to sit with his New England colleagues, turned the president's chair over to Benjamin Harrison of Virginia. As was the custom then, acting-president Harrison read out the resolution that had been under debate, slowly, giving full weight to each phrase and word. "Resolved: That these United Colonies are, and of right ought to be,

John Adams, by Peale

149

free and independent States; that they are absolved from all allegiance to the British Crown, and that all political connection between them and the State of Great Britain is, and ought to be, totally dissolved."

Then the roll call began, the names ringing out through the crowded hall, "Massachusetts . . . New Hampshire . . . Rhode Island . . . Connecticut . . . New York . . . ," unconsciously forecasting a future when that same roll call would echo out, "Alabama . . . Arizona . . . California . . . Colorado . . . Connecticut . . . Delaware . . . ," intermingling the old names with those of lands unimagined in Philadelphia on July 1, 1776.

The vote was indecisive and the session adjourned, with some members feeling that calamity had been averted and others mourning a fading hope. The next day absentees from the July 1 session appeared. Staunch Caesar Rodney had ridden eighty miles through a rain-lashed night and took his place, still mud-spattered, beside his colleague, Thomas McKean, to set Delaware on the affirmative side. By the close of the session of July 2, 1776, the *ayes* had carried the question, despite rifts within individual delegations. As the weary John Adams wrote his wife, Abigail, who was looking after farm and family in Braintree, the day ought to be "commemorated, as the Day of Deliverance . . . even altho We should rue it, which I trust in God We shall not." The one great fact—Independence—had been established.

The increasing heat of July 4, 1776, with the thermometer climbing at a rate that surprised even seasoned Philadelphians, found a packed session in the State House, with Benjamin Harrison once more presiding. Clerks, already mopping their foreheads, were handing out copies of the final document that Jefferson, Franklin, Adams, and Livingston had put together. At once the heat was forgotten, as men muttered to their neighbors, ran fingers along salient passages, underscored them with pens, gestured in assent, or burst into angry opposition.

The vote of July 2 had established the fact of independence, and the work of Jefferson's Committee was to set forth just why that vote was justified, explaining to the whole world, to countries friendly or bitterly hostile, how the daring conclusion had been reached. And since the Virginian's Committee spoke in the name of the Thirteen States, thought and word had to be as acceptable in Georgia as in New Hampshire.

The immortal preamble went through with hardly a token challenge. Then the main body of the document was considered, and all at once tempers began to flare. Members hesitated as unexpected mental reservations occurred to them. They reddened in anger as they detected slurs on cherished beliefs or institutions. Nodding in approval over an assault on some grievance, they checked themselves as they felt the attack too sweeping, too dangerous.

Jefferson had made, and his colleagues had somehow allowed to stand, one bad tactical blunder. Himself a slaveowner by inheritance and force of circumstances, he lashed out at the institution of Negro slavery, calling it "this assemblage of horrors; this market where men are bought and sold!" Many members, Northerners and Southerners alike, were willing to keep pace with him in his denunciations. But he had included a hot and detailed charge against the Crown, apparently blaming George III and his predecessors for imposing slavery on the helpless and unwilling colonists.

There were dozens of objections to this part of the passage, not the least valid being that it formed an extremely weak plank in the whole structure; so the entire measure was lost, along with others that seemed to flow from Jefferson's red hair rather than from his cool mind. He demanded "eternal separation" from

Contemporary sketch of the signing of the Declaration

150

the British Crown and the British people, branding them as enemies from the beginning of time. A fellow Virginian, Benjamin Harrison, intervened skillfully and had the hot words tempered to express the thought that the United States would always look upon the British people, as upon the rest of the world, as "enemies in war, in peace friends."

Other articles were subjected to alteration or were struck out, but when the debate was over at last, the general sense of the great exposition of the cause was little changed. Thomas Jefferson could listen in gravely humble relief to the last paragraph of the resolution by which the Congress of the United States finally adopted the instrument that he and his colleagues had prepared: "And for the support of this Declaration, with a firm reliance on the protection of divine Providence, we mutually pledge to each other our Lives, our Fortunes, and our Sacred Honour."

Other measures followed, and the Declaration was ordered to be engrossed on proper parchment, since most of the copies in the hands of members and of clerks were by now crosshatched with thick lines, with deletions, interlineations, carets, and often with pungent marginal comments. The question of an official seal for the new United States was brought up, and the matter of design was left in the hands of Thomas Jefferson, Benjamin Franklin, and John Adams. The three considered many ideas that were less than appropriate, and even the final design they submitted was so bad that the majority rejected everything but the central motto *E pluribus unum*. Consequently, there was no official seal when the formal copy was ready for signing in August.

The Declaration is read to a group of citizens

Engrossed parchment and embossed seal were not needed to send this new Declaration out over all the Thirteen States. Philadelphia printers bent over their presses and rolled out copies which were snatched up before the ink was dry, bundled hastily, and shoved into saddlebags or crammed into the cabins of coastal vessels. On the eighth of July, Colonel John Nixon of the Philadelphia Associators (a militia unit that Benjamin Franklin had helped found in earlier troubled times, nearly thirty years before) read the Declaration from a hastily built platform in the green yard of the State House. The capital city apparently greeted Nixon's effort with knowing acceptance rather than with exultation. Every question remotely bearing on that proclamation had been argued again and again in every house and tavern. It was gratifying to hear, but not quite news. To some people it was rather less than gratifying at the time. Charles Biddle thought the whole performance infra dig., and wrote of it, "I was in the State House Yard when the Declaration of Independence was read. There were very few respectable people present." The Reverend Henry Muhlenberg, whose minister son, Colonel Peter, was even then at Charleston with his 8th Virginians, was torn between sympathy with the colonies and a native-born German's awe of established order—a struggle which his journal reflects: "This—The Declaration—has caused some thoughtful and farseeing *melancholici* to be down in the mouth; on the other hand, it has caused some sanguine *miopes* to exult and shout with joy. *In fine videbitur cuius toni.* The end will show who played the right tune." Yet he canceled out the rather acid tone of those thoughts when, writing to his friend Emmanuel Schultze, he burst out, "The young people are right in fighting for their God-given native Liberty."

In other parts of the country matters went differently. Washington's main army had moved down from Boston to Manhattan and Long Island, and as early as July 9, 1776, the Declaration was read to regiments of half a dozen states, drawn up in hollow-square formation at six o'clock that evening. In his formal order the commander in chief stated, "The General hopes this important

I do acknowledge the UNITED STATES of AME-RICA to be Free, Independent and Sovereign States, and declare that the people thereof owe no allegiance or obedience to George the Third, King of Great-Britain; and I renounce, refuse and abjure any allegiance or obedience to him; and I do   that I will, to the utmost of my power, support, maintain and defend the said United States against the said King George the Third, his heirs and successors, and his or their abettors, assistants and adherents, and will serve the said United States in the office of   which I now hold, with fidelity, according to the best of my skill and understanding.

Printed form of the oath of allegiance to be administered to American civil officers, 1776

151

Event will serve as a fresh incentive to every officer and soldier . . . knowing that now the peace and safety of his Country depends (under God) solely on the success of our arms." That night the gilded equestrian statue of George III, which had stood so far unmolested on the Bowling Green, was hauled down by the Sons of Liberty, and later melted into bullets for the young American army.

On the bright nineteenth of July, huge, bull-strong Thomas Crafts, friend of Paul Revere and Sam Adams, stepped out onto the east balcony of the State House in Boston and read the Declaration to a vast crowd that swarmed over the site of that misnamed Massacre of 1770. Abigail Adams was there, and later she wrote to husband John in Philadelphia how "The Bells rang the privateers fired the forts & batteries, the cannon were discharged . . . & every face appeared joyfull . . . After dinner the kings arms were taken down from the State House & every vestige of him from every place . . . & burnt . . . Thus ends royal Authority in this State. and all the people shall say Amen."

Not everyone looked down a high-lifted, disparaging nose as did Charles Biddle, or say a joyful "Amen" with Mrs. John Adams. Captain Alexander Graydon, 3rd Pennsylvania Battalion, reported with cautious appraisal, "The Declaration of Independency is variously relished here, some approving, some condemning—for my own part, I have not the least objection did I know my rulers and the form of government . . . popular governments I never could approve of . . . delaying [the Declaration] a while longer . . . would have kept the door open for a reconciliation, convinced the world of our reluctance to embrace it and increased our friends on t'other side of the water. . . . However, the matter is settled now and our salvation depends upon supporting the measure."

In the Congress members could share the feeling of the country at large, whether that feeling was despairing or joyful, that an immeasurably great step had been taken. Yet to them it could not stand as the be-all and end-all that it was to so many citizens. It was a single item, though a vast one, on the agenda, and there remained countless others to be solved. The Congressional mind had to be fixed on such matters of sheer existence as finance, possible foreign assistance, the relation of the main body to the thirteen Assemblies, and, most imminent and pressing, the intent of the Royal troops and Royal Navy, who were known to be stirring again after their Boston and Charleston failures.

There were individuals who realized that, Declaration or no Declaration, life must go on locally as well as nationally. In New Hampshire's Hillsboro County, farmer and Probate Judge Matthew Patten noted events in his faithfully kept journal. "August 1st. Col: Kelley according to orders from the Comtee of Safty published INDEPENDANCE in Amherst one of the Amherst Companies under Capt John Bradford and Lindborough company under Captain Clark attended under arms the Whole was conducted with decence and Decorum and the people departed in peace and good order The prinsaple Gentlemen of the County attended but not any who were suspected of being unfriendly to the country attended my Expences was 5/." Thus, with a magnificent disregard for spelling and punctuation, and with complete objectivity, Patten recorded the announcement and reception of INDEPENDANCE in Amherst, New Hampshire. He went on to add, without breaking sentence or paragraph, "I bot two scycles [sickles] from Means for which I paid 5/."

Whatever his inner thoughts and emotions might have been, he did not confide them to his diary, then or later. Like the Congress, he was aware of the continuing problems of existence, and his next entry, August 3, 1776, contains the single unadorned sentence, "We begin to reap our Rie"—surely using those same "scycles" that he had bought from Means.

The Liberty Bell in the Philadelphia State House

"These hardy knaves and stupid fools,
Some apish and pragmatic mules,
Some servile acquiescing tools,—
These, these compose the Congress!

"When Jove resolved to send a curse,
And all the woes of life rehearse,
Not plague, not famine,
    but much worse—
He cursed us with a Congress."
    —Tory Ballad, 1776

ARMS
AND
MEN

Recruiting and Training an Army

A British drill manual shows (from left to right) how to fix bayonets, charge, prime and load, fire, and "rest your firelock."

America's success in the Revolutionary War is all the more remarkable when it is considered that the contest was essentially one between a collection of inexperienced amateurs and an army of trained professionals. With a distrust of standing armies which has lasted into the twentieth century, the Americans had relied on militia for their defense, supplemented with volunteers for special emergencies. The colonial tradition was of short service for a single campaign—a habit which plagued George Washington until the end of the war.

Many Americans had been exposed to the rudiments of drill at militia "training days," others had seen combat against French or Indians; but Washington's first army was, as he observed, "a multitude of people . . . under very little discipline, order or government." The men, he said, "regarded an officer no more than a broomstick." Uniforms were almost nonexistent, ammunition scarce, weapons of every conceivable quality and type (since they belonged to the men who carried them), and the essentials of drill and camp routine almost unknown.

The British army also had its problems. Since commissions in infantry and cavalry regiments were purchased, the quality of officers was generally low. In this era of precise linear tactics, some authorities felt that it took as long as five years to make an accomplished soldier of a recruit, and that task fell on a fine but inadequate cadre of noncommissioned professionals. All too often the men they had to work with were the worst elements of British society, recruited from jails and slums.

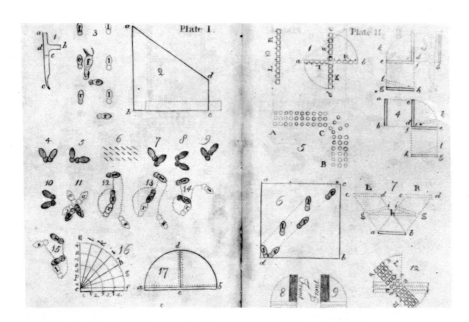

The Boston Tea Party awoke Timothy Pickering of the Salem militia to the need for a simple manual for colonial drillmasters, and he prepared An Easy Plan of Discipline for a Militia. *His drawings in Plate I at left include an all-purpose tool (top left) and, next to it, positions of feet for firing; a pattern for making cartridges (2); motions for right, left, and about face (7–11); and to the rear march (12–13). Plate II includes a diagram for wheeling by column of ranks (5); and offers an explanation of the oblique march (6).*

The 1775 engraving above depicts the plight of the poorly paid British soldier "Exposed to the Horrors of War" in America while tradesmen at home live in comfort. The recruiting sergeant below has a poor lot in tow.

The Infantryman's Weapons

Like most of the wars since history began, the Revolution belonged to the infantryman; and the chief weapon was the flintlock musket with its attached bayonet. The British redcoat was trained for, and excelled in, close-order line of battle, and the American had little choice but to accept this European style of fighting.

An experienced commander usually drew up his battle line just out of effective enemy artillery range, which put the two opposing forces about 500 yards from each other. The assault line formed, dressed ranks, and marched off toward the enemy as if on parade; and from this moment on, success or failure was in almost direct ratio to the discipline, training, and maneuverability of that line.

The large-bore musket shot a lead ball, sometimes molded by the soldier himself, contained in a paper cartridge made up in advance. Its maximum effective range was between 80 and 100 yards. "As to firing at a man at 200 yards with a common mus-

ket," a British expert observed, "you may just as well fire at the moon and have the same hopes of hitting your object." This put a premium on volley-firing—with loading and firing executed by command—which made up in fire power what it lacked in accuracy. Since the compact, solid mass of an attacking line made a perfect target for a similarly massed defending body at short range, speed was vital, and troops were taught to "load and fire fifteen times in three minutes and three-quarters." This meant a sustained fire of one shot every fifteen seconds, or about two effective volleys during an average charge.

Contrary to popular opinion, the American rifle was not a major weapon of the Revolution. Although it was extremely accurate at ranges up to 300 yards, it could not be equipped with a bayonet, and it took far too long to reload. All the weapons shown here, with the exception of the Ferguson rifle, are from the collection of Harold L. Peterson.

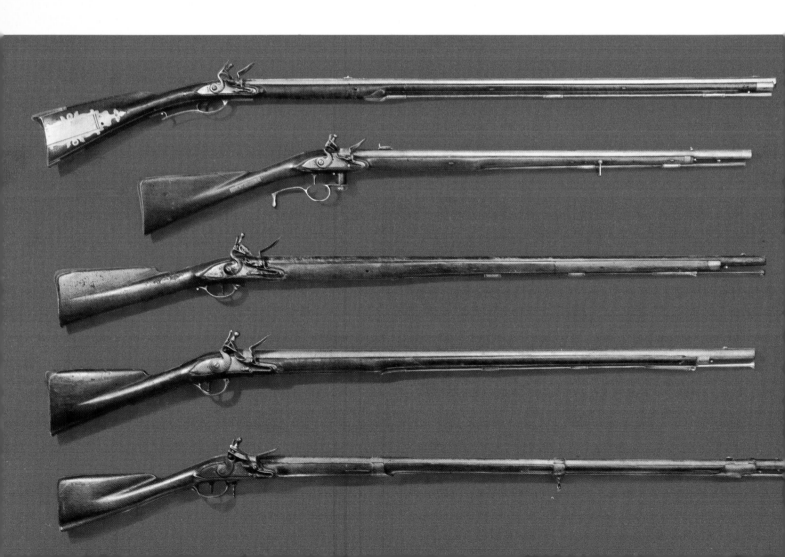

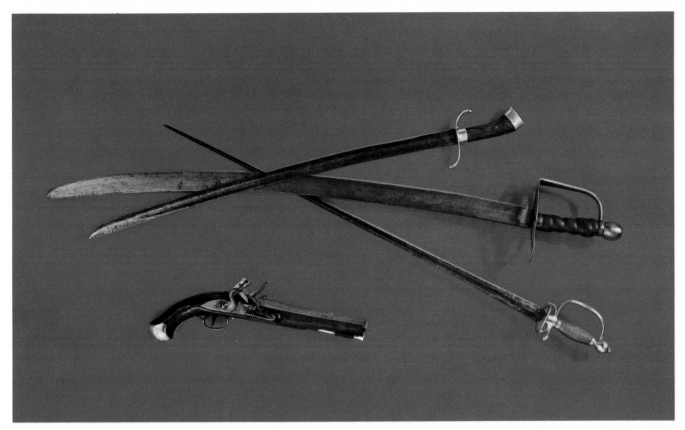

Although swords varied considerably, the three American weapons above illustrate the most popular types. The hunting sword (top) and the small sword (bottom) were worn by officers; the efficient heavy saber was favored by cavalrymen. The British pistol was also a cavalry weapon. By the time of the Revolution the halberd (below, left) was carried mainly as a symbol of rank by sergeants, but the spontoon was still used in combat. The tomahawk, standard for American riflemen without bayonets, was used by infantrymen as an extra weapon. At right are a French and a British bayonet.

Illustrated at left, from top to bottom: The American rifle—also called the "Kentucky" or "Pennsylvania" rifle—was developed as a frontier hunting weapon by German gunsmiths. Extremely accurate even at long ranges, it was an ideal gun for flankers, pickets, and other special troops. The Ferguson rifle was the only breechloading Revolutionary rifle. Invented by British Colonel Patrick Ferguson, this rapid-firing gun was a real innovation; but not over 200 were used in the war. This officer's model is from the Smithsonian Institution. Committee of Safety muskets were made by American gunsmiths under contract during the war. Most were patterned on the "Brown Bess" below. Calibers were about .75, and barrels 44" to 46" long. Most were replaced later with French muskets. The famous "Brown Bess" musket is thought to have been introduced into the British army by the Duke of Marlborough, and was a standard weapon for over 100 years. A .75-caliber smoothbore, the gun's name came from its brown oxidized barrel. The French Infantry musket was introduced into the war when the first shipments of arms were received from France. The gun shown here is the 1763 model.

This charming sketch, from a powder horn owned by Harold Peterson, is a unique contemporary drawing showing an American gun limbered up. The Continental uniforms have been depicted quite accurately.

Artillery in the Revolution

Americans had had less experience with artillery than with any other arm, since the cannon was far too cumbrous for use in the vast wilderness where Indian wars were fought. At the outset of the Revolution the few cannons in American hands were an odd accumulation of European-made guns, howitzers, and mortars. There were almost no trained gunners, and what knowledge Washington's Chief of Artillery, Henry Knox, had of the subject, came from British books like Muller's *Treatise of Artillery.*

In 1775 Pennsylvania and Massachusetts foundries began casting cannon, and French weapons were received later. Most fieldpieces ranged from 3- to 24-pounders, and horses or oxen, often with hired civilian drivers, provided their transport to the battlefield. Once there, the cannoneers used dragropes to maneuver their short-range guns into position, and employed them not to lay down a barrage, but to increase the infantry's firepower or to protect the flanks of the foot soldiers.

A drawing from C. W. Peale's diary shows how a cannon barrel was raised or lowered by means of an elevating screw.

158

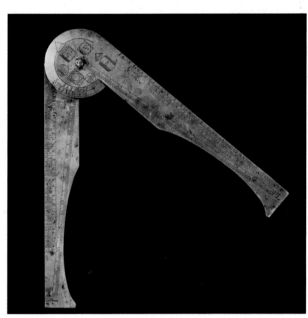

The frontispiece of Muller's Treatise of Artillery *(top, right)* shows several fieldpieces and mortars common during the Revolution, with gunners' tools and methods of firing. The brass gunner's calipers above were used to measure gun bore and size of cannon balls. Ammunition for the Continental Army's guns was transported in horse-drawn wagons like that at right, preserved intact except for the reconstructed wheels, which should be larger. American artillerymen suffered from a chronic shortage of powder, and Committees of Safety issued instructions for making saltpeter and gunpowder. The drawing below illustrates the eighteenth-century manufacture of saltpeter.

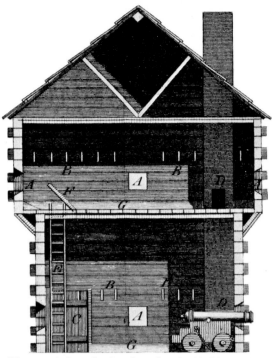

Thomas Anburey's plan for a frontier blockhouse shows cannon ports and musket loopholes on both floors.

Fixed Defenses

Until France's entry into the war, there were no engineering officers as such in the American army. This lack was recognized as early as 1775 by John Adams, who wrote Henry Knox, asking "what skilful engineers you have in the army; and whether any of them . . . have seen service."

Most existing forts dated from the French and Indian wars and varied from masonry structures like Fort Ticonderoga to hastily improvised field defenses. Almost all of them had been designed or erected by French and British engineers, and what little knowledge the Americans had of fortifications or the techniques of siege warfare came from the writings of European experts like Vauban.

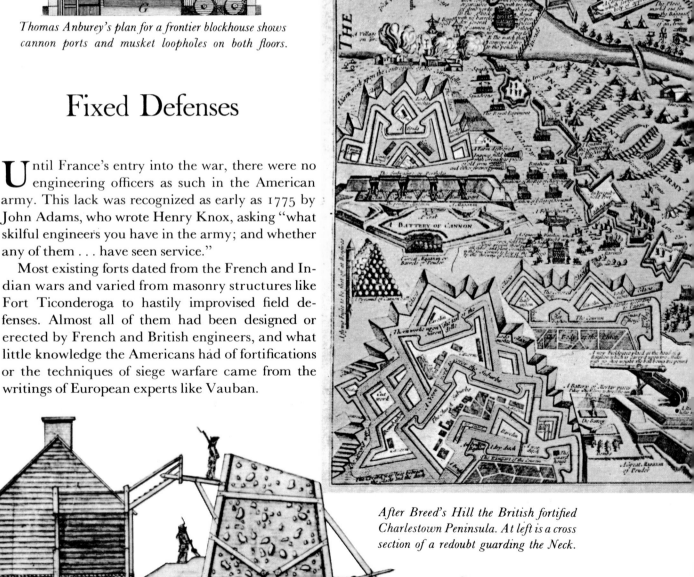

After Breed's Hill the British fortified Charlestown Peninsula. At left is a cross section of a redoubt guarding the Neck.

This rare English print, now in the possession of the Fort Ticonderoga Museum, illustrates a wide variety of military techniques and tools of the mid-eighteenth century. At the lower left is a town fortified according to Vauban's principles. At top left the procedures for defending against attack from the sea are shown, and at right are tools for construction work and gunnery.

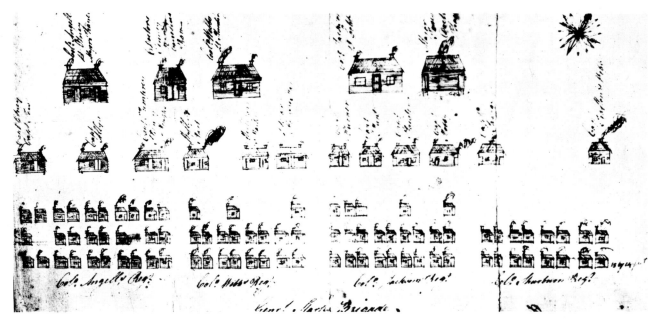

This contemporary sketch shows the camp of General Stark's brigade at Morristown, 1779–80. Although each small building held twelve soldiers, windows were not cut in them until spring. Larger huts were for officers.

The American counterpart of the Jersey was Newgate prison in Connecticut, "commonly called Hell." Loyalists, often chained, worked the underground copper mine.

Something of the dreadful conditions aboard the British prison ship Jersey *is evident in John Trumbull's drawing of starving Americans. The* Jersey's *rotting hulk was anchored off what is now Brooklyn, and here captured Americans were interned. The awful conditions aboard the ship gave rise to many atrocity stories, some of them undoubtedly true.*

Camps and Prisons

The painting below is based on excavations of a large British camp which was located near present 204th St. in New York.

For the pitifully equipped Continental Army, camp life, especially in winter, often caused more suffering than a battle. The deplorable sanitary conditions, with lack of proper clothing, food, and shelter, several times reduced Washington to a state "of scarce having any Army at all." At Valley Forge and at Morristown, where in 1780 his men endured the worst winter of the war, soldiers arrived in camp and pitched what tents they had on frozen ground. Then, often "without shoes and stockings, and working half leg deep in snow," they set about felling trees for a crude "Log-house city."

Far from weatherproof, these shelters were poor apologies for housing. Cold winds blew through crevices, ill-designed fireplaces filled the huts with choking smoke, and most of the men slept with only a thin layer of straw between them and the damp earth. The lack of food and prevalence of disease made these winter quarters a nightmare, yet the men, as Washington wrote, bore their distress "with as much fortitude as human nature is capable of."

If camp life was horrible, conditions in the military prisons of the time were indescribable, and a quick death on the battlefield was often preferable to the interminable agony and brutality common in the prisons of both sides.

AMERICAN INFANTRYMEN'S UNIFORMS AND EQUIPMENT
In 1780 a soldier in the Continental Corps of Light Infantry wore the blue coat with white facings at right, and the buff waistcoat and overalls beside it. His leather cap had a bearskin crest and black and red feather plume, while his shoes were the ordinary buckle-type (top right) worn by civilians. His weapon was the French musket with bayonet, for which he fashioned cartridges out of paper, black powder, and ball (on vest). These were carried in a leather cartridge box (right center). His blanket was secured within the red knapsack, on top of which may be seen a pair of ice-creepers used on winter marches, and a three-pronged holder for rush light or candle. Just to the left of the knapsack are a flint and a tinder box. The fringed, home-spun linen hunting shirt and tricorn hat at left were worn by a

rifleman. For his weapon (shown on page 156), the rifleman carried powder horn, lead balls, and a shot pouch (lower left), instead of cartridges. An axe or tomahawk was also part of his equipment. Both the uniformed Continental and the rifleman had a canteen (extreme left), and would have had with them such items as the folding knife and fork, fishhook and sinkers, Continental money, clay pipe, sundial-compass, dice, lead for writ- ing (on top of letter), small horn for salt, needle, scissors, and the hunting knife below them. The editors are indebted to the West Point Museum for the replicas of the Continental soldier's uniform and many other items; to H. Charles McBarron for the knapsack; to Washington's Headquarters and Museum at New- burgh, N.Y., for the hunting shirt; and to the Fort Ticonderoga Museum for most of the small items which are illustrated here.

The American Infantryman

A private in the Continental Army was paid less than $7.00 a month, out of which clothing was deducted. Congress specified that uniforms were "as much as possible" to be brown, with different color facings to distinguish regiments; but early in the war uniforms were the exception, not the rule.

A few state regiments like the Delawares and Marylanders were well uniformed and equipped, but the average soldier turned out in civilian clothes. Riflemen wore the conventional hunting shirt of brown or gray cloth; and the New Englanders who besieged Boston in 1775 wore "small-clothes, coming down and fastening just below the knee, and long stockings with cowhide shoes ornamented by large buckles." Varicolored coats and waistcoats, homespun shirts, and broad-brimmed hats completed their dress, and their arms "were as various as their costume." When a shipment of uniforms arrived from France in 1778, brown and blue coats with red facings were distributed to the state troops, and this was the first time that anything like uniform dress for a sizeable portion of the army was possible.

1. Americanischer Scharffschütz oder Jäger (Rifleman
2. regulaire Infanterie von Pensylvanien.

About 1775 a German engraver made the "accurate representation" of the "very durable and healthy" American rifleman above, basing it on a drawing by a Bavarian officer who had served with the British. At right are an American "sharpshooter" and a Pennsylvania regular infantryman (in brown), depicted in 1784.

Indispensable items in every American regiment were drums, which were the equivalent of the modern bugle. The routine of camp life and battle maneuvers were signaled by various calls on the drum. This colorful specimen is at Guilford Courthouse National Military Park.

Wahrhafte Abbildung der Soldaten des Congreßes in Nordamericka, nach der Zeichnung eines Deutschen Officiers. Die Mütze ist von Leder, mit der Aufschrift Congreß, die ganze Kleidung von Zwillich, überall mit weißen Franzen besetzt, die Beinkleider gehen bis auf die Knochel herunter. Die Meisten laufen barfuß. Ihre Feuer gewehr sind mit sehr langen Payonets versehen, welche Sie auch stat eines seiten gewehrs gebrauchen. C. P. Henning. exc. Nürnberg.

Only a handful of contemporary illustrations exist which purport to show American uniforms as such, and most of them appear on these pages. The riflemen in the German engraving above are dressed in fringed, coarse cotton cloth, and their leather hats carry the inscription "Congress." According to the caption, most of these men were barefoot. At left is a British representation of an American general. His plumed cap was made from a hat from which all but six inches of the brim was removed, and this latter turned up to make a "Liberty" cap-plate. The U.S. pennant below appeared in a 1784 German book.

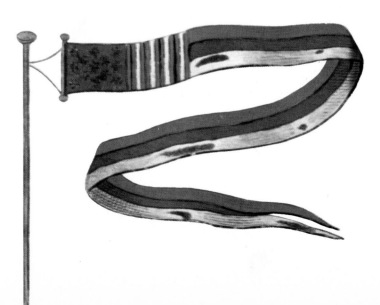

A Few Crack Regiments

Held the Army Together

At the core of the Continental Army was a handful of regiments without whose toughness, loyalty, and valor the story of the Revolution might have been far different. Washington was quick to see the folly of relying on militia and other short-term troops, and after the battle of Long Island he wrote to Congress declaring that "our liberties" might be lost "if their defence is left to any but a permanent standing army." He had seen the militia flee, disappearing "almost by whole regiments," while Haslet's Delawares and Smallwood's Marylanders had stood firm, holding off some of the finest troops Europe had to offer.

The Maryland regiment (left) shown departing from Annapolis on July 10, 1776, to join Washington, was composed of "men of honor, family and fortune," according to their Major, Mordecai Gist. Their dress uniforms were actually scarlet and buff, not blue-green as in this illustration; but at the Battle of Long Island they were clothed sensibly in hunting shirts or smocks of a brownish color. They were commanded by William Smallwood, whose portrait by Charles Willson Peale appears above. The regimental flag below belonged to the Philadelphia Light Horse Troop, another famous outfit which served throughout the Revolution, and it was carried at the battles of Trenton, Princeton, Brandywine, and Germantown.

In battle after battle, until war's end, a few Continental regiments formed the center of American strength and resistance. For example, the Delaware regiment that received its baptism of fire at Long Island was still fighting at Camden in 1780, and after that its decimated ranks were combined with Maryland companies to form a regiment. Later still, its surviving veterans were reorganized into an elite light company. And some of the Marylanders who had marched north with William Smallwood in 1776 to join Washington in New York were with the American army that left Williamsburg, Virginia, in 1781, headed for the siege of Yorktown.

Regimental flag, 5th Foot

Regimental flag, 33rd Foot

Regimental flag, 9th Foot

This British officer's uniform coat is faced with dark blue of the House of Hanover, indicating that he belongs to a Royal regiment. The coat's knee-length skirts are turned back for greater ease in marching. In the contemporary illustration of a British camp at right, the common soldiers' laundry dries on tents, while camp followers (far right) cook a meal. The commander's three-part tent is at center, guarded by sentries, and beyond, marked by small signs, are sutlers' or butchers' tents. Camp guards patrol in foreground, where the regiment's colors, drums, and stacked muskets are discernible.

The British Foot Soldier

In the eighteenth century, British regiments were raised by a favored officer or gentleman who was paid by the Crown for each soldier he enlisted. Commissions in his command were sold to such other officers or gentlemen who could afford them, and common soldiers were recruited by the formula: "By lies they lured them, by liquor they tempted them, and when they were dead drunk they forced a shilling [signifying enlistment] into their fists." Unreliable the system may have been, but it brought into the army tough, hardened, and often desperate men who made good soldiers.

An English regiment had ten companies—eight for line duty, one of light infantry, and a grenadier company. The elite grenadiers were picked for strength and courage, and given detached duty or posts of honor in battle; the fast light infantry was used for reconnaissance or skirmishing.

Uniforms, patterned after German models, were highly ornamental and often impractical. Scarlet coats had colored linings, facings, piping, lace, and brass or pewter buttons. Stiff collars and high leather stocks restricted movement of the head, and none of the awkward hats had a visor or brim to shield the eyes. To wash his white breeches, powder his hair, and clean brightwork and belts often took the British soldier three hours a day, but this was part of the discipline that made him so reliable in battle.

The German Mercenaries

At the outset of hostilities, Great Britain had a relatively small standing army, and when recruiting lagged the government fell back on the practice of hiring mercenaries to help fight the war. Possibly no move could have turned the colonists so irrevocably against the mother country, and the Declaration of Independence assailed George III for an action "unworthy the head of a civilized nation." When Russia failed to supply troops, England turned to the nearly 300 petty German princes. A treaty with the Duke of Brunswick produced 4,300 men, in return for £11,517 17s. 1½d., and twice that each year for two years thereafter. In addition, the Duke received "head money" of over £7 for each man furnished, with a similar payment for each one killed. "According to custom," three wounded counted as one dead man. All told, six German states—Brunswick, Hesse-Cassel, Hesse-Hanau, Waldeck, Anspach-Bayreuth, and Anhalt-Zerbst—sent nearly 30,000 men to America during the war, of whom 12,000 never returned home. Nearly 5,000 deserted to stay in the New World. The principality of Hesse-Cassel furnished not only the best of the mercenaries but the erroneous general title of "Hessians," since more than half of the troops came from there. In return for English blood money, their greedy ruler stripped his kingdom of one out of every four able-bodied males. As for the unfortunate soldiers themselves, they had been thoroughly disciplined to fight well for whatever cause in which they might be engaged.

These 1784 drawings, from Mrs. John Nicholas Brown's collection, show (top) men of the Prinz Carl Regiment and (right) a grenadier of the Landgrave's Third Guard.

Bucks County, December 14, 1776.

THE PROGRESS of the *British* and *Heffian* Troops through NEW JERSEY, has been attended with such fcenes of Defolation and Outrage, as would difgrace the moft barbarous Nations. Among innumerable other inftances the following are authenticated in fuch a manner, as leaves no doubt of their truth.

WILLIAM SMITH, of *Smith*'s Farm, near *Woodbridge*, hearing the cries of his daughter, rufhed into the room, and found a *Heffian* Officer attempting to ravifh her, in an agony of rage and refentment, he inftantly killed him; but the Officer's party foon came upon him, and he now lays mortally wounded at his ruined, plundered dwelling.

On Monday Morning they entered the houfe of SAMUEL STOUT, Efq; in *Hopewell*, where they deftroyed his deeds, papers, furniture and effects of every kind except what they plundered; they took every horfe away, left his houfe and farm in ruin, injuring him to the value of £2000. in lefs than three hours.

Old Mr. PHILIPS, his Neighbour, they pillaged in the fame manner, and then cruelly beat him.

On Wednefday laft three women came down to the Jerfey fhore in great diftrefs, a party of the American Army went and brought them off, when it appeared that they had been all very much abufed, and the youngeft of them a girl about fifteen, had been ravifhed that morning by a *British* Officer.

A number of young women in *Hopewell*, to the amount of 16, flying from this ravaging and cruel enemy, took refuge on the mountain near Ralph Harts, but information being given of their retreat, they were foon brought down into the *British* Camp, where they have been kept ever since.

The fine fettlements of *Maidenhead* and *Hopewell* are intirely broke up; no age, nor fex has been fpared; the houfes are ftripped of every article of furniture, and what is not portable, is entirely deftroyed; the ftock of Cattle and Sheep are drove off; every article of cloathing and houfe linnen feized and carried away; fcarce a foldier in the army but what has a horfe loaded with plunder; hundreds of families are reduced from comfort and affluence, to poverty and ruin, left at this inclement feafon to wander through the woods without houfe or cloathing.——— If thefe fcenes of defolation, ruin and diftrefs, do not roufe and animate every man of fpirit to revenge their much injured countrymen and countrywomen, all Virtue, Honour and Courage muft have left this Country, and we deferve all that we fhall meet with, as there can be no doubt the fame fcene will be acted in this Province upon our own Property, and our beloved Wives and Daughters.

Not all the atrocities attributed to Hessians were true, but the actions of Corn-wallis' army in New Jersey swayed many a neutral to the American cause.

Above, in blue and white, stand an officer, noncom, grenadier, private, and drummer of the Knyphausen Regiment. Only the jägers, former hunters and foresters who were used on detached duty, wore green. These fine troops (right) carried rifles, and their accurate fire was greatly feared by Americans. The miter-shaped brass hat belonged to a Hessian fusilier; the handsome regimental flag was captured by Washington at Trenton.

The Army of Louis XVI of France

Americans had seen splendid ranks of British red-coats, and the precise files of blue-coated Germans; but it is doubtful if either sight could equal the sheer pageantry of the French who arrived with Rochambeau in 1780. Most impressive of all were troopers of Lauzun's colorful Legion, dressed in light blue jackets trimmed with yellow. Their breeches were yellow, and they wore plumed caps and fur-trimmed capes.

There were four infantry regiments—the Soissonnais, in white coats with rose-colored facings and hats with white and rose-colored plumes; the Bourbonnais, in white and black; the Saintonge, in white and green; and the Royal Deux-Ponts, largest of the regiments, in blue coats with brilliant yellow facings and cuffs. What was far more important, nearly all of these troops were veterans of European combat. Superbly trained and equipped, they were truly the flower of Louis XVI's French army, and their commanding officer, the Comte de Rochambeau, was undoubtedly the best general France could have sent to America.

Musicians (top) were always the most colorfully uniformed troops in the eighteenth-century armies. Flanking the French drummers are (left) the flags of the Dillon and Metz regiments, and (right) the Soissonnais and Auxonne Artillery. The cartoon of Rochambeau drilling his troops is a 1781 British jibe at the French uniforms. The French print opposite shows, from left to right, uniforms of Soissonnais, Limousin, and Bretagne regiments.

N.º 1 SOISSONNOIS.
2.LIMOSIN 3.BRETAGNE.

Thomas Sully's painting shows Washington triumphant at Trenton

THE CRISIS

"These are the times that try men's souls: The summer soldier and the sunshine patriot will, in this crisis, shrink from the service of his country; but he that stands it Now, deserves the love and thanks of man and woman. Tyranny, like hell, is not easily conquered; yet we have this consolation with us, that the harder the conflict the more glorious the triumph."

THOMAS PAINE, *The Crisis*—DECEMBER, 1776

"MARCH 18, 1776. Boston is free at last," Dorothy Dudley exulted to her diary. "Today General Washington entered the town accompanied by Mrs. Washington . . . He has ordered five regiments and a portion of artillery . . . to march immediately to New York." The last of the British had left Boston on March 17. Now, no later than the morning of the eighteenth, five New England regiments, plus those Pennsylvania, Maryland, and Virginia riflemen who had not gone to Canada with Benedict Arnold, started for New York.

Little by little, as signs and portents pointed more and more to a British seaborne attack on New York, the bulk of the army of the blockade followed, and almost as soon as they arrived on Manhattan and Long Island, the men, characteristically, began to dig. A soldier from the Boston blockade would recognize many familiar faces and units. Here were John Durkee's 20th Connecticut, Loammi Baldwin (to be famous later as the developer of the Baldwin apple) and his 26th Massachusetts. Israel Putnam was flying about here, there, everywhere, and Henry Knox, now a full Colonel of Artillery, had brought his guns and wagons clattering down. Nathanael Greene scouted the terrain about Gravesend and the southwest shore of Long Island, picking out potential enemy landing beaches, surveying approaches that might bring an attacking force against the high ground that sheltered Brooklyn. The commander in chief himself quartered at Abraham Mortier's house in Lispenard's meadows, now the corner of Charlton and Varick streets.

There were also new troops at whom the New Englanders stared—men in brown coats with green or yellow or red facings, brown, black, or gray hunting shirts. They saw New Yorkers and Jerseymen and the files of the Pennsylvania Line. August brought company after solid company of the "Blue Hen's Chickens," John Haslet's Delaware Continentals who were to win fame second to none in the long years ahead. Men pointed at William Smallwood's Marylanders, drawn, it was whispered, from wealthy families of Annapolis by the Severn and from Baltimore. One of Glover's Marbleheaders could find plenty of food for reflection in what he saw. New England and New York, New Jersey and Pennsylvania, Maryland and Delaware—all signed on for the same cruise with a Virginia skipper at the helm!

Up and down Manhattan, picks and shovels bit into the dirt from gun positions at modern East 89th Street on down to the Battery. Men sweated and cursed as they hacked Fort Washington out of the solid spine of rock that still runs through the West 180's. Across on Long Island, Nathanael Greene and Rufus Putnam, cousin of General Israel, traced out works along the Heights that sloped down east to the flatlands and beaches beyond Brooklyn village. From the standpoint of sheer engineering this line was excellent. Militarily, it was a trap, since both men, and those who advised or aided them, made the customary beginner's mistake of trying to include far more territory than could possibly have been held by the force available, even though Washington's command now numbered close to 20,000, counting both Continentals and militia.

Down on New York's Battery, Henry Knox made a comparable slip in siting his unquestionably strong works and heavy guns. He wrote brother William Knox, "If [Howe] comes up like a man and brings his ships to before our batteries, there must the finest fight ensue that ever was seen." But the former bookseller was staking his whole plan of defense on the enemy doing precisely what he hoped would be done, rather than on the countless alternatives open to an attacking force.

Most ranks of the newborn army felt rather unhealthily confident. They were

Henry Knox's New York headquarters at No. 1 Broadway (building at left)

an army of 20,000 based on strong positions that were being constantly improved, and, above all, with powder in quantities beyond the wildest dreams of a few months or even weeks before.

Finally all the waiting and speculation came to an end. Daniel McCurtin, looking out at the sunrise of June 29 from a sea-front house, froze at his window. "I . . . spied as I peeped out . . . something resembling a wood of pine trees trimmed . . . the whole Bay was full of shipping as ever it could be. I . . . thought all London was afloat." An enemy fleet of more than one hundred sail anchored in the Lower Bay.

British troops occupied Staten Island, scouted the Jersey shore across the narrow Kill van Kull, but made no move toward Manhattan and Long Island. Toward the end of July more clumps and thickets of masts showed hard against the eastern horizon, and transports and warships closed in with the original fleet which had come down from Halifax. Black Dick Howe had brought heavy reinforcements from England to bolster his brother William's efforts, and with him a new element entered the war. Many of the transport decks were thick with blue instead of scarlet, and the sun picked out the glitter of miter-like brass helmets or shone dull on broad cocked hats. Troops hired by George III's agents from the German states had arrived.

The arrival of this new fleet had been expected by the American command and hence produced little shock. Then still another flotilla loomed up from the south through the sea-mists of early August as Admiral Sir Peter Parker brought the force under Clinton and Cornwallis from the Charleston debacle, eager to wipe out the disgrace of Sullivan's Island. Yet in the face of the greatest expeditionary force Britain had ever sent from its shores, there was a feeling of confidence among the Americans. After all, had they not smashed British attacks at Breed's Hill and Sullivan's Island?

Actually, Washington had placed the backbone of America's military strength in a trap that could have been deadly even for seasoned troops. His army was split between Manhattan and Long Island, with the North (Hudson) River, the East River, and Long Island Sound open to British warship and transport. Howe could strike when and where he pleased against either part of the divided American army, and his ships could prevent, in theory, any reinforcements being sent the threatened section. Military wisdom unquestionably should have prompted Washington to give up untenable New York and fall back into Westchester County, where Howe would have to seek him out and where the fleet could not follow. True, there was some Congressional pressure to hold Manhattan, but the decision was a military one, and Washington seems to have made few, if any, objections to the political arguments. He and his generals were facing formal war for the first time, and their theoretical knowledge did not cover the present situation.

The army was also badly staffed, Washington himself being forced to handle petty details that should have been taken care of by a field clerk. Greene complained that such triviality "confines my thoughts as well as engrosses my time. It is like a merchandize of small wares." When a fever took the Rhode Islander out of the picture for the time being, the already harassed Washington had to reshuffle the Long Island command.

It was finally decided that Israel Putnam would hold sway inside the main works on Brooklyn Heights while John Sullivan, now a full Major General, would command the troops posted out in the woods and farmlands on the American left. The right sector was given to William Alexander of New Jersey, a devoted, capable man known to most Americans as Lord Stirling through his

A view from New York Harbor, *c.* 1773, shows Trinity Church

Call for militia to meet Howe's threatened attack on New York

179

claim to that Scottish title. The new setup was more than shaky, with responsibility very hazily defined, especially between Putnam and Sullivan. Unfortunately time, which might have cured much of this, was lacking. These shifts in command took place in the third week of August just as the Howes began to move [*see* map, page 194].

Dawn of August 22 broke clear and hot with a breeze off the bay stirring the wheat about New Utrecht and Flatbush and Flatlands and rippling the water under Schoonmaker's Bridge. From the Heights and the observation post on the Ponkiesburg, American lookouts gasped in awe. Off Staten Island, frigates and bomb ketches spread their sails, stood in toward Long Island, and a great procession of barges sculled slowly along in their wakes—88 of them loaded with British and Hessian troops. Shrill music soared above them and the sun was bright on bayonets, on scarlet coats, blue coats, and high brass helmets. Wind ruffled the plumes of the 17th Light Dragoons, tossed the dark kilts of the Black Watch, and the cockades of green-coated jägers. On came the barges through the August morning, spilled their multi-hued cargoes ashore, headed back to Staten Island to reload. There was little, if any, opposition, and by the end of the day a good 15,000 men were landed under the critical eyes of Clinton, Cornwallis, and the Hessian Count von Donop.

Over on Manhattan, the American command watched the frightening smoothness of this amphibious move which might, of course, have been a feint to cover a still heavier stroke at New York itself. A merciful wind that held steady all day kept the British warships from tacking up the East River and allowed Washington to ferry over to the Brooklyn side as many men as he dared commit. Then the weather changed and until the twenty-fifth, Howe was unable to reinforce Clinton and von Donop, who stayed watching and probing in the flat country about the landing beaches. Washington, increasingly convinced that no feint was intended, managed to transfer more troops to Long Island. Actually, he had split his army neatly in two, with a waterway that could be controlled by the enemy lying between the halves.

Then the wind shifted and the ferrying from Staten Island began again; and old General Philipp von Heister proudly watched his big Hessian grenadiers actually standing at attention in their moving barges, with shouldered arms "and in column of march, preserving the well-considered pomp of German discipline." It must have been a terrifying sight for the Americans who manned the works or posts out on the open slopes. They must have realized that their only chance lay in a second Breed's Hill, with heavy lines of scarlet and blue moving against prepared positions.

But there was to be no Breed's Hill on Long Island. On the night of the twenty-sixth a column formed in the Flatlands area. Driving out into the dark were the 17th Light Dragoons, the 33rd West Ridings, the 71st Highlanders, the Guards, and twelve more regiments behind them, with no less than 28 fieldpieces clanking over the soft roads. Henry Clinton led, riding with memories of Breed's Hill and its slaughter. Cornwallis was there, bitter over wasted opportunities at Charleston, while Lord Percy thought perhaps of Lexington Green and a broken British column.

With this night move the fate of Long Island was really settled. The column, 10,000 strong, curved away from the heavy American center, wound through unguarded Jamaica Pass on the far north, and as the sun rose "with a Red and angry Glare," smashed into the left and rear of the defenses. There was predictable panic, for, as Chester Wilmot wrote of 1940, "Nothing in war is more unnerving than the unexpected," and John Sulli-

Officer of the German jäger corps

"I imagine that we shall very soon come to action, and I do not doubt but the consequence will be fatal to the rebels. An army composed as theirs is cannot bear the frown of adversity."
—Captain Francis Rawdon, August 5, 1776

180

van's entire left wing was crushed and broken, rolled south in shattering defeat.

There was a signal gun from the lowlands by the British center and left, and Hessian jägers and grenadiers, British line companies, and kilted Scots roared into action. Everything gave way. Riflemen, on whose deadly aimed fire so many hopes had been built, found that their clumsy weapons took far too long to reload. Lacking bayonets, they were engulfed by yelling, stabbing swarms of Germans and British. American gunners abandoned their pieces in the face of scarlet and blue lines that poured toward them, bayonets aslant.

Sometime during the morning of the twenty-sixth Washington came over to Brooklyn, but there was nothing that he or any other commander could have done. And there was consolation for him in only two points. Adverse winds still kept the British fleet out of the East River. And down at the American far right, where Lord Stirling commanded, Smallwood's Marylanders, their scarlet and buff hidden by brown smocks, and Haslet's Delawares in their blue and red were standing firm, taking the heavy assaults of fur-capped British grenadiers and the kilted 42nd Black Watch. An English officer in one of the attacking waves particularly remembered the Delawares, "their ranks full, their uniforms smart . . . their courage high."

But the rest of the army was crumbling about them. Stirling acted promptly to save what he could. He sent Haslet's men and most of Smallwood's in orderly retreat over terrain that was cut by marshes, little ponds, and Gowanus Creek. But he held back Major Mordecai Gist and some 200 immortal Marylanders and led them in incredible counterattack against the red and blue lines that were coming on around the gray stone walls of the Cortelyou house. Highlander, grenadier, and Hessian recoiled from this unexpected onset. Their lines wavered, seemed about to break. Then fresh troops raced up just as Stirling launched his sixth assault, and the Maryland survivors broke up into small groups, trying to fight their way back to their own lines. Of the 200, only Mordecai Gist and nine others succeeded. Lord Stirling himself was captured, surrendering his sword to old General von Heister in person.

By noon the whole action was broken off, the last of the American survivors tumbling dry-mouthed and shaken into the Brooklyn works, while General Howe sat down to compose a full, glittering report for Lord George Germain in London. Howe's actual accomplishment did not add up to much. He had cleared the approaches to the Brooklyn Heights works of a poorly placed American screening force. The main army was intact, if badly shaken, and now lay exactly where Howe, with his Breed's Hill memories, did not want it—behind good earthworks, protected on both flanks by water, and immune to any attacks by his fleet as long as the adverse winds held his brother's ships out of range. He decided to pull back to the flatlands to the east, and set sappers and engineers to constructing earthworks of their own, pushing closer and closer to the American lines. He would have to attack, sooner or later, and when that moment came, he wanted his troops to have a minimum of open ground to cover.

Within the American lines there was chaos and deep, bitter disillusionment as men wandered about trying to find their outfits. It was clear to the dullest that they had no chance in the field unless American firepower could smash bayonet charges before the attackers could close. There was nothing else with which to counter that weapon. There were few bayonets in the American lines, and fewer men who knew how to use them. Yet some semblance of order crept back into the works, for George Washington was there—outwardly calm, imperturbable, and confident, whatever doubts may have gnawed at him in his first big test as commander in chief. Units were sorted out, guards posted, and

German caricature of a Rebel soldier

"The rebels have some very good marksmen, but some of them have wretched guns, and most of them shoot crooked."
—*A Hessian Officer*

181

by late afternoon parties of riflemen crept out a good hundred rods from the works to fire on enemy posts.

Washington still clung to his belief that Brooklyn could be held, and in a gesture that invited disaster, shifted more units from Manhattan, apparently forgetting that a turn of the wind could bring the British fleet between him and his base. On August 28 the weather broke in a howling, rain-lashing nor'easter, but Howe's diggers kept on, drawing closer to the American lines. Appreciating the situation more clearly as hours went by, the Virginian concluded that after all he could not hold Brooklyn. With that conclusion the American army was placed in the greatest danger it had yet known. If the British received the slightest hint of evacuation, slaughter and mass capture must result.

Two factors tilted the scales somewhat in Washington's favor. The prevailing winds still kept the British fleet at bay. And among the regiments shifted by chance to Long Island were the blue-coated, white-trousered Marbleheaders led by John Glover. With great good fortune, Washington reached out for them and their unique skills, at the same time that he ordered a search for all available small craft. Near dusk, through blinding rain, Glover's men came silently out of the advanced lines and filed down to the drenched wharves and beaches, where they found other seafarers, Israel Hutchinson's 27th Massachusetts from Salem, ready to join them.

As darkness fell, line after line moved out of the Brooklyn works, were quickly herded into boats, and rowed in the deadest of hushes to the New York landings. Occasionally order broke down at the beaches, men panicked, brawled, and fought to get aboard, but quiet was always restored somehow and the oarsmen, working on few rations and less sleep, kept doggedly at their two-mile round trip. They dumped their loads at New York and sculled back time and again to the dark Long Island shore that might at any instant blaze out with the flashes of British muskets and artillery. This performance of Glover's and Hutchinson's men had none of the desperate intoxication of the charge of Lord Stirling, Gist, and the Marylanders, none of the bitter heroism of unnamed, uncounted men who turned to face bayonets with empty muskets. But it had a grim, dogged glory of its own.

There was deadly peril once more in the late hours as the wind died, but suddenly, miraculous as the gales that had tied down the British fleet, a dense fog blanketed shore and river. Thick and blinding, it held while the soldier oarsmen labored on through their sixth consecutive hour of rowing. They had snatched a whole army from defeat, death, and capture. More than that, they had ferried across all stores and equipment, leaving nothing behind except a few hopelessly rusted cannon.

In the stern of one of the last of John Glover's boats, Lieutenant Benjamin Tallmadge looked back toward the Brooklyn shore. His last glimpse showed him a very tall man, cloaked and booted, coming down slippery steps while a blue Marblehead arm stretched out to guide the commander in chief to the boat below. The whole withdrawal had been a magnificent feat. A British military critic wrote, "Those who are best acquainted with the difficulty, embarrassment, noise and tumult which attend even by day, and with no enemy at hand, a movement of this nature . . . will be the first to acknowledge that this retreat should hold a high place among military transactions."

There is little question that storm and sheltering fog, the devotion of the Salem and Marblehead men, the firm, cool grip of Washington that somehow exacted superb discipline from green troops, kept the British high command in utter ignorance of that evacuation hastily ordered on August 29, 1776. Major

Nathan Hale, carrying his coffin, is drummed to his execution as an American spy, September 22, 1776

"Rejoice, my friend, that we have given the Rebels a d--d crush . . . It was a glorious achievement, my friend, and will immortalize us and crush the rebel colonies."
—A British Officer, September 3, 1776

Baurmeister wrote his patron, Baron von Jungkenn back in Hesse-Cassel, "We had no knowledge of this [move] until four o'clock in the morning of the 30th." Then, guessing wildly, he estimated that "The entire American army has fled to New England, evacuating also New York. . . ."

The Hessian Major's estimate was militarily logical and, substituting Westchester County for New England, was probably the course that should have been followed. Nathanael Greene, now recovered from his crippling fever, urged it, with the rider that the city should be burned to deny its shelter to Howe. The commander in chief seems to have appreciated the menace implied by British naval control of all the waters about Manhattan, and agreed that Howe might "enclose us . . . by taking post in our rear." Yet he clung to the island, keeping his forces scattered from King's Bridge to the Battery.

At last, always urged by Greene and given a free hand by Congress, he decided to evacuate. But he had all his stores to move, transportation was very scarce, and he feared that "we shall not effect the whole before we shall meet with some Interruption." That "Interruption" drew closer and closer.

The Kip house, near which the British landed in Manhattan

With the onset of hazy September days Howe began to move, pushing his British and Hessians up the west shore of Long Island, and American posts on Manhattan could make out scarlet coats and blue around modern Long Island City and Astoria. What is now Welfare Island was occupied. British gun pits scarred Randall's Island and Ward's, and enemy shipping, at last wind-favored, ominously beat up the East River, up the North River.

The bulk of the American forces was massed on Harlem Plains, just north of present 125th Street; but far down at the Battery, at the tip of Manhattan Island, Israel Putnam and Henry Knox, with some 4,000 men and mounds of priceless ordnance and supplies, still lingered on in the face of that "Interruption" which the commander in chief dreaded.

"The last check on Long Island has sunk our credit to nothing."
—*Silas Deane, from Paris*

The fifteenth of September was a hot, glass-clear day, blurred now and then by a slight haze that was never thick enough to hide the British ships as they slid along the East and North rivers, gunports open. There was no need for concealment or for subtlety—a British landing force was under way. Barges from Long Island moved across the East River while frigates and ketches slammed shot ashore from the East 20's to the East 40's and beyond. British and Hessian officers were delighted by the picture: "The hills, the woods, the river, the town, the ships and pillars of smoke . . . furnished the finest landscape that either art or nature combined could draw . . . altogether grand and noble."

Barges grounded in the neighborhood of East 34th Street and big Hessian grenadiers in towering helmets, and quick-moving British light infantry spilled ashore. There were only militiamen in front of them, already badly shaken by the cannonading, and their panic spread contagion to more seasoned units in support. Soon Americans by the hundreds were flying in utter disorder to the northwest and the shelter of Harlem Heights. The attackers formed unhurriedly, pushed inland with no opposition, worked north as far as East 42nd Street, and then halted. The high command followed with more troops, and soon Howe, Clinton, and Cornwallis were installed in the Murray house on Murray Hill, then known as Inclenberg, while their men grounded arms in the meadows that stretched south from present-day Grand Central Station. Howe could see no need for hurry. Tory spies seem to have misinformed him that the entire American force was well north of the site of 59th Street. He could rest his men, regroup, and then swing on up the island.

Harlem Heights and the high ground toward the North River still form a

A warship of Admiral Howe's fleet off Manhattan Island in 1776

commanding, cliff-like stretch. From it, one looks down at the west end into a weird scoop of a giant trowel called the Hollow Way, which led to the river at Martje David's Vly. To the south was more high ground, now the site of Columbia University and Barnard College. Southeast, the rise was notched by McGowan's Pass, and straight down the center of the island was a rolling, wooded, broken tract, bounded on the west by Bloomingdale Road and on the east by the Boston Post Road. In modern terms, that tract is Central Park and its environs, with Amsterdam Avenue on the west, and 2nd or 3rd Avenue on the east. On these heights, by afternoon of September 15, lay the bulk of the American forces.

From the Point of Rocks, almost midway along the face of the Harlem escarpment, from other high lookout posts, Americans suddenly stared and pointed south. Drama was moving along the roads that formed the boundaries of the great central wilderness. Bright scarlet uniforms were coming north along the eastern road, and over the western highway thousands of drab men lurched on with the sound of their scuffed boots for drumbeats. Aaron Burr was guiding Knox, Putnam, and the forgotten Battery command toward safety, hidden from the orderly British advance by the rough, wooded country that separated the forces. Neither column had any notion that it was engaged in a life-and-death race, but if the fleet-footed British light infantry broke through McGowan's Pass and rolled out onto the flats, the fugitives in the American files would be cut off.

The slow-moving drama flowed on. Once watchers saw British flankers fan out into the rough country to the west. By luck, they never reached high ground that might have shown them the Bloomingdale Road. Knox and Putnam came on, attacked only by racking fatigue and the heavy burden of known defeat. Then their men spilled out into the deep scoop of Martje David's Vly, scaled the Heights, and the rest of the army opened ranks to let them through.

With nightfall, the British halted just beyond McGowan's. Morning, thought Howe, would be time enough for a good strong push against the Heights and the shattered, uncertain men who held them. Once more, he was presenting his enemies with the priceless commodity of time.

Up on the dark Heights a beaten force lay on its arms, apparently ready to fall to pieces at the lightest touch. Yet there was in that mass a hard, solid core, and its hardest, solidest part was represented by a tall, cloaked Virginian who sat with his subordinates, fully aware that the weight of the all-important decision—what to do next—rested on his shoulders alone. He had seen his troops break in panic that very morning. Would they be any more reliable now? George Washington made his decision.

Before dawn Lieutenant Colonel Thomas Knowlton of Connecticut, who had known the rail fences on Breed's Hill, was on the move. Cool and courageous in battle, Knowlton was, said a contemporary, "six feet high, erect and elegant . . . courteous and affable . . . favorite of his superiors, idol of his soldiers." Down into the Hollow Way he led about 100 Connecticut Rangers, all picked men, and on the south slope they collided with light infantry. Knowlton's men stood firm, exchanging fire with the enemy until the sudden skirl of bagpipes brought on masses of the Black Watch. Then, carefully and in excellent order, Knowlton broke off and made a leisurely retreat.

Not unnaturally, this move was interpreted by the British as flight, and a general forward movement was almost contemptuously begun. Immediately Washington saw an opportunity to draw the enemy's light infantry down into the Hollow Way. Orders snapped out, and Archibald Crary of Rhode Island drove south with 150 men of Nixon's Massachusetts brigade, sup-

The Hollow Way, as seen from the British lines, with the Hudson at left

Colonel Thomas Knowlton, sketch by John Trumbull

ported by Andrew Leitch and some tough riflemen from the 3rd Virginia.

There was immediate contact. Jeering scarlet lines poured into the Vly, were checked, and, incredibly to both sides, faltered. The Yankees were attacking, and in the open, not from behind walls! More troops poured down from Harlem Heights, with Reazin Beall's Maryland militia pressing on with them. George "Joe Gourd" Weedon raced into action with the rest of the 3rd Virginia. Then, in a magnificent gesture, Washington committed the very militiamen who had fled so ingloriously just the day before at Kip's Bay, saw them stand almost toe-to-toe with the very units which had slashed so hard over on Long Island.

Suddenly the British began to retreat! Through a field of buckwheat on the site of Barnard College, through an orchard went kilt and bearskin, with New Englanders and Marylanders and Virginians in pursuit. Through fringes of smoke to the south men could see the last of the British and Hessian reserves being hurried forward at the double. The little reconnaissance was developing into a general engagement which was more than Washington dared risk. Wisely and coolly he ordered a retirement which, said young Tench Tilghman of Pennsylvania, was greeted derisively, for "the pursuit of a flying enemy was so new a scene that it was with difficulty that our men could be brought to retire . . . they gave a Hurra! and left the field in good order."

This startling American achievement was a national one, not sectional. Troops from many states had been committed to battle and there was nothing to choose between them. Washington's force had been transformed by him and by its own efforts from a mob into an army, and every man on the Heights knew it. Joseph Reed, sensing this, wrote, "You can hardly conceive the change it has made. . . . The men . . . feel a confidence which before they had quite lost." Such confidence, of course, could evaporate, as Reed realized when he added, "I hope the effects will be lasting."

Losses, too, were national, not sectional, and the army had to mourn, among many others, Colonel Thomas Knowlton of Connecticut and Major Andrew Leitch of Virginia, hard-hitting spearheads of the assault.

This whole new script, ad-libbed so outrageously by the Americans, seemed to throw the shadows of Breed's Hill deeper and deeper over Howe and Clinton. They could hardly have been cheered by Count von Donop's not too tactful report that except for Hessian intervention, all the British and Scottish troops would have been captured. A frontal assault on the American position was only one of the several courses open to Howe. Making use of his naval strength, he could have struck flanks or rear, or bypassed Washington entirely; but Howe's mind dawdled among his alternatives and for days he did nothing, his seeming paralysis possibly intensified by a disastrous fire that gutted the city of New York on September 21.

Inactivity clamped its deadening hold over the American forces, though for different reasons, and Adjutant General Joseph Reed had cause to recall his cautious words, "I hope the effects will be lasting." Glamor of victory ebbed notably in all ranks. Supply problems were almost insuperable, as were those of equipment. Men cheered when reinforcements from New England marched down over King's Bridge, then muttered in discouragement when they saw that the new troops brought little beyond their weapons and empty powder horns and cartridge boxes. Desertion assumed serious proportions, there was insubordination, and the commander in chief wrote home to cousin Lund Washington: "Such is my situation that if I were to wish the bitterest curse to an enemy on this side of the grave, I should put him in my stead with my feelings." Still he clung to the position on Harlem Heights, knowing that he was too weak to

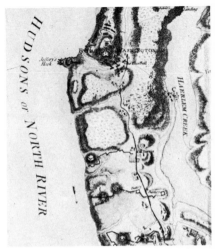

Part of a map of upper Manhattan, showing the area of the Battle of Harlem Heights; Fort Washington is at the top

European engraving of the burning of New York in September, 1776

185

Plan of Fort Washington

"'Tis God that girds our armor on,
And all our just designs fulfills;
Through Him our feet can swiftly run,
And nimbly climb the steepest hills."
—*"The American Soldier's Hymn"*

attack in force, yet fearing that he might be too weak to withdraw in safety.

Something had to be done before Howe, as Washington realized, "might enclose us . . . by taking post in our rear." There were long conferences in what is now known as the Jumel Mansion, high on the bluffs above the Hudson. Lord Stirling attended with John Sullivan, who, like Stirling, had been captured on Long Island and exchanged. Up from the south came Charles Lee, mentally relishing the Charleston laurels won for him by Peter Parker's naval mishaps and the unshakable courage of William Moultrie and his men. Lee at once echoed the earlier advice of Nathanael Greene: Get off Manhattan and up into Westchester County! Now!

By October 16, evacuation was decided upon, with one deadly reservation: Fort Washington, on a rock-reef in what are now the West 180's, was to be held by its garrison of 2,000, isolated and with all communication with the Jersey shore cut off by British cruisers. It was high time for the rest of the move. Howe had started butting his barges and sloops up the East River, obviously seeking a landing in Westchester and then a quick swing west toward the Hudson, to bottle up Washington's forces.

The American move was mortally slow. Like the maddening creep north from New York to Harlem Heights, this shift was severely hampered by lack of transport. Shaky carts and famished horses had to be leapfrogged in short hauls that conserved strength but wasted time alarmingly. Men outmarched their rations, ammunition, stores of all kinds. Units lost their way, blundered here and there, dribbling off little trickles of deserters. But always through mud or darkness or the breathless swelter of Indian-summer days, soldiers looked up to see their tall commander in chief riding on, outwardly calm. There was something in the way he sat his horse or nodded in silent approval over work well done, and then rode on, immutable, unshakable, that kept many men willingly in their places in a column, that lightened a little the galling weight of a musket, that smoothed out a killing slope, that gave a man spirit enough to growl "Come on" to a lagging comrade.

Howe's progress up the East River suffered from his own inertia, from faulty intelligence that put Hessians and British ashore at Throg's Neck in the face of an unfordable stream guarded by Edward Hand's black-shirted Pennsylvania riflemen, and also from the presence at Pell's Point of John Glover, who lay there like a wary old bull seal, with a skeleton brigade under his orders. Against Pell's Point, with its Marbleheaders and the others of the little brigade, went the bulk of the landing strength on October 18. Unlike Greene or Anthony Wayne, Glover had no flair for war, but he did have common sense, courage, and a bone-deep belief in what he fought for. "I did the best I could and disposed of my little party to the best of my judgment," he reported later. Now cautiously, now daringly, he committed his troops, feinting here, falling back there. He lost a few men, but he carried on a fine delaying action, conning his command as though it had been a ship beating through shoal waters. When dusk fell he withdrew successfully across little Hutchinson's River and bivouacked "after fighting all day without victuals or drink . . . the heavens over us and the earth under us," as he wrote later.

Although it was a small action, it underscored once more the fact that no matter how flimsy an American force appeared to be, it was more than apt to lash out, hard and dangerous. And the triumph was more than psychological. Had Glover's brigade disintegrated like the troops at Kip's Bay, pursuit would almost surely have brought the dreaded British bayonets smashing into Washington's long, straggling retirement, a few scant miles from Pell's Point.

Howe dallied about the foreshore through ten days that were invaluable to Washington. On the twenty-eighth he pushed west, screened by clouds of light infantry and jägers, toward the Bronx River and the village of White Plains. His van was rather roughly handled by a small force under General Joseph Spencer of Connecticut, who used much the same tactics that Glover had at Pell's Point. Then Howe struck the main American position, sited on three hills, the highest of which, Chatterton's, on the far right, was the most weakly held, due probably to a mixture of oversight and inexperience.

Holding Chatterton's Hill was General Alexander McDougall of New York, one of the earliest and hottest of the Sons of Liberty. His 1,600 men were made up of more-than-dubious militia, with his own 1st New York, Ritzema's 3rd New York, and Webb's 19th Connecticut, these last units still suffering from the shock of Long Island. But behind them were the Maryland and Delaware Line, grimly and properly proud of their record to date.

Toward this weak and exposed position Howe threw his main attack. Blue and red gunners of the Royal Artillery rolled their pieces forward, smothering Chatterton's crest with their fire. When the bombardment lifted, heavy lines of Hessian brass helmets and blue coats, British cocked hats and bearskins and scarlet coats went plunging and floundering across the Bronx River, battling their way up the slopes. There was a long, confused struggle among autumn-bare trunks and dead leaves, with the green militia levies showing surprising stamina and cohesiveness.

Then out of nowhere came a pounding of hooves, the hollow booming of cavalry kettledrums, and the 17th Dragoons swept down on the exposed militia in a swirl of red plumes, brass helmets, and the silver lancing of long sabers. It was the very first formal cavalry charge of the war, and its impact on the raw American militiamen must have been frightful. The unexpected was showing once again its power to unnerve, and the militia and nearby units broke for the woods. Other units held, and, stiffened by the Marylanders and Delawares, were able to retire, unhurried and with ranks intact. The British historian Trevelyan commented: "The Delaware regiment, which had learned on Long Island that prisoners are not easily made unless they make themselves . . . fought sullenly and composedly . . ."

Howe had won Chatterton's Hill but had completely missed his main objective, the destruction of Washington's army. Worse, he made no attempt to interfere with the withdrawal of his quarry to the high ground of nearby North Castle on the night of the thirty-first, nor did he reach out to block the supply roads from New England over which the Americans received "good flour, beef and pork in plenty, with grog to wash it down."

A good flow of rations and a trickle of new equipment, added to the memories of the Hollow Way, Pell's Point, and many phases of the fighting about White Plains and Chatterton's Hill, acted as a powerful tonic on the Thirteen States and their army in the field. What was not apparent to them or to their army was the fact that every move that had been made so far was merely a prolongation of the very first retirement into the works on Brooklyn Heights. Each was part of a series of continuing actions in which, at most, successful withdrawal had been made in the face of superior, if rather slackly handled, strength.

The picture suddenly changed. In early November, Howe made a night move back to Manhattan. A hastily summoned American council of war had pondered that never-ending military question: what is the enemy going to do now? Unfortunately, the council completely misread British intentions and wrongly foresaw an immediate enemy move into the Jerseys. American troops were

"These dreadful people ought rather to be pitied than feared; they always require a quarter of an hour's time to load a rifle, and in the meantime they feel the effects of our balls and bayonets."
—*Colonel von Herringen*

A British army kettledrum

shifted across the Hudson at once, leaving a force at Peekskill on the east bank and one in the Highlands on the west.

It was a stunning blow to learn that on November 16, a force of British and Scottish, the Rall and the Alt Lossberg Hessians had taken Manhattan's Fort Washington. Worse was to come. On the twentieth, moving surely under the aegis of the Royal Navy, another force crossed the Hudson to the west, fell upon Fort Lee and nobbled it up, nearly seizing Nathanael Greene in the process. So all Manhattan was now British, plus a strong lodgment on the Jersey shore. Hundreds of cannon, muskets by the thousand were lost, huge stores of ammunition, along with tents, blankets, tools, and clothing. Irreplaceable troops were gone for good, units like Colonel Moses Rawlings' Maryland and Virginia riflemen, and the dead Colonel Thomas Knowlton's picked Connecticut men.

To cap everything, the American army, small enough to begin with, was split three ways. Gaunt Charles Lee clung to the heights about North Castle on the Croton River, guarding the approaches to New England. General William Heath, whose service had begun on that fateful April 19, 1775, lay with another command at Peekskill. And the main body under Washington, with Greene seconding him, was falling back through New Jersey, beyond the Hackensack, beyond the Passaic, on to Newark with the low Watchung mountains, off to the right, frowning through late November mist and drizzle. The pace had to be smart, for Lord Cornwallis—who had not known Breed's Hill and its paralyzing slaughter as Howe and Clinton had known it—was driving after the main American contingent with strong columns of Hessians and British. In contrast to the ten days Howe took to cover seventeen miles between Pell's Point and the Bronx, records show that Cornwallis' men devoured a good twenty miles in a single day.

Newark could not be held, and Washington's rear guard pulled out just ahead of the onrushing jägers. Across the Raritan there was an unlooked-for, if brief, breathing spell at New Brunswick, but death and desertion trailed along with the staggering ranks. A British officer was shocked to see that "many of the Rebels who were killed . . . were without shoes or Stockings, & Several were observed to have only linen drawers . . . without any proper shirt or Waistcoat . . . also in great want of blankets . . . they must suffer extremely." They did. But most of them kept on.

On command level, there was serious trouble. Washington sent dispatch after dispatch to Charles Lee, ordering him to bring his force across the Hudson and join the main body. Lee, always playing some weird game of his own, treated the commander in chief's courteous letters coolly, if not insolently. At last he moved, and in a shocking display of carelessness allowed himself to be captured by a detachment from the 16th Dragoons under Colonel Harcourt, though the guiding spirit seems to have been the young Cornet (modern 2nd Lieutenant, Cavalry) Banastre Tarleton. Luckily, Lee was far from his command, which pushed on unmolested to join Washington. Horatio Gates sent 500 men down from Ticonderoga, while Colonel John Cadwalader brought up 1,000 Philadelphia Associators along with Nicholas Haussegger's Pennsylvania Germans. Out of New Jersey and across the Delaware, where he had smashed or seized every available craft on the north bank, Washington could count nearly 6,000 men, many of them, by his own grim account, "entirely naked and most so thinly clad as to be unfit for service." In a private letter he confessed that unless he had many more men, "the game will be pretty well up." The approaching end of the year would bring with it the expiration of most enlistments.

Luckily William Howe lent a helping, if involuntary, hand. No army, he de-

The first page of Thomas Paine's famous pamphlet

clared in effect, ever campaigned in the winter, so he pushed a chain of posts out into New Jersey from the main Manhattan base, beginning with Amboy and New Brunswick, and on to the college town of Princeton. The Delaware front was to be held by the 42nd Black Watch at Bordentown, while the post of honor, Trenton, was entrusted to the Rall, the Alt Lossberg, and the von Knyphausen regiments in recognition of past service, particularly Fort Washington. Cornwallis began packing for a bit of home leave, Clinton sailed off to occupy the pleasant Rhode Island town of Newport, and winter closed down on the Delaware. Ice thickened from a skin to a shell, became soggy, pitted, and broken under sudden warm rains, froze again. As Christmas arrived, the river was in full flood, jammed with great, massive sheets of ice as broad as threshing floors that spun and whirled down from the upper reaches. Any soldier could tell at a glance that the Delaware River in icy spate was utterly impassable, militarily speaking.

Yet on the night of December 25 there was a booming and banging from the dark, ice-choked flood, where sixty-foot Durham boats were being marshaled by men in remnants of blue and white uniforms. Once again the commander in chief was calling on the peculiar skills of John Glover's Marbleheaders. The roads from the interior were astir, and New Hampshiremen, Virginians, New Yorkers, Pennsylvanians bent into gale-driven sleet as they made for the river and the waiting boats, their course "tinged here and there with blood from the feet of men who wore broken shoes"—or no shoes. "It will be a terrible night for the soldiers," wrote an officer, "but I have not heard a man complain."

The Durham boats shoved out into the awesome flood, laden with shivering men or with Henry Knox's guns and horses. Vast ice slabs crashed into the sides of the craft, lunged under bows, ripped into sterns, were fended off by Glover's men before they could smash down on thwarts. And all the time oar and pole worked on in skilled, freezing hands—to the north bank, back to the south, to the north again.

By four in the morning there were nine long miles to cover before wintry dawn. There was no smoking or talking or halting or straggling—surprise was essential on the road that led to sleeping Trenton and its garrison of tough German professionals. The column split [see map, page 202]; John Sullivan, replacing the captured Charles Lee, took Glover's brigade and Arthur St. Clair's and Paul Sargent's along the river highway. Nathanael Greene swung inland to the Pennington or Scotch Road with the commands of Adam Stephen, Hugh Mercer, the Frenchman Roche de Fermoy, and Morris' troop of Philadelphia Light Horse. Soaked muskets became useless, but Washington ordered: "Tell General Sullivan to use the bayonet. I am resolved to take Trenton." And for once bayonets were available. Ice formed on the roads. Men fell in a clatter of equipment, were pried to their feet, went stumbling on. Overhead the eastern sky began to pale. The columns broke into what a soldier later called a "long trot."

The hundred-odd scattered houses of Trenton lay silent under the storm, and ice glinted on picket fences, orchards, and the hulking stone barracks built to house Royal troops during the old French wars. A few of Colonel Rall's command were beginning to moan as they wakened to face thundering post-Christmas hang-overs. Outposts were weak and unready.

Sometime after half past seven on the morning of the twenty-sixth, Herr Leutnant Andreas Wiederhold of the Alt Lossberg, in command of a picket out on the Pennington Road, saw movement, then heard shots, running feet, shouts in the lightening air. The sentry's cry, *Der Feind! Heraus! Heraus!* (The enemy! On your feet!) was the first warning the garrison had of the attack that

The chain of British posts established by Howe in New Jersey

Detail from Emanuel Leutze's famous painting of Washington crossing the Delaware River

189

Colonel Rall's Trenton headquarters

was even then breaking. Wiederhold fell back on the next supporting body under Hauptmann Ernst Eber von Altenbockum.

It was too late. There was a horrible din down by the river and along the Pennington Road, for John Sullivan had kept pace with Washington and Greene. Henry Knox's fieldpieces began to slam out. Mercer's men went in with the bayonet. Farther south, John Glover's amphibious command, still driving hard after their killing work on the river, smashed across the Assunpink.

On high ground at present Princeton Avenue, Washington appeared with his staff, and threw in Lord Stirling's brigade, spearheaded by George Weedon's 3rd Virginia. Americans under Captain William Washington and Lieutenant James Monroe (later to assume a far higher title) cut down the gunners about two Hessian fieldpieces. Arthur St. Clair's brigade was in, and John Stark, leading its right element, "dealt death wherever he found resistance and broke down all opposition before him."

As their firearms dried out, riflemen took aim and muskets began to pop all along the line. Rall, still dazed from his holiday celebrations, raged up and down King and Queen streets, bravely trying to rally his men. Then he was down, mortally wounded. Sullivan swung his whole command up from the river to meet St. Clair crashing down from the north, and the remnants of the Trenton garrison downed arms in a dripping, wintry orchard.

The whole affair had lasted less than three-quarters of an hour. Washington collected his men, assembled some 900 prisoners, arranged for immediate transportation of important captured stores, and by noon was marching upriver again, hurrying the whole mass over the nine miles that lay between Trenton and the ferries. The river was, if possible, more dangerous than it had been the night before. Captured Germans viewed the crossing with horror, but no one in Washington's column seems to have worried much about getting back. Weren't Glover's men still there?

News of the Trenton victory ran through the army and the country like a bolt of electricity. It had been a real offensive, not a counterattack like the Hollow Way, and had been won largely by the bayonet, a weapon which the Americans were not supposed to understand—or even possess. In exulting, men and soldiers forgot that the triumph could have been far greater, for the original plan had contemplated two other landings farther downstream by Cadwalader and Ewing, but these had been balked by river conditions. (After all, Glover's men couldn't be everywhere.)

The success was heartening enough as it was. Had Washington been able to keep his Trenton men as a nucleus about which to build an army for the rest of the war, he could have presented a formidable threat to the British, on land at least. But the commander in chief was never to have a veteran army. Days were flicking off the calendar, bringing mass expiration of enlistments nearer.

An American jibe at enemy soldiers, entitled "British Heroism"

The new year of 1777 came and the army still held together somehow. Henry Knox and Thomas Mifflin had toiled from unit to unit, begging, cajoling: Just six weeks more. The commander in chief added his personal pleas. Officers and men listened in sullen silence, then men growled to each other, "I'll stay if you will." By December 30, Washington was writing, "I have the pleasure to acquaint you that the Continental Regiments from the Eastern Governments have, to a man, agreed to stay six weeks beyond their term of enlistment . . ." And assured of a little more time, he took his men across the Delaware to Trenton once again.

Soon the ragged army was in a deadly trap. The energetic Cornwallis, whose home leave had been canceled after Trenton, rushed nearly 8,000 well-clothed, well-equipped men over from Princeton to the town on the Delaware, to oppose the American force of some 5,000, which had its back to the river. Tragedy seemed inevitable. But as weather had stretched a protecting arm over the American army at Long Island, keeping the British fleet helpless, now once again it intervened, and biting winds began to freeze the sodden fields and mud-track roads. If the freeze held, the army could move. But where? At a council of war, one officer made the staggering suggestion that there should be no retreat. Instead, the whole force was to slip out by night past the British left and plunge deep into New Jersey.

At one in the morning of January 3, 1777, the desperate march began, with a few devoted souls remaining in the works about the Assunpink to raise a din with pick and shovel, and keep fires stoked to assure the British that their prey would still be there in the morning. The rest of the army moved out almost on tiptoe, gun wheels muffled in sacking and cannoneers holding the trace chains to silence the slightest clank.

The route was ghastly, far worse than the average abominable back road of the time. Newly opened, its surface was studded with tree stumps against which men stumbled in the silent dark, on which horses barked legs. "We moved slow," wrote one man in the column, "on account of the artillery, frequently coming to a halt . . . when ordered forward again, one, two or three men in each platoon would stand, with their arms supported, fast asleep; a platoon next in rear advancing on them, they, in walking . . . would strike a stub [stump] and fall." All count of time was lost, men being absorbed in the labor of raising and planting one foot, and bringing up the other. Day broke, "bright, serene, and extremely cold, with a hoar frost which bespangled every object," as Major James Wilkinson wrote.

Other eyes were taking in the new day. Out of Princeton, headed for Trenton and the expected bagging of Washington and his men, marched the 17th Leicesters and the 55th Borderers. Lieutenant Colonel Charles Mawhood of the 17th rode in command, mounted on a plump brown pony. A pair of spaniels, drunk with the glory of the drums and the tramp of gaitered legs and the keen bite of the morning, yiped and scampered about after their master's pony. Then, off to his left, Mawhood sighted the flicker of bayonets heading for the bridge over Stony Brook on the Trenton road, a vital link in British communications. Reacting promptly, he swung his column around to head off Mercer's column, detached by Washington to destroy Stony Brook bridge. The two forces met and the confused melee known as the Battle of Princeton was on.

There was violent fighting in William Clark's orchard beyond a neat Quaker meetinghouse, and soon the Borderers and the Leicesters were in with the bayonet among Mercer's mortally slow-loading riflemen. Panic struck nearby militia, spread, and another Kip's Bay loomed. Mounted on a white horse, the commander in chief himself raced out far into the van, in the thick of bullets and bayonets. An aide, watching, flung his cloak over his eyes to shut out what he was sure was the death of his chief. When the smoke cleared, Washington and his white horse were still there, plunging from this knot of fugitives to that.

Henry Knox's guns began to pound across the frosted meadows. Over a ridge came the swift ranks of Daniel Hitchcock's Rhode Island and Massachusetts brigade, with Edward Hand's hard-shooting Pennsylvanians on its right. Mawhood's lines shook, frayed out, then broke away in flight, gasping and running along the road that led to Trenton.

Pursuit was too dangerous, since the firing would have been heard down by

Detail from Trumbull's preliminary sketch for his painting of the engagement at Princeton

Detail of Trumbull's sketch of the death of General Hugh Mercer at Princeton

the river and strong forces would be sent out by Cornwallis to investigate. Washington led his men on into the college town of Princeton and found some of the South Lancs still there trying to rally about Nassau Hall. Up came Knox's guns again. Captain Alexander Hamilton directed a round at the college building, and the fight was over.

It had been another American victory in the open, with militia rallying from panic to close with tough British units. But a price had been paid. Hugh Mercer was mortally wounded. Colonel John Haslet, whose Delaware regiment was absent on recruiting duty, had fallen with him, and the "Blue Hen's Chickens" would listen in vain in later actions for that rallying voice. Captain John Fleming of the 1st Virginia had called calmly to his company at the opening of the action, "Gentlemen, dress your ranks before you make ready to fire." Now he was gone, as was Captain Daniel Neil, whose New Jersey gunners had broken up a dangerous British rush at their very muzzles.

Princeton was no place to linger, with the main British force at Trenton surely aroused by now and very likely hurrying up the road from the Delaware. The commander in chief spoke longingly to his generals of the town of New Brunswick, great British supply base which was known to contain the paymaster's chests bulging with hard, minted money. But two nights without sleep and the killing march from the Assunpink to Princeton had finished the American army as a combat force for a day or two. It was decided to push on deeper into New Jersey, toward Somerset Court House and thence to the high natural bastions of Morristown and the rich hinterland that lay beyond. At least Washington's columns could chuckle, as Henry Knox did, over the arrival of Cornwallis and his men at Princeton, far too late for pursuit, "in a most infernal sweat—running, puffing and blowing and swearing at being so outwitted."

So the army of the United States, unfed and unrested, struck out for the western highlands. In a sense, the long, long retreat that had begun at Brooklyn in August came to an end when Morristown was reached. William Howe and his lieutenants had won battles, but not a campaign, since Washington's army was still in being.

Trenton and Princeton produced far-reaching results. Howe pulled in his most advanced posts, leaving the whole state of New Jersey virtually free of Royal troops. The Jersey people, Tory and Rebel alike, had suffered sorely at the hands of the King's men and their allies during that occupation, and began to look more and more trustingly on the new nation. The heavy Loyalist core that had existed before had softened, if, indeed, it had not entirely melted away. In other parts of the country, men on recruiting duty found it a little easier to fill up their quotas. Continental currency was not quite so hard to put into circulation. Ports and farms were more willing to release supplies to commissary officers.

Morristown was well chosen as winter quarters. It lay on a steep-sided plateau, and the only avenue of enemy approach ran through broken, wooded ravines, potential deathtraps for the rather inflexible British formations and their ponderous German colleagues. Washington informed Congress that he intended "to watch the motions of the Enemy and avail Myself of Every favourable Circumstance."

And watch was about all the General could do, as his pathetically small army dwindled still more. The six-weeks men went home. New units were slow in replacing them, but Howe, Cornwallis, and von Knyphausen were blind to this frightening weakness. The snow-covered bastions of Morristown were guarding a secret as well as an army.

The presence of the Royal Navy gave Howe an overwhelming advantage in the New York campaign. British warships cruised the Hudson River almost at will, with utter contempt for the feeble American defenses.

The War Shifts to New York

General Howe's evacuation of Boston in March, and Admiral Parker's repulse at Charleston in June, 1776, left the British with no American base from which to sustain the war. New York seemed an obvious answer to this dilemma. Its capture would provide not only a fine harbor in the heart of the colonies, but control of the Hudson River, a vital link in the interior water route to Canada. As George Washington knew well, a British hold on the Hudson would "stop the Intercourse between the northern and southern Colonies, upon which depends the Safety of America." Alert to the "infinite importance" of New York, Washington rushed his army south from Boston. The events that ensued, late in 1776, marked the nadir of the American cause.

In this 1777 English print, Sir William Howe wears the Order of the Bath, awarded for his victory in the Battle of Long Island.

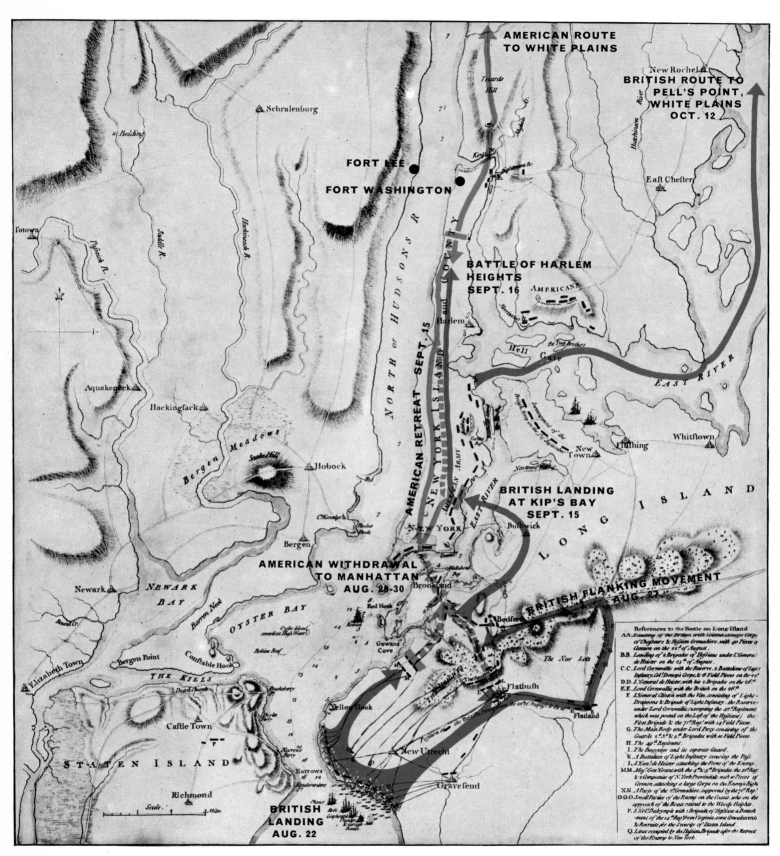

AMERICAN ROUTE
TO WHITE PLAINS

New Rochel

BRITISH ROUTE TO
PELL'S POINT,
WHITE PLAINS
OCT. 12

East Chester

FORT LEE

FORT WASHINGTON

BATTLE OF HARLEM
HEIGHTS
SEPT. 16

AMERICANS

Harlem

Hell Gate

EAST RIVER

Whitstown

BRITISH LANDING
AT KIP'S BAY
SEPT. 15

New Town

Flushing

Schralenburg

Building

Totowa

NORTH OR HUDSON'S R.

AMERICAN RETREAT SEPT. 15

NEW YORK ISLAND and COUNTY

Aquakenack

Hackingsack

Bergen Meadows

Hobock

Snake Hill

Bergen

LONG ISLAND

AMERICAN WITHDRAWAL
TO MANHATTAN
AUG. 29-30

New York

Bushwick

Brookland

Bedford

BRITISH FLANKING MOVEMENT
AUG. 27

Newark

NEWARK
BAY

OYSTER BAY

Red Hook

Gowans Cove

The New Lots

Round Cr.

Bergen Point

Constable Hook

Flatbush

THE KILLS

Elizabeth Town

Dutch Church

Flatland

Castle Town

Yellow Hook

New Utrech

STATEN ISLAND

Narrows

Richmond

Gravesend

Scale — 3 Miles

BRITISH
LANDING
AUG. 22

References to the Battle on Long Island

The movements of the opposing armies (British in red, American in blue) during the New York
campaign are superimposed on the so-called "Howe War Plan" map made in October, 1776.

194

The British
Invasion Begins

A British officer, Archibald Robertson, sketched this view of the British fleet and camp on Staten Island in July, 1776. In the left background is Long Island.

As soon as American troops arrived in New York they were put to work on the fortifications of Manhattan and Long Island. While they dug, the greatest expeditionary force in Great Britain's history slowly assembled in the harbor: ten great ships of the line, twenty frigates, and hundreds of transports carrying 32,000 seasoned troops. British and Hessians disembarked on Staten Island, and soldiers on both sides waited for Howe to make his move.

The mobility provided him by the fleet under his brother, "Black Dick" Howe, gave the English General several choices. He could land on Manhattan or on Long Island, or he could move up the East or Hudson rivers to trap America's only army. Washington, strangely blind to this latter possibility, failed to move. With some of his troops on Manhattan, some on Long Island, his force was split in two by the East River, which should have been the preserve of the Royal Navy. Sir William Howe made up his mind at last, and on August 22, 1776, British and hired German soldiers waded ashore, unopposed, on the western end of Long Island.

The Royal Navy quickly took control of the Hudson by sailing right past the poorly manned American shore batteries. This aquatint shows the gallant but fruitless Rebel attempt to attack the frigates Phoenix *and* Rose *with fire ships.*

One bright spot in the Long Island disaster was the resistance of the American right wing. Maryland and Delaware Continentals withdraw across Gowanus Creek after checking the British long enough to let the rest of the army escape.

The American Disaster on Long Island

The Battle of Long Island on August 27 revealed much about the two opposing commanders. Howe's battle plan was brilliantly conceived and executed, yet he failed to finish off his defeated enemy. On the American side, Washington and his subordinates did not do well in their first real tactical test, but when the survival of his army was at stake the commander in chief rose to the crisis.

The battle was actually decided almost before it began by the American commanders' failure to cover the extreme left of their lines. Howe exploited this quickly by sending 10,000 men through unguarded Jamaica Pass to fall on the unsuspecting American left flank with devastating impact. At the same time, German and British divisions hit the center and right of the line, and only a steadfast rear-guard action under William Alexander, the self-styled Lord Stirling, prevented a complete rout. The demoralized colonials retreated to their vulnerable defenses on Brooklyn Heights, having suffered over 1,000 casualties. But, inexplicably, Howe stopped. Instead of a hard, decisive stroke, he contented himself with digging approaches to the fortifications.

Thus far, unfavorable winds had providentially kept British warships out of the East River, but Washington saw that it was only a matter of time before he would be under attack from the Royal Navy in his rear and by Howe before him. On the night of August 29, under the cover of rain and a blessed fog, John Glover's Marblehead regiment and former sailors from Salem ferried the entire American army of 9,500, with all its baggage and equipment, across the river to Manhattan. As it was to do again and again, Howe's quarry slipped away.

Israel Putnam (left) was in general command on Long Island; the right wing of his army was led by William Alexander, Lord Stirling (above). John Glover (right) and his amphibious Marbleheaders evacuated the troops to Manhattan. The sketches of Putnam and Glover were drawn by Trumbull.

The retreat from Long Island was praised even by the British. So effectively was silence maintained in the ranks and by Glover's "hardy, adroit, weather-proof" men who manned the boats, that instead of an entire army, Howe captured only three stragglers who had lingered behind to plunder.

Redcoats Enter
New York City

These German engravings give a rather distorted European view of the British army's

Even after the Americans eluded him at Long Island, General William Howe still had an opportunity rarely given a field commander—that of destroying the principal army of the enemy. By sending an assault force up the Hudson or Long Island Sound, Howe could have trapped the retreating Rebels and cut them to pieces, almost at leisure. Well aware of this, Washington nevertheless decided to make a stand north of the city. For one thing, his demoralized men were in no condition for immediate retreat; for another, he desperately hoped to give them one success. The chance was not long in coming.

Before Washington could move all his army and stores north to Harlem Heights, the British landed at Kip's Bay, scattering the militia there. Then Howe let opportunity slide through his hands by dawdling at the beachhead while some 3,000 Americans slipped out of the city to the Harlem lines. The British had the port they wanted, and would hold

Captain Archibald Robertson of the Royal Engineers sketched the unopposed landing at Kip's Bay. It was preceded by such a withering fire from the British frigates that the terrified American defenders fled their posts "with the utmost precipitation."

1776 occupation of New York. They show (from left to right) the landing, the triumphal entry, and the disastrous fire which soon swept the city.

it for the rest of the war, but the American army still existed. On September 16 crack British and German outfits were lured into a trap at Harlem Heights and dealt a stinging setback. This "brisk little skirmish" bolstered the morale of Washington's troops; and after Howe's prize, the city of New York, was largely consumed by fire, the commander in chief wrote his cousin: "Providence, or some good honest fellow, has done more for us than we were disposed to do for ourselves."

The bloody game of cat-and-mouse continued. In October Howe tried what he should have done earlier, and landed a force in Westchester; but John Glover's men fought him off just long enough for the main army to dig in at White Plains. Here again Howe's attack failed to bring off a final showdown. Washington moved north to North Castle, plagued by wholesale desertions and expiring enlistments; while Howe, frustrated once more, gave up the chase and returned to consolidate his hold on New York.

At Harlem Heights, a skirmish that almost developed into a full-dress battle, American troops gleefully witnessed the rare sight of the enemy's backs. The 42nd Highlanders, the famous Black Watch, are shown here retreating under a heavy fire.

This painting by Dominic Serres shows the frigates Rose *and* Phoenix *and their tenders forcing the Hudson River passage in October, 1776. The view is to the north, with Fort Lee at left, Fort Washington at right.*

England Commands the Hudson

The New York campaign was George Washington's first real test as a strategist, and although he had lost the city he had managed to save the little army which was, in reality, the Revolution. Once it was realized that Howe was not going to test their North Castle defenses, the American forces were "in high spirits, loath to give an inch to their enemies." But "their enemies" were preparing to teach Washington a bitter lesson.

In the hope of retaining control of the Hudson, the Americans had built two strongholds on the river's rocky heights. Fort Washington in northern Manhattan, and Fort Lee, opposite it in New Jersey, were heavily garrisoned; but their ineffectiveness in blocking the river was apparent when British warships sailed past their harmless fire, and went as far north as Tarrytown. After the loss of New York, Washington and his generals had discussed the evacuation of Fort Washington, "but finally nothing

concluded upon." The indecision was disastrous. Leaving the Rebel army at North Castle, Howe marched south and sent 8,000 troops against the fort on November 15. The strike was well led and manned, and after a courageous resistance the defenders surrendered.

Howe's bag was stupendous. In addition to nearly 3,000 prisoners, he acquired 146 cannon, 12,000 rounds of artillery ammunition, 2,800 muskets, and 400,000 cartridges. It was one of the most expensive American defeats of the war. Washington, unable to send any assistance, watched the battle from Fort Lee in a rage of frustration. Four days later Charles Cornwallis surprised Nathanael Greene and the Fort Lee garrison across the river. Greene and his men barely escaped capture, leaving behind another invaluable store of supplies. The city of New York was securely in British hands, and now the way to New Jersey lay open.

The attack on Fort Washington (above) was mounted from three directions. Hessian mercenaries stormed the fort itself, partly visible on the high ground at center, in the main attack. The other two thrusts, made by British troops, one by way of the Harlem River in the foreground, were aimed at the fort's outposts. In the right background, below the New Jersey Palisades, the British frigate Pearl can be seen shelling American positions from the Hudson.

Cornwallis' move against Fort Lee (below) was reminiscent of Wolfe's approach to Quebec in 1759. He embarked 4,000 men in flatboats, landed north of the fort, scaled the Palisades, and rapidly moved to cut off the fort's garrison. The Americans were warned in just enough time to abandon the position, leaving everything, even their half-prepared breakfasts, behind. Both water colors are by Thomas Davies, a British officer who witnessed the battles.

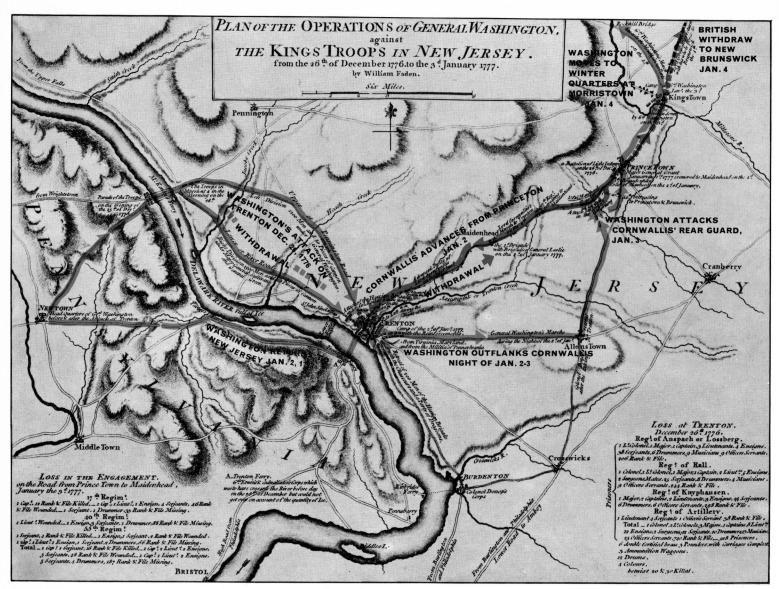

PLAN OF THE OPERATIONS OF GENERAL WASHINGTON,
against
THE KINGS TROOPS IN NEW JERSEY.
from the 26th of December 1776.to the 3d January 1777.
by William Faden.
Six Miles.

This contemporary British map indicates the routes of Washington's attack on Trenton and his later maneuvers around Princeton. The American troop movements are shown in blue, those of the British in red.

Retreat Through the Jerseys

The retreat through New Jersey was a costly one for the Americans. At one point they had to burn their tents for lack of transport.

With the fall of the Hudson River forts Washington's troops—"the wretched remains of a broken army," now reduced to less than 3,000—retreated south through New Jersey. In energetic pursuit was Cornwallis, a capable general who had the killer instinct that Howe lacked. Time and again the Rebels barely slipped away. The Americans were leaving Newark just as the British entered the town; at New Brunswick Washington reported to Congress, "The Enemy are fast advancing, some of 'em in sight now." Then Cornwallis halted. The ever-cautious Howe ordered him to wait for the main army, and Washington escaped across the Delaware, gathering up all available boats to thwart further pursuit.

As 1776 drew to a close the balance sheet was scarcely favorable to the American cause. On the one hand was the delivery of Boston and victory at Charleston; but these were far outweighed by the failures in Canada, the defeats at Long Island, Fort Washington, and Fort Lee, and the loss of New York and New Jersey. In three months Washington had seen 5,000 of his men taken prisoner, including, on December 13, General Charles Lee, although that event might have been a blessing in disguise. On the retreat through New Jersey, Thomas Paine was writing *The Crisis*—"These are the times that try men's souls"—and Washington was saying of his plight, "No man, I believe, ever had a greater choice of difficulties and less means to extricate himself from them." Once again, the rival commanders could be measured by their actions. While Howe was content to garrison a chain of posts in New Jersey and retire to winter quarters in New York, Washington plotted a counterstroke born of desperation.

"Necessity, dire necessity, will, nay must, justify my attack," the commander in chief wrote to one of his officers. On December 31, unless a victory were achieved to encourage re-enlistments, expiring terms would shrink the American "Grand Army" to 1,400 men. The objective, for which Washington coined the watchword "Victory or Death," was Trenton. On Christmas day the army filed down to the Delaware, and John Glover and his invaluable Marbleheaders began to ferry it across the dark, ice-clogged river.

General Charles Lee was captured in a New Jersey tavern by men from the same British regiment he had led in the Seven Years' War.

The Delaware crossing in a "storm of wind, hail, rain and snow" ranks with the evacuation of Long Island as a great tactical masterpiece of the war. Washington is the central figure in Edward Hicks' painting.

Washington's twin columns hit two sides of Trenton in perfect synchronization, spreading out to cut off escape routes. The well-handled American artillery repeatedly cut up the Hessians before they could form, and in all the confusion the formally trained Germans were at a loss to improvise defenses. The print above shows the American charge into the town at the beginning of the battle, which soon developed into chaotic street fighting. John Trumbull's painting (right) catches the drama of a great moment in the Revolution, the Hessian surrender. Washington offers a generous hand to the mortally wounded Rall; on the white horse at right is Nathanael Greene. Henry Knox's Pennsylvania headquarters, surrounded by his "artillery park," is at left.

The Desperate Gamble Pays Off

This German drawing shows the Trenton captives being marched through what is meant to be Philadelphia. The Hessians had been told that they would be killed and eaten if captured by the Rebels.

Even granting the weakness of Washington's army, the British position in their thin chain of New Jersey posts was somewhat tenuous. Howe, troubled by signs of guerrilla warfare and noting that the population had not flocked to the King's colors as expected, admitted that the chain had "rather too large links." Nevertheless, Colonel Johann Rall, commanding the Hessians at Trenton, viewed the Americans with scorn and did not bother to fortify his post. "Let them come," he said. "We want no trenches. We will go at them with the bayonet." So his soldiers celebrated their lonely Christmas at the rum barrel, while Rall was too busy with cards and wine to heed warnings that the Rebels were astir.

On paper, the plan Washington had formulated did credit to a professional. A thrust was to be made at Bordentown to keep that garrison occupied; while another crossing at Trenton would cut off the enemy escape route. At McKonkey's Ferry, nine miles above Trenton, the main division of 2,400 men and eighteen of Knox's cannon were to cross. As it turned out, this was the only division able to negotiate the ice-clogged Delaware, which placed a heavy burden on the element of surprise if the plan was to succeed. Fortunately, surprise was complete and victory total. Rall was killed, over 1,000 of his men fell or were captured. The elated Americans, withdrawing across the river, had only four wounded.

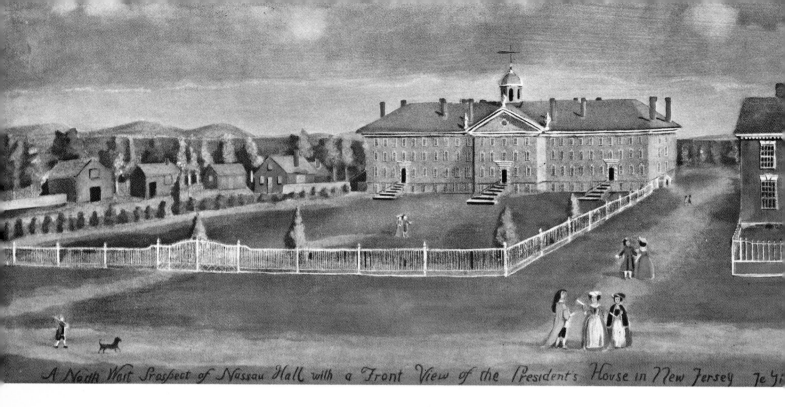

A North West Prospect of Nassau Hall with a Front View of the President's House in New Jersey

The print above shows Princeton College's Nassau Hall and, at right, the home of the college president. Both were sacked during the Hessian occupation, and Nassau Hall was the last refuge for British troops during the Battle of Princeton. After Captain Alexander Hamilton brought up a cannon and decapitated with one shot a portrait of George II in the prayer hall, the garrison, "a haughty crabbed set of men," filed out and surrendered.

The painting of the Battle of Princeton (right) is by William Mercer, the deaf-mute son of the American General who was mortally wounded in the fighting. The first stage of the battle, fought in the fields south of town, was between the American advance guard and British en route to join Cornwallis at Trenton. The redcoats had the upper hand until George Washington and the main force came up and attacked, putting them to flight.

Victory at Princeton

om an old print Feb 1809

The Trenton surprise disconcerted the British high command momentarily, and American strength was wildly exaggerated as Rebel patrols ranged through southern New Jersey. Then, by January 1, 1777, Washington was across the Delaware again to strike his supposedly disorganized foe. Instead, he found himself in grave danger, trapped by the hard-driving Cornwallis. Only a superb delaying action on January 2 prevented an attack which would have driven the Americans into the river at Trenton. Cornwallis planned to "bag the fox" the next morning, but during the night Washington's men slipped out of their lines and moved around his flank to hit the British rear guard at Princeton. With the commander in chief shouting "It's a fine fox chase, my boys!" the Americans routed the Princeton force. The British supply base at New Brunswick lay exposed, but the exhausted "ragged scarecrows" were fought out, and Washington had to take up winter quarters at Morristown. His brilliant campaign had forced Howe to abandon nearly all of New Jersey, and brought hope to what had seemed a hopeless cause.

Washington reviewing his ragged army at Valley Forge

THE MAKING
OF AN ARMY

"... *you might have tracked the army from White Marsh*

to Valley Forge by the blood of their feet."

GEORGE WASHINGTON

FROM his headquarters on the edge of Morristown Common, the commander in chief watched his army settle itself in log huts on the south slope of Thimble Mountain, ready to face still another winter in the field. Despite the lingering glow of Trenton and Princeton, the future must have appeared ominous to him, for all his never-failing outward calm. Clothes were in very short supply, and provisions flowed in the thinnest of currents through the western passes. Smallpox broke out, and Washington had to set up isolation areas and struggle with the then almost impossible problem of camp sanitation. Since an idle force rots quickly, troops were set to work building a fort of sorts, about which there grew up a legend that it was planned simply to give them something to do. Most fittingly, it has been called Fort Nonsense.

Then, as the weeks passed, life in and about Morristown began to improve. Washington used special powers granted him by Congress to commandeer supplies, and his men ate better. New troops came in and older formations decided to stay on. Into the little hill town came Martha Washington, always cheerful and brisk, and began entertaining modestly for the wives of other officers. March brought news from Portsmouth, New Hampshire, that the brig *Mercury,* out of Nantes, had docked there with 364 cases of arms, bales of "Cloath," caps, stockings, shoes, "Necloathes," and, most important, 11,000 gunflints and 1,000 barrels of Lavoisier's superlative powder. *Mercury* brought word, too, of no less than 34 similar ships clearing French ports for America. The drab, workaday firm of Hortalez et Cie was functioning with quiet efficiency. Logistically, the year 1777 was opening most propitiously.

Exchanged prisoners began to appear on the plateau. Huge Daniel Morgan, known to the army as the "Old Wagoner," reported and was given command of the 11th Virginia. Return Meigs was assigned to Henry Sherburne's Connecticut regiment, while Christian Febiger, the Dane, with Breed's Hill as well as Canada on his record, took post as second-in-command of Morgan's Virginians.

So the main American army budded with the new spring of 1777, taking shape and size to a degree that was miraculous to those who could look back on the starved, ragged 4,000-odd who had struggled south to the Delaware in December, 1776. Yet with all its growth, it had frightening weaknesses—officers whose knowledge was often only rudimentary, troops who could barely execute the simplest maneuvers, equipment and arms little above survival level. And events were gathering on the horizon of time to test this and other American commands to the utmost. As summer came on, Lake Champlain was once more astir with bateaux and sloops and small frigates, heading south for Ticonderoga under the breezy, flamboyant leadership of "Gentleman Johnny" Burgoyne. Closer to the heart of things, William Howe embarked thousands of his best British and Hessian troops at New York and headed out into the Atlantic hazes. His great flotilla could have any number of objectives. George Washington would have to reason out its true aim, and the smallest mistake in his reasoning could be fatal.

Through the early summer weeks, a tall, red-haired young Frenchman was beating his way from South Carolina to Philadelphia. Though he was not yet twenty, his mind and sympathies had become deeply involved in the American struggle by what he had read and heard, and he had abandoned wife, family, and career to offer his services to the new nation.

To Philadelphia came Marie Joseph Paul Yves Roch Gilbert du Motier, Marquis de Lafayette. Congress cast a more than jaundiced eye on his open-armed enthusiasm, remembering earlier "volunteers" from Europe, who had

Marquis de Lafayette

210

descended on Philadelphia with extravagant claims for rank and pay which seemed to be based on the most shadowy military backgrounds. Cheerfully the Marquis accepted the snub, and soon Congress was in a mild state of shock as it learned the details of the Marquis' requests. He did want the rank of major general, but would serve without pay. He did not even want a command, asking only to be "near the person of General Washington till such time as he may think proper to entrust me with a division of the army."

Soon the Marquis and Washington met, and from that meeting sprang a deep, enduring friendship. The army had moved down from Morristown Heights into Bucks County, Pennsylvania, where Lafayette joined it at its camp near Neshaminy Bridge. He found a desperately ragged force, uneasily poised, ready to move to the coast should the mysterious flotilla of the Howes materialize out of the summer mists, yet at the same time looking north over its shoulder toward the far Champlain Valley where Burgoyne was moving. On August 22, after a flood of rumors, there was authentic news of the British, and John Adams wrote Abigail: "It is now no longer a secret where Mr. Howe's fleet is . . . it is arrived at the head of Chesapeake Bay . . . His march by land to Philadelphia may be about sixty or seventy miles."

The twenty-fourth brought fine weather, and Philadelphia turned out along Front and Chestnut streets to see George Washington leading the American army through the city to meet Howe, Cornwallis, and von Knyphausen. There was a small advance guard and then the commander in chief, most carefully dressed in blue and buff, escorted by Henry Knox and Tench Tilghman and the young Marquis. For more than two hours Washington's men flowed over the cobbled streets—the main army of the United States, which had begun to take on an identity of its own. After a lull of two days, more troops poured through the brick city, and a paroled American officer watching the passage of the whole army was impressed. "Though indifferently dressed," he wrote, they "held well burnished arms and carried them like soldiers, and looked . . . as if they might have faced an equal number with a reasonable prospect of success." Such a comment from a civilian would have meant little, but the paroled officer had seen his comrades in action and had standards of judgment to apply. Whatever the "reasonable prospect of success" might be, the main American army marched out to meet it.

Howe had landed his troops—weakened, sick, their numbers depleted by the long weeks below decks on a broiling summer sea—at Head of Elk. He had to rest and refit his men and scour the country for transport and cavalry horses, most of his having died on the time-wasting voyage. Then he gathered his British, Hessian, and Tory forces and began moving north.

The two forces, British and American, edged closer and closer to the placid ripples of Brandywine Creek, with Painter's Ford in its middle reaches and Chad's some three miles downstream. On the morning of September 11, four young girls "were walking in the road . . . close by Polly Buckwalter's Lane." They saw horsemen on the road to Kennett Square, riding through the fields under tall elms. The quartet could hardly have known that the troopers were a patrol thrown out by General "Scotch Willie" Maxwell and his Jerseymen, and they kept on with their walk. A horseman called, "Girls, you'd better go home!" "Why?" asked one of them. "Because the British regiments are coming up the road." One of the girls, Elizabeth Coates, remembered looking down the road and seeing them "in great numbers," and then scurrying home just ahead of the foremost fringes of the Battle of Brandywine Creek.

They were not in great numbers—just a Tory command under Major Patrick

Satire on the table manners of Hessian General von Knyphausen

211

Ferguson, a gifted man as well as an honorable, skilled soldier, destined to fight out his life a few years later on a Carolina mountaintop. Behind him was a screening force, spearheaded by the always dangerous 23rd Welch Fusiliers. Unfortunately the American command misread numbers as thoroughly as had little Elizabeth Coates and her friends and, worse, misread intentions. This advance was a mere diversion, and Howe's main strength was curving far upstream toward unwatched Brandywine fords to fall heavily on the American right rear, another version of the Long Island maneuver. And again the blow was to strike New Hampshire's John Sullivan, always able, never lucky.

On came the shattering attack, pouring down from Scanneltown, out of Osborne's woods, and a complete roll-up of the whole American line along the Brandywine seemed inevitable. Units broke and teamsters panicked, sending their heavy wagons rocking and roaring along toward Chester. Washington, finally alive to the main point of danger and shaking off his earlier conviction that the real blow was to come on his left by "Polly Buckwalter's Lane," sent Nathanael Greene with a whole division of Virginians to Sullivan's aid.

There were four hard miles to cover on foot and over broken country; then hard fighting in a defile near the peaceful Birmingham meetinghouse. The Virginians met the British advance, checked it, then fell back slowly and in good order, struggling for each copse and outcropping until darkness forced an end to the action. Off on the American left more solid blows had fallen, but Wayne fought his ground well, used what guns he had skillfully, and managed to withdraw most of his command from the field in the September dusk.

As darkness fell over the retreating army, the poison of disintegration spread evilly. The commander in chief retreated with Greene's division, which, still solid despite its killing double-time march and hard fighting, butted on through the mass of fugitives like a heavy log working down a flume. Perhaps it was the example of the Virginians led by the wheezing Rhode Islander, but soon the routed men discovered some reservoir of stamina. Scattered squads began to find their proper platoons, platoons their companies. Captain Enoch Anderson of the immortal Delawares remembered that night with grim pride. "I saw not a despairing look, nor did I hear a despairing word. We had solacing words always ready for each other—'Come, boys, we shall do better another time.'—Had a man suggested, or merely hinted the idea of giving up,—he would have been knocked down, and if killed, it would have been no murder."

Little by little order was regained, and the whole army trailed over the bridge at Chester Creek, and beyond the village of Chester. Close to midnight the spent and weary commander in chief sternly reminded himself that he was a servant of the United States and responsible for the army of those states. He read a report for Congress prepared by an aide, which concluded, "Notwithstanding the misfortune of the day, I am happy to find the troops in good spirits," and added to it, "I hope another time we shall compensate for the losses now sustained."

In view of the unquestionable defeat along the Brandywine, this conclusion may seem too optimistic. Yet Washington, reviewing events in his mind, could find many vividly bright streaks across a somber picture. Sullivan's collapse had been due largely to the fact that his men had been too green to maneuver promptly enough to meet the unexpected British rush. Greene's march with the Virginians had been a minor epic, with "Joe Gourd" Weedon's leading brigade covering the four miles to Sullivan in 45 swift minutes and then going

A recruiting broadside for a Loyalist regiment, 1777

John Trumbull's sketch of General Anthony Wayne

into furious action. Regimental and brigade commanders had shown initiative and resourcefulness, and the young Marquis had gone ahead with Greene and Washington, plunging in among Sullivan's breaking troops in an effort to stem them, until a British bullet caught him in the thigh and put him out of action. The next day he was able to write his wife, "Dear Heart," that *messieurs les anglais . . . wounded me slightly in the leg, but it is nothing . . . for the ball did not touch bone or nerve."*

Another heartening point that passed unmarked, but may have been more important than anything else, was that Greene, a Rhode Islander, took a Virginia division into action while Wayne, a Pennsylvanian, held the left with New Jersey troops as well as men from his own state. The army had come a long, long way from 1775, when men roared in fury at the thought of being commanded by a man from another town.

Washington fell back toward Philadelphia while Howe tardily occupied Chester, fifteen short miles from that city. Congress, temporarily blind to the fact that it lay in the certain path of the next move, dallied, moved to Lancaster, and then made for the little town of York, which, to its uneasy surprise, found itself the *de facto* capital of the United States of America.

The army showed promptly that Washington's confidence in all ranks on the night of Brandywine was not misplaced. Howe swung to the west of Philadelphia, and at once what cavalry there was, now under General Casimir Pulaski, pushed out vigorously to meet him, with Generals Wayne and Maxwell pressing close behind with infantry. Solid contact was made with Hessian jägers and grenadiers, and an all-out fight loomed. Then a terrific storm broke on the sixteenth, its appalling cloudburst soaking powder and muskets. The terrain became a quagmire, and Hessian Major Baurmeister wrote that "we sank to our calves." The Americans suffered worse than the Hessians from this drenching, due to faultily made cartridge boxes that acted as miniature reservoirs, ruining most of the ammunition. "A most terrible stroke to us," Henry Knox wrote mournfully as he totted up the damage. So instead of more action there was a long march through the downpour, a series of wet encampments, until finally the supply base at Reading Furnace was reached and dried-out boxes refilled.

More American troubles boiled out of the fall air, for as Howe reached the Schuylkill one of his foraging parties blundered into a little-known spot called Valley Forge and gobbled up an unguarded American depot which held "3800 Barrels of Flour, Soap and Candles, 25 Barrels of Horse Shoes, several thousand tomahawks and Kettles and Intrenching Tools and 20 Hogsheads of Resin." To cap this loss of priceless matériel, the usually alert Anthony Wayne allowed himself to be trapped in bivouac near Paoli by a British force that swept down into his camp, using only the bayonet. Since this was a weapon that the Americans rightly feared and hated, there were cries of "Massacre" as hot as they were unjustified.

The Paoli debacle ended everything save indecisive maneuvering for the time being. By September 26, Washington had established a camp at Pennypacker's Mill (today's Schwenksville) on Perkiomen Creek, a confluent of the Schuylkill; and on that same day Lord Cornwallis led British and Hessian grenadiers into Philadelphia. The map maker Montresor saw them enter "amidst the acclamations of some thousands of the inhabitants," though he added the comment that the crowds were "mostly women and children." The rest of the Anglo-German force took up posts at Germantown.

William Howe had won another North American victory that could be well displayed in dispatches. Off parchment, it did not look so impressive. He had

Lafayette wounded at the Battle of Brandywine Creek

British satire on Howe's capture of Philadelphia

wasted weeks of fighting weather by keeping his formidable army wallowing at sea, out of action and powerless to influence the progress of Burgoyne's invasion from the north. He had captured Philadelphia, but this could have been accomplished by a quick move up the Delaware instead of the dreary, interminable course that he chose up the Chesapeake. And once again he had missed his main objective. Washington's army was still very much in being, as it had been after Long Island, after White Plains, and after the retreat through the Jerseys.

The loss of Philadelphia, capital of the new nation, was a staggering blow, yet its effects evaporated quickly and men began to look at each other in sheepish surprise. True, the chief American city was in enemy hands, but Congress was functioning in York, and the army lay undisturbed above Germantown. A more insidious line of thought cropped up as people considered that army. Was the right man really in command of it?

Civilians asked this question in undertones, and their worries were reflected in all ranks of Washington's force. Adjutant General Timothy Pickering, meeting Nathanael Greene, said, "Before I came to the army, I entertained an exalted opinion of General Washington's military talents, but I have since seen nothing to enhance it." The Rhode Islander, perhaps remembering the commander in chief's hesitation about evacuating Fort Washington in '76 (and forgetting that that position had been held largely on his own advice), agreed. "Why, the General does want decision," he said. It was far easier to recall past shortcomings than to dwell on the grim determination of the winter march through the Jerseys or the daring strokes at Trenton and Princeton.

Washington must surely have been aware of such rumblings; but calm and unshaken as ever, he now studied what he had to work with, counted swarms of incoming militia, and pondered the British positions about Germantown. At command-level meetings he began hammering home a new thesis—forget Brandywine; forget Paoli; don't live with past setbacks except to learn from them; and *attack*. Many of his generals listened slack-jawed with surprise, then began to nod agreement in growing confidence.

Germantown, core of the enemy's advanced strength, was a village of small houses and stone mansions strung along the main highway leading to Philadelphia. Washington's planned move against it was an ambitious one. A heavy column under John Sullivan was to strike straight down the Germantown Road, while a second, led by Nathanael Greene, broke in from the east, joining Sullivan at an obscure crossroads deep in the British-Hessian position. Perhaps this plan was too ambitious, better fitted for a force of seasoned, well-trained troops backed by flawless professional staff work. There were other drawbacks, for while the Germantown Road was wide and well surfaced, very few lateral roads cut into it. Thus Greene would be out of touch with the main body until he made contact with Sullivan at the spot where School House Lane and Luken's Mill Lane crossed the main thoroughfare. However, few, if any, high-level objections were made and there was little talk now of the General's lack of decision.

Seven P.M. on October 3, 1777, saw the attacking forces on the march, with nearly twenty miles to cover before contact could be made with the enemy. By three A.M. Washington and Sullivan were inside the British picket lines. As dawn approached, an autumn mist rose with the sun, wrapping the whole sloping countryside in a ghostly, glowing pall. At Mount Airy the first contact was made. British camps were overrun, sleepy grenadiers and light infantry staggering into formation were broken, obstinately re-formed, and were swept back in

By ORDER OF HIS EXCELLENCY
Sir William Howe, K. B.
General and Commander in Chief, &c. &c. &c.

PROCLAMATION.

I DO hereby give Notice to the Inhabitants of the City of Philadelphia and its Environs, it is the Order of His Excellency, that " No Perfon whatever, living " within the faid City and its Environs, fhall appear in " the Streets between the Beating of the Tattoo, at Half " an Hour after Eight o'Clock in the Evening, and the " Revellie in the Morning, without Lanthorns: And all " who fhall be found abroad, within the Time aforefaid, " will be liable to be examined by the Patroles, and con- " fined, unlefs they fhall give a fatisfactory Account of " themfelves." And I do hereby enjoin and require the Inhabitants, and all others refiding in the faid City and its Environs, to pay ftrict Obedience to the faid Order, and govern themfelves accordingly.

Given under my Hand at Philadelphia, this 9th Day of January, in the Eighteenth Year of His Majefty's Reign.   JOS. GALLOWAY,
Superintendent-General.

Proclamation ordering a curfew in British-occupied Philadelphia

the yelling, stabbing onrush. The American striking force surged ahead, suddenly buoyant with the elixir of seldom-tasted victory. Musketry banged and crackled, adding its smoke to the sticky dawn mists.

British drums began echoing out the call to retreat, and William Howe, riding out from Philadelphia, found himself caught up in a recoiling swirl of scarlet coats and beat about him with his sword, roaring, "For shame, Light Infantry! . . . it's only a scouting party." Then masses of Americans, gunners manhandling fieldpieces out in front, loomed through the smoke and fog, and blasted off a hot hail of grapeshot. A British officer remembered that cannonade as well as Howe's "For shame," and wrote, "I never saw people enjoy a charge of grape before, but we really all felt pleased . . . to hear the grape rattle about the commander in chief's ears after he had accused the battalion of running away from a scouting party."

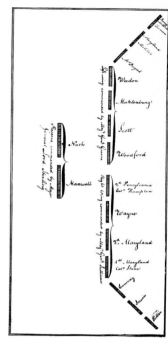

The American plan of battle at Germantown shows the divisions of Greene and Sullivan leading, with Stirling in reserve

But the sands of the American attack were running out. At the east of the Broad, the great house of Benjamin Chew, looking very much then as it does today, seemed to shoulder up through the mists like a haunted castle. Six companies of the 40th Regiment barricaded themselves behind its thick walls and fired on all passing Americans. Scotch Willie Maxwell's Jerseymen tried to clean them out, were repulsed, began sniping at the windows instead of pushing on to join the rest of Sullivan's command that was striking heavier opposition each moment. Timothy Pickering, who had been narrowly missed by a bullet, found Washington and several other generals in a nearby field, pondering the problem of the impromptu stone fort. The logical move would have been to detach a small force to contain the defenders and push all other men as far forward as possible. But Henry Knox, most deeply read militarily of all those present, dug back into his well-stored mind for precedent and came up with a fatal answer. According to Pickering, the former bookseller said, "It would be unmilitary to leave a castle in our rear." So more infantry was thrown against the house. Fieldpieces were brought up and maintained a useless fire that might have turned the scales had it been employed in another part of the field. In the southern meadows American ammunition was beginning to run low. Militia units fired on each other in the persistent fog and fled, their panic spreading to other units. Commands falling back to draw more ammunition found their movement to the rear an irresistible impulse, began to break and run. Sullivan's force, victorious up to now, was falling apart about him. A seventeen-year-old Massachusetts veteran, Private Joseph Martin, noted a simultaneous stiffening of British resistance and shrewdly attributed it to the enemy having heard Americans calling to one another that they were out of ammunition.

Off to the east, Nathanael Greene was moving, but he was late, due to a gross staff miscalculation of the distance his men must cover in their curving march. When the column finally came into action, Adam Stephen's command collided with masses of unknown infantry in the mist, and both groups opened fire before Stephen discovered that his opponents were Anthony Wayne's men. Then fresh British troops struck Greene's columns, spent by their unnecessarily long march into action. There was blind fighting in smoke and mist. Greene lost some guns, and then fell back in reasonably good order, covered by Casimir Pulaski's raw cavalrymen.

American assault on the Chew house

Off to the west, the men in John Sullivan's command were grudgingly leaving the field that they had come so close to winning. "The enemy kept a civil distance behind, sending every now and then a shot after us and receiving the same from us," soldier-pamphleteer Thomas Paine wrote some time later.

It is possible that many of the marchers would have welcomed stronger enemy action, if only for the chance it would have given to stop and face about. For new march orders had come down to these men who had plodded sixteen to twenty miles to fight an action that had ended in exasperation and disillusionment. Now they learned that they would not return to their starting point, but instead push on to their old camps about Pennypacker's Mill, 24 miles away. The Delaware Continentals were a tough, enduring lot of men, but even they acknowledged that the day had been a trying one. Once at the Mill, Captain Enoch Anderson wrote, "Here we old soldiers had marched forty miles. We eat nothing and drank nothing but water on the tour."

The cost of October 4 had been heavy. American casualties in all grades totaled about 1,000 men, with General Francis Nash, who had brought on his hard-fighting North Carolinians, among the dead. Yet, as the Iron Duke was to say of Waterloo, "It was a damned close-run thing." All ranks knew that they had come close to victory. On a far larger scale than at the Hollow Way, they had smashed hard into highly capable, seasoned British and German formations, had seen them break into flight or throw down their arms, beaten for the moment. Soldiers' tales of the day drifted back into the various states, and soon civilians, too, were saying, "Maybe *next* time . . ."

Other eyes took note of this strange fight. "Eminent [foreign] generals and statesmen," wrote British historian Sir George Otto Trevelyan, "were profoundly impressed . . . that a new army, raised within the year and undaunted by a series of recent disasters, had assailed a victorious enemy in its own quarters and had only been repulsed after a sharp and dubious conflict." Particular attention was paid to the events of October 4 in Paris, where Benjamin Franklin pointed out to Foreign Minister Charles Gravier, Comte de Vergennes, that the American army had a most astonishing way of bouncing back, alert and dangerous, after each flooring. All in all, the Battle of Germantown was a substantial rung in the ladder of world opinion up which the United States of America was slowly climbing.

Sir William Howe was either too much or too little impressed by the sudden American onsurge, and made no serious effort to hit Washington's army, which, from its very presence, interfered with the overland flow of supplies into captured Philadelphia. Turning his attention to freeing the sea route to that city, he flung relatively heavy forces against two little American strong points that blocked the approaches in the lower Delaware River—Fort Mifflin just above Hog Island, and Fort Mercer, near Red Bank on the Jersey shore. Colonel Christopher Greene, ably seconded at Fort Mercer by a young French engineer, the Chevalier de Mauduit du Plessis, smashed a powerful Hessian attack. Out in flimsy Fort Mifflin, Colonel Samuel Smith, late of Smallwood's Marylanders, and Major Simeon Thayer of Rhode Island endured, with their men, terrific bombardments from ship and shore, holding out until November 15, when they slipped across to Mercer under cover of darkness. Soon afterwards, Greene and du Plessis abandoned that fort and struck overland for Washington's army. The Delaware was now British from Philadelphia to the sea, but one entire and irreplaceable month had been dribbled away by Howe, and his generals could reflect glumly that two small American commands in amateur fortifications had proved extremely tough.

Like the army, the Congress of the United States of America had also managed to keep together through the year 1777. Quite comfortably lodged in the town of York, it held its meetings and dreamed ambitious plans. Month by

American print of two Royal Navy ships attempting to clear the Delaware River in 1777

month it struggled along through the inevitable fogbanks of human frailties and errors, never quite sure what its powers were, perpetually irritated by the exasperating cantankerousness with which, at one time or another, each of the Thirteen States mocked at the efforts and decrees of its own elected representatives.

And yet in this dark year one vital step was cleanly accomplished. Since the very beginning there had been no definition of just what this "new nation" of which men spoke really was. Was it a mere loose league of individual states, or a leagued state?

In the stirring early summer of '76, Richard Henry Lee of Virginia had boldly asked that question, and state-minded men from each of the Thirteen had exploded in hot anger. Even to think about the problem was to exceed by far any delegated powers. Lee held firm, and moved that "a plan of confederation be prepared and transmitted to the respective Colonies for their consideration and approbation." Against heavy opposition, Farmer John Dickinson and others were named to a committee to prepare "Articles of Confederation and Perpetual Union."

On November 15, the very day that Major Thayer was planning his successful withdrawal from the mudbanks of Fort Mifflin, the Articles of Confederation were finally adopted and sent on to the various states for "consideration and approbation," a process which was to drag on until spring of 1781. The Articles were makeshift. They dodged issue after issue, leaving the Congress of the United States of America almost entirely dependent on the collective wishes of the states. In fact, Congress was authorized to call on the states for whatever was thought necessary, and the states, collectively and individually, were empowered to refuse if they saw fit. Yet the concept of "Perpetual Union" was definitely embodied in the Articles, and from them, weak and unworkable as they were, was eventually to come the Constitution of the United States, that instrument of unity that was to bend under innumerable unguessed and unforeseen strains down to the present—bend, only to spring back once more.

As the last days of November, 1777, trickled away, most of the delegates to the Congress of the United States packed up and left for their homes, a move that a good part of the army of the United States would have been happy to follow. Numerically, Washington's command, now at Whitemarsh, was nearly 11,000 strong, with Continentals heavily predominating. A great American victory over Burgoyne had been won in the north, and down into Pennsylvania trooped seasoned units like James Varnum's brigade, John Glover's, John Paterson's, as well as Daniel Morgan's riflemen.

This strength was largely illusory, since each day's reveille brought thousands of men closer to the expiration of their time. Constant campaigning had gnawed at the equipment of every soldier, and tattered clothes were patched and patched again. Blankets were scarce, shoes more so. Rare as hard money was, the commander in chief offered a reward of ten dollars *in coin* for a "substitute for shoes, made of raw hides." Individual states were helping, but not intelligently. Governor Patrick Henry of Virginia sent a load of clothing, not for general distribution but for his state troops alone, and most other states acted as narrowly, if at all.

Food could have been plentiful but its flow was cut off by poor transportation arrangements and a civilian tendency to hoard. Lieutenant Colonel Henry Dearborn wrote resignedly: "This is Thanksgiving Day . . . but God knows we have very little to keep it with, this being the third day we have been without

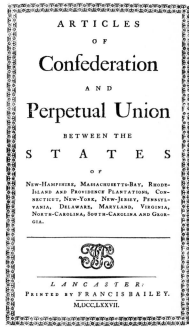

ARTICLES
OF
Confederation
AND
Perpetual Union
BETWEEN THE
STATES
OF
NEW-HAMPSHIRE, MASSACHUSETTS-BAY, RHODE-ISLAND AND PROVIDENCE PLANTATIONS, CONNECTICUT, NEW-YORK, NEW-JERSEY, PENNSYLVANIA, DELAWARE, MARYLAND, VIRGINIA, NORTH-CAROLINA, SOUTH-CAROLINA AND GEORGIA.

LANCASTER:
PRINTED BY FRANCIS BAILEY.
M,DCC,LXXVII.

The title page of the Articles of Confederation, published in 1777

"There was a Continental Thanksgiving ordered by Congress . . . our country, ever mindful of its suffering army, opened her sympathizing heart so wide upon this occasion as to give . . . each and every man half a gill of rice and a tablespoon full of vinegar!"
—*Private Joseph Martin, 1777*

Troops at Valley Forge

flour or bread . . . Upon the whole I think all we have to be thankful for is that we . . . are not in the grave with many of our friends."

Too weak to mount an attack, too wise to count on Howe's lethargy, Washington decided to move out of reach of any sudden Anglo-German coup. His selection of a site for winter quarters could hardly be termed ideal, but pressure, civilian as well as military, narrowed his field of choice, forcing a compromise.

Twenty-odd miles to the west and a little north of Philadelphia, the placid Schuylkill is joined on its eastward course by Valley Creek flowing up from the south. At the junction of the two streams the ground east of the creek rises swiftly to a 250-foot crest, then straightens out into a rolling two-mile plateau. There was little to mark this terrain on a map, just a ford across the Schuylkill known as Fatland, or Fatlands—and an old forge on the ravine-like creek that travelers called the Valley Forge.

Toward this plateau the main army of the United States headed in December, as the air sharpened and powdery snow began to sift through pine and oak limbs. It was a bare thirteen miles, if that, from the Whitemarsh camps, but more than a week was spent in covering them. Baggage wagons went astray. Snow thickened, became stinging sleet, softened into pelting rain. The freeze came swiftly and the wretched, boggy roads stiffened into knife-ruts that slashed at rag-bound feet. Washington said "you might have tracked the army . . . to Valley Forge by the blood of their feet."

The main column reached the plateau on the afternoon of December 19, and exhausted, chilled men lurched to their camp sites and lighted fires. For rations they had only what they might scrape out of their haversacks, and soon even the fires became a menace, for all their cheerful glow. Broken boots dried too quickly, cracked and split. Foot-wrappings charred and fell away from bruised, bleeding soles. Nothing very much happened in the Valley Forge lines. Men simply set their teeth and stayed alive, and thus kept alive the army that was the active expression of their cause, quite unaware of the deep glory of what they did. Theirs is an old story, told and retold, but as historian Christopher Ward wrote, "Not once too often."

Winter could not be faced in tents, and on the very first day orders went out to build huts to a prescribed pattern. Short of tools and nails, weakened men forced themselves into the woods, felled trees, split out boards, kneaded clay to plug up wall-chinks. Street by street a hut-city slowly rose, until at last the commander in chief felt free to quit his own leaky tent and move into the gray field-stone Isaac Potts house close by the junction of creek and river, a step which he had sternly refused to take as long as his men were under canvas.

Food began to trickle into Valley Forge. The flow dried up, appeared again, stopped, in a frightening pattern that was a nightmare for every man in authority. Soap was as rare as meat and flour, and bruised feet and chapped hands festered. Dirty rags brought on an itch that only soap and water could cure. Drafty huts, sunless and damp inside, were powerful allies of sickness and infection. Surgeon Albigence Waldo of the 1st Connecticut, who had been in the field since '75, was shocked by what he saw. "There comes a Soldier, his bare feet are seen thro' his worn-out shoes, his legs nearly naked from the tattered remains of an only pair of stockings, his Breeches not sufficient to cover his nakedness . . . his whole appearance pictures a person forsaken & discouraged. He . . . crys . . . I am Sick, my feet lame, my legs are sore, my body covered with this tormenting Itch."

There was even a shortage of water on the plateau, and some units had to send men on a two-mile round trip to fill heavy buckets at the creek and lug

GEORGE WASHINGTON, Esquire,
GENERAL and COMMANDER in CHIEF of the Forces of the United States of America.

BY Virtue of the Power and Direction to Me especially given, I hereby enjoin and require all Persons residing within seventy Miles of my Head Quarters to thresh one Half of their Grain by the 1st Day of February, and the other Half by the 1st Day of March next ensuing, on Pain, in Case of Failure, of having all that shall remain in Sheaves after the Period above mentioned, seized by the Commissaries and Quarter-Masters of the Army, and paid for as Straw.

GIVEN under my Hand, at Head Quarters, near the Valley Forge, in Philadelphia County, this 20th Day of December, 1777.

G. WASHINGTON.

By His Excellency's Command,
ROBERT H. HARRISON, Sec'y.

LANCASTER, Printed by JOHN DUNLAP.

Washington requisitioned supplies at Valley Forge, 1777

them back. Clothing went fast. Officers mounted guard in old padded dressing gowns or in blankets slung poncho-wise. Money was of little use. Wealthy Colonel John Laurens of South Carolina helplessly watched his last pair of breeches crumble about him, and Surgeon Waldo took darning lessons from a brother officer. The men were worse off. A guard was seen standing his post properly and presenting arms while standing on his hat to keep his bare feet out of the snow.

Yet the army still held together, to the utter astonishment of the numerous foreign officers now attached to or serving in it. No troops that they had known, they declared, could or would have kept the field under such conditions. In late February the commander in chief rode out some miles along the York Pike to meet still another foreign officer whose letters to the Congress and to himself had agreeably startled him by their modesty and repudiation of rank. On that rutted road the Virginian met Baron Friedrich Wilhelm Ludolf Gerhard Augustin von Steuben, late of the armies of Frederick the Great of Prussia, and the oddly assorted pair took to each other at once.

Von Steuben's military background was by no means as exalted as his dossier made out. Actually he was a half-pay Captain, not Lieutenant General as set forth in his record. More, he had been a good fourteen years out of work when he first met Benjamin Franklin in Paris. But Franklin had sized him up at once as a valuable man, connived at—if he did not actually prepare—the von Steuben dossier, as a means of impressing Congress, and packed him off to America. In this benevolent deception Franklin probably performed his greatest service to the American army.

The Prussian, not wanting a fixed command, at once flung himself into the seemingly hopeless task of making fighting formations out of Washington's regiments. He spoke some French, very little English, and was forced to rely on the services of his secretary, the Frenchman Pierre Duponceau, Colonel John Laurens, or Lieutenant Colonel Alexander Hamilton to translate his ideas from German to French to English. But by some magic of his own he managed to establish an immediate entente with the hungry, ragged, sick men who reported to him for drill.

Beginning with small groups, the indefatigable Baron toiled from sunrise to sunset and later, beginning with what would now be called the School of the Soldier. He corrected such details as the placing of men's feet at attention, simplified the manual of arms, smoothed out such elementary moves as right-face and left-face. When his first group of control guinea pigs suited him, he sent them back to their commands to spread his teachings, and began on another lot. Soon he progressed from squad to platoon to company to regiment, and then on to whole brigades and divisions, until heavy masses could maneuver smoothly and in unison. A new American army was born on the bleak plateau of Valley Forge.

From the army's standpoint, the commander in chief made another appointment nearly as important. Thomas Mifflin having retired as Quartermaster General, Washington named Nathanael Greene as successor. Greene, whose first love was service with troops, protested long and loud, then threw himself into the work wholeheartedly. Limping about the countryside on endless, wearing searches, he uncovered great caches of abandoned and forgotten matériel, and had them lugged back to the great camp on the Valley Forge plateau.

On top of such windfalls, the food problem was providentially eased by an unusually early and heavy run of shad up the Schuylkill past Sullivan's lines.

Inspector General von Steuben

"With regard to military discipline, I may safely say no such thing existed. . . . The formation of the regiments was as varied as their mode of drill, which consisted only of the manual exercise."
—Baron von Steuben, 1778

With the first warning ripples of crowded fins breaking the surface, men plunged into the river armed with pitchforks, shovels, baskets, and broken branches to heave the squirming fish onto the soggy banks. Other details rushed up barrels and salt to store away the ever-increasing surplus. When it seemed likely that the run would sweep out of reach upstream, Major Henry Lee's Virginia dragoons charged into the river and milled their horses about. The rush was checked, and a long stretch of the Schuylkill became a seething mass of shad, an inexhaustible supply depot that writhed and jumped and twisted. There were tons of fresh fish to eat, tons more to be salted down against possible lean weeks ahead.

The ultramasculine severity of the camps was softened when Martha Washington, always a gallant campaigner, came up from Mount Vernon and threw herself into army life. The dank hospitals knew the memory of her warm smile and her words that somehow touched every man in the stark wards. A small *salon* grew in a flimsy addition to the crowded Potts house to which the officers flocked. Huge Baron de Kalb might be seen bowing beside John Sullivan, Gimat with Anthony Wayne, and the flamboyant Pulaski waiting his chance to speak along with Alexander Hamilton. Colonel Elias Boudinot of New Jersey thought the first lady of the army was "almost in a mope for want of a female companion" and wrote Mrs. Boudinot to come at once. Later Lady Stirling appeared, then Lucy Knox and Kitty Greene, the last being a magnet for lonely foreign officers as she accomplished the difficult feat of turning a respectable stock of textbook French into passable conversation.

To offset this tranquilizing influence, two men with a talent for starting nerve-rasping discord under the calmest of conditions came into camp. Benedict Arnold reported, still semi-invalid from his wound received fighting against Burgoyne, and at once drew a terse rebuke from Washington for attempting a rather lavish banquet, drawn from army stores, for a select guest-list of twenty. Few accepted Arnold's invitation and it was noted that many officers who had served under him in Canada were markedly cold toward him.

In Major General Arnold's wake stalked gaunt, ugly Charles Lee, recently exchanged after his '76 capture. Lee was unchanged. Disregarding the visible results of von Steuben's training, he disparaged everything he saw and produced plans for "The Formation of the American Army," since "I understand it better than almost any man living." He hoped, too, that he should stand "well with General Washington . . . I am persuaded . . . that he cannot do without me." On top of this he broached the rather startling theory that American troops could never defeat British troops, no matter what the circumstances, and in a final flourish, confided to Elias Boudinot that Washington was not fit to command a sergeant's guard.

It was May 5, 1778, and the slanting rays of the sun were spanning the deep slash of Valley Creek to light up the plateau whose regular lines of huts and tents looked almost pastoral against the soft green of the coming summer. In all headquarters, duty officers were reaching for quill, ink, and sand as they stared at the new order that had just come in from the commander in chief to be entered in all orderly books. Dozens of nibs traced out the words: "General After Orders. 6 o'clock—P.M.—It having pleased the Almighty Ruler of the Universe propitiously to defend the cause of the United States of America and finally by raising us up a powerful friend, among the Princes of the Earth . . ."

Captains and subalterns could well stare as they copied the text, for it was the prelude to a staggering announcement. Encouraged by the defeat of Bur-

Martha Washington, by Peale

A French print showing Washington with a copy of the Alliance in his hand

goyne, further heartened by the display of strength and morale at Germantown, France had declared itself an ally of the United States of America. French funds and supplies would now be available in generous quantities and the subterfuge firm of Hortalez et Cie could be liquidated. More than this, the French army and navy were to co-operate wholeheartedly.

It cannot be said that joy over this announcement was universal. Many men felt that France would intervene principally to damage Britain, and then try to establish a French North American empire, reaching from the Arctic to the Gulf of Mexico. Older Americans had bitter memories of French officers leading murderous raids against the frontiers in earlier days. Bigots cursed any alliance with a Catholic power. Few seem to have grasped the fact that the entry of France into hostilities would inevitably turn what had begun as a struggle between England and a group of its colonies into about as complete a World War as the times permitted.

Sir Henry Clinton, who had most reluctantly taken Howe's place as commander of all British forces in North America, was made immediately aware of the altered scope of the war. Orders from London, received almost as soon as he installed himself in Philadelphia, directed him to send 5,000 men to the West Indies for an immediate attack on French St. Lucia, and another 3,000 to St. Augustine in Florida. He was to embark his Philadelphia command for New York, and North America was to be, for the time being, a relatively minor theater.

The evacuation orders posed a very awkward problem for Sir Henry. Not only was shipping woefully short, but he also had to think of the thousands of Tory civilians who had flocked to Philadelphia during the tinsel-gaudy days of the occupation, just as Howe had had the Boston Tories on his mind in '76. Clinton states that he had no intelligence from England of any French naval forces moving toward North America, but he was shrewd enough to reason that, with the new Alliance, hostile warships might appear in the waters between New York and Philadelphia at any time. Hence he did not dare transport soldiers and civilians in time-consuming installments by water.

Ships of the line of French Admiral d'Estaing's squadron

With a sureness of decision that was too often lacking in him, he issued firm orders. Available shipping would be used for the Tories, sick and wounded troops, and such heavy matériel as could be crowded on board. As for the army, it would march overland through the eastern fringes of New Jersey to Sandy Hook. This could be a highly dangerous operation, since it would present the flank of his long columns, encumbered by innumerable heavy wagons, to an American attack sweeping in from the west. And Washington now enjoyed a numerical superiority in addition to the initiative.

At three in the morning of June 18, 1778, Clinton began to cross the Delaware, and in seven hours had his command on Jersey soil, ready for its long, exposed march.

Up in the gray stone Potts house by the Schuylkill, intelligence of a move by Clinton was known as early as June 1, and Washington was soon presented with a commander's dream, the chance of hitting a strung-out enemy from the flank with a strong, compact force. The situation obviously called for action, since existing roads sharply limited the course that the Anglo-German retreat must follow. According to his custom, Washington called councils of war (which the irreverent Alexander Hamilton likened to a gaggle of midwives), apparently not noting that one of the chief stumbling blocks to decision was prickly professional Charles Lee, to whom many of the amateur generals still deferred. This seasoned expert announced that he was "passionately opposed"

General Charles Lee

to an attack on Clinton. Was anyone naïve enough to dream that mere Americans could stand up to British regulars? The thing to do, as Lee preached constantly, was to sit tight at Valley Forge and see what happened.

Lee's pessimism infected many senior officers as well as juniors. Then, at one meeting, Washington asked the opinion of a handsome and very junior Brigadier, and at once struck sparks. Anthony Wayne's answer was hot and terse. "Fight, sir!" he snapped. Nathanael Greene, Lafayette, and John Cadwalader closed ranks at once with Wayne. But they were a minority of four, and discussions dragged on while Clinton's army made its crossing of the Delaware into New Jersey and the chance of striking it while split by that river was gone forever.

Meanwhile the Anglo-Germans were facing a killing march. The weather turned tropical, with savage downpours. Innumerable bridges over ravines and creeks had been broken down by American militia, and vital hours and days were swallowed up in repairs, for there were no less than 1,500 wagons to jolt and jar along with the columns. Under these circumstances the rate of march was often less than six miles per day.

When Philemon Dickinson's Jersey militia and Daniel Morgan's riflemen appeared on his flanks, Clinton had no way of knowing that these troops were merely for observation, or that cloying deference to Charles Lee's professional background was still keeping the main American army anchored at Valley Forge. Not until June 23 did Washington finally shake off the hypnosis of Lee's prestige and shift the bulk of his command across the Delaware at Coryell's Ferry. By the twenty-fifth, he was angling sharply down through Rocky Hill and Kingston, his mind fully made up to launch a strong blow against Clinton's rear. Already Generals Charles Scott and William Maxwell were close to the British line of march with Dickinson and Morgan. Promptly Washington backed them with Anthony Wayne and Enoch Poor's New Hampshire brigade.

Then came the question of over-all control of the striking force. Military etiquette, all powerful in those days, decreed that it must go to Charles Lee, second only to Washington in the tables of organization. For a moment the gods smiled on the American army, and Lee scorned the assignment as not important enough for him. Vastly relieved, Washington detailed Lafayette to the command, and the young Frenchman and Wayne moved out briskly. Then the gods stopped smiling.

Finding that the command now included some 6,000 men, Lee suddenly began to storm and shout that the job belonged to him and he wanted it. Washington reversed himself and assigned the command to Lee, who went galloping off to the American camp at Englishtown and took over from Lafayette. Enthusiasm, youth, and devotion were supplanted by sour defeatism. Lee issued no orders and fobbed off his subordinate commanders with evasive answers all through the night of June 27, despite the fact that his command could clearly hear the rumble of heavy wagons moving north out of reach beyond Monmouth Court House. Dawn of the twenty-eighth brought no change, even when Philemon Dickinson reported that he was engaged with a force that seemed to be falling back. Actually, Dickinson and his Jersey militiamen had struck the very cream of the enemy—three fine brigades of British infantry, two heavy battalions of British grenadiers, all the Hessian grenadiers, the Coldstream Guards, two battalions of British light infantry, the 16th Dragoons, and Colonel John Simcoe's excellent Tory light cavalry, the Queen's Rangers. Characteristically, Lee made no move to extricate Dickinson from trouble.

Providentially, orders snapped down from Washington. General Charles Lee was to attack at once. The rest of the American army was moving up to his support. So at last Lee's fifes and drums shrilled and muttered and the American Advance Corps began to move. Underestimating the number of men ahead of him, Lee told Wayne to take 600 Pennsylvanians and two fieldpieces and strike the British rear. Anthony Wayne, handsome and eager, drove ahead, smashed through some loose formations, hit unexpected strength, and wisely took position at the edge of a long, swampy ravine and sent back to Lee for support. With that message, the last coherent move of Lee's force evaporated into the sweltering air of June 28, 1778.

Charles Lee, self-acknowledged master of the art of war, scattered his command over the broken terrain as though spilling torn paper from a sack, and then apparently forgot about it. No orders reached the firing line where Clinton increased the pressure against Wayne. Behind Wayne, regiments and brigades marched and countermarched aimlessly, undirected. Units improvised, advanced, retired in accordance with what a commander could see or guess of the immediate situation. Lafayette, still cheerfully in action, although without troops, urged a general advance all along the line and received Lee's chilling reply: "Sir, you do not know British soldiers. We cannot stand against them."

Out at the swampy ravine, Wayne's men, now backed by Scott's Virginians, fought on doggedly, fully expecting an answer to Wayne's plea to Lee. Instead, out of the smoke the busbied Queen's Rangers pounded down on them in a wild charge, followed by the 16th Dragoons. At Chatterton's Hill near White Plains, the rush of a few cavalrymen had been enough to stampede an American brigade. Now the Steuben-trained men under Wayne and Richard Butler and Scott stood firm, fired steady volleys, and then dashed in among the troopers with the bayonet. The roles were reversed, and Sir Henry wrote that his horsemen had "to retreat with precipitation upon our infantry." Wayne gathered his men, re-formed them, and tried to link up with American units that he was sure *must* be on his right and left.

There was no one on Wayne's right or his left. Lee, without notifying any save the units nearest him, had ordered a general retreat, leaving Wayne and the others stranded. Somehow, the young Pennsylvanian managed to get his men and their supporting guns off the field.

The course of this retreat lay along the Englishtown Road that ran on through the low hills, cut by more swampy ravines. Some units moved back in good order, while others broke in unmistakable panic. Added to the unexplained turn of affairs, the weather was fiercely hot now, reaching a good hundred degrees. Officers and men began to collapse among the heat waves that shimmered over the sticky grass, increasing the general confusion.

Then someone noticed a dust cloud coming up from Englishtown, and men stopped in their tracks to stare at a man in sweat-stained blue and buff on a huge white horse. Among the starers was a young, red-haired Frenchman whose sloping forehead streamed perspiration. The Marquis de Lafayette never forgot that sight. Washington's "presence stopped the retreat . . . his calm courage . . . gave him the air best calculated to excite enthusiasm." Over and over the Marquis told how Washington rode "all along the lines amid the shouts of the soldiers, cheering them by his voice and example and restoring to our standard the fortunes of the fight. I thought then, as now, that never had I beheld so superb a man." Somewhere en route Washington encountered Charles Lee, sent him to the rear, and took over full command himself, this

Washington (right) relieving Lee of command at the Battle of Monmouth

"It is not a field of a few acres of ground, but a cause, that we are defending . . ."
—*Thomas Paine, 1778*

brief meeting leading to Lee's court-martial and ending his further participation in the war.

George Washington undoubtedly made errors as a general. But this day as a leader he was close to flawless. Without a touch of the theatrical, he had only to show his unshakable courage, his matchless integrity and devotion, and their combined alchemy fired men from New Hampshire and Rhode Island, New Jersey and Virginia, Delaware and North Carolina, and made them one with him and his strength and his convictions.

But the chance of a major coup had been lost by Charles Lee's failure, and the rest of the day slammed and crashed out its course as British and Hessian counterattacks thundered down on the re-forming American lines. Wayne was in action again, with Stewart's Pennsylvanians and Ramsay's 3rd Marylanders. Up came Varnum's Rhode Islanders and Henry Livingston's 4th New Yorkers, with Virginians and more Pennsylvanians. Nathanael Greene swung his division in on the right, and Lieutenant Colonel Edward Carrington of Virginia brought up his guns across Wemrock Brook to enfilade a sweep against Wayne. Von Steuben, watching, saw all this reshuffling under deadly pressure and thought that his trainees moved up "with as much precision as on ordinary parade and with the . . . intrepidity of veteran troops."

Hard and firm as any troops on the field, the exhausted British pushed their counterattack relentlessly. There were the 42nd Black Watch, light infantry, grenadiers, and the Guards. The 37th Hampshires and the 44th Essex regiments and the dragoons were in, driving and smashing alongside the towering helmets of the Hessian grenadiers. Scarlet coats and blue littered the trampled grass, struck down by the heat as often as by American bullets. As the British came on, superbly unflinching, their morale must have suffered at the sight of American units advancing, shifting ground, sideslipping, falling back with a precision and effectiveness that they could not have shown prior to the advent of von Steuben.

Late afternoon ended the action, with Clinton withdrawing in good order after a last wild and vain fling at Wayne's line by a magnificent grenadier battalion under Lieutenant Colonel Henry Monckton, whose dead body fell at the very feet of Wayne's panting, staggering men. Washington combed the field for troops fresh enough for a counterattack of his own, found Woodford's Virginians and Thomas Clark's North Carolinians, and issued orders. But the word "fresh" is relative. Woodford's men and Clark's were steady and willing, but dark fell before they could be committed.

During the night Clinton continued his retreat, satisfied that he had saved his immense wagon train that was now far along on its way to Sandy Hook and an easy crossing to Manhattan and Staten Island. The American commander in chief disposed his force for the night in the fields. His immediate task finished, he found a tall man in blue and buff, smoke-blackened, asleep without cloak or blanket under an apple tree. The master of Mount Vernon then lay down under that same tree, spreading his own cloak over himself and the exhausted Marquis de Lafayette.

Monmouth may be called a drawn battle, since the Americans held the blood- and sweat-soaked terrain, or a British defensive victory, since Sir Henry accomplished his purpose of getting army and baggage safely to Sandy Hook. Stalemate or victory, that twenty-eighth of June, 1778, marked the last time that the two main contending armies were to meet in the field. For the rest of the war, all the fighting would be carried out by subordinate armies or by detachments from them.

"The victory of that day turns out to be much more considerable than at first expected . . . Tell the Philadelphia ladies that the heavenly, sweet, pretty redcoats, the accomplished gentlemen of the Guards and Grenadiers have humbled themselves on the plains of Monmouth."
—General Anthony Wayne to Richard Peters, July 12, 1778

The surprise night attack on Anthony Wayne's division at Paoli, near Philadelphia, was a virtual slaughter. Here the British troops, using only their bayonets, inflicted over 150 casualties, while losing less than 10 men.

Howe Moves Against Philadelphia

By spring of 1777, General William Howe had completed plans for what was to be his last attempt to put down the rebellion. Apparently he assumed that Burgoyne's invasion from Canada could reach Albany unaided while he took "the rebel capital" at Philadelphia and subdued Washington's army. After that, presumably, there would be time to join Burgoyne in Albany. When his opening maneuvers in New Jersey failed to lure Washington into battle, Howe drew back to New York, embarked over 15,000 men in a huge fleet of 260 ships, and headed out to sea. This "strange coasting voyage" consumed a month of summer campaigning time, and when Howe finally landed at the northern tip of Chesapeake Bay, fifty miles from Philadelphia, Washington lay in wait blocking his path to the city.

The ensuing fight at Brandywine Creek on September 11 was, like Long Island, an example of Howe's favorite flanking technique, and resulted in a decisive victory. But unlike Long Island, it found his enemy still ready and able to fight again. Howe followed with a bloody surprise attack on Anthony Wayne at Paoli, and then sent Cornwallis into Philadelphia. It was an uneasy conquest, however, for Washington's army lay nearby, menacing and dangerous. Another fight would be necessary before Philadelphia was secure, and meantime, Burgoyne was still thirty miles from Albany and—without the expected help from Howe—in serious danger.

225

The Battle of Germantown

"Mad" Anthony Wayne (above), along with John Sullivan, led the drive on the center of the British line.

At right is the attack by Wayne's and Sullivan's troops, shown in the background advancing on both sides of the main Germantown road. Some 120 redcoats took refuge in the Chew house (actually more imposing than shown here), and the Rebels wasted an hour trying to rout them out. This painting, and that of the Paoli action, page 225, were done by artist Xavier Della Gatta in 1782, probably for a British officer who witnessed the engagements.

The battle fought in the village of Germantown, five miles from Philadelphia, must be classed as one of the Revolution's most important actions. Here, for the first time in three years of war, Washington felt ready to risk a major offensive against the main British army. Washington's battle plan of October 4, which called for a huge pincers-movement, was probably too complex; and a "most horrid fog" that settled over the field made co-ordination between his four attacking columns all the more difficult. His soldiers did not lack resolution, however. Wayne's men, in particular, smarting from their mauling at Paoli, were in a vicious mood, and these troops, with those of Greene and Sullivan, overran a sizable number of the enemy.

For a moment "Trophies lay at our feet," as General Weedon described it, then suddenly everything came unstitched. Two American columns collided

in the blinding fog and fired on each other; one element wasted precious time trying to reduce the fortress-like Chew mansion instead of bypassing it; and a British counterattack caught many Rebels out of ammunition. Once the American assault had spent its force, the men were compelled to withdraw, but "nobody hurried." This amateur army, with all its ragged staff work and poor liaison, had nearly won the field.

Most of the soldiers could agree with Weedon, who wrote: "Though the enterprise miscarried, it was worth the undertaking." Washington noted that his men "behaved with a degree of gallantry that did them the highest honor." He had discovered that "the enemy are not proof against a vigorous attack, and may be put to flight when boldly pushed." This fact was also observed by the French, who were considering intervention in the war.

The Hard Lesson

Howe received a gaudy farewell from his officers in Philadelphia, the largest party of its kind ever seen in America. Called the Mischianza, its theme was "a fantastic exhibition of sham chivalry"

The Howe brothers' inactivity in Philadelphia inspired the widely circulated satire below. The Admiral's flagship Eagle (background) is abandoned as he and the General drowse over a punch bowl. The cow of British commerce is milked dry by France, Spain, and Holland while America removes its horns. A distraught Englishman at right cannot rouse the British lion.

Undaunted by the Germantown repulse, Washington virtually blockaded the British in Philadelphia, forcing Howe to call on the Royal Navy for help in opening the Delaware to supply ships. At length the stubbornly held American forts along the river were taken—but at the cost of one 64-gun ship, one sloop, and three badly cut-up battalions of crack Hessian grenadiers. Then Howe settled comfortably in Philadelphia to wait for spring. The winter, however, brought him bad news. Burgoyne's army was captured, and worse, France, with its fine army and growing navy, had declared for America.

In May, Howe was relieved by Sir Henry Clinton, who was informed by Cornwallis that he faced "a situation which, I fear, you will not find a bed of roses." Ordered to send 5,000 troops to the West Indies and withdraw to New York, Clinton could do little more than conduct a holding operation.

Only twenty miles from Philadelphia, Washing-

# of Valley Forge

ton, in a classic understatement, described Valley Forge as "a dreary kind of place and uncomfortably provided." Although the men suffered horribly and "remained whole days without provisions," the army emerged from the "winter of discontent" a far more potent striking force. The Prussian von Steuben had pounded a system of drill and military formations into the troops, and Clinton's planned withdrawal to New York soon offered Washington a chance to test his new army.

The troops at Valley Forge were virtually shelterless, and Washington immediately put them to work building log huts. This vignette is from a nineteenth-century bank note.

Although they were good individual fighters, the Americans' ignorance of the elementary principles of drill or maneuvering often put them at a fatal disadvantage against their well-trained enemy. Von Steuben (at right) set out to change all this, and incidentally kept the men well occupied during the Valley Forge winter.

Despite his claims, the genial Baron von Steuben was only a captain, not a former Prussian general; but he was a superb drillmaster. Exasperated with the raw recruits, he would begin "to swear in German, then in French, and then in both languages together," finally pleading for someone to "swear for me in English." But his "fits of passion . . . rather amused than offended the soldiers." Ralph Earl's portrait shows him in the uniform of a major general. The decorations are European except for the blue Order of the Cincinnati.

Charles Lee's removal at Monmouth inspired this sketch by Kosciuszko, titled "A Suspended General."

Howe's departure from command marked the end of the ineffectual Philadelphia campaign. The seizure of the enemy's capital, a prized strategic concept in European warfare, had proved worthless, simply because the colonists did not have enough of a government to need a capital. Washington's army, the real heart of the rebellion, still existed, and was toughened now by battle experience and von Steuben's training. Against it, Clinton got off to a poor start. On May 20 he had a fine chance to destroy Lafayette and a third of the Rebel army that had ventured across the Schuylkill to Barren Hill; but the Frenchman neatly marched his men to safety before the trap was sprung. Von Steuben's efforts had paid their first dividend, and the young Marquis imagined the British returning to Philadelphia "much fatigued, and . . . laughed at for their ill success."

Clinton's problem now was to get his army to New York. Sending it by sea was too risky, considering the possible arrival of a powerful French fleet in American waters, so he decided to risk a long march through New Jersey to Sandy Hook. He was more than halfway there before Washington overrode Charles Lee's vehement objections to an attack and set off in pursuit. That the ensuing battle near Monmouth Court House on June 28 was not a clear-cut American victory can be blamed on Lee. He had superseded Lafayette as field commander, and the attack on Clinton's rear guard was going well when Lee inexplicably ordered a retreat. As Clinton launched a counterthrust against the baffled Rebels, Washington brought up the main force, fired Lee on the spot in a rare burst of temper, and, with his troops deploying like professionals, stopped repeated attacks by Clinton's elite corps. It was the war's last major battle in the northern theater, and Washington could write to Congress with pride: "We forced the enemy from the field and encamped on their ground." By July the British were back in New York, and the Rebels camped at White Plains to keep an eye on them.

Handsome Marquis de Lafayette was to have had a major command at Monmouth, but was replaced by Lee at the last minute.

Major Battle in the North

Washington galloped his great white horse into the mass of Americans thrown into confusion by Lee's order to retreat, and rallied the troops. "Cheering them by his voice and example . . . never had I beheld so superb a man," Lafayette recalled. This romantic early 19th-century painting of the Monmouth battle shows the grim General receiving a captured British standard as the fight rages on. At the right a wounded officer receives first aid.

General John Burgoyne, by Sir Joshua Reynolds

THE TURNING POINT

"The fortune of war, General Gates, has made me your prisoner."

GENERAL JOHN BURGOYNE—OCTOBER 16, 1777

"Beg your pardon my Dear Sir—had it from my Lord Fiddlefaddle. He'd nothing to do but cut 'em off pass the Susquhanna and proceed to Boston possess himself of Crown point—then Philadelphia would have fallen of course and a communication opend with the Northern Army—as easily as I'd open a Vein."

A British armchair strategist, 1779

A NEW betting-book was being opened at ultra-fashionable Brooks's Club in London, and members crowded about to watch a handsome, florid man record the first wager. That entry read, and still reads (if the betting-book survived World War II), "John Burgoyne wagers Charles [James] Fox one pony [fifty guineas] that he will be home victorious from America by Christmas Day, 1777." Few doubts, if any, assailed genial, gregarious Major General John Burgoyne. Not long before, his military treatise entitled with characteristic flamboyance "Thoughts for Conducting the War from the Side of Canada" had been approved in the highest quarters, and the major portion of the execution of those "Thoughts" entrusted to him.

Basically, the plan was sound. With a strong Anglo-German force, Burgoyne was to sweep up Lake Champlain, capture weakly held Ticonderoga, drive south across the narrow land bridge that separated the lake from the upper Hudson, and then push on gloriously to Albany. At Albany, his command was to be joined by a mixed body of British, Hessians, Tories, and Indians under Lieutenant Colonel Barry St. Leger coming down the Mohawk River from the base at Oswego on Lake Ontario. Then the united forces would act as an anvil for the smashing sledge-hammer blow that Sir William Howe was to launch north up the Hudson from New York [see map, page 251].

It was hoped that the main American army under Washington would be forced to come up out of the Jerseys to counter this blow. In that case it would surely be crushed along with lesser American commands, and armed resistance to the Crown would be at an end. If "Mr." Washington, as he was usually termed in official British correspondence, refused to move, then the British (in complete control of the great waterway that ran from New York Harbor to the St. Lawrence, broken only by that land bridge between lake and river) could effectively seal off New England from the rest of the country. The tons of supplies and the thousands of men that flowed out of those four states would dry to a trickle and the spine of rebellion would be snapped.

Accomplishment of this sweeping design, however, depended on its three elements—Burgoyne, St. Leger, and above all Howe—moving in perfect accord and harmony. From the start, liaison would have to be flawless, and this was complicated by the fact that London, whence the formal orders must flow, treated New York and Canada as separate areas of command.

This aspect does not seem to have concerned Burgoyne in the least. He himself would bring ample authority from London to set his own and St. Leger's expeditions in motion, and he had been assured by Lord George Germain that Howe would be alerted in ample time and with positive orders. Charles James Fox's fifty guineas were as good as in the Burgoyne exchequer, and the affable playwright-general embarked once more for the New World with no recorded worries that Germain's instructions to Sir William Howe might be disconcertingly vague, or that they might reach that General when the latter had already committed himself deeply in some other theater.

On May 6, 1777, the ship bearing Major General John Burgoyne dropped anchor in the magnificent fjord-like reaches of the St. Lawrence between the reddish cliffs of Levis and the awesome rock-mass of Quebec. Burgoyne hurried ashore to seek out Carleton, who had been shamelessly passed over in the whole matter of the expedition, and totted up the pluses and minuses of the task. The troops were in excellent shape, the Brunswickers and Hessians among them having been favored through their first frozen Canadian season by a winter so mild that, for years afterwards, the habitants spoke of it as "the German winter." The subordinate British commanders were first-class, and as for the

Germans, Burgoyne had previously formed a sincere liking and respect for their leader, Baron von Riedesel, an honest, competent, straightforward soldier.

One British liability had unexpectedly been turned into an asset. An administrative snarl had sent astray a complete supply of new scarlet uniforms. As an emergency measure, the traditional long coattails had been chopped off for patching, and the cocked hats of the line companies had been trimmed down to skullcap dimensions. The resultant garb was distinctly unorthodox, but the men, rid of the dangling tails and the clumsy cocked hats, would be far more mobile in the broken, heavily wooded country that lay ahead of them.

Intelligence was excellent, and Burgoyne learned that Ticonderoga was commanded by a former British officer, Major General Arthur St. Clair, whose 2,000 American troops were known to be definitely substandard in morale, health, and equipment.

Then minuses began to pile up. Attempts to recruit a strong Tory corps had failed utterly, a bare hundred or so having rushed to the colors instead of the expected thousands. Canadian enlistments had been as bad. About 400 Indians, a disappointing total, would be present under the rather loose control of two Frenchmen, La Corne St. Luc and Charles de Langlade, and it was reliably reported that the London decision to use Indians against the misguided colonists was swinging thousands of waverers away from the Crown. Worse was to come. Horses were in very short supply, and Canadians were refusing to sell or rent their wagons for transport, so carts and gun carriages would have to be hastily thrown together out of green wood. One extra burden was supplied by Burgoyne himself, for he insisted on weighting down his columns with 138 pieces of artillery, ranging from the lightest calibers to lumbering 24-pounders. Many of these were to be mounted on ships or in captured forts, but a good 42 were to accompany the infantry through the wilderness, a number far in excess of their needs. The nightmare of Breed's Hill was strong in Burgoyne's mind, and he was determined that if he met entrenched Americans he would smother them with artillery fire before a single British or German infantryman attacked. Actually, once Ticonderoga was passed, there were no American forts worthy of the name, no prepared positions. But by dragging this mass of guns and munitions overland, Burgoyne was giving his enemy time to build earthworks where none had existed before.

One final damper was dropped by Carleton. Howe had written him, mentioning casually that 1777 would find the main British force busy in Pennsylvania, although a token raid or two *might* be made north up the Hudson. Burgoyne's optimistic, sanguine mind apparently discounted this shocker, and he reasoned that Howe's letter to Carleton must have been written before instructions from London had reached him, canceling out that absurd Pennsylvania notion!

So smiling John Burgoyne headed west up the St. Lawrence to pick up the force he was to muster along the Richelieu River. His rolling laughter, his undying *bonhomie*, his genuine concern for the well-being of all ranks, an eighteenth-century rarity, met quick response. Grenadier Lieutenant William Digby of the 53rd Shropshires wrote that the genial General "engrossed their warmest attachment . . . idolized by the army, his orders appearing more like recommending subordination than enforcing it . . . he was the soldier's friend."

In the false dawn that crept in over the shaggy ramparts of the Green Mountains, bringing with it the first day of July, 1777, a vast flotilla pushed out from the Anglo-German camps about Crown Point on Champlain's west shore, poised for the opening blow of the campaign.

Major General Baron von Riedesel

"When Jack, the king's commander,
Was going to his duty,
Through all the crowd
he smiled and bowed—
To every blooming beauty . . ."
—"The Fate of John Burgoyne,"
1777

Some of Burgoyne's Indian allies

The winds that sifted down from the high lift of the Adirondacks flowed over the mile-wide throat of the lake, swerving against the sails of ships that were almost frigates, of trim pinnaces, sloops, and ketches, sending ripples against the rough sides of uncounted bateaux and gundalows. The waters reflected a foretaste of autumn. There were Indians painted ocher and crimson and saffron and green and blood-red. Images of scarlet coats with willow-green, buff, and yellow facings danced among the ripples of the small craft, while the blue of Brunswicker and Hessian mixed with the light green of the jägers. Burgoyne had no firsthand knowledge of the German units, beyond the fact that their regimental records were good. But that rocking line of bateaux carried British history. The 21st Royal Scots Fusiliers dated back to 1678. They had fought at Bothwell Bridge and Killiecrankie, at Blenheim and Malplaquet. The 9th Norfolks and 20th Lancashires were nearly as venerable, and the 47th North Lancs had stormed Louisbourg and Quebec, had marched the tragic road from Boston to Concord, had struggled up the fatal slopes of Breed's Hill.

Looking south, Burgoyne may have felt less assured. In advance and along the flanks of the line glided a score of long war canoes, freighted with hideously painted allies. The red men were born warriors, requiring little in the way of supplies and munitions, yet Londoners might ask awkward questions. Could a gentleman make war leagued with savages, especially when those savages were to be used against transplanted Englishmen? Burgoyne had his answer ready. He had made a speech to the red men, telling them that they must make war in civilized fashion; wounded and prisoners were not to be scalped or tortured, and noncombatants, especially women and children, were to be held sacrosanct.

Many British officers and men had served in the past with Indians, knew something of their psychology, spoke a little of their tongue. Yet for some unknown reason, most of the Indians were assigned to cover the left wing, composed of von Riedesel's Germans. The Baron had had little or no contact with this alien screen, nor had his officers. How, then, could he be expected to command, direct, or control them, or see that they obeyed Burgoyne's naïve speech?

Burgoyne's army on Lake Champlain

About three miles above Fort Ticonderoga, where St. Clair waited, the British plunged ashore on the west bank. Von Riedesel's ponderous Germans spilled out on the swampy east shore, their mission to close in on the American works on Mount Independence just across from Ticonderoga.

No troops could have been worse prepared for what they found than the Brunswickers. They were in utterly primeval forest, with deadfalls and windfalls where immense trunks were stacked like the jackstraws of a drunken Titan. Sinister East Creek oozed evilly into the lake, its banks sloughing into a viscous muck where a man could neither walk nor swim. This morass wandered aimlessly, and a soldier used to the ordered waterways of the Brunswick plains could, and often did, crack physically and mentally as he tried to beat his way forward. The air was like a steam room. Faces were scarlet under grenadier's helmets or heavy cocked hats. Double cuffs galled sweaty wrists, and white breeches shrank over heat-swollen legs. Sabers, haversacks, and muskets caught against branches, banged against arms and knees, sent men sprawling into green-topped muck, while mosquitoes hovered in whining clouds and the silent, nearly invisible black flies settled on raw necks and bleeding hands. Time and the wilderness were fighting on the side of the Thirteen States.

Things went better on the clean west shore where Burgoyne could have moved even more confidently had he been able to guess that St. Clair, his in-

236

telligence channels choked by the few Indians ahead of the British, knew only that a hostile force had landed, and had no way of estimating its size, composition, or immediate objectives. Axes rang on the west shore, huge boles toppled, were cut up to make corduroy roads for Burgoyne's heavy guns, and a formal siege of the Gibraltar of America loomed.

But there was to be no siege. Lieutenant Twiss of the Royal Engineers had been prowling west and south of the fort, his professional eye alert. Sometime about July 3, he called the attention of Burgoyne's second-in-command, Major General William Phillips, to a high peak known as Mount Defiance, whose crest commanded a superb view of the interior of Fort Ticonderoga and the waterway running south.

The Americans had failed to fortify the crest, believing the slopes to be inaccessible. Phillips, an artillery officer, did not share this belief, announcing firmly that "Where a goat can go a man can go and where a man can go he can drag a gun." An approach of sorts was hurriedly hacked out, guns were manhandled up this killing ascent to the very peak, and a secret battery installed there. When the time came, its guns could slam down into Ticonderoga, smash the works on Independence, make pulp of any evacuation.

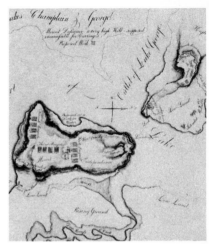

Trumbull's drawing of Fort Ticonderoga (center) and its outposts

Burgoyne could afford to chuckle richly over his champagne with the pretty mistress he had brought down from the St. Lawrence. "Old Ti" was demonstrably his, and he need not fear any Breed's Hill on the shores of Champlain. Soon Barry St. Leger would come sweeping down the Mohawk in the second phase of the "Thoughts," and at that very moment Sir William Howe *must* be marshaling a strong force to sweep up the Hudson.

Well before daybreak on July 6, Brigadier General Simon Fraser, in command of the British Advance Corps (the massed light infantry and grenadier companies of all regiments), received word that the American lines were deserted. Further scouting showed that more than 200 boats had slipped south toward Skenesboro, now Whitehall. All at once great fires flared on Mount Independence across the lake.

Warned by carelessly exposed troops on Mount Defiance or, as some accounts hold, by an accidentally discharged piece of the ultra-secret battery on the crest, Arthur St. Clair had seen his deadly peril, and during the night of the fifth had managed to slip his raw, unsteady troops across the bridge of boats that connected Ticonderoga and Independence. Gathering up the garrison of the latter post, he headed through the darkness along a cart track that ran southeast to Hubbardton and Castleton before it swung west to Skenesboro at the very head of Champlain, while his mass of shipping sculled south to the same point. St. Clair's move would have been perfect had not the barracks and supply dumps of Independence been prematurely fired, against his own strict orders. Those fires told Simon Fraser, a skilled, seasoned veteran, that the east bank was clear as well as the west. He formed his men, drove them hard across the bridge of boats, which St. Clair's careless subordinates had failed to destroy, and picked up the American trail.

Grenadiers and light infantry plunged on into the night through steep, wooded hills and deep, narrow valleys. Dawn found the Advance Corps keeping up a murderous pace that would have done credit to tough frontiersmen. Gentleman-volunteer Thomas Anburey of the 29th Worcesters stated later that this stage of the pursuit lasted from 4 A.M. until 1 P.M. with no real halts. Somewhere along the route Baron von Riedesel appeared, reporting that his own men, who were supposed to link up with Fraser's, were hopelessly strung out along the east shore. Fraser, impatient, decided to push on alone with his Brit-

"I think we shall never defend a post until we shoot a general. After that, we shall defend posts, and this event, in my opinion, is not far off . . . We must trifle no more."
—*John Adams to Abigail Adams, August 19, 1777*

John Trumbull's sketch of General Arthur St. Clair

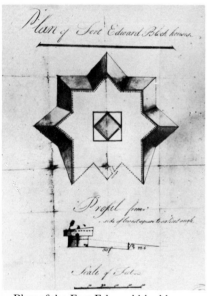

Plan of the Fort Edward blockhouse

ish, the Baron vowing to do his best to catch up. The day was ground away under the boots of the Advance Corps and Fraser was finally forced to call a halt, with reveille set for 3 A.M. of July 7.

A silent reveille set the British moving again, with still no sign of the Baron's Germans. Then, at dawn, Fraser's van stumbled onto the New Hampshires of Colonel Hale (not the famous patriot-spy), who had not so much as a single guard out. Drums clattered, orders snapped among Fraser's men, and at once there was flight, panic, and surrender near a hamlet called Hubbardton.

Unexpectedly, St. Clair's rear, under Colonel Francis and Colonel Seth Warner, rallied, struck, and the pursuit was brought to a jarring halt. Muskets flashed through smoke in the Vermont meadows, and Fraser began to lose heavily as drab American formations looped about the British left. Real disaster hung above the smoke clouds. Then from Fraser's left rear a fearful din arose. Drums boomed, oboes and brass echoed louder, and German voices could be made out, roaring a Lutheran hymn. The Baron had come up at the vital moment with just enough of his quick-moving jägers to prop up the British line.

Action was broken off. Understandably spent, British and Germans collapsed on the bloody grass. There was no pursuit. Indeed, both the Baron and Fraser were so impressed by American resilience that they actually dug in where they were, admittedly fearing another Rebel smash. Thomas Anburey, reflecting on the lessons of his first day of action, said that "the exertions of the day had so far wearied me that, drinking heartily of rum and water, I laid down in my [grenadier's] bearskin . . . and did not awake till twelve the next day."

The American survivors of Hubbardton moved on, caught up with St. Clair's main column, and continued to ruinous little Fort Edward near the great westerly bend of the Hudson. Von Riedesel and Fraser rested their men and then pushed on west to Skenesboro, where the rest of their army was lying.

At the field-stone house of Philip Skene, late Major of His Majesty's forces, proprietor of Skenesboro, and claimant of uncounted wilderness acres to the south and west, John Burgoyne had ample grounds for laughing with his very warm friend, Mrs. Commissary. True, he had not trapped St. Clair's force at Ticonderoga, but what of it? The whole Rebel force was hopelessly shattered; unnumbered prisoners had been taken, along with vast amounts of stores and all the Rebel barge-flotilla. Some British officers were shaking their heads over the rough handling given the ancient 9th Norfolks at tottery wooden Fort Anne to the south, but as far as Burgoyne could see, nothing was left to complete fulfillment of the "Thoughts" except a mere twenty-mile march to the Hudson and thence to Albany for that joyous meeting with St. Leger and Sir William Howe.

Those twenty miles, however, hung heavy on the minds of a few of Burgoyne's officers. They knew that the "Thoughts" recommended the water route Champlain–Lake George–Hudson River–Albany; yet here was the author, confidently scrapping the Lake George part, which would have floated heavy guns and stores while the troops kept to a known road on the left bank. Instead, he would plunge overland through those twenty wilderness miles, where hardly a trail existed.

Burgoyne's choice is more than puzzling. It may be that Philip Skene, by no means averse to having his vast acres improved with a road built by the British army straight south to the Hudson bend, managed to talk the genial commander into that course. Whatever the reason, the steamy, mosquito-infested job was begun. By inches a road was gnawed through virgin forest, and not even the presence of skilled Canadian axemen could speed the work much. To impede their progress, General Philip Schuyler, American area-commander, had combed the Hudson Valley for woodsmen, found tools for them, and sent them north to add to Burgoyne's days and miles. Ahead of the crawling advance these woodsmen felled trees across trails, adding to existing deadfalls. Trunks jarred over brooks, dammed them, and formed pools and made viscous swamps where there had been sure footing. Ravines were choked, each log adding its girth to a stack that had to be laboriously cut up and hauled aside by the advance.

Some of Burgoyne's contentment had been seriously disturbed by La Corne St. Luc, the white-haired French noble, a courtier off the trail and a savage on it. St. Luc knew from his younger days the effect of Indian raids on advance settlements and on civilian morale. Now he kept growling to the affable British commander, *"Il faut brutaliser les affaires,"* demanding a freer hand for himself and his Indians. Burgoyne held fast to his original orders that the Indians make war only on troops, not civilians. As the slow advance brought his men into territory with more and more cabins and isolated farms, certificates of protection were given to those settlers who swore allegiance to the Crown. But what good would such documents be when flourished in the face of illiterate Indians? The point was most important, since Skene had been whispering for weeks that soon the expedition would come into country aswarm with Loyalists just waiting the chance to flock to the colors.

Tragedy struck close to home. Drunken Indians brought into camp a scalp whose luxuriant tresses were quickly identified as those of young Jane McCrea. She could have been written off as just another frontier girl, victim of a deplorable misunderstanding; but she happened to be the fiancée of Lieutenant David Jones of Colonel John Peters' little band of Tories. Worse, she had been staying with an elderly widowed cousin of General Simon Fraser of the Advance Corps. Yet Burgoyne's hands were tied, for when he attempted to arrest the culprit Indian, he was faced with a mass walkout of braves which he could not afford. The whole McCrea affair had wide publicity and produced deep repercussions on Rebel and Tory alike. More, it provided Americans with a rare propaganda item.

By July 29, 1777, the advance finally broke out of the miasmic forests and stood with an almost hysterical sense of relief in honest, open rolling meadows. Men forgot what lay behind them, the twenty wilderness miles spanned by forty bridges, one of them two miles long—twenty miles that had cost at least 26 irreplaceable days. Many officers expected that a light, mobile force would be thrown across the Hudson for a swift dash to Albany and the meeting with St. Leger and Howe. Instead, the whole force went into camp in the meadows about Fort Edward while the maddeningly slow procession of heavy guns came wambling over the wretched road from the head of Lake George. Round trip after round trip had to be made while the summer days dropped one by one from the calendar.

Burgoyne settled himself and Mrs. Commissary in the old Smythe house and waited for his power to assemble. Orders went out stripping the entire command of all superfluities. Surplus stores, baggage, clothes, and personal effects were to be sent back to Ticonderoga for storage (except for thirty carts earmarked for Burgoyne's own belongings, his traveling cellar, and the extensive wardrobe of Mrs. Commissary).

The twinkle in Burgoyne's eye was heavily dimmed and his fine chin went slack on August 3, when a weary courier arrived at the Smythe house with a

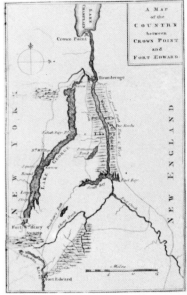

This map shows the "Drown'd Lands" south of Fort Ticonderoga through which Burgoyne's redcoats marched

Tadeusz Kosciuszko

letter from Sir William Howe. Congratulating his colleague on the taking of Ticonderoga, Howe went on to say, almost as an afterthought: "My intention is for Pennsylvania, where I expect to meet Washington, but if he goes to the northward . . . and you can keep him at bay, be assured I shall soon be after him to relieve you. After your arrival at Albany, the movements of the enemy will guide yours. Success be ever with you."

This was enough to rock any general back on his heels. Howe was *not* coming north unless Washington moved there, and even then Burgoyne was supposed to bear the brunt of the American blow until Howe, never noted for speed, came to help out. But Burgoyne rallied quickly. His own orders said simply, "Go to Albany," so there he would go. So far the Rebels had given him very little trouble, and the few of them left in this theater were massing at a place called Stillwater, twenty miles down the west bank of the Hudson. It did not occur to him to wonder just what the Rebels might be doing there, or to speculate on how a skilled Polish engineer named Tadeusz Andrzej Bonawentura Kosciuszko might be aiding them, enhancing their known and feared genius at digging. Instead, Burgoyne kept Howe's bad news strictly to himself and set about gathering supplies for his last leap south. After all, St. Leger was surely on his way down the Mohawk, and the combined forces could spend a comfortable winter in Albany and see what spring might hold for them.

At that moment, Barry St. Leger, a cool and experienced soldier, was closing his lines about old Fort Stanwix on the upper reaches of the Mohawk, about 100 crow-miles from Burgoyne. St. Leger's command consisted of about 500 British and Hesse-Hanau troops, an equal number of well-trained Tory units, and, as local advisers, Tory leaders Sir John Johnson and Colonel John Butler. With him, too, were swarms of Canadian axemen for road work and, most important, 1,000 Indians under the famed Mohawk chief Joseph Brant, also known as Thayendanegea.

Stanwix proved unexpectedly stubborn. Colonel Peter Gansevoort and Lieutenant Colonel Marinus Willett, both of the 3rd New York, had worked miracles in repairing the neglected fort and keeping its garrison of some 750 in fine combat-readiness. They managed to beat back all enemy blows, and took alert countermeasures against the siege.

Stanwix did not stand alone. In early August a long column wound west up the lovely Mohawk Valley. Out of little settlements like Stone Arabia, German Flats, Palatine, Deerfield, and Fairfield came the militia of Tryon County, 800 strong, following Brigadier General Nicholas Herkimer—a veteran of the old wars who, though Valley-born, spoke German more readily than English. Every man knew what would happen if Stanwix fell and Brant's Indians struck their fat farms and prosperous hamlets. Even more they feared the return of the Johnsons and Butlers, whose rather feudal notions of life they had battled for years. In fact, the impending clash almost belongs in the annals of Valley feuds rather than in those of the Revolution.

Alerted by scouts and spies, St. Leger sent out heavy details of Johnson's and Butler's Tories, as well as Brant's Indians, to circle Stanwix and head off Herkimer's relieving force. On August 6, 1777, the Tryon County men, despite their little screen of friendly Oneida Indians and their own skilled scouts, stumbled into a carefully laid ambush in a ravine on the south bank of the Mohawk, near a place called Oriskany. All day long a fearful wilderness battle raged, with little groups of former neighbors and relatives often opposing each other, clawing, slashing, and stabbing. Before dusk, the Tryon County men were in full re-

"The great bulk of the country is undoubtedly with the Congress, in principle and in zeal; and their measures are executed with a secrecy and dispatch that are not to be equaled. Wherever the King's forces point, militia . . . assemble in twenty-four hours."
—*General Burgoyne, August, 1777*

240

treat down the Mohawk, carrying with them Nicholas Herkimer, out of action with a wound that was to prove mortal.

In little better shape, the Tories and Indians, terribly mauled, returned to the lines about Stanwix, only to find that in their absence the alert Marinus Willett had sallied from the fort, driven off the few guards in the Indian and Tory camps, and returned without the loss of a man but with about everything that was portable from their tents and lodges. This loss cost the Indians every shred of equipment and their scanty but vital reserve rations. Adding this to the heavy casualties they had suffered at Oriskany, they found their enthusiasm for further service under the Great White Father across the seas vanishing, and began to desert.

St. Leger's coup had beaten back the relieving force, and now he turned his attention to the siege, pushing his approaches nearer and nearer. Then, about August 21, he began to receive rumors that Major General Benedict Arnold was storming up the Mohawk with 3,500 Continentals. The rumors were true, except in point of numbers, for Arnold had with him only 1,000 Continentals and militia, whose arrival would make Gansevoort's force just about equal to St. Leger's.

Others heard the rumors. Tories and Indians began to panic. On the twenty-third, St. Leger broke camp and started a hasty retreat for his Oswego base, abandoning all his artillery, ammunition, and supplies, and was cruelly harassed on the march by his former Indian allies. Thus the stroke from the west was canceled out for good. Never again would formal warfare, as practiced by His Majesty's troops, threaten the Mohawk Valley. However, there remained the Johnsons, the Butlers, and the Indians. The settlers along the Mohawk would hear from them again and again until the rich earth itself would seem charred and bleeding.

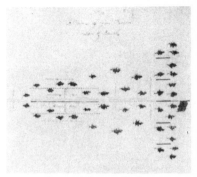

Colonel Barry St. Leger's order of march

Summer days were placid along the upper Hudson, Burgoyne, confident of Mohawk successes, had new plans to mull over. To the east in the Hampshire Grants, or Vermont, were great masses of Rebel stores and uncounted horses to be had for the taking. And once again came the same old story, which bedeviled British generals to the end of the war, of innumerable Loyalists fairly panting for the appearance of the Royal colors, begging to be allowed to form regiments for the King.

Burgoyne began planning a swift coup to the east that would yield provisions, stores of arms, and horses for the artillery and wagon trains. The animals could also be used by the beautifully trained veteran von Riedesel dragoons, who had thus far been plodding along with the rest of the army in boots that weighed twelve pounds per pair, not counting ponderous spurs.

Logic seemed to call for a dash by Tories, British light infantry, and jägers, mobile troops that could cover ground, attain an objective, and get out ahead of any trouble. Instead, Gentleman Johnny turned to his good friend Baron von Riedesel to carry out the raid. The only excuse for such a choice was that the Germans held the east of the line, and to have leapfrogged British troops across them would have been a severe affront to cherished military honor.

Errors began multiplying. To spearhead this lightning stroke into enemy country were the lumbering, overequipped dragoons under Lieutenant Colonel Friedrich Baum with their heavy boots, sabers, and carbines. In a pathetically hopeful gesture, each dragoon carried a halter to secure the prized mount that would be his once the objective was reached. Back of them came a mass of Brunswick grenadiers, only a little more mobile than Baum's men,

A British attack on Howe's inactivity at the time of Saratoga

and two of Captain Georg Pausch's Hesse-Hanau guns, dragged by famished horses. As an afterthought, a picked handful of British light infantry, a few Tories, and a cloud of Indians were detailed to cover the advance. On August 11, Baum's command set out from Fort Miller by the Hudson, crossed the Battenkill, and plunged into the near-virgin, hilly country to the east. A last-second switch in orders changed the objective from Manchester to a village known as Bennington.

The army watched Baum depart in all confidence and then, for the moment, forgot about him. Down the forest trails that led from Champlain bowled a *calèche* containing a very trim young lady ("a dancey little body"), whose wide blue eyes and rosebud mouth were deceptively demure and innocent. Baroness Friederike, or "Fritschen" as her husband called her, had arrived with three other von Riedesel ladies, Gustava, aged six, Friederike, three, and Caroline, whose first birthday had been celebrated in America. Installed near Fort Anne on Wood Creek, the Baroness settled down in the role of a soldier's wife and began to write long letters to her parents in Wolfenbüttel in Brunswick about the vast forests, how she learned to cook bears' paws, and about the other women present. (There were very pointed, almost audible sniffs concerning the ménage at the Smythe house.) Then the Baroness went to work, persuading Burgoyne to let herself, her daughters, and the pregnant Lady Acland accompany the army on its southward advance.

Soon vague reports came back from Baum's absurd "Flying Column." Some horses and cattle had been picked up, but there was trouble with the Indians, and Skene (probably the only English-speaking member of the force) could not control them. They terrified Tory and Rebel settler alike, shot all loose horses for the sheer joy of it, and slaughtered cattle not to eat but to get the highly prized cowbells that hung about their necks. Also there were rumors of militia massing about Bennington. Nonetheless, Baum was pushing on.

Sometime before dawn on August 15, a message was received from Baum asking for reinforcements. There were no further details, but the call in itself should have been a danger signal. Burgoyne ordered out Breymann and his Advance Corps to march to Baum's relief. Here again the choice was odd. Breymann's grenadiers were little more mobile than Baum's men. Worse, there raged between the two leaders a bitterly hot feud.

In a pouring rain Breymann and his cumbersome command took the road over which Baum had marched, knowing little of their mission beyond a misleading sentence in Burgoyne's orders to the effect that it was "in consequence of the good news received from Baum"!

Breymann never did reach his hated colleague. Rain fell, roads became ribbons of mud, the column was hampered by wheeled vehicles that never should have been brought along, and Breymann's military pedantry was so intense that he kept halting his men to align their ranks properly. Rate of progress rarely exceeded a half-mile per hour. On the afternoon of the sixteenth, the relief column met scattered bodies of armed civilians whom Breymann mistook for eager Tories. Sharp fire from front and flanks quickly disillusioned him, and an obstinate fight began along the road to Bennington. By dusk, Breymann's ammunition was gone, his two pieces lost, most of his horses shot, and he was wounded. He ordered a retreat, still ignorant of the fact that a bare mile from the point of his farthest advance Baum's whole command had been wiped out a few hours earlier, only nine survivors reaching the base.

The retreat was harassed until long after dark by one of the oddest forces to appear in the whole war. It was not an American army, but a New Hamp-

Baroness von Riedesel

John Stark directing troops at Bennington

242

shire one, raised chiefly by John Langdon, Speaker of the General Court, who had pledged his personal fortune, his plate, and his goods to finance it. It was commanded by Brigadier General John Stark who, after Trenton, had retired in a huff at army routine and the blindness of Congress to his merits, and he assumed the leadership solely on condition that there would be no damned Continental foolishness in the business. He grudgingly accepted Colonel Seth Warner's Continentals (the same who had fought at Hubbardton), but only because most of Warner's men were from the Hampshire Grants. Still more reluctantly, he included in his ranks some hundreds of men from western Massachusetts brought north by the belligerent Parson Thomas Allen of Pitts-field. With this strange array, Stark had, in two consecutive engagements, put out of action for good over 800 of Burgoyne's solid Germans.

Back at the Hudson word came to headquarters, first of Baum's disaster and then of Breymann's repulse and retreat. Yet Burgoyne, with his dramatist's sense of timing, rode out to meet Breymann's wreckage and greeted the haggard men as though they had been conquerors, managing a brief but florid speech thanking them for "their very pretty little success" which the enemy would feel "most severely." Meanwhile, La Corne St. Luc and most of the Indians, disgusted perhaps that matters were not sufficiently "brutalisé," went back to Canada, and with them went the eyes and ears of Burgoyne's army.

A week after the twin engagements known as the Battle of Bennington, Burgoyne was rocked by news of St. Leger's failure at Fort Stanwix. To his credit, Gentleman Johnny did not panic. He wanted to fall back to Fort Edward, possibly to Ticonderoga, but his orders from London specified that he must push on, regardless of what others did or failed to do. He wrote Lord George Germain that "my orders being positive to 'force a junction with Sir William Howe,' I apprehend I am not at liberty to remain inactive." Not one to underplay the situation's drama, he added: "The Hampshire Grants . . . a country unpeopled and almost unknown in the last war, now abounds in the most active and rebellious race on the continent, and hangs like a gathering storm upon my left."

Prisoners captured by Rebels at Bennington

September 15, 1777, was a magnificent fall day along the Hudson. The whole command, British and German, was across on the west bank and passed in review, bands playing and flags romping. Burgoyne, with his mental eye on an invisible audience, swept off his hat to the marching columns and shouted "Britons never retreat!" Then the flimsy bridge of boats that spanned the river was broken up, cutting the last link with Canada and the Ticonderoga base as the curtain rose on the last act of the tragedy. A brand-new campaign had begun, regardless of what the original "Thoughts" contemplated. The objective was narrowed to a very simple one: Get to Albany. No officer or man of the expedition seems to have thought beyond that point, for it was as far as the mind could carry. Enemy resistance was still shadowy, but outposts were ambushed silently by night, details met with unexpected bursts of fire from dense woods.

Once on the west bank, matters worsened. Day became no safer than night. A foraging party of thirty was snapped up. Pickets had to be doubled, trebled. The terrain was still wilderness, but it was broken now by well-kept fields, solid houses, sawmills, gristmills, stout barns.

The slow march went along a wood-girt, narrow plain by the river, through which deep stream beds ran down to the Hudson. The countless bridges over these miniature canyons had been wrecked, and once more the army halted while the wheeze of saw, the smack of axe filled the air. New structures had to be built to support Burgoyne's guns, wagons, and the thirty-odd carts that enabled the commander to take the field as a gentleman should. One mile a day and halt. Half a mile a day and halt, each hour yielding priceless dividends of time to the largely unseen enemy.

The march south was blind as well as slow. The river plain was open enough, but the rugged shoulders jutting out from the heights were heavily wooded, masking what lay beyond. No dominant hill or peak afforded an observation post, and if an agile man swarmed to the crest of a great oak or pine, he looked out into more branches, more leaf-masses.

Then the army, waking in the misty river meadows, heard a new sound—the ghostly patter of distant drums off to the south, a sound like the feet of squirrels racing over a shingled roof. At last Burgoyne knew in a general way where the main enemy strength lay. There was hasty reconnaissance that found cart paths leading inland to the shelf-like heights in the west, clearings, an abandoned farm with a weed-masked cabin, the holding of one Freeman whose unharvested wheat rippled in the wind. Farm and clearing seem to have dazzled Burgoyne, the few open acres transforming themselves in his mind into sweeping country where his men could fight like civilized soldiers instead of whacking about like irregulars or Indians. Soon he issued orders that have puzzled military students ever since.

General Simon Fraser was to take the Advance Corps and follow a foul track that eventually led into Freeman's western fields. Burgoyne himself would lead the line companies of four fine regiments onto the Freeman lands, while von Riedesel pushed three Brunswick regiments down the river road. Thus three bodies were to start out, completely out of sight of one another. When someone in Burgoyne's party guessed that the columns were abreast, a signal gun would be fired for a general advance.

Despite a pre-dawn start on September 19, it was almost one o'clock before elements of Burgoyne's party broke into the Freeman clearings and nosed warily ahead toward the silent woods at the south edge. Suddenly there was movement under those trees, made by half-seen men with fur caps and long rifles. Somewhere an unearthly turkey-gobbling broke out. With the crack of rifles, every British officer in the advance was shot down. Noncoms and privates began to topple, then the open stretches were alive with lean men in fringed shirts, rifles alert. Daniel Morgan's rifle corps had struck the first blow of the Battle of Freeman's Farm.

The rush of the riflemen, probably not more than a company strong at this point, carried them across the clearing where they collided, almost fatally for them, with Burgoyne's main body. They managed to break off, fled to the shelter of the south woods, and the bulk of the British occupied the Freeman fields that ran east and west for some 350 yards. There was no enemy in sight, but the eerie, nerve-twanging gobble wailed its gibberish among the trees, Daniel Morgan's individualistic way of rallying his companies.

The south woods were filling fast. More and more fur caps, broad hats, and hunting shirts could be made out. Rifles flashed quicker and sharper, joined now by the duller reports of muskets as Joseph Cilley's New Hampshire Continentals closed up with Morgan. It was a bad situation for a general trained in formal war. There was nothing to strike against, no way of estimating enemy strength. Nonetheless, Burgoyne calmly ordered the signal gun fired to tell Fraser and von Riedesel that the grand advance had begun. He had no way of knowing it, but he had reached the high-water mark of the invasion. Never

A British caricature of an American rifleman

"Both armies seemed determined to conquer or die. . . . They were bold, intrepid, and fought like heroes, and I do assure you, sirs, our men were equally bold and courageous and fought like men fighting for their all."
—*John Glover to A. Orne, September 21, 1777*

244

would Englishman or Brunswicker pass the south edge of Freeman's lands.

Burgoyne's companies, firing sturdily at the tree-masked targets, began to suffer heavily. Cannoneers and gunner officers were picked off before a piece could be loaded. There was a rush for the shelter of the north woods. Morgan and Cilley followed hard, only to find the relative positions exactly reversed. Now the British were firing from cover into an exposed meadow. Morgan's turkey-call bubbled out its message and the Americans fell back, yielding the deadly open spaces to the British. For three hours and more the two forces swayed back and forth across the clearing while British losses swelled to a frightening figure. Regimental lines closed up again and again while companies shrank to platoons and platoons to squads. Exhausted, hungry, ragged British officers and men were magnificent, giving ground with bitter reluctance, driving forward again, unflinching, in the face of a gale of rifle fire that was, to them, almost a new form of warfare.

A woodcut of the Battle of Freeman's Farm

Menacingly, the arc of American fire spread about the British left. Burgoyne, superb in fresh scarlet and white, rode unhurriedly among his men as bullets ripped his coat. His hat was pierced, but he only laughed and waved it above his head as his men cheered him hoarsely. But the British hold on the clearing shrank as men in patched scarlet coats pitched to the trampled grasses.

All at once, beyond the left of the tough old 9th Norfolks, blue coats and brass helmets appeared among the trees. Out from the hidden east burst von Riedesel with the Rhetz regiment and two of Georg Pausch's cannon. Pausch's guns went into quick action, the Rhetz files closed on the British left. Yankee drum and turkey-call faded away to the south and British and Brunswicker dropped to the ground, utterly spent. As at Hubbardton, a British force had been saved from possible destruction by the arrival of German troops on its left.

Burgoyne returned to his headquarters in the Great Ravine and somehow managed to transmute what he had seen into a golden victory. Actually, British losses topped the 600 mark, with the 62nd Wiltshires reporting only 60 men fit for duty. As for the triple advance, the strongest element, Fraser's Advance Corps, had hardly come into action at all; the Baron's downriver sweep had been called off and his men luckily diverted to save Burgoyne's center at the very last moment. Yet to his men Burgoyne was still the beloved commander. Sergeant Roger Lamb of the 9th wrote that he "shunned no danger; his presence animated the troops for they greatly loved the General."

Gentleman Johnny's hopes were sent skyward again no later than the twenty-first. A messenger from Sir Henry Clinton in New York managed to slip through the American lines with a letter. "You know my good will and are not ignorant of my poverty," wrote Clinton. "If you think 2,000 men can assist you effectually, I will make a push at [Fort] Montgomery in about ten days. But ever jealous of my flanks if they make a move in force on either of them I must return to New York to save this important post. I expect reenforcement every day. Let me know what you wish."

It must have been the reference to "reenforcement" on which Burgoyne pinned his hopes, for he was soldier enough to know that a demonstration by 2,000 men against Fort Montgomery far below West Point could have little effect on that mysterious enemy, barely seen if sorely felt, lying somewhere to his immediate south. He decided to hang on and wait on events.

The halted invasion dug in solidly, and Rebel pressure steadily increased. There was constant sniping. The Anglo-German lines were raided almost nightly. Rations dwindled and the remaining horses had to be fed on leaves.

"At no time did the Jews await the coming of the Messiah with greater expectancy than we awaited the coming of General Clinton."
—*German Soldier, 1777*

Desertions, especially among the Germans, increased. Officers, busy day and night, grew gaunt and shaky. The Baroness, installed with her daughters in a log cabin, noted that her husband went days on end without a chance to change his clothes or sleep for more than a few minutes. The weather grew colder, and since all spare gear had long ago been sent back to Ticonderoga, all ranks suffered. A pack of wolves descended from the north to howl dreadfully in the dark nights as they pawed up half-buried bodies or closed snapping jaws on helpless sick and wounded.

Rebel formations captured several hundred prisoners about Ticonderoga. John Stark swooped out of the Hampshire Grants and pressed downriver far enough to bring Burgoyne's priceless string of supply bateaux and barges under fire. As October came on it was obvious that the invasion force would have to do something on its own, whatever Clinton might or might not attempt far down the Hudson. Burgoyne consulted with his leading generals and on October 7, 1777, launched the weirdest, most inexplicable coup of his entire campaign.

Under a sun that beat down from a cloudless sky, 1,500 men stood waiting among the golden stalks in a wheat field beyond the Freeman clearings. Faded British scarlet glowed ember-like on the right. In the center was the solid blue of Brunswick units. On the far left, facing a steep downslope, were the ragged bearskin caps of British grenadiers. The command was far too strong to be the "reconnoisance in force" that Burgoyne called it, but it was too weak numerically to launch a real offensive. Burgoyne was a born gambler, and he may merely have been pushing his stakes onto the table to see what his shadowy enemy would do. If this were the case, Gentleman Johnny was facing loaded dice. All that can be said is that he, and those with him, faced them gallantly.

Sometime after two o'clock, the dice rolled across the board in a series of stunning thuds. Up the blind slope, where the grenadiers stood under Major Acland, swept General Enoch Poor's brigade, smashing in among the bearskins and shattering those elite troops. Off to the right, Dan Morgan's turkey-call bubbled and gobbled as the riflemen and Henry Dearborn's infantry struck at the Earl of Balcarres' rear. The Germans were rocked back, shredded, cut up, driven from the center by Ebenezer Learned's brigade. The whole wheat field snarled with bullets and cannon shot, and the long, drying stalks were pulped under heavy, broken boots. Burgoyne, the Baron, and Simon Fraser struggled heroically to rally their men, but riflemen high in the treetops sent bullets drilling unerringly down. Burgoyne's hat and uniform were riddled once more. Off to the right, Fraser and Balcarres strove to re-form the light infantry and the 24th South Wales Borderers. Suddenly Fraser crumpled in his saddle, mortally wounded by one of Morgan's snipers.

The rout became complete, and the survivors reeled back into fortifications that had been hacked out during Burgoyne's weeks of hopeful waiting. There were two strong points in advance of that main line, the so-called Balcarres and Breymann redoubts, and into the first poured the wreck of the young Earl's command. The Germans made for the main works, leaving Breymann and his grenadier garrison unsupported.

Sometime during this phase of the action, Benedict Arnold, whose exact whereabouts and movements during the whole campaign are still hotly debated, appeared on the scene. Either joining up with General Learned's pursuing units or hurling them along in his wake, Arnold led a furious smash against the Balcarres redoubt only to meet with intense resistance from the garrison and remnants of the light infantry and the Borderers. Balked here,

The death of General
Simon Frazer, by West

and losing more men in the vain onrush, he swung his men to the left, cleared out the light works between the two redoubts, and then sent some of Morgan's men at the Brunswick grenadiers. These tough fighters seem to have been in the process of withdrawal when the blow fell, and little more than a token volley appears to have been fired before the grenadiers fled back to the main line. Breymann was shot down, possibly by his own men, as he tried to stem the flight; and Benedict Arnold, urging his big horse through a sally port, caught a parting bullet in the same leg that had been smashed in the blizzards before Quebec on New Year's day, 1776. He was to be out of action for a long time, and when he took the field again, it was to be against his own countrymen.

The disaster of what may be called the Second Battle of Freeman's Farm rendered every line of Burgoyne's "Thoughts" purely academic. The invasion force was finished as a combat entity, and on the night of October 8 the remains of the army formed in a pouring rain and began a slow, perilous march north along the Hudson with the haven of Ticonderoga as objective. Supply wagons bogged down axle deep and had to be abandoned. Roaming bodies of Rebel militia snapped up laden barges and bateaux. Luckily for the beaten force, the American commander, Horatio Gates, was very tardy in applying pressure to the northward move, but Burgoyne failed to profit by his adversary's laxness, and it was not until October 9 that his army managed to cross the Fishkill, a confluent of the Hudson. Possibly hoping for a breathing spell, Burgoyne dug in there, on the heights of Saratoga.

Major General Horatio Gates, by Peale

Then Dan Morgan was up and across the Fishkill with Learned, and drenched British sentries could see masses of Brigadier General John Fellows' Massachusetts militia closing in from the east. British and German eyes turned longingly north, where the road to Ticonderoga still lay open if only Burgoyne would give the word to move. Then, on the thirteenth, the wambling road on the west bank was suddenly acrawl with the enemy. Unpredictable General John Stark had dragged his feet after Bennington, but now he abruptly slammed the door of the northern corridor, ringing down the curtain on the final act of Burgoyne's tragedy, leaving nothing but a brief epilogue to be spoken near the village of Saratoga.

There were negotiations, florid and orotund, for Horatio Gates could pose and gesture nearly as effectively as his opponent. On October 17, in accord with the "Convention" (not "capitulation") to which Gates had agreed, British and German troops filed out of their works and formally laid down their arms near the ruins of a fort built by Baron Dieskau, a Saxon General in the French service, in the 1750's. This simple ceremony was a very sore point in the myriad tangles of eighteenth-century military honor, and Gates, not usually the most generous or tactful of men, stepped out of character long enough to order that no Americans be present to witness the stacking of muskets, drums, and flags.

Drama reasserted itself when Gates and Burgoyne, the former gravely unobtrusive in plain blue and the latter gleaming in scarlet and white under a wildly plumed hat, watched the weaponless men of the invasion force pass in review. First came the British, sullen, silent, and by no means convinced that they had been beaten. They have never, in all their long history, made good prisoners of war, and throughout the captivity which they were now entering proved as cantankerous and exasperating to their captors as the most arrant Yankee could have been. Panache could hardly have been expected from the Germans, who, sent off to a war in which they had no interest, accepted

A German version of Burgoyne's surrender

defeat as stolidly as they would have met victory, for, barring the chance of individual loot, defeat or victory merely meant the end of campaigning. So these lost, homesick thousands marched docilely on, taking with them unnumbered forest pets. Young deer minced along, and bear cubs padded clumsily by gaitered legs. Leashed foxes moved sleekly with their owners, and raccoons chittered and clowned as they perched on knapsacks. These were the Germans' *spolia opima*, the pitiful rewards of hard campaigning.

These prisoners came out of the haze of war to face a real shock—the sight of the ordered ranks of Gates' army, of Morgan's and John Glover's men, of Abraham Ten Broeck's Albany militia. They had seen their foes before, but rarely en masse, and some marchers wrote that they felt they were seeing a new race of men. There were oddly clothed young boys and old men in the militia ranks, and Negroes who presented arms as free men along with free men. Faces, several Germans noted, were lean, the men's bodies rangy. Paunches were few and tall men seemed the rule rather than the exception.

The prisoners' curiosity was blanketed by a dread of jeering outbursts from the supposedly ill-disciplined ranks, who might conceivably add a shower of stones to barbed taunts. Yet the march went on past rank after rank of impassive, motionless Americans. This silence had been ordered by Gates and that ordering does him credit. That the order was so uniformly obeyed, as both British and Germans testified, was to the credit of every silent man standing beside his well-kept firearm.

After the passage of the troops, a solid *calèche* rocked out of the German lines, bearing the von Riedesel ladies into captivity along with their husband and father. The little Baroness wrote, "In the passage through the American camp I observed, with great satisfaction, that no one cast us scornful glances. On the contrary they all greeted me, even showing compassion on their countenances." The little party was taken directly under the wing of General Philip Schuyler, not only along the Hudson but also later in his Albany mansion.

After such amenities, the last vestige of courtesy and generosity passed out of the picture. Gates, the niggling, pettifogging side of his nature coming uppermost, broadcast his triumph in many quarters, but omitted the one man to whom he should have reported at once. General George Washington learned of the wreck of the invasion only by accident, a good two weeks after Burgoyne's capitulation. The relative stature of the two men may be gauged by the fact that Washington wrote Gates at once, warmly congratulating him on his "signal success" and confining any well-merited rebuke to the mild ending, "I cannot but regret that a matter of such magnitude . . . should have reached me by report only, or through the channel of letters, not bearing that authenticity which the importance of it required, and which it would have received by a line under your signature, stating the simple fact." It is a further measure of Gates that he did all he could to prevent and then delay the dispatch of his now idle forces to the main army, recovering from its near miss at Germantown.

As to the prisoners, known to history as the "Convention Troops," Gates had promised and over-promised to an extent far exceeding his legal powers, without the slightest reference to the Congress or to General Washington. This resulted in the unfortunate troops being tossed about, with Congress repudiating many of Gates' pledges made at Saratoga in the name of, but without the sanction of, Congress. Sent to Cambridge, the prisoners languished miserably in Massachusetts, then were ordered out on another killing march that took them down into Virginia and later into Pennsylvania, where most of them stayed until the end of the war.

"The Horse America throwing his Master," a British comment on Burgoyne's defeat and the subsequent French alliance

"Q. What kind of men compose the Congress?
A. It consists of obscure, pettifogging attorneys, bankrupt shopkeepers, outlawed smugglers, etc., etc."
—A Loyalist Catechism, 1778

248

St. John's on the Richelieu River served as a staging area for Burgoyne's expedition. The two larger ships, the Royal George *(left) and* Inflexible, *escorted the flotilla of transports up Lake Champlain to Ticonderoga.*

Burgoyne's Strategy for Invasion

The interior water route between New York and the St. Lawrence River held an almost hypnotic attraction for Revolutionary strategists. Ethan Allen, Montgomery, Arnold, and Carleton had struggled for its control; in 1777, Major General John Burgoyne entered the contest. His "Thoughts for Conducting the War from the Side of Canada" called for Burgoyne to move south to Albany, where he would meet Colonel Barry St. Leger's force driving east through the Mohawk Valley. Howe was to march north from New York to join them. To George III it seemed to be "on a proper foundation," for if Washington tried to stop Howe he would be an easy target for the combined forces; if he did not, New England would be knocked out of the war. The plan, however, required the closest co-ordination between the three divisions, and this, as it turned out, was its fatal flaw.

The British "considered their toils to be nearly at an end" when they reached the Hudson after a brutal wilderness march. As shown here, they advanced along its east bank, transporting the army's heavy baggage in bateaux.

Failures Plague the British

With Barry St. Leger (left) at the siege of Fort Stanwix were some 1,000 Iroquois and an insane Tory named Hon Yost Schuyler, whose ravings the Indians believed to be the voice of the Great Spirit. Benedict Arnold held Hon Yost's brother hostage, and, through him, forced the madman to spread rumors among the Indians that a large American force was approaching. This ruse caused the terrified red men to desert St. Leger.

Misfortune dogged Burgoyne's "Thoughts" from the start. A slip-up in London caused Howe's orders to arrive after he had already committed himself to taking Philadelphia, eliminating any chance of his aiding Burgoyne. Then St. Leger failed utterly. His force, composed largely of Indians, was to cut in behind any Rebels who moved north to challenge Burgoyne. As he laid siege to Fort Stanwix, which guarded the Mohawk Valley near present-day Rome, New York, his Indians were thrown into a panic by rumors that Benedict Arnold was about to fall on them with a huge American force— a ruse initiated by Arnold himself. The Indians turned on their erstwhile allies, and St. Leger's redcoats were driven right out of the campaign.

Burgoyne had started with a stunning success, taking Ticonderoga, the so-called "Fortress of America," without a fight on July 6. But instead of continuing by water via Lake George and along the upper reaches of the Hudson, Burgoyne pushed straight south through primeval wilderness. This punishing march forced him to send almost the entire left wing of his army to seize badly needed stores at Bennington, where militiamen under John Stark cut it to ribbons. Informed at last of the fact that no help was forthcoming from Howe, Burgoyne could withdraw or fight his way through Horatio Gates' army to reach the comparative safety of Albany. He elected to honor his dictum that "This Army Must Not Retreat."

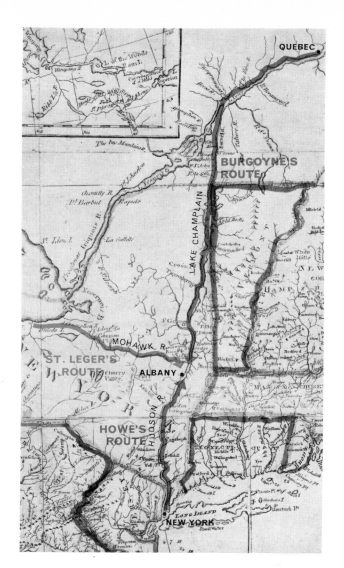

Philip Schuyler (above) effectively slowed Burgoyne's advance until Gates took command. Burgoyne's grand strategy is superimposed on the 1777 map at right. The half-Hessian, half-Tory force sent to Bennington was "warmly engaged" by Stark's militia and virtually annihilated. Below, the mortally wounded commanders, Baum of the Germans and Pfister of the Tories, are carried from the field. Burgoyne lost some 900 of his men in this action, the Rebels only 70.

The Two Battles
of Freeman's Farm

Having decided to push on to Albany, Burgoyne could either continue down the Hudson's undefended east bank, crossing the river near Albany, or cross farther north to challenge Gates. Under the direction of the Polish engineer Tadeusz Kosciuszko, the Americans had thrown up strong works on the west bank, and Burgoyne, in the best British tradi-

tion, chose to attack. On September 19 his attempted breakthrough at Freeman's Farm was repulsed, largely by Daniel Morgan's riflemen, and a second effort there on October 7 was also turned back. The painting above shows Benedict Arnold, on a white horse, leading a charge in this battle. At the right British General Simon Fraser is carried from the field, supposedly a victim of sharpshooter Tim Murphy, visible in the tree at upper left. After losing 1,200 men in these two engagements, Burgoyne's situation was desperate. As he began to withdraw the remnants of his army to entrenchments at Saratoga, he was pursued by a force which now outnumbered him three to one.

The Significance of Saratoga

Burgoyne tarried in his Saratoga lines for four days, trying to find some way out of his dilemma. Then John Stark appeared with 1,100 men from the Hampshire Grants, blocking his last northern escape route. "Numerous parties of American militia . . . swarmed around the little adverse army like birds of prey," a British sergeant wrote, and Hessian General von Riedesel recalled, "Every hour the position of the army grew more critical, and prospect of salvation grew less and less." Finally, on October 14, Burgoyne asked for surrender terms, and Gates allowed him virtually to dictate the resulting "Convention of Saratoga."

Although the subsequent execution of this agreement suffered from bad faith on both sides, doing credit to neither, this in no way dims the luster of a great American victory. The surrender of an entire British army with all its equipment had a tremendous psychological impact on the American cause. While Gates claimed the victory, the credit must go to others—among them Benedict Arnold, who blunted St. Leger's drive and who, with the superb Daniel Morgan, wrecked Burgoyne's attempts to break through at Freeman's Farm. France had already been impressed by the Americans' conduct at Germantown, and news of the surrender of over 5,000 crack British and German troops gave impetus to a momentous decision. Louis XVI officially recognized the new republic, and on February 6, 1778, signed a Treaty pledging full military support to the United States.

The British evacuated Ticonderoga and Crown Point and gave up all hope of using the Hudson-Champlain route. Clinton, who had started up the Hudson toward Burgoyne, hastened back to New York, and by the end of 1777 the British held only that city, Philadelphia, and Newport. Six months later they abandoned Philadelphia, and the center of activity began shifting toward the South.

Trumbull's painting of the surrender has Burgoyne offering his sword to Gates, who returned it and invited his opponent to dine with him in his tent. Also shown are Morgan (in white) and Philip Schuyler (in mufti, right).

Above is a view of the British camp, made shortly after the Second Battle of Freeman's Farm. General Fraser's funeral procession is visible near the base of the hill at right.

At right is the prison camp of Burgoyne's army at Charlottesville, Virginia. Congress refused to parole the so-called "Convention Troops," rightly suspecting that the British planned to send them back into the war.

Benjamin Franklin, by Charles Willson Peale

THE QUEST
FOR ALLIES

"Firmly assure Congress of my friendship. I hope that

this will be for the good of both nations."

KING LOUIS XVI OF FRANCE—MARCH 20, 1778

IN THE days immediately following the outbreak of hostilities, before the word "Independence" had been more than whispered in the shady streets of Philadelphia, the collective minds of the Continental Congress turned almost instinctively to the question of support, open or tacit, from Europe. While many factors guided the delegates' thoughts into this channel, three major ones were obvious at once to any man surveying the state of the Thirteen Colonies. First, to survive, financial aid was essential, since Britain had not encouraged the accumulation of capital in its colonies. Next, supplies of all kinds must be found and a steady flow arranged from Europe into America, for British policy had frowned upon any extensive colonial manufacturing, curbing it by such legislation as the so-called Iron Act of 1750, which shut down hard on the American production and processing of iron. And finally, to prosecute a war the colonies most certainly had to obtain the support of a large, efficient, up-to-date fleet to checkmate British control of the seas and waterways.

Finance and supplies could be secured through negotiation, assuming that a European power with sufficient available risk capital for covert loans to the colonies were willing to risk an open breach with England. The question of a manned fleet, which could hardly be purchased or hired, obviously involved an outright alliance with some foreign power, with some country ready and willing to step into the picture as an active ally or co-belligerent. Appreciation of the importance of these three points was by no means universal among delegates to the Congress. The problems inherent in foreign entanglements, in fact, caused many level-headed men to shy away from even thinking of them. But quiet, sometimes furtive, explorations of these and other questions went on.

It was quite obvious that supplies and financial aid would be obtained from countries whose wish for British defeat overrode the ever-present possibility of American collapse. Such help—whether in cash or kind—could be regarded as a calculated risk by the hypothetical lender, who might lose his stake but would not have committed any official overt act of hostility against England. And where might such a lender be found? The field narrowed down to France, which Louis XV's minister, the Duc de Choiseul, had brought back into very fair shape after the staggering losses of the Seven Years' War. If France could induce other powers, such as Holland and Spain, to join in secretly, the risk of loss might be spread.

As to the fleet, France, now under Louis XVI, stood alone as a possible source, and to tap this would mean establishing such hope in Paris of American victory as to make outright alliance promise ultimate success. Otherwise, French ministers could visualize an American debacle, with France left alone to face an outraged England which would already be in high gear for war.

For the moment, the question of alliance with any foreign power held so many highly touchy points that it, and the naval aid that might accompany it, was pushed into the background to be contemplated only by the most desperate and daring. It is being wise after the event to hold that sea power should have engaged the closest attention of the whole country. Yet surely it must have been clear that water-borne transport had thus far predominated in American life to the extent that roads had been little developed, particularly in the agricultural South. As the war went on, it was found that the cost of moving wheat overland from Virginia to the army in New Jersey was prohibitive, for the transport animals used up more forage en route than they brought the troops. More obvious still, as the war went on, was the fact that American armies were chained to a wretched interior road system, while the British commanders, with control of the seas, were able to

Caron de Beaumarchais

move by water up and down the coast and strike when and where they chose.

So foreign finance and supply, along with other problems, held the attention of Congress, and as early as November, 1775, a Committee of Secret Correspondence, under benign Benjamin Franklin, was instructed to put out feelers to foreign powers. Other minds, in far-off Europe, had been moving along the same general track, and in the winter of 1775–76, a French agent, Bonvouloir, masquerading as a Flemish trader, appeared in Philadelphia. Highly secret meetings were held between Bonvouloir and Franklin's Committee, and American hopes soared until it was found that the Frenchman's visit was strictly an exploratory one, and that he had no powers to negotiate. However, he did take back to France a sober report that the "ardor and determination" of the Americans were incredible.

The Secret Committee would have liked something more concrete than Bonvouloir could offer, but at least it was encouraged to broaden its field of activity. Arthur Lee, a Virginian living undisturbed in England, was authorized to sound out various European embassies in London, while Silas Deane of Connecticut was chosen to go quietly to the French Court as a sort of undercover agent for both the Secret Committee and the Commercial Committee of Congress. Deane, on the surface, was singularly ill-equipped for his task. He spoke no French and was utterly ignorant of diplomatic usages. Yet somehow he managed to offset these shortcomings through resoluteness, honesty, and courage—qualities that also saw him through the bitter abuse that followed completion of his mission.

Arthur Lee

It may be added that Silas Deane had another gift, one which Napoleon later held to be essential for a good general—he was lucky. Even before he arrived in Paris, mysterious wheels were turning under the astute hand of Charles Gravier, Comte de Vergennes, French Minister of Foreign Affairs, who had fought successfully for a policy of granting money and supplies to the new nation across the Atlantic. Vergennes and his followers seem to have had no wish to regain their own lost colonies, which they looked upon as a drain rather than as a strength. But they did look on the loss of British North America as England's ruin, with France taking the island kingdom's place as the leading power of the world. Already substantial shipments of French supplies had been made to America through the utterly private firm of Pliarne, Penet et Cie, which had been able mysteriously to purchase weapons directly from French government arsenals.

So Deane reached France to find his main job done for him. And very soon afterward there materialized the shadowy firm of Hortalez et Cie, headed by the never-shadowy, ever-flamboyant Caron de Beaumarchais.

Diplomatic successes abroad were not matched by military triumphs at home. Howe's campaigns in New York and the Jerseys clearly pointed to the fact that something would have to be done quickly in the way of outside aid. There were blistering debates in Congress, and the dread word "Alliance" kept reappearing until it was finally crushed by an opposition controlled largely by John Adams. He had been ashamed, Adams cried, to hear "so many Whigs groaning and Sighing with Despondency and whining out their fears that We must be subdued unless France should step in."

One vitally important move sent the ablest and wisest of all Americans of that day, seventy-year-old Benjamin Franklin, to France. His mission: to step up aid of all sorts and to effect a Treaty of Commerce and Amity with that country. Perhaps the alliance idea had not been quite scotched, for Franklin was specifically authorized "to press for the immediate and explicit declara-

Silas Deane

tion of France in our Favour, upon a Suggestion that a Re-union with Great Britain may be the Consequence of a delay." This would undoubtedly have made France a co-belligerent, and an out-and-out alliance would have been the next logical step.

Outwardly unimpressed with the strong probability that if his ship were picked up by British cruisers he would be hanged for high treason, Franklin calmly set sail on October 27 on the armed sloop *Reprisal,* which was laden with Carolina indigo to cover the cost of the voyage. With him went his two grandsons, Temple Franklin, seventeen, and Benjamin Franklin Bache, seven. The never-old septuagenarian spent his time quite happily on *Reprisal,* noting daily temperature readings of air and water, and musing on the true nature of the Gulf Stream. Landing near Quiberon Bay, the scene of the French navy's stinging defeat in 1759, the man from the New World found that France was opening its arms to him. Crowds followed him, besieged his quarters en route to Versailles and Paris, gave balls and dinners in his honor. He could hardly have expected such a welcome, but it did not seem to disturb his unshakable equilibrium, for on the road he took approving note of "six or seven country women . . . on horseback and astride; they were all of fair white and red complexions but one among them was the fairest woman I ever beheld."

The simply garbed Franklin is welcomed at a French reception in 1778

He was at Versailles on the twentieth and at Paris the next day, and the ardor with which he was welcomed did not abate in the slightest. In the past he had corresponded with many scientists and intellectuals, men like Diderot, d'Alembert, and Lavoisier. His reception in such circles might have been taken for granted, but he swept France like a benign contagion. Portraits, busts, statuettes of him appeared everywhere. His face smiled out from enameled brooches, studs, and watches, and was printed on coarse cotton handkerchiefs and on finest silk and lawn.

Soon he was installed in the then suburb of Passy on the right bank of the Seine, finely lodged in the Château de Chaumont, which was put at his disposal gratis by the owner, Donatien le Ray. He quickly saw his proper role and as quickly fell into it. By no means averse to smart clothes, Franklin sensed that the French wanted to think of him as a sort of rustic philosopher, as the "natural man" so hymned by Rousseau. Very well. He dressed the part, wearing a fur cap and very plain clothes and walking abroad with a long, patriarchal staff of apple wood. His gray hair he wore unclubbed and falling nearly to his shoulders, and in this homely garb drew about him a worshiping entourage of French ladies—notably Madame Helvétius, and Madame Brillon, with whom he is reported to have played chess while Madame soaked in her bath.

A good deal of this odd mixture of gallantry and rusticity may be taken as what modern Intelligence would call "cover." Under it, work went on furiously. Arthur Lee came over from England to help him and Silas Deane, and Franklin left many of the details of the commercial treaty to them while he, peering wisely over the tops of his spectacles, steered a steady course that might lead to far bigger stakes. Carefully keeping clear of court intrigues, where people tried to involve him in de Choiseul's attempt to oust Vergennes in favor of someone who might take more direct action, he dropped a word here, chatted amiably there, and more and more ships began to clear French ports bound for America. American privateers, which soon swarmed thicker in European waters, preying on British commerce, found that they could put in at French ports for refitting.

Lord Stormont, British Ambassador at Paris, fumed and spluttered at Vergennes: "It is a fact, sir, a Part of the force of this Country is directed against us . . . All human things have bounds beyond which they cannot go. We are

Victor Hugo made this sketch in 1836 of Franklin's house at Passy, France now come to the utmost Verge of these Bounds." Vergennes was able to soothe Stormont, but it was increasingly harder to do so as time went on. And all the while Franklin professed very little interest in any formal military alliances, which might well bind America beyond "its True interests." So firmly and pleasantly did he state his position that Louis XVI's ministers, buttonholing each other at Versailles, wondered if Monsieur Franklin could be *induced* to accept an alliance for his country, assuming that such a proffer were made.

The news of Germantown and of Burgoyne's surrender seems to have thrown a sudden fright into Vergennes. His agents let him know through various channels that Lord North, British Prime Minister, had been in touch with Franklin, Deane, and Lee. Suppose England offered Franklin such terms that the philosopher-diplomat of Passy could not afford to refuse! Much of Vergennes' carefully and cautiously built structure would come tumbling down.

In secret councils Vergennes unveiled his qualms. "Events have surprised us, they have marched more rapidly than we could have expected. The time lost, if any, is not entirely our fault, but there is no more to be lost. . . . They [the Americans] want positive facts and effective assurances, capable of counterbalancing the definite offers of England." Yet it is likely that at this time Vergennes' idea of "effective assurances" was limited to increased material aid, he still being fearful of involving France in open war with England.

Comte de Vergennes

Louis XVI has often been portrayed as the chief checkrein on an impetuous Foreign Minister and on his country in general, even to the point of scowling at the very thought of French officers going to America as volunteers. Lafayette, in particular, is generally supposed to have fled France against royal order, with a *lettre de cachet* hanging over his head. According to M. Albert Krebs of the Bibliothèque Nationale, however, the young Marquis left France with full royal blessing, the *lettre de cachet* and the secret embarkation from a Spanish port having been carefully rigged to forestall any British complaints that highly placed nobles were openly sailing to join the Rebels on French ships and from French ports.

The Treaty of Alliance, when it finally flowered, appears as the work of Louis himself. M. Philippe Erlanger cites a letter from Vergennes, dated January 8, 1778, to the French Ambassador at Madrid, Montmorin, which contains the flat statement, "The supreme decision was taken by the King. He did not take it under the influence of his ministers."

So, in the early weeks of 1778, Vergennes presented, with inward misgivings, a draft treaty to the American Commissioners, which added military provisions to those of commerce and amity that the American Congress had authorized in 1776. At least the Count could console himself with the virtual certainty that Spain, too, would enter the war as a result of the French action, for Montmorin had written him, "Be sure, Sir, that in whatever manner France is dragged into the war, Spain will follow." The logic of events would, he felt, be bound to break down any misgivings the Spanish Foreign Minister might have.

King Louis XVI

Strolling about the great gardens in Passy, sunning himself on the southern pavilion that jutted out from the Château de Chaumont, peering approvingly over his spectacles as workmen installed Franklin lightning rods on the *poivrières,* America's senior statesman could mull over the terms and realize that they reflected an international meeting of minds. True, the military Alliance was to take effect only in the event of war between France and England, but the trend of events made this a virtual certainty. When this occurred, America was to pledge itself to the defense of the French West Indies and not to make peace without the consent of France. On its part, France guaranteed the independence of America and promised to continue hostilities until that great aim had been gained. And, keeping in mind the opinion of the French Ambassador to Madrid, a secret clause was inserted, making room for Spain—just in case His Catholic Majesty should change his mind.

On the evening of Friday, February 6, 1778, Benjamin Franklin discarded those somber clothes which most Parisians insisted were Quaker garb, and donned a magnificent, if slightly out-of-date, coat of figured blue Manchester velvet. His astonished colleagues Deane and Arthur Lee were stunned by the sudden burst of elegance. Smiling, Franklin told them that he had worn it new to a special hearing of a Parliamentary committee in London, back in '74. At that meeting Alexander Wedderburn had attacked him violently for his part in the transmission to the Massachusetts General Court of the private Hutchinson-Oliver letters concerning doings in that colony. This had been one of the greatest humiliations in Franklin's life, and though he had carefully kept the coat, he had never worn it since that day in 1774.

Now, he explained, he was giving that coat "a little revenge," for the three Americans were going into Paris on a most important mission. That evening, in Vergennes' offices in the Hôtel de Lautrec, a cuff of figured blue Manchester velvet brushed across the formally engrossed copy of the Treaty as its wearer put his name to the great instrument that bound France and the United States of America in firm alliance.

Some attempts were made to keep the Treaty a secret until all possible French ships then at sea could be moved out of the path of British cruisers and raiders. But on March 20, Louis XVI made formal avowal by receiving the American Commissioners at Versailles. Word had spread and crowds gathered. With his sure touch, Franklin did not disappoint them. His Wedderburn coat was carefully packed away, and he descended from his coach without wig or sword—in a somber brown coat, spectacles perched on his nose, a plain white hat under his arm—and sailed majestically into the palace. After him came Silas Deane, Arthur and William Lee, and Ralph Izard of South Carolina, all in formal court dress. If the gaping crowds outside had been impressed by Franklin's display of sturdy republican simplicity, the courtiers inside were bowled over.

There was a private audience with Louis of France, and the Duc de Croÿ noted that the King spoke with unusual warmth and grace, asking Franklin to assure Congress of his friendship: "I hope that this will be for the good of both nations." The silver-haired patriarch "very nobly thanked [the King] in the name of America, saying: 'Your Majesty may count on the gratitude of Congress and its faithful observance of the pledges it now takes.'" Later Vergennes gave an elaborate dinner and took the party to call on the royal family, where pretty little Marie Antoinette was so carried away by Franklin's charming simplicity that she abandoned her beloved gaming table to talk with the philosopher of Passy. And when the lure of high stakes became too strong for her, she commanded that he stand beside her while she played on.

Franklin, Deane, and Arthur Lee might mentally write "Mission accomplished" against the treaty item. It still remained for the Congress in Philadelphia to ratify, and for the moment time seemed to be running against the French-American pact. Early in 1778, Lord North had laid before Parliament his so-called Conciliatory Propositions, measures intended to end hostilities. Their provisions were long and involved, but they at least showed on the part of the ministry a keen desire to receive the turbulent and unruly colonists back in the Empire once more. Almost every important point of friction was

CONTINUED ON PAGE 264

A Ramberg sketch of Franklin's audience at the French Court

The Treaty of Alliance

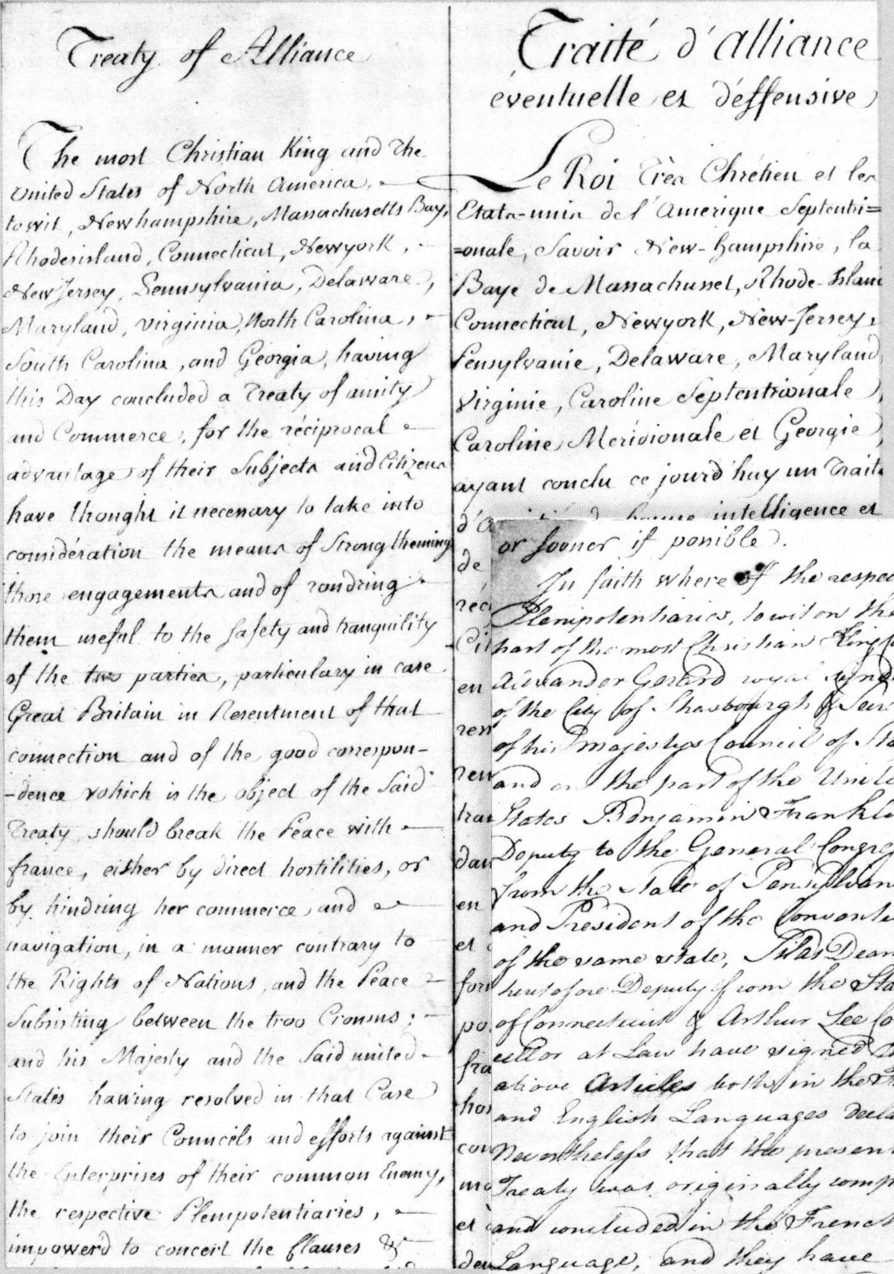

Treaty of Alliance

The most Christian King and the United States of North America, to wit, New hampshire, Massachusetts Bay, Rhodeisland, Connecticut, Newyork, New Jersey, Pennsylvania, Delaware, Maryland, Virginia, North Carolina, South Carolina, and Georgia, having this Day concluded a Treaty of amity and Commerce, for the reciprocal advantage of their Subjects and Citizens have thought it necessary to take into consideration the means of strengthening those engagements and of rendering them useful to the safety and tranquility of the two parties, particulary in case Great Britain in Resentment of that connection and of the good correspondence which is the object of the Said Treaty, should break the Peace with France, either by direct hostilities, or by hindring her commerce and navigation, in a manner contrary to the Rights of Nations, and the Peace Subsisting between the two Crowns; and his Majesty and the Said united States having resolved in that Case to join their Councils and efforts against the Enterprises of their common Enemy, the respective Plenipotentiaries, impowerd to concert the Clauses &

Traité d'alliance éventuelle et déffensive

Le Roi Très Chretien et les Etats-unis de l'Amerique Septentrionale, Savoir New-Hampshire, la Baye de Massachuset, Rhode-Island, Connecticut, Newyork, New-Jersey, Pensylvanie, Delaware, Maryland, Virginie, Caroline Septentrionale, Caroline Meridionale et Georgie, ayant conclu ce jourd'huy un Traité d'amitié, de bonne intelligence et

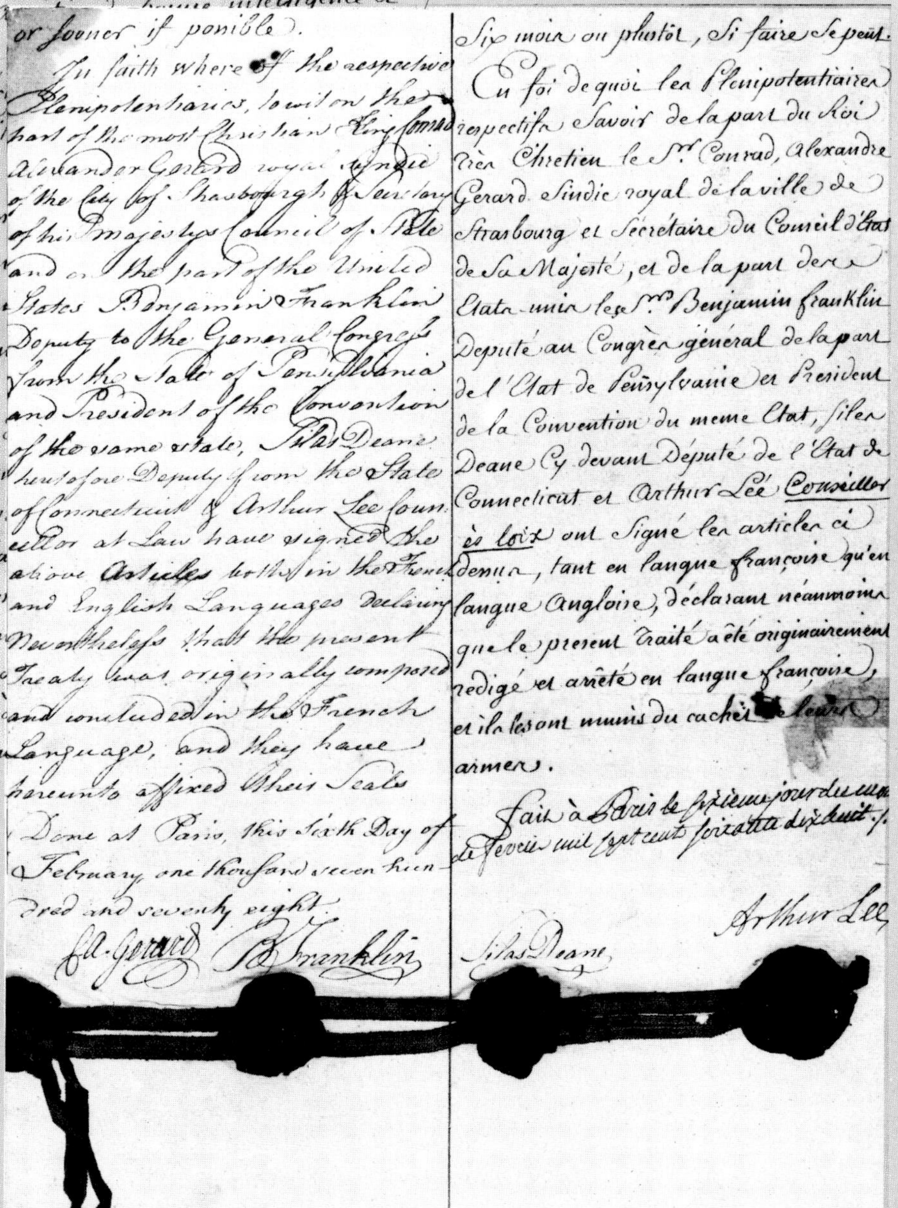

or sooner if possible.

In faith where of the respective Plenipotentiaries, to wit on the part of the most Christian King Conrad Alexander Gerard royal Syndic of the City of Strasbourgh & Secretary of his Majestys Council of State and on the part of the United States Benjamin Franklin Deputy to the General Congress from the State of Pensylvania and President of the Convention of the same state, Silas Deane heretofore Deputy from the State of Connecticut & Arthur Lee Councellor at Law have signed the above Articles both in the French and English Languages declaring Nevertheless that the present Treaty was originally composed and concluded in the French Language, and they have hereunto affixed their Seals

Done at Paris, this sixth Day of February one thousand seven hundred and seventy eight.

C.A. Gerard B Franklin

Six mois ou plutôt, Si faire se peut.

En foi de quoi les Plenipotentiaires respectifs Savoir de la part du Roi Très Chretien le Sr. Conrad, Alexandre Gerard Sindic royal de la ville de Strasbourg et Secrétaire du Conseil d'Etat de Sa Majesté, et de la part des Etats unis les Srs. Benjamin Franklin Député au Congrès général de la part de l'Etat de Pensylvanie et President de la Convention du meme Etat, Silas Deane Cy devant Député de l'Etat de Connecticut et Arthur Lée Conseiller ès loix ont Signé les articles ci dessus, tant en langue françoise qu'en langue Angloise, déclarant néanmoins que le present Traité a été originairement redigé et arrêté en langue françoise, et ils les ont munis du cachet de leurs armes.

Fait à Paris le sixieme jour du mois de fevrier mil sept cent soixante dix huit.

Silas Deane Arthur Lee

The first and last pages of the Treaty of Alliance, which was written in both French and English, are shown here. This vital document was signed in Paris, in February, 1778, by France's Minister to the United States, Conrad Alexandre Gerard, and by the three American representatives, Benjamin Franklin, Silas Deane and Arthur Lee.

CONTINUED FROM PAGE 262

abolished, even that sorest of sore spots, the Parliamentary claim of the right to tax. There should be an immediate conference with the former colonists; Lord North added yearningly that there was "so much affection left in that country [America] toward this, that barely to enter on a discussion is half the business." Sweet reason, not threats, oozed from every line of the Propositions.

It took a hot fight to get this measure through Parliament, but North finally won out—his victory somewhat marred by a statement from his own party members that the proposals proved "the affection of the indulgent, injured mother, even to her most degenerate, refractory, guilty children." Whig members muttered acidly that while Acts of Parliament might make a rebellion, they could not repeal one.

North's plan very possibly would have met with quick acceptance a few months earlier. How would it fare in 1778? The cards seemed stacked against the new French Alliance, since North's proposals reached Congress at a time when that body had had no news of any sort from its mission to France in nearly a year, when the army was just emerging from Valley Forge, and when the British military and naval hold on the country seemed unshakable.

The impact of the Propositions on Congress was surprising. They were unanimously rejected, with a rather nastily barbed rider to the effect that England could not be trusted, since "upon the first favorable occasion" that country would again be swayed by "that lust of domination which hath rent in twain the mighty empire of Britain."

Whatever dissent there might have been outside Congress was smothered by the receipt of the French Treaty on May 2, and its ratification two days later.

Admiral d'Estaing's French fleet arriving at the mouth of the Delaware

The military side of the Alliance bore quick fruit, which proved to be hard and bitter. On July 8, 1778, just a few maddening days after Clinton's risky overland evacuation of Philadelphia and the fight at Monmouth Court House, a strong French fleet, convoying transports, appeared off the Delaware Capes, and then nosed north along the coast toward Sandy Hook where the British were still embarking men and supplies for the short jump from the Jerseys to Manhattan. The British ships in the area were heavily outgunned and outnumbered, but French Admiral d'Estaing, rightly or wrongly fearing the loss of his ships in unknown shoal waters, decided not to join action, and Clinton's evacuation was completed without interference.

Washington sent Alexander Hamilton to the coast to confer with d'Estaing. He found the French commander eager enough to fight and to co-operate with his new allies in any way that he could. However, he was hampered by orders from Paris which strictly limited his time on the North American coast and decreed a fairly prompt departure for the French West Indies to guard against British coups in that quarter. Such naval orders were now, as in the future, to hamper full co-operation between the allies, often evoking American wrath and disgust. What many Americans failed to grasp, as they failed to grasp certain similar British problems, was that France, like England, was now fighting a World War in which the Thirteen States were merely one theater, and not necessarily the most important one.

There was enough leeway, however, for a swift blow, and Washington and the Admiral mapped out a land and sea attack against British-held Newport, Rhode Island. D'Estaing was to sweep on and land his troops, while from the interior a strong American force struck down in a pincers-movement. In command of the Americans was John Sullivan, the New Hampshire General who had about everything that a good leader needed except luck.

The joint attack promised very well. In the last days of July the French ships closed in on Newport. Sullivan, his command bolstered by additional Continental regiments and New England militia, moved south out of Providence to the Tiverton ferry and Seaconnet Passage. Then the whole movement began to come apart. Hot-tempered Sullivan quarreled violently with the French brass (not unjustifiably, Lafayette thought), and action slowed to a halt as August came on. Then a reinforced British fleet stood up the Sound. D'Estaing, whose troops had not yet been fully disembarked, reloaded his transports and put out to sea, ready for action. His plans and those of his British opponent, Admiral Richard Howe, were shattered by a storm of hurricane proportions. The eventual return of fair weather found both fleets scattered and badly damaged. Howe put back for New York, while d'Estaing sailed north to Boston to refit. When his ships were finally repaired he had no choice but to sail for the West Indies, his officially rationed time in North America having run out.

As for Sullivan's force, abandoned willy-nilly by d'Estaing, it soon found itself pinned on the northern part of Newport's island by strong British units. Disaster threatened and hung poised, but good fighting, in which a Negro regiment under Christopher Greene distinguished itself, allowed Sullivan to withdraw to Seaconnet beaches. There familiar figures shuttled about in expertly handled craft of all sorts as once more John Glover's Marbleheaders exerted their peculiar skills to salvage a beaten American command.

So the first tangible results of the Alliance petered out into nothing, and men began to wonder if after all there had not been something rather worthwhile in those Propositions of Lord North.

Barring d'Estaing's ill-fated flurry off Newport, long months rolled by before the average man could detect any change in the situation as a result of the French Alliance. The main British and American armies, destined never again to meet in the northern theater after Monmouth, remained largely quiescent, with Clinton holding fast to his Manhattan base and adjacent territory, and Washington lying defensively alert a little way up the Hudson in the neighborhood of Haverstraw Bay.

Fringe-warfare went on, savage and bloody. Long Island Sound was scored with the wakes of small craft as each side launched raids that had no bearing on the course of the war. Great South Bay's waters boiled under what became known as "The Whale-boat War," with small parties sculling back and forth to pounce on supplies that they felt desirable or on people whom they felt objectionable. There was British participation in some of this, but a good deal of the fighting seems to have been the playing out of local grudges to their utmost conclusion. Westchester County became a place of horror, a sort of no man's land—roving bands ripping up with fine impartiality any objective weak enough to promise success and rich enough to hold loot. Off in western New York state, Joseph Brant and Walter Butler swept out in murderous, fiery raids in which there was little to choose, as far as savagery went, between Indian and Tory. Here again, the fight may be looked upon as the struggle between Indian and settler, between big landholder and small farmer. It had little or no effect on the conflagration that began over colonists' rights.

Very real, but not yet evident on the surface, was the shift in war-focus that was inevitable with the entry of a European power of the American side. The struggle became virtually global. British units began to embark from Manhattan and sail south for British Florida or the West Indies, hitherto unthreatened. Gradually the whole emphasis of the war shifted to the southern states

This French map shows American and British positions during the Newport siege

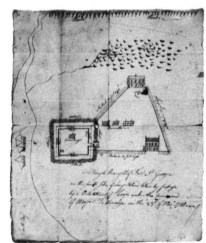

American Major Benjamin Tallmadge's sketch of Fort St. George on Long Island, which he raided in 1780

under orders from London. By making them the main theater of action it was possible, given British control of the seas, to shuttle troops swiftly from a West Indian station to the Carolinas and vice versa, a maneuver that did not have to be considered until the entry of France into the war.

Aside from this important strategic aspect, an old, familiar will-o'-the-wisp danced before British eyes, the same *ignis fatuus* that had drawn Clinton and Peter Parker to the Carolinas in '76, that had sent Baum and Breymann into the Hampshire Grants in '77—the vision of thousands of eager Tories waiting, poised, to snatch up arms and join the King's troops in blowing the rabble Rebels off the face of the earth. "Beat the Americans with Americans" became an intoxicating slogan. Organize and equip these swarming Loyalists, support them with regular troops! It was all so simple and logical; but it overlooked the facts that, so far, Tories had not been militarily effective, save on the smallest of scales; that they had shown no talent whatsoever for organizing themselves; and that they had never appeared in the field in important numbers.

This emphasis on the South put an added burden on Sir Henry Clinton. He was under orders to operate in that theater; yet he could not detach too many troops from Manhattan without laying his northern base open to a swift blow by Washingon. At headquarters a fairly satisfactory program was finally mapped out. Five thousand troops were embarked for St. Lucia in the West Indies, and a mixed force of British, Hessians, and Tories—some 3,500—tramped onto other transports. Their target: Savannah, Georgia.

Weakened by London rather than by enemy action, Sir Henry Clinton considered his situation there in Manhattan and its environs. A conscientious if uninspired soldier, he felt bound to explore all possibilities for the profitable employment of what resources he had left. There was the Hudson, a natural barrier between the four New England states and the rest of the confounded Rebels. The idea of British control of the river had often been in staff minds, notably during Burgoyne's disastrous plunge south from Canada. Clinton could recall with satisfaction his own small coup during that time, which gave him Fort Montgomery and allowed him to burn Esopus, now Kingston.

The picture was different in 1779. There was no force coming down from Canada. But if he were able to drive upriver and seize the towering rock mass known as West Point, a bare fifty miles to the north, a chain of posts between there and Manhattan could be an extremely annoying check on the flow of men and supplies out of New England.

The move may have been exploratory, but in any event, on May 30, 1779, Clinton pushed some 6,000 picked troops upriver in 70 sailing vessels and 150 flatbottoms. About 35 miles above New York, this force poured ashore and easily captured two American forts, one at Stony Point on the west bank, the other at Verplanck's Point on the east, just opposite. Then Clinton had his men dig in while he watched Washington hastily shift troops between Stony Point and vital West Point. The American commander was also deeply troubled because the two newly taken forts covered King's Ferry, a link in the principal highway from New England.

American reaction came swiftly. On the night of July 15, a picked force of some 1,300 men under Anthony Wayne made a secret and killing march over dark mountains, swept in on Stony Point, and took it with bayonet alone, in one of the perfect set pieces of the war. Another body came down the east bank and hit Verplanck's Point. It was beaten off, and Stony Point was abandoned after Washington decided it would be too difficult to hold. But Wayne's victory bore fruit far beyond the lift it provided to public and army morale.

The storming of Stony Point

Clinton's losses in men and matériel had been considerable, and the debacle at Stony Point completely discouraged him from attempting any offensive move.

As Sir Henry lapsed into inactivity, a summer calm hung deep over the Hudson Valley. Towering West Point still shouldered up above the river, the American flag flying high over the works that were being extended there. Even a very cautious British commander in New York could not forget it, although it might seem beyond his immediate reach.

Benedict Arnold

A nation may hunt for allies in an attempt to gain important ends. So may a commander, without stirring from his base; or a potential ally may seek him out. In Clinton's case the latter happened.

Down in Philadelphia, Major General Benedict Arnold, still nursing his Freeman's Farm wound, was installed as military commander. He had taken as his second wife the beautiful Tory, Peggy Shippen. He entertained lavishly with fine china and plate, which caused local eyebrows to jump, since Arnold was perennially hard up. Eyebrows jumped still higher when it was noted that he seemed to seek out as intimates many wealthy Tories who had not evacuated with Clinton before Monmouth.

The explosive Arnold, brushing aside criticism implied or spoken, was happy enough with his gorgeous Peggy and the manner in which the pair lived. Or he would have been happy except for that damned crowd of civilian busybodies known as the Congress, who were always prodding him for accountings of public funds he had expended. Congress began asking other questions, such as why the General was so free in giving passes for the round trip between British-held New York and Philadelphia. There was the matter of his use of public wagons for private ends, and charges that by using his office he was buying goods very cheaply and reselling to the public at a high profit. Other charges kept cropping up as they had since the start of his military career. Some were obviously trumped up and some still look tenable, to put the matter conservatively.

Arnold raged and stormed at Congress, virtually told that august body to mind its own business, and went on enjoying his life in general, as far as his wrath allowed. Also he began making casts, like an angler whipping a trout pool. In New York, Major John André, elegant, foppish adjutant to Sir Henry Clinton, began receiving mysterious letters through devious channels, hinting strongly that a highly placed but unnamed American officer might offer "his services to the commander-in-chief of the British forces in any way that would most effectually restore the former government and destroy the then usurped authority of Congress, either by immediately joining the British army or cooperating on some concealed plan with Sir Henry Clinton."

In the dull spring of 1779, John André had been toying with the possibility of approaching some top American officer via a bridge of gold, and he leaped at the bait so temptingly flicked. Codes were devised, fresh channels opened, and the Major found at once that he had no starry-eyed dreamer to deal with, but a hardheaded practical businessman, now revealed as the celebrated Benedict Arnold, who wanted substantial monetary rewards figured down to the last farthing, rank in the British army, and possibly a title for his services. Correspondence became animated, then acid, and André reluctantly closed the file.

A year later, in June of 1780, André was surprised to find the issue suddenly brought to new life and the General's proposals far more concrete. Arnold spoke of obtaining the command—and here André's breath must have quickened—at *West Point*, fifty miles up the Hudson! This appealed greatly to Sir Henry, who had André write at once of his interest, adding that steps would

Arnold's wife, Peggy, with their child

A map of West Point, showing the chain blocking passage on the Hudson

A wash drawing by Ramberg of André's capture by Rebel militia

be taken to keep Arnold's coattails clear of any suspicion. Also he spoke of an "ample stipend."

On this last point negotiations threatened to break down, for there was a discrepancy between Clinton's definition of "ample" and Arnold's. The Connecticut General wanted a lump-sum payment and also a specified number of pounds sterling per head for every American soldier that he was able to turn in to the British as prisoner of war. Dickering and haggling dragged on, while Arnold began prudently to turn his possessions into cash, banking the proceeds in British-held New York through various obliging agents.

In late July, Washington recalled Arnold's earlier clamorings for a field command and gave him the American left wing. Somewhat to his surprise, Arnold began to twist and squirm. His Excellency must have misunderstood. What he really wanted was to be in charge at West Point, not to lead troops in the field. However this may have struck Washington, he had the orders changed, and Benedict Arnold was sent up the Hudson as of August 3, 1780. Now there were very few "ifs" left in the long-drawn-out bickering and bartering. Arnold and Clinton came to terms.

On September 23, 1780, Major Benjamin Tallmadge, Washington's Chief of Intelligence, was on patrol with troopers of his own 2nd Dragoons in the Westchester County-Fairfield County area. The whole district had been buttoned up as tightly as was possible in those days, for the commander in chief himself was riding east with an escort to confer at Hartford with Comte Donatien de Rochambeau, leader of the French forces which had landed at Newport in July. The greenest trooper of Tallmadge's command could see the importance of making sure that no Tory or British force could snap up General Washington. Tallmadge, of course, was fully aware of the risks. Other matters were gnawing at his mind, too. From West Point, General Arnold had been deluging officers at Westchester and Fairfield posts with meaching, flattering letters, quite unlike his usual terse, rather angry style. From Tallmadge, Arnold had demanded complete data on all secret agents working under the Major. Since such information could be divulged by Washington alone, this summons could be side-stepped easily enough even by a field officer of dragoons. But one Arnold letter had contained a curious rider, directing Tallmadge to forward instantly to West Point one John Anderson from New York, should the latter appear in the Major's area. Tallmadge thought it was asking a good deal of him to send an unvouched-for man fresh from British Manhattan, particularly as he had known Arnold for many years and had a low opinion of his principles and motives.

The dragoon patrol ended. Tallmadge returned to his quarters, where a real bombshell awaited him. Dragoon Lieutenant Colonel John Jameson informed him that a man named John Anderson had been picked up by some militiamen close to the Westchester no man's land. With the name John Anderson, an ugly picture began forming in Tallmadge's mind. The man Anderson had been trying to get through to the British lines, and there was something damnably wrong about the whole matter. In his shoes had been found detailed plans of the West Point forts, data on ordnance, and digests of confidential orders issued by Washington. The oddest thing was that the prisoner had a pass signed by Arnold, and some of the documents seemed to be in Arnold's handwriting.

As for Anderson, he was already on his way, under heavy guard, to try to explain to Arnold himself how he had come by the papers, and frankly, Jameson would not care to be in Anderson's shoes, knowing Arnold's temper. Yes, a letter to Arnold describing the papers had gone on with Anderson, and the captured papers were on their way to General Washington. They would catch him on his return from Hartford.

Tallmadge, with his Intelligence background, was aghast. He wrote later that he wanted to take very direct action, which might well have been to surround the Beverley Robinson house on the east bank across from West Point with dragoons and arrest Arnold there. Jameson, as Tallmadge's superior, may have forbidden such a course, for the most the Major could wrest from him was a promise to recall the prisoner and his guard. The letter, Jameson held, *must* go through to Arnold. Intercepting the guard at Old Salem, Tallmadge found the prisoner to be a shabby civilian who at last threw off his disguise, revealing himself as Major John André, Adjutant General to Sir Henry Clinton.

In the meantime, as hours slipped away, the gods of chance thoroughly scrambled the timetables of the couriers sent to Arnold and Washington respectively. Washington took an unexpected route on his return from Hartford, and the messenger missed him completely. The rider for Arnold reached the Beverley Robinson house while Arnold was at breakfast with his military family. The letter he bore must have been a fearful shock to Benedict Arnold, but he masked it completely, excused himself, bade a hurried farewell to Peggy, and plunged off down the long slope to the Hudson where his official barge was, as usual, waiting for him.

He boarded it, ordered the crew to row him not across to West Point but downstream where H.M.S. *Vulture* rode at anchor, waiting for the return of the passenger that it had brought north, Major John André. Arnold brusquely told the *Vulture's* captain, Andrew Sutherland, that André had gone ashore as planned, that the two had had a long talk in the Joshua Hett Smith house on the west bank, and that André had been captured later. Arnold does not seem to have told anyone that he had advised André to try for the British lines overland instead of via the *Vulture,* or that the unfortunate Major had, at Arnold's urging, changed his uniform (which would have made him a mere prisoner of war) for civilian clothes, which sealed his fate as a spy under military law and custom.

H.M.S. *Vulture* eventually put back for New York with Arnold aboard. There was no chance now of handing over West Point; yet Arnold seemed to think that Clinton had come out very well in the whole deal. André could be exchanged, and the British command was gaining the services of the renowned hero of Quebec, Valcour, and Freeman's Farm. In addition, news of Arnold's change of sides would rock the American nation to its foundation.

On the east bank, by the Beverley Robinson house, events moved predictably. Washington finally put in an appearance and was given the papers found on André. West Point was immediately strengthened and its garrison increased. Clinton, horrified at André's capture and status, argued and stormed, demanding the Major's release. Washington stood his ground. The prisoner had been taken out of uniform within the American lines, where he had come with the avowed purpose of plotting with the now-exposed traitor, Arnold, to wreck the army of the United States.

If events were predictable, the conduct of one man was not. Foppish dandy John André, with a lifetime of genteel scheming behind him, should by all logic have cracked up pitiably. Instead, he stood forth during the court-martial and the sentence of hanging as a gallant man of high courage and unshakable nerve, and these qualities shone brightly until the final snap of the hangman's noose about his neck. Benjamin Tallmadge wrote to his friend, Colonel Samuel Webb, "By heavens, Colonel Webb, I never saw a man whose fate I foresaw

André made this sketch of himself on the day before his execution

269

An effigy of Arnold, made by Charles Willson Peale, paraded in Philadelphia

whom I so sincerely pitied. . . . He seems to be as cheerful as if he was going to an assembly. I am sure he will go to the gallows less tearful of his fate and with less concern than I shall behold the tragedy." Unnumbered Americans felt as deeply and keenly as did the Connecticut Major.

So John André died, a casualty in Clinton's search for an ally and in Arnold's search for rank and money. As for Arnold, he set about at once cashing in on his venture into infamy, his final rewards probably falling far below what he had hoped for, since he now had nothing with which to bargain. He was finally made a British Brigadier (he had been an American Major General, so he actually lost a step), was handed the sum of £6,315 sterling and a pension of £500 per annum for his pretty Peggy. Tossed in almost negligently were British commissions for his three sons by his earlier marriage to Margaret Mansfield of New Haven, and pensions of £100 per annum for each of his children by Peggy. This was hardly a fortune, but it was the best that he could manage. He had no leverage to apply, no more secrets to betray for a few more pounds. Given permission to recruit an Arnold Legion among the Tories, he could scarcely have been elated, nor Clinton impressed, when barely enough men turned out to make up a major's command, much less a brigadier's.

The need for money occupied the minds of many men as 1780 wore on into 1781, but nowhere was it more desperately felt than by Benedict Arnold's former commander in chief, General George Washington. Behind Washington's dilemma lay the financial struggle which had engaged the Congress ever since the colonies chose to become the United States of America. Although the French Alliance eased that problem, it hardly solved what had become a downhill battle for economic survival.

To be sure, Congress was authorized to request from the individual states such funds as were needed for the common good, but it had not the least semblance of power to enforce compliance. The states considered each request and were quite free under law to meet them fully, in grudging part, or to ignore them with bland irresponsibility. A good share of the trouble lay in the fact that each state was apt to think of itself as being in temporary wartime alliance with its twelve fellow states. In this respect, the army was far ahead, nationally speaking, of the country as a whole.

States tended to conduct private wars with England, maintaining what amounted to their own navies and armies, like the New Hampshire force that smashed Baum and Breymann at Bennington. They even sent their own agents abroad to compete with national appointees such as Franklin, Deane, John Adams, and Arthur Lee, much to the embarrassment and harassment of the latter group. And every step taken by a state on its own drew away urgently needed strength from the central government.

Very early in the war, Congress began the issue of paper money. Forced to such a step by the acute shortage of currency, it soon found that the clank and clatter of printing-presses set up such a delightful harmony that it quite drowned out any warning whispers that, after all, those engraved bits of paper were backed by nothing but a hope that lay in the distant future. A contemporary observed acidly that men were "struck by the charm of converting a piece of paper not worth a farthing into a 30 dollar bill."

The states joyously followed the example of Congress and soon presses were spewing out valueless paper money from the Merrimac down to the Savannah. At the start, most people accepted such fiat money willingly enough. As times grew darker, laws were passed forcing such acceptance, and where people

A 36-shilling note designed and engraved by Paul Revere in 1775

proved reluctant, boycotts, imprisonment, or the rough work of city and town mobs were called quite effectively into play. Naturally enough, the value of such paper money varied widely from state to state. Rhode Island notes might be worthless in Massachusetts while passing at a discount in Pennsylvania or Maryland. Commodity prices jumped alarmingly, and individuals and groups began to hoard against the next skyrocket ascent. Urban and rural interests clashed and farmers withheld their produce in an effort to win higher prices from city consumers. Abigail Adams wrote husband John: "The merchant scowls, the farmer growls and everyone seems wroth that he cannot grind his neighbor." Mechanics and laborers suffered, for while their scale of pay rose to the point where potential employers howled in anguish, the cost of living was always bounding along well in advance of each increase.

Speculators rushed into the field and paper fortunes were made, lost, made again. They cornered supplies of shoes, clothes, vital supplies, and sold them at huge profits while Washington's troops wrapped rags about their feet or wound quilts around themselves in place of unobtainable breeches.

The busy Dutch West Indies port of St. Eustatius, from a 1781 drawing

Privateers swarmed out of every port, returned heavy with captured goods and chests of prize money. But such windfalls rarely benefited the country as a whole, since Congress had no way of channeling specie into the national treasury. Merchant shipping, evading British cruisers, glided south to the West Indies and traded with complete disregard for which country owned which island, touched at the great entre-pôt of Dutch St. Eustatius—or "Statia" as it was usually called—and returned richly laden. Individuals made fortunes and home ports flourished, but very little economic lifeblood was pumped into the national veins. Hard money remained so scarce that a bonus of ten dollars in coin induced hundreds, perhaps thousands of men to stay beyond their enlistment terms in the winter of 1776–77.

In times of acute distress Congress followed many courses that can only seem weird now. In 1777, for example, it began making drafts on its agents abroad, hoping that by the time the instruments were presented to Franklin or Deane or John Adams for honoring, those public servants would have managed somehow to secure important loans from the government to which they were accredited. The agent in question rarely, if ever, had advance warning of these drafts, and if he did receive some hint he was left in ignorance of the total sum demanded. Franklin protested wearily: "Ever since I entered into office, they [the drafts] have not only plagued and perplexed me, but they have invariably consumed the resources on which I have formed a reliance." In effect, Congress unwittingly was canceling out its agents' salaries before those individuals received them.

Luckily, many men who had accumulated important cash reserves or quick credit were more than willing to place their private resources at the service of their country. Robert Morris, member of Congress and, in 1781, first occupant of the office of Superintendent of Finance, was also the guiding spirit of the firm of Willing, Morris and Co. This spectacularly successful concern had a Midas touch with shipping, privateering, brokerage—buying or selling anything that could be bought or sold on a large scale. Public opinion being far less censorious then than now, Morris unabashedly profiteered, holding goods for a jump in price before selling to the army. The phrase "conflict of interests" was unknown in the eighteenth century, and if used would not have been understood, so Morris employed the inside knowledge which his governmental positions afforded him to further his own private ends. The cynically-minded may say "Why not?" to Morris' unflagging readiness to pledge his ever-swelling wealth

Robert Morris, by Peale

to Congress, to make loans out of his own capital; but many others, nearly as wealthy, held back, fearful of losing their stake.

In 1772 there arrived in New York from Lissa, in Poland, an unobtrusive, thoughtful man named Haym Salomon. He throve on Manhattan and built up a quietly solid reputation as a broker whose word was never called in question, whose paper was always good. When Washington evacuated New York in '76, Salomon stayed on, and people who envied him muttered back of their hands that it was quite in character, that to him money was money and there was an end of it. When Salomon was suddenly arrested by the British on a charge of spying, held in close confinement, and then grudgingly released, it led to talk of bribery, of money passed in high British circles. The year 1778 again found Salomon in jail, but this time hints of golden keys to jail doors died as a court-martial pronounced the death sentence on him, once again for spying for the Americans.

Somehow Salomon managed to escape, fled to Philadelphia, and, quietly resuming his brokerage business, rapidly recouped his fortunes. Many people were surprised when inquiries from members of Congress brought a quick, unstinting response from the Salomon coffers and sound money flowed out in a time of great need. Individuals in tight places sought him out and were given relief, and the Salomon ledgers carried the names of Thomas Jefferson, James Madison, and Thomas Randolph. Never showy, Haym Salomon built a reputation for deep integrity as well as financial shrewdness. When Dutch and French subsidies began to flow into America, they passed through Salomon's hands, and he was also formally appointed paymaster to Rochambeau's French expeditionary force in 1781.

But grudging contributions from individual states, occasional windfalls in the form of captured goods or treasure, the efforts of men like Robert Morris, Haym Salomon, and others, or doles from foreign governments had never been enough to provide anything like a solid, substantial treasury for the United States of America. And because of this, the commander in chief of the Continental Army was deeply troubled in the summer of 1781.

Out of the east had come the long white columns of French infantry, screened by the Duc de Lauzun's sky-blue cavalrymen, pouring across Connecticut and onto the banks of the Hudson where Washington's army was massed. The commander in chief conferred with Rochambeau. They talked earnestly about the little force under Wayne and Lafayette, sparring with Cornwallis down there on the York Peninsula in Virginia, and, particularly, about the movements of a powerful French fleet under Admiral de Grasse. Could a picked French-American force march down the continent to Virginia and take advantage of what was known about de Grasse and his warships?

Militarily the plan was feasible. But in the back of Washington's mind was the numbing realization that his war chest was empty. Robert Morris, Superintendent of Finance, was consulted and reported ruefully that he saw no hope of any important supply of hard money until late autumn—and this was only August. Rochambeau summoned his army treasurer, talked earnestly and privately with him, and then sought out Washington. The French military chest, which had not been replenished since the debarkation at Newport over a year ago, contained gold to the equivalent of some $40,000. If Rochambeau's American superior would do him the honor of accepting half this sum . . .

By this single, wonderfully generous act, Rochambeau set in place the last plank in a bridge to Yorktown and the surrender of an entire British army under Lord Charles Cornwallis.

272

THE WAR
AT SEA

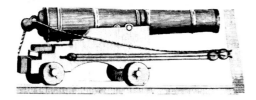

The Importance of Sea Power

Even when it became clear that the American war would require a maximum effort, the British government ignored the advice of men like Secretary-at-War Viscount Barrington, who felt that "the Americans may be reduced by the fleet, but never can be by the army." When, after three years of war, the rebellion persisted, and an entire British army had been lost at Saratoga, Barrington's words took on the ring of prophecy. British land forces were based on the sea and on the navigable rivers leading from it, and after France's intervention in 1778 and Spain's entry in 1779, England's success depended on its ability to keep its communications intact. From 1778 on, the conflict between mother country and colonies was a full-scale World War.

The battleship of the eighteenth century was the ship of the line, mounting upwards of 64 guns which could hurl over half a ton of metal in one broadside. An example of these ships is the 90-gun *Sandwich*, shown on the previous page. Lighter-armed, fast-sailing frigates—today's destroyers and cruisers—were used as the eyes of the fleet, as convoy escorts, and, especially in American waters, for blockading and to support the army.

The stakes in the war at sea were high, including the rich trading areas of the West Indies, India, and the Mediterranean; while even the British Isles were threatened by invasion. In America George Washington realized that the navies would cast the decisive vote in the conflict. Only "if we had the command of the seas," he believed, could the army undertake "to convert the war into a vigorous offensive."

Life aboard a warship is pictured below in a cutaway view of a French two-decker. Captain's cabin (8) and officers' mess (14) are at the stern; crew's quarters (11) and mess (17), amidships. The brig (23) is deep in the hold, along with stores and magazine (26).

Naval architecture in the age of sail had its decorative aspects. The contemporary view above shows the bow quarter, stern, and stern quarter of a mid-eighteenth-century British ship of the line. The royal figurehead on the bow is apparently one of the Georges.

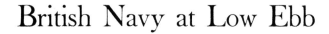
A contemporary described the Earl of Sandwich as "Too infamous to have a friend, Too bad for bad men to commend."

British Navy at Low Ebb

The British navy was singularly unprepared to face its new enemies. From unchallenged supremacy at the end of the Seven Years' War it had fallen into decay and disrepair. Corruption permeated the Admiralty when the Earl of Sandwich became First Sea Lord in 1771, and this only accelerated the decline, for Sandwich was as unprincipled in public life as in his private affairs. When an official complained that "desertions from ships and hospitals are beyond imagination [60,000 men deserted or died from disease between 1774 and 1780]. The discipline of service is entirely lost. . . . The dockyards . . . are in a wretched disabled state," Sandwich replied that he had "neither leisure nor inclination to enter into a discussion upon the subject."

The navy was too weak to apply an effective blockade of French and Spanish ports, so enemy squadrons sailed at their pleasure. What few new ships England had were cheap and of inferior quality. Although British admirals were imbued with the idea of firing into enemy hulls and fighting to a finish, they were hamstrung by the *Fighting Instructions*, virtually unchanged in 75 years, which generally limited them to an attack from the windward in a rigid line of battle to engage ship to ship.

The Revolution found the Royal Navy probably at the lowest point in its proud history. The Duke of Richmond, writing to an admiral, summed up the feeling throughout the service: "I would determine not to trust Lord Sandwich for a piece of ropeyarn."

This painting shows the launching of the 74-gun Alexander at Deptford dockyard in 1778. A similar ship of the line is at right

The engraving at left, by James Gillray, shows a navy press gang abducting a London tailor, despite the strenuous efforts of his womenfolk. The state of the Royal Navy was so bad that impressment was officially sanctioned. These gangs raided the water front areas and merchant ships for seamen; and sometimes even "the gaols were swept."

277

Gabriel de Sartine (above) was France's Minister of Marine during most of the Revolution. At right is a French navy signal book of the period. Signal pennants flown by the admiral's flagship in the center of the line of battle were relayed to the ships of the van and rear divisions by frigates.

France Rebuilds Its Fleet

In contrast to England's ports, where warships lay crumbling in Rotten Row, France's dockyards were bustling with activity as the Revolution began. Under the capable direction of the Duc de Choiseul and Gabriel de Sartine, the French navy rebounded strongly from its disastrous defeat at Quiberon Bay in 1759. Beautifully designed and built ships came off the ways, and captains were rigorously drilled in maneuver and absolute obedience to orders.

Yet French naval philosophy was quite different from the victory-at-any-cost English tradition. The fine ships were not to be risked in all-out decisive action, but preserved to fight another day. Consequently, French admirals often accepted the defensive leeward position in battle, with its open line of withdrawal, and aimed at the enemy's sails and rigging to cripple pursuit.

Commodore La Motte-Picquet aptly summarized France's objectives in the war when he wrote, "the surest way of conquering the English is to attack them through their trade." As for Spain, its policy was dictated by visions of taking Gibraltar and Minorca in the Mediterranean, and Jamaica in the West Indies. Fortunately for England, the Bourbon powers were frequently at odds, and while their combined fleets gave the allies a numerical superiority, the Spanish ships "all sail so badly that they can neither overtake an enemy nor escape from one," as a French officer admitted. Their first joint effort, an attempted invasion of England in 1779, was driven out of the Channel not by the Royal Navy but by a typhoid epidemic, storms, and divided counsels in Paris and Madrid. Even so, the very sight of a huge enemy fleet boldly sailing up the Channel moved a British captain to remark, "What a humiliating state is our country reduced to!"

Toulon was the major French Mediterranean base. Ships'
guns and cannon balls are in the foreground. France split
her fleet between Toulon and the Channel port of Brest.

French naval architects, at work below, scientifically re-
fined principles of design to produce ships that generally
sailed faster and better than their English counterparts.

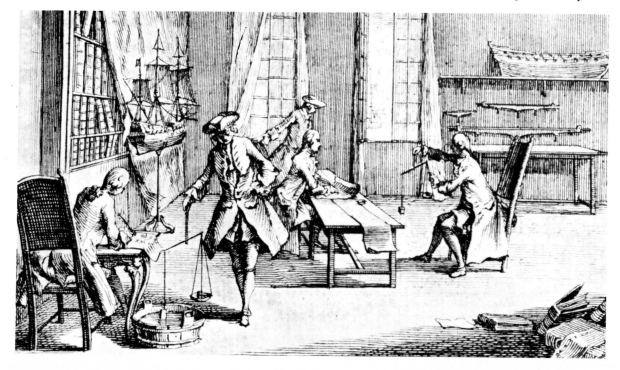

First Test of the Alliance

The alliance between the United States and France immediately threatened British control of American waters. Admiral Richard Howe had only six ships of the line, far too few to oppose a substantial French squadron. Philadelphia was clearly indefensible, and when Clinton abandoned it in favor of New York, his evacuation offered Washington and the French their first opportunity for a combined blow.

The Comte d'Estaing sailed from Toulon in April, 1778, with twelve ships of the line, bound for North America. A normal Atlantic passage would have brought him to the Delaware River in time to trap Howe's fleet in the process of loading Clinton's heavy baggage, and would have left Clinton's army high and dry. But d'Estaing made such a lethargic crossing that he missed the chance by ten days.

Howe had reached New York and saw Clinton and his army, somewhat battered from Washington's attack at Monmouth, safely across the bay to the city. On July 11, the French fleet appeared. Although his firepower tripled that of Howe, d'Estaing threw away another chance to crush the British fleet, refusing to believe that his heavy ships could cross the sand bar at the harbor mouth.

In late 1776 the British had seized the fine anchorage at Newport in Narragansett Bay, and this was the Frenchman's next objective. He was to co-operate with John Sullivan's Rebel army to besiege the Newport garrison. On July 29 the French fleet arrived and the siege was soon begun. The intrepid Howe, still outnumbered but determined to "profit by any opportunity which might offer," made sail for Newport.

D'Estaing moved out of the bay to meet him, and the two commanders maneuvered for position for two days. Finally, on August 11, they were about to come to grips when a mighty gale, remembered afterward as the "great French storm," scattered the fleets. D'Estaing put into Boston to refit his damaged ships and, despite Washington's requests, refused to resume the Newport siege. Without his help, Sullivan had no choice but to abandon operations. D'Estaing departed to seek colonial advantages for France in the West Indies, leaving behind shattered American hopes for a decisive victory in 1778.

Painting dark-visaged "Black Dick" Howe (above) Copley flattered his subject with a florid complexion. The Comte d'Estaing (below) was a good soldier, but lacked naval experience.

The seizure of Newport (above) by Sir Henry Clinton in December, 1776, was a neatly executed amphibious assault. In this contemporary water color, landing barges wait while five frigates lay down a barrage to drive away the few defenders. The landing was unopposed. After the British abandoned Newport in October, 1779, it became the foremost American base for the French navy.

Above is the French fleet (foreground) at the entrance to New York Harbor in 1778. Howe lay behind Sandy Hook, but the Comte d'Estaing made no attack, thinking his ships unable to negotiate the channel at right. Below, the 90-gun Languedoc, *dismasted by the storm that struck the opposing fleets off Newport, is pounded by the British* Renown, 50. *Darkness saved d'Estaing's flagship.*

The Conflict Widens

The area of the Lesser Antilles (left) in the Caribbean was the scene of constant naval action during the war. The chief French base was Fort Royal on Martinique; England's important bases were at Barbados and, after its capture in 1778, St. Lucia. The main battle fleets were forced to quit the West Indies for safer latitudes—usually North America— during the violent July-to-October hurricane season.

For the next two and a half years, except for an abortive French venture at Savannah in 1779, the fight between England and her enemies for control of the seas was waged in European waters and in the West Indies. The Caribbean islands—the richest trading area in the world—were prime targets, and the tropical waters echoed constantly to the thunder of naval broadsides.

In 1778 and 1779 France seized Dominica, St. Vincent, and Grenada, while St. Lucia fell to the British. The British were overjoyed by George Brydges Rodney's destruction of a Spanish squadron off Cape St. Vincent, Portugal, in January, 1780, one of the few decisive naval actions of the war. Then Rodney moved to the West Indies and severely injured England's newest enemy by taking the Dutch island of St. Eustatius. In 1781 his opponent, the Comte de Grasse, added Tobago to France's conquests. Throughout this island war French defensive tactics frustrated every British effort at a finish fight.

In America the stage was set for the climax of the war as Cornwallis entrenched at Yorktown. In July, 1781, de Grasse made the momentous decision: instead of sending half his force home as ordered, he notified Washington that he was sailing with his entire fleet of 28 ships of the line for Chesapeake Bay and Yorktown.

Above, French troops storm the defenses of St. George on Grenada in 1779. The British attempted to recapture the island, but were driven off with six warships crippled.

Below, Rodney's flagship Sandwich *under full sail at the moonlit battle off Cape St. Vincent. Of eleven Spanish ships, one blew up (background) and six were captured.*

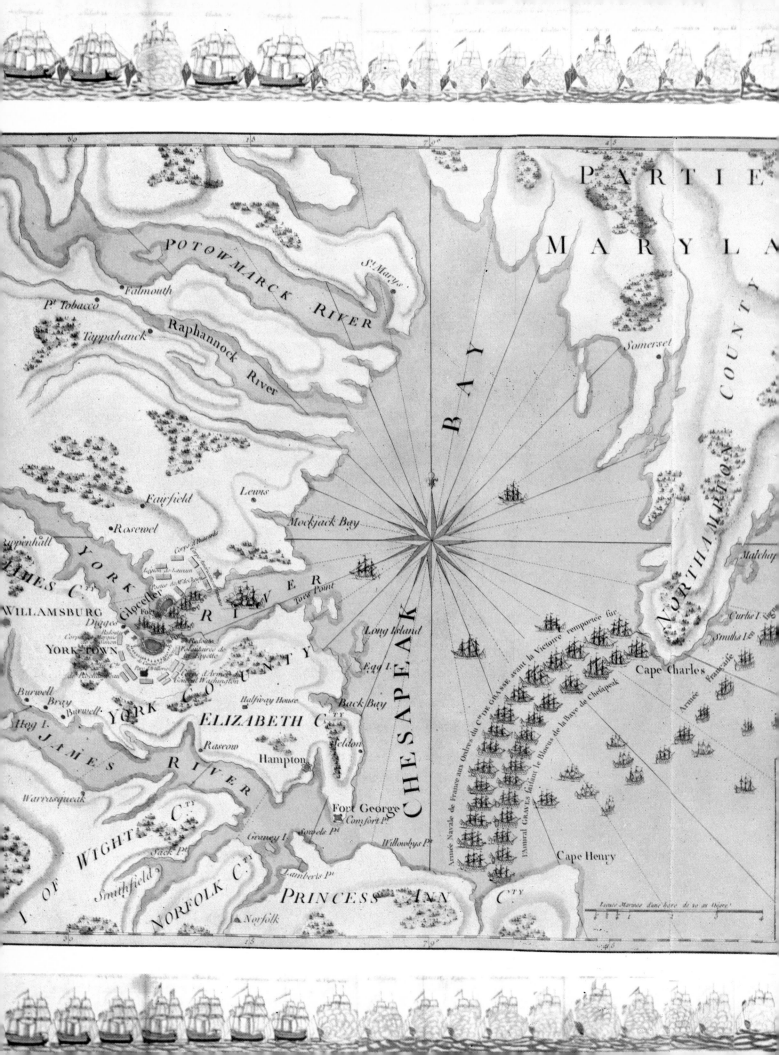

PARTIE

MARYLA

POTOWMARCK RIVER

Falmouth

P.ᵗ Tobacco

Tappahanck

Raphannock River

St. Marys

Somerset

BAY

Fairfield

Lewis

Rosewel

Mockjack Bay

NORTHAMPTON COUNTY

Malchap

Cuppenhall

JAMES Cᵗ

YORK

Corps d'Hussards

Legion de Lauzun

Postes de M.ᵈᵉ Choisi

RIVER

Toes Point

WILLAMSBURG

Diggss

Glocester

Fort

RIVER

Curtis I.

Smiths Isᵗ

YORK TOWN

Corps Marine du General Steuben

Redouttes Volontaires de fayette

Camp d'Armee du General Washington

YORK COUNTY

Long Island

Egg I.

Cape Charles

Armee Françoise

Burwell

Bray

Burwell

Halfway House

ELIZABETH Cᵗʸ

Back Bay

Armee Navale de France aux Ordres du Cᵗᵉ DE GRASSE avant la Victoire remportee sur

Hog I.

JAMES

RIVER

Rascow

Seldon

l'Amiral Graves faisant le Blocus de la Baye de Chesapek

Warrasqueak

Hampton

CHESAPEAK

Jack Pᵗ

Fort George

Comfort Pᵗ

Cape Henry

I. OF WIGHT Cᵗʸ

Graney I.

Sewels Pᵗ

Smithfield

Willoughys Pᵗ

NORFOLK Cᵗʸ

Lamberts Pᵗ

PRINCESS ANN Cᵗʸ

Lieues Marines d'une lieue de 20 au Degre

Norfolk

Comte de Grasse   *Thomas Graves*

French Sea Power Traps Cornwallis

As the Revolution entered its seventh year, the French navy had so far prevented England from concentrating its forces to win the American war, but the colonists were very close to losing it from sheer exhaustion. In the late spring of 1781 Washington wrote, "If France delays timely aid now it will avail us nothing if she attempt it hereafter. We are at the end of our tether and now or never our deliverance must come."

His deliverance, in the form of de Grasse's 28-ship fleet, cleared Haiti in August for Chesapeake Bay, taking a little-used route to elude pursuit. Rodney had departed for England, leaving Samuel Hood in command. Informed of de Grasse's departure, Hood cracked on sail with 14 ships of the line, and, unwittingly, passed the Frenchman en route. After looking in at the empty Chesapeake on August 25, Hood sailed to New York to join his senior officer, Admiral Thomas Graves. Aware of neither the size nor the whereabouts of de Grasse's fleet, the two Britons went looking for Admiral Barras' small squadron based at Newport. The elusive de Grasse slipped into the Chesapeake on August 30, blocking Cornwallis' escape by water, and the 3,000 troops he landed enabled Lafayette to hold the quarry until the main French-American army should arrive. The whole operation was a masterpiece of strategy and timing.

When Graves and Hood rounded Cape Henry on September 5, still seeking Barras, they were startled to find "a number of great ships at anchor which seemed to be extended across the extreme of the Chesapeake." De Grasse immediately stood out to sea. Graves formed his line but bungled the attack; only part of his ships engaged, and they were badly mauled. For several days the fleets sparred for an opening and then de Grasse hustled back to his anchorage to find that Barras had arrived. He now had 36 ships of the line to Graves' 19. When Graves asked Hood for suggestions the reply came back that "Sir Samuel would be very glad to send an opinion, but he really knows not what to say in the truly lamentable state we have brought ourselves." Unable to give "effectual succour" to Cornwallis, Graves sailed off to New York, leaving an entire British army with no choice but surrender.

This map shows the allied siege of Yorktown, the French ships blocking Chesapeake Bay, and the action of the subsequent Battle of the Virginia Capes. Above and below, unique contemporary water colors from a French logbook illustrate the two lines firing broadsides in the battle.

England Regains the Initiative Too Late

With the Yorktown fiasco the Royal Navy reached its nadir. During the next year vigorous leadership by Rodney, back in command in the West Indies, and Black Dick Howe, called out of retirement to command the Home Fleet, removed some of the tarnish from the navy's reputation.

De Grasse returned to the West Indies in 1782, took St. Kitts despite some fine seamanship by the outnumbered Hood, and then prepared to attack Jamaica. But Rodney's quick pursuit forced the Frenchman to try to shake his tormentor. On April 12, when two French ships collided, Rodney had the long-awaited pleasure "to find . . . it in my power to force the enemy to battle." The Battle of the Saintes began harmlessly enough with the two lines passing in opposite directions, exchanging broadsides. Suddenly the wind shifted, throwing the French into disorder. Ignoring the *Fighting Instructions,* Rodney broke through the enemy line in two places. At close quarters British fire was deadly, and by sundown five French ships had struck, including de Grasse's magnificent 110-gun flagship *Ville de Paris.* Hood's pursuit brought in two more prizes.

Six months later, when Gibraltar repulsed the strongest Spanish attack of a three-year siege, and Howe forced his way through to the Rock with a badly needed convoy, England could sit down at the peace table with some of her honor restored.

Samuel Hood had an original flair for naval tactics. During the war he, Rodney, and Howe stood out in a sea of generally mediocre naval officers.

Mosnier's fine portrait captures the imperious, crusty George Brydges Rodney. While a good tactician, Rodney rarely took his captains into his confidence, declaring "I require obedience only, I don't want advice."

Below, Gibraltar's guns pound the supposedly unsinkable floating batteries spearheading the Spanish attack on the Rock in September of 1782. All ten of the batteries were sunk or burned.

t left, Rodney's 90-gun flagship Formidable *rakes a French ship of the line (under sail, right) n the heavy fighting following the breaking of the line in the Battle of the Saintes. One French 74 badly damaged (left), while another, her bowsprit and foremast overboard, is at the extreme right.*

The first navy fleet commander, Esek Hopkins, is shown at left in an idealized English print. Behind him are the Rebel "Rattle-snake" and "Pine Tree" flags. James Nicholson (above, left) lost the navy's frigates Virginia *and* Trumbull. *Nicholas Biddle (above, right) captained the ill-fated* Randolph *(opposite page).*

The Birth of
an American Navy

Despite a solid maritime tradition that gave the colonies a reservoir of capable commanders and experienced seamen, America produced little in the way of co-ordinated naval activity during the Revolution. A general poverty of resources prevented the construction of ships larger than frigates; more important, the lack of centralized government hampered the establishment of a strong Continental Navy. Most of the warships available were siphoned off into the state navies—jealously established to protect only their own coastlines—or were commissioned as privateers.

The war had barely begun when Washington organized a fleet of small craft during the siege of Boston. His little navy brought in some 35 British supply ships whose cargoes proved of great benefit to the fledgling army. In late 1775 Congress made a beginning at a national navy by authorizing the construction of thirteen frigates "for the protection and defence of the United Colonies."

Early in 1776 Esek Hopkins was placed in command of the navy's first squadron, a makeshift collection of ships dispatched to plague English naval installations. Hopkins, flying a flag which bore "a lively representation of a rattlesnake," attacked Nassau and came off with a considerable store of military supplies. His cruise was virtually the only planned major operation undertaken by the navy. More frequently, naval captains like John Paul Jones became commerce raiders. Even this role was difficult, for the navy had to compete for seamen with state-commissioned privateers offering less discipline and more prize money. William Whipple of the Marine Committee wrote, "you may depend no public ship will ever be manned while there is a privateer fitting out."

All told, 53 ships served in the navy during the war. Of the thirteen original frigates, only four were at sea by 1777, and one, the *Hancock,* was soon captured by the 44-gun *Rainbow.* Ironically, it was the *Hancock,* renamed *Iris,* that took the last of the thirteen, the *Trumbull,* in August, 1781.

Despite the efforts of men like John Adams and Robert Morris, America was not strong enough to create an effective navy where none had existed before. William Ellery of the Marine Committee admitted that "The Conduct of the Affairs of a Navy as well as those of an Army We are yet to learn."

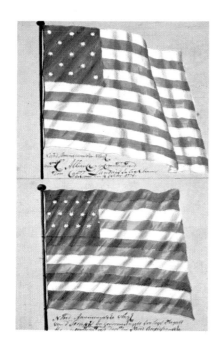

At left is a 1779 Dutch water color of two American naval flags, the top one flown by the Alliance, the other by John Paul Jones' prize, the Serapis (page 294). Above, the Continental frigate Alliance engages two British ships in 1781. The Atalanta (left) has struck, but the Trepassey (right) fought on some time before surrendering.

In March, 1778, off Barbados in the West Indies, the 32-gun Continental frigate Randolph, Captain Nicholas Biddle, challenged the Yarmouth, a 64. Biddle was punishing his opponent severely when, as shown below, a shot struck the Randolph's magazine and blew her to pieces, killing Biddle and over 300 of his men.

The State Navies:

This British plan of the Penobscot action indicates the position of the Massachusetts fleet when Sir George Collier's squadron arrived, as well as the American retreat up the Penobscot River.

The history of the state navies (eleven colonies had their own fleets) closely parallels the state militia establishments which posed a constant problem for Washington. Like the militia, the state navies were activated when danger threatened at home; otherwise, although their ships could have been employed usefully in other theaters of operation, they were of little help to the Continental service.

There were exceptions, of course; the Connecticut navy devoted its handful of vessels to procuring sulphur from the West Indies for the manufacture of gunpowder. However, the majority of the state navies simply patrolled their own rivers and harbors to drive off British and Tory privateers. South Carolina lost most of her ships with the fall of Charleston in 1780, and Virginia's naval force was largely destroyed by the raids of Benedict Arnold in 1781. Toward the end of the war, with both the Continental and state services cut to pieces, Philadelphia mer-

A Dubious Asset

chants had to fit out their own ship, the *Hyder Ally*, Captain Joshua Barney, to convoy their trade in the Delaware and in Chesapeake Bay.

A prime example of the wastage of resources was the Massachusetts navy's expedition in the summer of 1779. The object was Maine's Penobscot Bay, a haven for Loyalists driven out of Boston and a base for enemy privateers. Nineteen armed ships, twenty-odd transports, and some 3,000 sailors and militia troops were raised; but the inept American command allowed the British fort to withstand a siege until a British rescue squadron, including a 64, arrived. At once the Massachusetts fleet fled up the Penobscot River. As recorded in a logbook, the British "pursued the . . . Rebels & Drove them before us without the Return of a single shot." Every ship in the American flotilla was taken or destroyed to prevent capture. The disaster threw Massachusetts $7,000,000 into debt, nearly knocking the state out of the war.

The British captured Joshua Barney three times. Exchanged twice, he escaped once, and commanded the cruiser Hyder Ally *late in the war. He was 25 when Peale painted him in 1784.*

Above, Barney's 16-gun Hyder Ally *engages and takes the* General Monk, *20 guns, in Delaware Bay in 1782. A British frigate (left) and a brig (aground, right) failed to aid their consort.*

In Dominic Serres' painting at left, the British sail into the Penobscot River as the Rebels burn their ships to prevent capture (background). The 64-gun Raisonnable *(left) pursues an American vessel whose captain "was obliged to Strik all thou Contray to my well."*

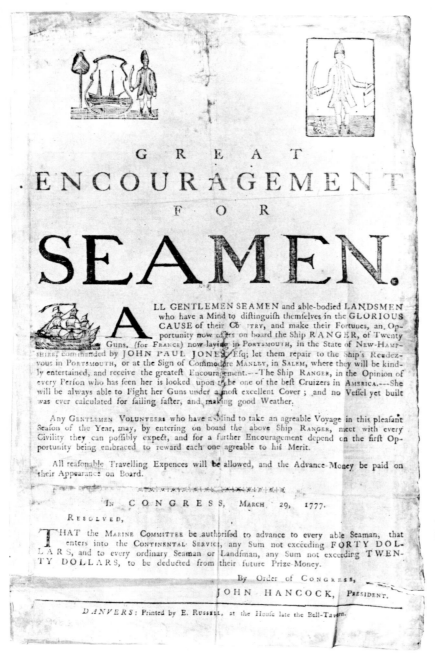

Privateers and Commerce Raiders

Above is Gustavus Conyngham, American priva-teersman whom the British called the "Dunkirk Pirate." The 1777 poster at left called for "Gen-tleman Volunteers" to serve on Jones' Ranger.

The fine print of John Paul Jones at right shows him as the very apotheosis of the gallant sea dog. The panel depicts the Richard-Serapis *fight.*

While the British had little to fear from the Continental or state navies, they were plagued by swarms of American privateers. During the course of the Revolution, the Rebels fitted out some 2,000 raiders which damaged Britain's commerce by over $18,000,000. The hope of prize money was a powerful incentive for privateersmen. Skyrocketing marine insurance rates angered England's strong merchant class, prompting John Adams to write, "it is by cutting off supplies, not by attacks, sieges, or assaults, that I expect deliverance from enemies."

Yet little of the plunder aided the American war effort. British military convoys had powerful es-

corts, which only Continental frigates had the temerity to attack. Many privateer captains sold their prizes in European ports to the highest bidder—often, since the American treasury was empty, right back to the enemy.

The most daring of the commerce raiders was John Paul Jones. Jones began his career in the 18-gun *Ranger,* with which, in 1777, he attacked the British port of Whitehaven, raided the Earl of Selkirk's castle, and took a Royal Navy war sloop while circumnavigating Ireland. Back in France, he had to wait a year for another command, a converted merchantman he named the *Bonhomme Richard.*

Jones' Great Victory

John Paul Jones' voyage to fame began in August, 1779, when he left L'Orient with a small squadron. His flagship, *Bonhomme Richard*, was a slow East Indiaman, refurbished and mounting 40 guns of dubious quality. The little fleet circumnavigated the British Isles, taking prizes. On September 23, off Flamborough Head in the North Sea, Jones sighted a British convoy, escorted by the 50-gun *Serapis*.

Jones' battle with the *Serapis* was one of the bitterest fought in the age of sail. Lashed together most of the time, the ships pounded each other "with unremitting fury." At the battle's height, called upon to surrender, Jones supposedly replied: "I have just begun to fight." Finally, mainmast overboard and crew decimated, the *Serapis* struck. Her captain testified that "the American ship was dominated by a commanding will of a most unalterable resolution."

The print above, of an incident which is probably apocryphal, shows Jones shooting a sailor trying to strike the Richard's *flag.*

At right the Serapis, *on fire, her mainmast shot away, is raked by the* Richard *(left) at the climax of the battle. The shattered* Richard *had to be abandoned and sank two days later.*

Francis Parsons' portrait of the Cherokee warrior Cunne Shote

FRONTIERS AFLAME

"If I attach myself to the mother country, which is three thousand miles from me, I become what is called an enemy to my own region; if I follow the rest of my countrymen, I become opposed to our ancient masters . . . how should I unravel an argument in which reason herself has given way to brutality and bloodshed?"

HECTOR ST. JOHN DE CRÈVECOEUR

ALL through the clanging months and years when the seaboard and immediate hinterland of the United States were masked by the smoke pall of its formal struggle against England, another type of warfare went on unabated. It flickered, burst into full flame, ebbed, died, only to blaze forth again along the inland frontiers and in the mysterious, little-known regions that lay beyond them. This border strife, which had had full and cruel being before the break with the mother country and which was to continue long after the Anglo-American conflict became a memory, belongs in the record of the years of the Revolution, although often it had little or nothing to do with words spoken or written in the rose and white State House in Philadelphia in 1776.

The chief figure in this concurrent conflict was the Indian, whether backed by white allies or operating on his own. He would have been on the warpath regardless of the relationship between the Thirteen States and England. To the Indian, the whites in the north—the ones who clung to lakes and rivers, who built few settlements and fewer towns—were the people to tie to, be they French, as in the beginning, or the later English. Such whites were his allies against the ever-pushing settlers to the south, against those men who were slowly eating into the Indian lands and eroding the Indian way of life. The red man could live with the trapper, the *voyageur,* the *coureur de bois,* with the landless man whose quest was for pelts. But the whites who built a cabin and owned a plow, the people who felled the forests, who built roads and brought in wheeled vehicles, who launched craft of great carrying-power on the rivers —these were the mortal enemies of the Indian, no matter how friendly the cabin builder, the road maker, or the boatman might be by nature or how pacific his intentions.

Before the Revolution settlers had been slipping along river valleys, through wild passes, across ranges, and into the trans-Appalachian lands legally closed to them by the British government. They had trickled into western Pennsylvania, into modern West Virginia, and into the area now known as Kentucky, guided in increasing numbers into the latter by Daniel Boone via new-found Cumberland Gap and Boone's Wilderness Road. All in all, these settlers were a hard, driving lot, intent on owning and clearing land, and possessed of a callous disregard for the tribes they encountered. Shawnees, Delawares, Miamis, Ottawas, Cherokees, Chippewas, Foxes struck at them sharply, were struck with equal ferocity. And with the advent of war, these Indians found a strong ally in the British along the eastern Great Lakes.

Lieutenant Colonel Henry Hamilton—who was to earn the name of "Hair Buyer" from Americans along the frontier—was the commanding officer of the British post at Detroit. He set to work at once supplying the tribes with arms, ammunition, rum, blankets, and the usual trade-trinkets of Indian commerce, and sent them south with his blessing. There was no need for an Ottawa or Miami chief to think twice about such support. In the old days the French along the northern lakes and rivers had always armed the Indians against the pushing, striving intruders to the south. Now the English, replacing the French, were acting in the old familiar way, and the years from 1775 on became hideous ones for the settlers.

Alive to the plight of those outlying citizens, Congress tried to mount several expeditions in 1777 and 1778 whose objective was always Detroit, reasoning soundly that if the main source of Indian munitions was crushed, the western peril would be appreciably eased. But all these ventures ended in failure and frustration, England remained in its role of Protector of the Wil-

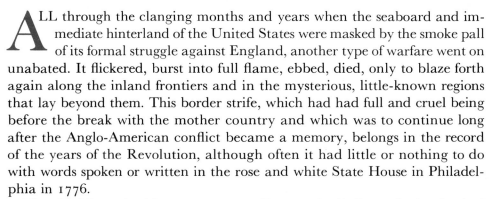

Bargaining for furs—detail from a 1777 map of Canada

Pen and ink sketch of a frontier cabin, from a manuscript diary

derness, and Indian raiding parties swooped out of the forest where and when they chose.

In that shadowy area known as Kentucky, the Indians' "Dark and Bloody Ground," a Virginia-born surveyor—big, tough, red-headed, shrewd, and not long past twenty—began to study the situation and reason out ways and means of controlling it. His name was George Rogers Clark, and he had ample data on which to base a plan of action and to appreciate the need for it. His diary for 1777 was studded with ghastly entries. "June 5. Harrod & Elliott went to meet Col. Bowman . . . Glen & Laird arr^d from Cumb^d Danl Lyons who parted with them on Green River we suppose was killed going into Logans Fort. Jno Peters & Elisha Bathy we expect were killed coming home from Cumb^d. 13. Burr Harrison died of his wound rec^d the 30th of May. 22. Ben. Linn & Saml Moore arr^d from Illenois. Barney Stagner sen^r killed beheaded ½ Mile from the Fort . . ."

George Clark's mind was working far beyond the mere defense of forts like Logan's, and late in 1777 he went to Virginia, sought out Thomas Jefferson, George Mason, and Richard Henry Lee, and outlined his thoughts. Briefly, these were to hit British-fed supply centers in what was called the "Illinois country," that area bounded by the Wabash and Miami rivers on the east, the Illinois on the north, the great Mississippi on the west, and the Ohio on the south. Out of this quadrangle, he held, came most of the supplies that made possible Indian raids on Kentucky. Most of the white inhabitants, Clark reported, were French, living docilely enough under British rule but by no means attached to it.

The main settlements were Kaskaskia, at the mouth of the Kaskaskia River on the Mississippi, about fifty miles south of St. Louis; Prairie du Rocher, about seventeen miles north of Kaskaskia; Cahokia, north again and just below modern East St. Louis; and Vincennes on the Wabash in present-day Indiana. Making Kaskaskia the chief objective, Clark reasoned, would have a dampening effect on the Indians, open communication with the friendly Spaniards across the Mississippi, and greatly improve the fur trade—all of which would be of inestimable value to Kentucky and also to Virginia, which exercised control over that new territory.

Jefferson and his colleagues, convinced by the big young surveyor, laid siege to Governor Patrick Henry, and soon the Burgesses voted Clark £1,200, with authority to requisition flatboats and supplies and to raise several companies of riflemen. The Burgesses were under the impression that this force was for the defense of Kentucky, care having been taken *not* to tell them that Clark's secret orders covered the capture of Kaskaskia and, if possible, Detroit itself.

Clark mustered his command at the Falls of the Ohio, near present Louisville, and found to his chagrin that he had a bare 200 men. Shrugging off this disappointment he embarked his force on June 26, 1778, and shot the rapids of the Ohio River. The sun went into total eclipse, to the terror of the superstitious, but Clark hailed it as a good omen and his boats rode the broad current west until they landed at old Fort Massac, nearly opposite the mouth of the Tennessee River. Hiding his boats, he drove his command north, striking across trackless prairie and forest, depending for supply on what each man carried.

It was a killing march, and at the end there were two long, foodless days before the riflemen sighted Kaskaskia on July 4. The settlement was unguarded and fell to Clark without a shot or any hostile reaction. He at once sent Captain Joseph Bowman on with a small detachment and presently had news that neither Prairie du Rocher nor Cahokia had offered the slightest resistance.

Indian warrior with his grisly trophy, from a 1789 engraving

Clark set about quickly to organize his bloodless conquest and began to show a rare tact and understanding in dealing with the largely French inhabitants. Almost to a man, they cast off allegiance to the Crown of England, won over by a firm guarantee of freedom of religion and by good treatment from the men of the expedition. More than that, allies were found in the settlements, and Père Pierre Gibault volunteered to make the long trek overland to Vincennes on the Wabash and endeavor to talk his fellow Frenchmen into following the lead of Kaskaskia and Cahokia. Père Gibault was eminently successful, and by August, Clark had sent Captain Leonard Helm with a small force to occupy Vincennes and the frontier-post, Fort Sackville, that guarded it [see map, page 315].

Kaskaskia, Prairie du Rocher, Cahokia, Vincennes, and invaluable Fort Sackville—every one of George Rogers Clark's immediate objectives had fallen into his hands without a shot being fired, with no losses at all through enemy action. Such a coup was completely out of line with the usual pattern of wilderness warfare. But Clark's hold was something less than tenuous and his over-all position could only be described as perilous. Of all this he and his lieutenants were keenly aware, and the whole situation was calmly estimated.

First, there were the always deadly Indians who, without much effort, could easily have erased every victorious entry that Clark had made in his ledgers. But that leader had somehow developed the gift, so strikingly displayed in later years by his younger brother William Clark on the immortal expedition with Meriwether Lewis, of dealing with Indians of all kinds. Through August and September he met with chiefs and tribal delegations from such dreaded nations as the Chippewas, Ottawas, Miamis, and Foxes. Speaking carefully, never promising what he could not fulfill, edging around sore points, anticipating their demands, he managed to arrange a truce of several months that was strictly observed by both sides.

His command was small to begin with, and soon Clark was faced with the same gnawing problem that plagued other American commanders along the eastern seaboard, the shrinkage of his force through expired enlistments and desertion. Supplies he must have if he were to keep together what was left to him. Luckily, contact had somehow been made with Oliver Pollock, an American merchant based at New Orleans and a devout believer in Clark's aims. Pollock tossed a good part of his capital and credit into flatboats that were worked up the Mississippi to Cahokia, and the expedition's supply problem was solved for the time being.

A third threat, as dangerous as Indian attacks or starvation, lay in the British base at Detroit. Lieutenant Colonel Henry Hamilton, in charge of that post, was a tough, energetic soldier, admirably fitted for a frontier command. As soon as word came to him of the fall of the four southern posts, he saw at once that the next step could be Detroit itself. No man to sit and wait behind log walls, Hamilton prepared a counteroffensive, a move that Clark could not parry by parley or by accumulating more supplies.

Although Hamilton's military strength was sapped by demands in other theaters, he was able to scrape together some 175 Europeans, mostly French militiamen, and 60 Indians. All precedent, all military teaching told him to postpone his move till spring, that it was far too late in the year for a wilderness march. Nonetheless, Hamilton set out from Detroit with his scratch force on October 7, 1778, bound for Vincennes. His route is an appalling one as it is traced out today on maps old or new, stretching from the shores of Lake Erie down the Maumee to the Wabash and on to that post in the southern reaches of Indiana. He seems to have had plenty of boats, but there were long portages.

A 1780 sketch of Detroit

300

Rivers and tributaries that floodwaters had sent meandering far from their known courses swamped barges and ruined provisions. That his column reached Vincennes on December 17 a cohesive fighting force is a tribute to his military skill and courage, even though there was no combat at the end of the long journey.

At the sight of the invading force, the people of Vincennes rushed to proclaim their allegiance to England. The local militia decided that there was no point in fighting, and Captain Helm and his few men were made prisoners of war. Like Clark, Hamilton had gained his objective without a shot and without casualties, and his obvious course, of which he was fully aware, was to repeat the whole American invasion plan in reverse, moving against what was left of Clark's force at Kaskaskia and Cahokia. The task looked simple enough, since he had knocked out the main prop of Clark's whole plan by the capture of Vincennes. Hamilton set about gathering supplies for his plunge to the west, but, as he probably had to call on the Detroit depots for much of what he needed, time slipped by. He seems to have been little concerned by this, however, since a mild winter had flooded the great flat stretches between him and the Mississippi, spreading out a formidable military barrier that would hamper his enemy as much as it would him.

Clark's march to Vincennes

The news of the fall of Vincennes threw the people of Kaskaskia and Cahokia into a first-class panic and Clark, his own force now whittled down to about 100 men, would have been helpless had Hamilton moved against him. The prudent thing would have been to slip out to the south, back across the Ohio, content with what damage had been done to British prestige and organization. Clark and the men with him took a different view of the matter. There they were on the banks of the Mississippi, there was Hamilton at Vincennes, 180 miles to the east. Therefore, they reasoned, we'll attack.

Clark and his lieutenants, powerfully aided by the unwavering Père Gibault, argued, pleaded, and cajoled until the population slowly began to regain heart. Some local militia were induced to join the Kentucky riflemen, men drifted north from "la Belle Rivière," and by February 6, 1779, George Rogers Clark could muster nearly a man for each of the 180 winter miles that separated him and Hamilton. This would be no mere wilderness march that would have been routine for most of the men. Thaws and floods had turned much of the country to the east into a vast lake whose depth varied from inches to feet. Once under way, nightfall would have to find the command on high ground, or the men would have no choice but to sleep in the shallowest water they could find, praying that sudden freshets might not drown them as they rested. On the surface, the whole attempt seems foolhardy today, but it did not impress Clark that way, his thoughts even reaching beyond Vincennes to Detroit.

For the first few days of the winter march, the men were in high spirits. The water over the flooded land was rarely more than a few inches deep, game was plentiful, and the weather mild as the column splashed across modern Randolph and Washington counties. By February 13, Vincennes was a mere twenty miles away and the Little Wabash was reached. High water had widened the stream and two whole days were spent in ferrying the expedition to the east bank—or to as much of it as was above the surface. And here their luck began to run out.

The surface waters were deeper and men sloshed along through icy, waist-high floods. Game had vanished, driven to some mysterious higher ground, and supplies ran low. On the seventeenth, the Embarrass River blocked the march,

301

sent men floundering north and south along its bank looking for possible fords. By the eighteenth the command was across, pushing on through slowly deepening water to the Wabash itself, hauling the sick and exhausted along with them in canoes; but they could not pass over the Wabash until February 20. Here a stray Frenchman from Vincennes was captured, and from him Clark learned that Henry Hamilton had not the least suspicion of the waterlogged advance from the west. If the latter had known about it, he could hardly have been blamed for taking the threat lightly. On the twenty-first, the march covered little more than three miles, with men half-wading, half-swimming through shoulder-deep water, rifles and powder held high above their heads. The next day showed virtually no progress as the men grew weaker and weaker from scant rations and their days of exposure to winter weather.

February 23 brought a crisis. Men hung back, their hoarse voices croaking of inability or unwillingness to go farther. Clark merely took to the water once more, shouting "Follow me!" while Captain Joseph Bowman skirted the rear with 25 riflemen who had orders to shoot any stragglers. This seems to have been the worst part of the march, with water still shoulder-high. More and more men had to be towed in canoes. Those on their feet tripped and fell in deep water, then clung to a rotten log or sodden tree until stronger hands rescued them, much as Arnold's men had helped each other up the Height of Land during the march to Quebec.

At last dry ground was reached, a tree-masked strip barely two miles from Fort Sackville, key to Vincennes. Here the command boldly lit fires, dried out their clothes, and ate the last rations, their spirits little lifted by news from another captured Frenchman that some 200 more Indians had joined Hamilton in the fort. And Clark's ammunition was almost gone.

Bad news cuts the legs out from under some men, merely numbs others. To George Rogers Clark it always seemed to act as a stimulant. Now he reacted strongly and at once. Carefully hiding his weaknesses from the Frenchman, he sent him on to Hamilton in Sackville with a message that was magnificent in its lack of ambiguity. Hamilton was informed that Clark was going to capture Sackville that night; that friends of the United States should stay quietly in their homes; that those still holding to England should join the garrison in the fort.

This done, Clark cheerily formed his men into two small divisions and marched them into Vincennes and down the main street, drums beating. Once in the streets, he divided and subdivided his shrunken ranks, sent them swinging through side streets, back to the main thoroughfare, into side streets again, trying to create an impression of far larger numbers than he actually had.

The ruse was successful. No habitant fled to Fort Sackville. Instead, eager men guided the invaders to secret caches of ammunition, and soon Clark's sodden, leathery men were filling pouches and powder horns from this unsuspected windfall. Rumors reached the fort, and the Indians faded out over the palisades and through sally ports and embrasures, their interest in Hamilton and his command evaporating in the misty February air. One chief was so overwhelmed by whispers of endless American legions swarming into Vincennes that he opened futile negotiations to join Clark and his men.

At sunset, Clark marched his command out of the settlement and toward the fort, drums still beating, and opened rifle fire against it. Some accounts state that these shots were the first warning that Hamilton had of Clark's approach, but in view of the messenger bearing the ultimatum and the fearful din of the American drums in the town, this hardly seems likely.

Clark's Long Knives firing on Fort Sackville at Vincennes

"Smart firing all night on both sides. The cannon played smartly, not one of our men wounded . . . fine sport for the sons of Liberty."
—American Officer with Clark

The fort itself was enough to convince any book-soldier that it could not be taken by a force like Clark's. Its eleven-foot palisade walls enclosed a space of three acres, and at each corner a wooden bastion towered a good twelve feet above the palisade, each bastion mounting three fieldpieces, a vital weapon that Clark did not possess. The garrison of Sackville was less than 100 men, but they were well protected and amply supplied with food, water, and ammunition. The average frontier force and frontier leader would have loosed a few rounds at the heavy log walls, burned a few outbuildings, and melted away into the wilderness. But there was nothing average about this force or this leader, as had been shown all through the February water-march and was further emphasized now. Irregular forces are apt to despise fighting from behind works almost as much as the digging of them. Nonetheless, the night of February 23 was spent throwing up entrenchments opposite the main gate of Sackville, and by dawn approaches had been pushed within thirty yards of the walls.

With the first light, Hamilton's guns began to thud out from the high Sackville bastions, but Clark's men still refused to follow precedent. Either unaware of or unimpressed by the theory that frontier troops cannot stand up against artillery fire, the riflemen began picking off the gunners methodically, and by the end of the day, after some parleying, Hamilton and his little force surrendered. The victory was made complete when Captain Leonard Helm slipped up the Wabash to capture a water-borne supply column hurrying to the fort.

Hamilton surrenders his sword and the Vincennes garrison to Clark

E xcept in exertion expended and territory covered, the campaign had been a small one; but it nailed down the whole Illinois territory for Virginia, and hence the United States, for the rest of the war. The eastern reaches boiled on, however, year after long year. Little bands and miniature expeditions roamed and ravaged back and forth with varying success. American leaders were always just about to gather enough strength to take Detroit. Indians, sometimes alone, sometimes with British or Tory formations, kept up a hot southward pressure. The Indian-raised white Simon Girty fought and burned and scalped and tortured up and down present Ohio and Indiana, much as he would have had there been no Crown behind him. Joseph Brant, deserting his favorite battleground of the Mohawk Valley and adjacent country, wrecked a Pennsylvania force near the mouth of the Big Miami and then pushed on toward the Falls of the Ohio, hoping to run George Rogers Clark to earth. However, such was Clark's prestige that the Indians under Brant gave up, and the Tory Rangers with them showed no wish to close with the tall Virginian. So the whole party eventually drifted back to Detroit.

To add to the unending variety of this whole confused, murderous war in the wilderness, a Spanish force under Captain Eugenio Pourré brought off a march that was in many ways comparable to Clark's move against Vincennes, and took British-held Fort St. Joseph in southern Michigan. In late 1782, Clark was in the field again, pushing into Ohio, wiping out Chillicothe and other Shawnee towns to bring the curtain down on the war in the west, so far as hostilities between England and the United States were concerned. The end of fighting found Americans still controlling the Illinois country, while the British hold was very shaky on the great tracts that lay between Lake Erie and the Ohio River. To George Rogers Clark goes most of the credit for those provisions in the Treaty of Paris that gave Kentucky and all the Old Northwest Territory to the United States.

The Indians, however, were not signatories of that Treaty, and the same sort of war, without overt British support, dragged on and on. In 1794, United

Hamilton appended his reasons for capitulating to the surrender agreement

CONTINUED ON PAGE 306

Overleaf: A British copy of Lewis Evans' 1755 map of the northern colonies and, to the west, the Indian country of the Ohio Valley

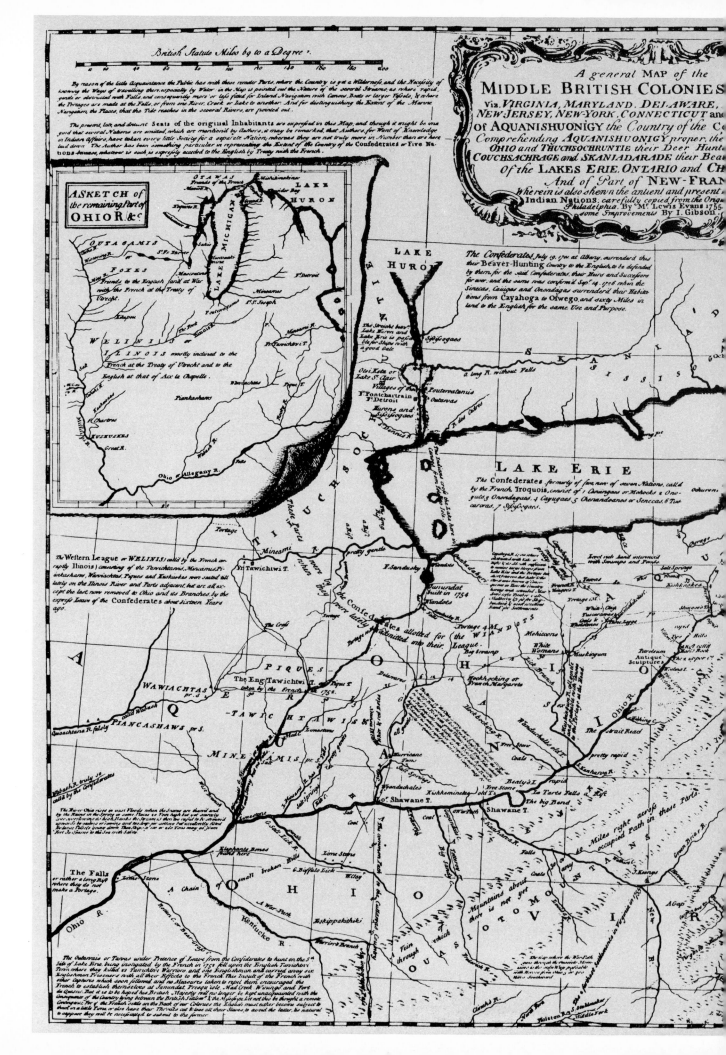

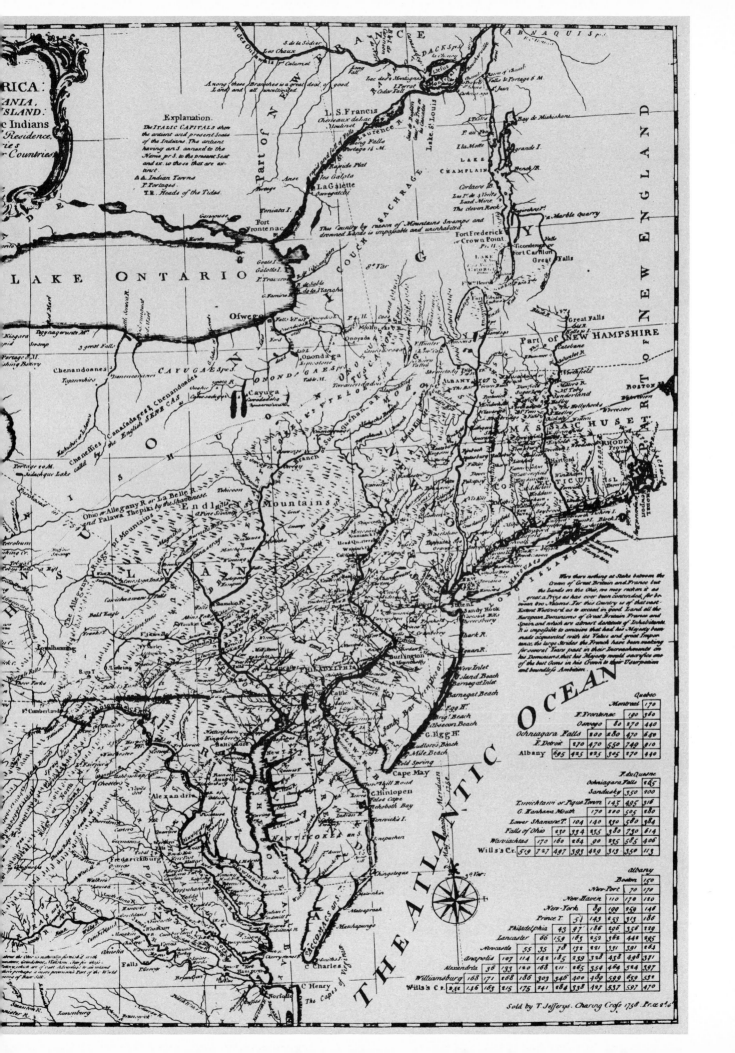

CONTINUED FROM PAGE 303

States troops under General Anthony Wayne were to win a great victory over the Indians at Fallen Timbers on the Maumee River, thereby canceling out unlucky Arthur St. Clair's debacle near the same spot in 1791. Back and back the Indians fell, always fighting, dotting the pages of history with the records of wars that began when the first arrow was drawn against the first arquebus in the seventeenth century, not ending until the dawn of the twentieth. The Revolution broadened the scope of some of these conflicts, giving the Indians new weapons and new allies, but it did not alter the basic nature of the struggle between European and aborigine.

A testimonial issued by Sir William Johnson to Indians loyal to the Crown

Through 1778, hot, bitter appeals for help had been pouring in to the Congress and to Washington's headquarters from the Mohawk Valley, from the Wyoming Valley in northeastern Pennsylvania, from Cherry Valley well to the west of Albany. The Johnsons and the Butlers with their grimly named "Destructives" had been scourging these and other centers of settlement with devastating raids whose planning was excellent and whose execution hideous. Joseph Brant and his Indians had thrown themselves into the burning and butchery and torture with an expertness and zeal that made earlier depredations, savage as they were, appear mild by comparison.

Thin-stretched as his strength was by the demands of the major war against England, Washington could not brush aside the ghastly details that poured in to him. Most of the settlers in the stricken areas were quite solidly opposed to the Crown and must be shielded somehow. Besides, their territories held fine productive farms which constituted an invaluable, accessible granary from which the main army drew supplies.

But what could be spared without seriously weakening the force that must be ready to meet any British stroke out of New York? Bit by bit an Order of Battle was drawn up from the depleted rosters of Washington's army, a course mapped out, and an objective assigned [see map, page 318].

The over-all plan was a daring one, almost hazardously so, since it contemplated two columns starting from widely separated points, driving on through the wilderness, meeting at a prearranged spot and time, and then going on together. The objective of this twin stroke, whose plans were completed in the spring of 1779, was very simply defined in Washington's final orders. The country of the Six Nations was to be invaded with "the total destruction . . . of their settlements and the capture of as many prisoners . . . as possible." Prisoners of all ages and sexes were to be held as hostages, being "the only kind of security to be depended on" for the future good behavior of the Indians, in the commander in chief's opinion.

Mohawk leader Joseph Brant, or Thayendanegea, after Romney's portrait

The lands of the Six Nations extended roughly from Lake Ontario south to the Susquehanna, with the Catskills of New York closing in on the east and Lake Erie on the west. Their settlements, which Washington had marked down for destruction, were no huddles of wigwams. The tribes had actual towns studded with good houses, sometimes of stone with glazed windows, and the adjoining orchard tracts showed years of careful husbandry. Politically, the Six Nations had kept step with their architecture and cultivation. They had a sort of constitution and a code of law, the whole forming a pattern of life that might have survived peaceably with the ever-oncoming white settlers. Unfortunately, tribal life had lagged in development. The women—and only the women—tended the fine farms and orchards. Men were above such sordid tasks. War—which may be translated as indiscriminate, bloody raiding—and hunting alone were worthy of masculine attention. Such a tribal frame of mind made peace a mere breathing spell between raids and forays, an unthinkable, unattainable end. So against the Six Nations marched the twin expedition.

Command of the larger American column, which was to move north through Pennsylvania and into New York state, was given to General John Sullivan, perhaps to soothe his feelings which had been so rasped by the Newport-d'Estaing debacle of the preceding year. Under him was an unusual collection of brigade and regimental commanders. For his first brigade, he had General "Scotch Willie" Maxwell of New Jersey, a tested, seasoned soldier, with colonels like Elias Dayton and Mathias Ogden to support him. Then came New Hampshire's Enoch Poor, with Joseph Cilley and Henry Dearborn among his regimental officers. Edward Hand of Pennsylvania, who had done very well with his riflemen on many fields, headed the 3rd Brigade, with others of his own state such as William Butler, Daniel Burchardt and his Germans, and James Parr with a detachment of Morgan's own riflemen.

The second column, under General James Clinton of New York, was to strike downstate from the Mohawk and link up with Sullivan near the New York-Pennsylvania line. This command was smaller, but numbered four New York Continental regiments under men like Colonel Peter Gansevoort, who had been outstanding in the turning back of Barry St. Leger's drive in '77, Philip van Cortlandt, and Baron Frederick Weissenfels, a former British officer who had lived in New York since 1763.

James Clinton's expeditionary force assembling at Canajoharie, New York

Each column included various special detachments as well as pack horses and artillery, with about ten pieces from Colonel Thomas Proctor's 4th U.S. Regiment being assigned to Sullivan's command. When the accompanying impedimenta is totted up, it does seem as though both expeditions were too elaborately organized for a quick-striking invasion of Indian country, with so many bateaux, wheeled vehicles, and guns detailed for the task.

Sullivan reached the assembly point for his column at Easton, Pennsylvania, on May 7, 1779, and at once delays began. Supplies were slow in coming. He also found that he would have to hack out a wilderness road some 23 miles through forest lands to pass along his guns, wagons, pack horses, and the great herd of cattle that, bit by bit, would be converted into rations for his column. Like Burgoyne's axemen, Sullivan's soldiers slowly drove a road onward through country where there had been little more than deer-trails before, and it was June 23 before field headquarters were set up at Wyoming. Here again he had to wait through no fault of his own. The rudimentary supply system of the army simply could not keep pace with him, and was woefully slow in replacing provisions and ammunition that had spoiled on the march from Easton. Glimpses of road conditions show through the stained pages of old diaries and letters written by men who, accustomed to rough going though they were, found themselves appalled by the terrain. Sergeant Thomas Roberts of the 5th New Jersey found strength to note on June 21: "Marched 20 Milds throug the Grate Swamp wheare theare was not A hous nor fense nothing but Rocks and Mountains and a Grate part of it was as Dark as after Sun down When it was Noon day. at times the Sun Was not to Bee Seen that for the timber the Swamp so thick you Cold not see 10 foot. Wee Incamped that Day at the End of the Shades of Death." Roberts also wrote of disciplinary troubles. "One of Colln. Spensers men Run the Ganlet Through 3 Regiments and Everey man had a whip and one [other man] had one hundred lashes at the post. thear Crime was for painting themselves threthhging [threatening] Two officers Lives as Indians." Another night "The woolves mad a wonderfool noys all around us wich Semed Verey Destresed."

Up at Canajoharie on the Mohawk, General James Clinton was astir. He had more than 200 bateaux ready and a three months' supply of rations. By June 17 he began to batter his way south across country that was wooded, hilly, and scored with a few very bad roads, to Otsego Lake, almost twenty miles from the Mohawk. His bateaux were bulky and heavy, and the four-horse hitches that he used for each boat must have been woefully inadequate for such terrain. Inadequate or not, by June 30 he was able to write Sullivan, still based at Wyoming, that his little force was at Otsego and ready for orders. When those orders did come, far later than the high command had hoped, the level of Otsego Lake was falling and Clinton's bateau-fleet, which carried supplies for himself and Sullivan, might have been immobilized. Many commanders would have thrown up their hands and sat and waited for the rains to raise the lake-level again. But Clinton had the main outlet dammed. The waters rose and his flotilla started out again, little delayed. The New York General had anticipated by nearly a century Colonel Joseph Bailey's feat of damming the Red River in Louisiana and thus saving Union gunboats supporting General Nathaniel Banks in the latter's ill-starred 1864 campaign.

On July 31, 1779, Sullivan's column left Wyoming, bound for Tioga, where Clinton was to meet him. With him went 120 bateaux, 1,200 pack horses, and 700 head of cattle. But long before his junction with Clinton, he struck his first blow of the invasion, Edward Hand's riflemen and Enoch Poor's New Hampshire brigade smashing into the village of Chemung. Here was something new for the troops, at least those from the eastern states. There were "between 30 & 40 Houses, some of them large and neatly finish'd; particularly a Chapel and Council House." There was no resistance, and Chemung flamed up in a "glorious Bonfire and wide fields of grain and vegetables were ruin'd." If this seemed a ghastly desolation, the troops could recall that out of such villages came Indians who had been burning and killing and torturing through the Mohawk Valley and the Susquehanna.

As to the commander in chief's concern about seizing hostages, this point seems to have been overlooked by all conducting the march. At Chemung and subsequent targets the invaders found empty streets, deserted houses. This was

A pre-1800 pencil sketch of a typical white settlement in the Mohawk Valley: the cluster of

hardly surprising as neither Sullivan nor Clinton made the slightest attempt at secrecy. Reveille each day was marked with a cannon shot which must have echoed far up the valleys and intervals, rolling over cornfields and orchards. On the march, regiments kept to strict formation, drums beating, colors flying, and fifes playing.

This strongly suggests two points. Neither commander had the least fear of a Braddock-like ambush and massacre which their march-order, as shown in surviving charts, clearly invited. And neither was in the least bit interested in the injunction concerning hostages. Sullivan and Dearborn, for example, were seasoned soldiers, and they must have been fully aware that the need for detailing men for prisoner guard or escort would have peeled down their force to the point where a very small Indian band could have wiped it out. No doubt Clinton, though less experienced, was led along the same train of thought by sheer common sense.

On August 22, Sullivan's advance scouts sighted Clinton's column pushing down from Otsego. The two commanders met at Tioga and the now unified force pushed on, with the earlier pattern of the march repeating itself. Another town, deserted like Chemung, was surrounded and burned: "one of the Neatest of the Indian towns . . . with good Log houses with Stone Chimneys and glass windows." Men in Clinton's column could recall that there had been solid chimneys and glazed windows in towns like German Flats and Stone Arabia before the Indians had raided them.

The march went on, and Dearborn's men and Poor's and Gansevoort's saw flame and smoke gush out over Queen Esther's Flats. Soldiers who remembered farms along the Merrimac or the Raritan went glumly about the business of wasting fields whose richness showed every sign of husbandry as fine as anything the white man knew. Here were acres of "Cucombars, Squashes, Turnips, Pompions." Cornfields showed ears an awesome two feet in length. Squaw-labor had ranged neat rows of "beans . . . Simblens [sometimes called pattypans or summer squash] watermelons and pumpkins such as cannot be equalled in Jersey." It seems odd that in the midst of such lavishness the ration problem existed for any man, but Henry Dearborn one day "eat part of a fryed Rattle

"At French Catherines . . . the Indian Fires were still burning in many Places but they had evacuated the Place all except an old Squaw that could not Travel."
—Diary of Lieutenant Obadiah Gore, Jr.

abins shown here was at the confluence of the Mohawk (foreground) and Hudson rivers

John Sullivan, by R. M. Staigg

Snake . . . which would have tasted very well, had it not been Snake."

Empty towns, empty fields—yet the men must have known that somewhere ahead of them the woodlands rustled and stirred with the men of the Six Nations, falling silently back and back. Then, near present Elmira, New York, the joint command tripped into a neat ambush laid for them by Indians and Tories. This could have been fatal to men from the coast where Indians had hardly been known for a century; but John Sullivan, James Clinton, Henry Dearborn, and Peter Gansevoort were alert and ready. The ambush was sidestepped, then smashed in a circling movement, riflemen to the front. Henry Dearborn, totting up the action of August 29, 1779, made a terse summation. "The Enimy . . . left the field . . . with precipitation & in great confusion, pursued by our light infantry about 3 miles." Lieutenant Obadiah Gore, Jr., recorded with approval the behavior of the "Riffle Corps," and noted that "the Troops were much animated with this Days Success."

The victory had cost Sullivan just three men killed, but the Indians and Tories were so battered that little opposition was met from then on. Scant booty was taken, some of it of a very odd nature. Lieutenant William Barton, 1st New Jersey, learned that riflemen had found dead Indians after the fight. He "skinned two of them from their hips down for boot legs; one pair for the Major [Daniel Piatt] the other for myself."

Kanadaseagea, a Seneca metropolis of eighty houses set in flourishing orchard country, went up in flames along with Schoyere and Canandaigua, Honeoye and Kanagha. At last the command reached Genesee—Chinesee as some diarists render it—about twenty miles south of modern Rochester, New York, and marked its farthest western penetration by sending nearly 130 buildings up in flames. And there the invasion force turned back, marching easily enough through clear September weather, Clinton slanting off to the Mohawk country and Sullivan rolling south. The latter reached his starting point, Easton, Pennsylvania, on October 15, 1779, and sent his formal report to John Jay. Summing up his achievements, he said "there is not a single Town left in the Country of the five [sic] nations," except for one spot far west of Genesee. No mention was made of the prime objective of the whole weary, cruel business—the securing of hostages—and Washington, thanking the New Hampshire General warmly, seems to have forgotten this point.

Tactically, the whole northwest sweep was a distinct success. Strategically, it was a fairly complete failure. Its ultimate aim had been to protect the frontier settlers. Instead, the Six Nation tribes had been rolled clear back to the British post at Niagara. Their year's crops were smoke and ashes marking Sullivan's and Clinton's progress. All their accumulated supplies were lost beyond any hope of recovery. The Indians huddled under the British flag, dependent on the Crown for survival. They were destitute. Also they were still armed, and their furious eyes turned toward the horizon behind which lay the hated settlements.

All through 1780 and 1781, Indians and Tories, singly or together, struck again and again at the Mohawk settlements in a crescendo of fury that made former raids seem like routine peacetime maneuvers. Then, not long after Cornwallis' drums had beaten out the message of his surrender by the York River, Colonel Marinus Willett, partner of Gansevoort at Stanwix in '77, cornered the last of Walter Butler's men at Jerseyfield near West Canada Creek in a blizzard. Walter Butler was killed, his force smashed. There was no pursuit, Willett writing in his report: "In this situation, to the compassion of a starving wilderness, we left them." The hard core of British-trained and

Marinus Willett, by Ralph Earl

British-equipped Tories was broken for good and there was no real rallying point left for the Indians, although Brant did return with his tribesmen for another raid or two in 1782, striking at Fort Dayton and the country about it. But the last real menace to the valley had ended there on the banks of West Canada Creek.

Other areas, other theaters, burned and bled through the war, sometimes saved by help from Washington's army, sometimes by state troops like George Rogers Clark's. Often the inhabitants fought off Indian attacks unaided, just as often they succumbed, cursing the help that did not reach them, which could not possibly have reached them. And as the frontiers expanded, pushing west and south and north, this war went on—a war that had begun long before the Revolution and which would rage on for a century or more.

E ver since the British warships and transports had limped away after their futile attack on Charleston in 1776, the southern states had known peace of a sort, or at least the absence of formal warfare. Their governments had contributed powerfully to the American cause in men and supplies, had strained their credit to the cracking point to bolster the main effort. But no campaigns comparable to those in New Jersey and Pennsylvania had rolled up and down their coasts and inland valleys, no desperately toiling columns of trained European soldiers had wasted the land and its towns. Instead, bands of Whigs and Tories had raided each other's areas, plundering, burning, and killing. Roving groups took advantage of local unrest to shoot up, with a careless impartiality, any center that promised loot. Like the war in the west and along the Mohawk, these were manifestations of older feuds and quarrels that had come into being with the states themselves, at least so far as the Carolinas and Georgia were concerned.

When formal warfare did return to the South, late in 1778, the backbone of the invading army was British. But out in front of it there were usually compact, highly mobile Tory units, testing once again the theory of "conquering America with Americans." Strangely enough, these Tories were not local levies, for South Carolinians showed the same reluctance that had been noted in other areas about swarming out to the Royal colors. Here were the Volunteers of Ireland, raised and trained on the Philadelphia water front by Lord Rawdon, and operating under him. Banastre Tarleton's hard-riding files had been gathered in New York and the Jerseys. Lieutenant Colonel John Harris Cruger came from the Hudson to serve with rare distinction in the South, and the able cavalry Major, John Coffin, was a Boston Tory.

Whatever their origin, whoever their leaders, these Loyalist formations brought civil war into the Carolinas. Wherever they went they turned the conflict into bitter, violent, brutal fighting, and they were resisted in the same terms by local Whig units. Up the Wateree, up the Congaree, bloody combats swirled, with the torch ready on either side and quarter unknown. In May of 1780, Tarleton and his Legion overtook a mixed force under Colonel Abraham Buford of Virginia at the Waxhaws, near the North Carolina border. Buford, cornered, tried to surrender. His signals were mistaken by Tarleton, possibly deliberately, and a horrible butchery of Buford's men, including the wounded, followed. Down on the coast in the Georgetown area, British Major Wemyss led a band as violent as the Mohawk Valley "Destructives," burning houses and wantonly killing sheep and cattle in his own version of a scorched-earth policy. Sometimes odd mistakes were made. To many officers who had served in the north, the Church of England meant steadfast loyalty, while Dissenters were all confounded Rebels. In the Carolinas, the picture was apt to be re-

Tarleton's massacre of Abraham Buford's command at the Waxhaws

versed. Hence Dissenter settlements were marked down for destruction by commanders unfamiliar with the local picture, and violent raids fell on groups of Loyalists who had been unwavering since earliest days.

Other sore points began to chafe in this half-rebellion, half-civil strife. South Carolina was conquered territory and plundering went on regardless of the politics of the sufferers. Slaves were snapped up, loaded on ships, and sent to the West Indies for sale to plantation owners there. Sweeping orders went out impounding all weapons discovered in civilian hands, and isolated Tories found themselves helpless in the face of raids by vengeful Whigs. Tory voices were raised in anguished protest when it was found that able-bodied males were liable for incorporation, willy-nilly, into the armed forces of the Crown. As in other areas, Loyalists were beginning to find that neither combatant would allow them to remain peaceful spectators of the great struggle.

On the American side there were also manifestations of this civil conflict. Until Nathanael Greene came along and, with rare genius, put these forces to work in the way they could be most effective, men like Francis Marion, Thomas Sumter, and Andrew Pickens waged a shadowy sort of *maquis* warfare which frequently constituted the only substantial American opposition in a given area.

Of them all, the swarthy little Marion—a man who rarely spoke—understood this kind of warfare best. Sumter was handsome, recklessly brave, and a natural rallying point, but his value was diminished by a fierce hatred of authority and control that made men like John Stark seem like parade-ground automatons. Colonel Andrew Pickens pretty well matched Marion and Sumter in daring, skill, and devotion, and if he was less imaginative than Marion, he was also far more co-operative than Sumter. As time went on South Carolina was roughly divided between this trio and their lieutenants, with Marion ranging inland from the coast, Sumter operating in the center, and Pickens in the west, although these informal spheres of influence were rather fluid.

All three understood—Marion best of all and Sumter the least—the vital difference between guerrilla bands and organized armies. The properly functioning guerrilla band never tries to hold territory. It must side-step open combat, must devote itself to eroding enemy forces and cutting off supplies and supply routes. It hits and runs, unless in overwhelming strength, and the most important item is the running, the getting away after striking, the avoidance of being pinned down.

Up and down South Carolina and into North Carolina actions were fought —at Flat Rock, at Thicketty Fort, at Rocky Mount, Hanging Rock, and Old Iron District. As a rule these were successful when the various bands stuck to their true mission. Disaster fell when they tried to act like formal armies. Taken action by action, these strokes amounted to little, but in the aggregate they seriously slowed down Cornwallis' plans for conquering the South.

Largely for convenience's sake, the end of the Revolution is usually assigned to that date on which Cornwallis' men marched out of Yorktown to stack their arms before the combined armies of France and America. But the war on the frontiers was far from over. In the South, well into 1782, there would be scuffles, raids, and savage encounters largely between Whig and Tory—extensions of conflicts that had existed before the war and would continue after it. The same was true in the far reaches of the bloody Mohawk Valley, while beyond the Allegheny mountains the fighting would go on for thirteen more years, during which more Americans were killed than in all the major Revolutionary battles combined.

"The difficulties I have had to struggle with have not been occasioned by the opposite army (they always keep at a considerable distance, and retire on our approach) but [by] the constant incursions of refugees, North Carolinians, and back-mountain men, and the perpetual risings in the different parts of this province."
—Cornwallis to Clinton, January 6, 1781

This view of Detroit was made in 1794. A French outpost from 1701 until 1760, for the next 36 years it was held by the British, and was used after 1775 as a base for their attacks on the American frontier.

The Struggle for the Northwest

British Lieutenant Colonel Henry Hamilton

The first white man's permanent home in what is now Kentucky was built in 1775, and while the war continued on the eastern seaboard, thousands of other Americans surged over the Appalachians to lay claim to the virgin western lands. On the northern and southern flanks of these settlements were Indians who had watched the American's inexorable westward progress and who had determined that he should go no farther. In this they found the British more than willing allies. Lieutenant Colonel Henry Hamilton, British agent at Detroit, was despised by Americans as the "Hair Buyer" for supplying the red men with weapons, ammunition, and liquor, and for supporting their raids on remote outposts.

Not until 1777, when frontier fighter George Rogers Clark presented a plan to Governor Patrick Henry of Virginia, were effective steps taken to loosen England's hold on the Old Northwest. Supported by Thomas Jefferson, George Mason, and Richard Henry Lee, Clark gained Henry's support, and received secret orders authorizing him to raise a command to attack Kaskaskia and, if feasible, Detroit.

Describing the fearful march to Vincennes (above), one of Clark's men wrote: "Having no other resource but wading this . . . lake of water, we plunged into it with courage, Col. Clark being first." The inspired leadership of Clark (left) gave the U. S. control of a vast territory in 1779.

The Long Knives

One of the great campaigns of the Revolution began late in June of 1778 when a band of Kentucky "Long Knives" under George Rogers Clark set off down the Ohio River in a string of flatboats, bound for Kaskaskia. Clark's mission was the conquest of the entire "Illinois country," that huge area included in the present states of Ohio, Indiana, and Illinois, which was held by the British and their allies, the Shawnees, Delawares, Miamis, and Ottawas. For this task, Clark had just under 200 men.

Leaving their boats below the mouth of the Tennessee River, Clark's frontiersmen headed off through prairies and trackless forests, their only food and equipment what they carried on their backs. Kaskaskia was taken completely by surprise, and Prairie du Rocher, Cahokia, and Vincennes fell quickly into Clark's hands. These successes were an imminent threat to Detroit, and on October 7 Lieutenant Colonel Henry Hamilton led some 200 whites and Indians south against Vincennes, taking it easily from the few men Clark had there.

Two months later the audacious Clark was moving against Hamilton, this time with about 180 men. By February 13 Vincennes was only twenty miles

The 1778 map at right shows the area of George Rogers Clark's campaign of 1778–79. His men covered the 180 miles from Kaskaskia to Vincennes in 18 days, often without food, and marching through icy water. Henry Hamilton called it a military feat "unequalled perhaps in History."

Epic Campaign

away, but floods had driven off all the game, and the hungry men had to push on through icy water that was often shoulder-deep. Always out in front, Clark inspired and drove his half-starved, frozen troops until they reached a point, two miles from Vincennes, where they could build fires and dry their clothes. A captured Frenchman brought news that Clark's approach was still unknown in the town, but he added the sobering note that 200 Indians had just joined Hamilton's force.

Although his ammunition was nearly exhausted, Clark resolved to attack that very night. At dusk he had twenty American flags attached to poles, spaced them at wide intervals along his line of march, and started his little army off on a zigzag course toward the town. The defenders, believing they were attacked by twenty companies, held out through the night, but the next morning Clark received Hamilton's offer to surrender.

Few campaigns in history on which so much depended have been conducted with more resourcefulness and daring. Clark's magnificent victory gave the United States complete control of the Old Northwest for the rest of the war

Heading south from Canada in
allies to fight in civilized fashion,

Sir William Johnson's large fortified house at Johnstown was the scene of frequent
Indian councils. Johnson died just after haranguing visiting Mohawks here in 1774.

The Six Nations Strike

The Revolution turned the Mohawk Valley into a dark and bloody battlefield, torn by a savage conflict between Rebel, Tory, and Indian. A focal point of the struggle was Tryon County, which had been dominated for years by the wealthy landowner Sir William Johnson. He had exercised great influence over the Six Nations of the Iroquois, and after his death in 1774 his son, Sir John, and his son-in-law, Colonel Guy Johnson, continued to do so. Leagued with them were Tories John Butler and his son, Walter, and the Mohawk chief Joseph Brant. From bases in western New York, British, Loyalists, and Indians swept down on unprotected settlements in New York and Pennsylvania, spreading disaster and terror in their wake. Although this warfare provoked cries of outrage even in England, it served the British by destroying crops needed by Washington's army, kept the Americans on the defensive and away from English bases in the west, and forced local men to stay at home to protect their families, instead of joining the army.

*American propagandists capitalized on the murder of Jane Mc-
Crea by Burgoyne's Indians, although she was a Tory's fiancée.*

77, Burgoyne ordered his Indian *t his instructions were of no avail.*

Benjamin West painted this ominous portrait of Colonel Guy Johnson and his Mohawk ally, Chief Joseph Brant, in London in 1775. The remarkable Brant had been educated in Connecticut by Eleazar Wheelock, founder of Dartmouth College, and is said to have aided in the translation of religious books into the Mohawk tongue. While in England he was entertained by James Boswell and had his portrait painted by Romney. After his return to America he was secretary to Guy Johnson, who succeeded his father-in-law as Britain's Superintendent of Indian Affairs.

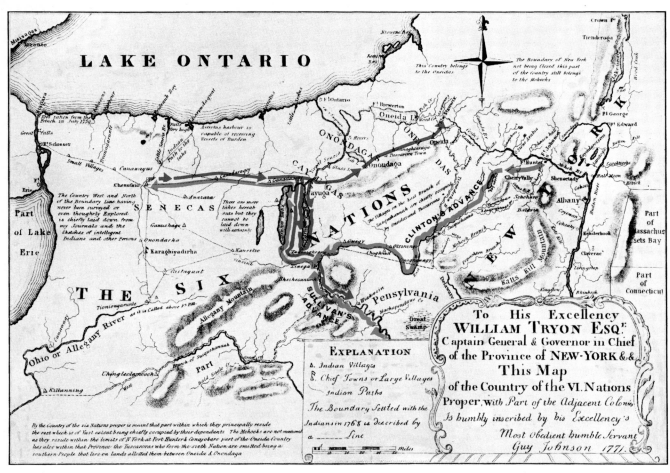

The routes of the punitive expedition of Clinton and Sullivan (advance in blue, return in red) are shown on Guy Johnson's 1771 map of the area. The two forces met at Tioga for the combined attack on the Six Nations.

The Indians' Power Is Broken

Alonzo Chappel's gory painting of the Wyoming Massacre (right) shows Colonel John Butler's Tories and Indians falling upon the local militiamen who went out to meet their attack. Butler claimed 227 scalps as a result of the fight, while he lost only three men.

This gruesome cartoon is a 1780 English attack on the King's employment of Indian allies against the Americans. George III shares a cannibal feast with an Indian chief, and behind the fat bishop a sailor appears, carrying scalping knives, crucifixes, and tomahawks.

In 1778 the frontiers of Pennsylvania and New York erupted in a series of barbarous Tory and Indian raids. Late that spring Colonel John Butler headed south from Fort Niagara with nearly 1,000 whites and Indians, striking toward the lovely Wyoming Valley near Wilkes-Barre, Pennsylvania.

The settlers there had some warning of the approaching attack, and many of them took refuge in the forts which had been built for this purpose, while another Butler, the patriot Colonel Zebulon, led several hundred local men and militia out to meet the enemy. Almost at once the Americans were thrown into confusion, and the savages fell upon them with tomahawks and knives. Not more than sixty Americans escaped death or capture, and the Tories and Indians laid waste to the whole valley, and destroyed every house in Wilkes-Barre.

As news of this and other frontier massacres reached Washington, he realized that he must put an end to these attacks not only to protect American settlements, but to insure the safety of his own lines along the Hudson. In 1778 he laid plans for a campaign which would destroy the power of the Six Nations. Beyond the military reduction of the enemy, Washington proposed to devastate the Indians' land at a time when their crops had reached maturity, thus removing the primary source of food from the Iroquois and the British garrisons.

During the spring of 1779 the four forces which were to participate in the campaign began to assemble. Daniel Brodhead was to move north from Pittsburgh into Seneca country; Goose Van Schaick was to attack the Onondagas; James Clinton would strike west along the Mohawk and join the main expeditionary force, under General John Sullivan, at Tioga for the major push. On August 22, 1779, Clinton met Sullivan, and four days later this army of 4,000 men headed into Indian country.

Almost immediately they made contact with a force of Tories and Indians at Newtown, and although no more than twenty men were lost on both sides, the Indians were so discouraged that they offered no further resistance during the campaign. One after another, Indian towns and fields were put to the torch, and by the time Sullivan's main force reached Tioga again on September 30, the lands of the Iroquois were in ruins, and the Confederacy of the Six Nations was broken forever.

A cavalry skirmish after the battle at the Cowpens, South Carolina, in 1781

STRUGGLE
FOR THE SOUTH

"We fight, get beat, rise, and fight again."

GENERAL NATHANAEL GREENE—1780

Contemporary map detail by Ozanne, of the French-American siege of Savannah

The death of Polish cavalryman Casimir Pulaski in the attack on Savannah

IN LATE 1778, under the new ruling from London which marked out the South as the main theater of war, British sails began to break the horizon off the South Carolina and Georgia coasts. Down from New York came warships and transports, unloading British, Hessian, and Tory units under Lieutenant Colonel Archibald Campbell at Tybee Island at the mouth of the Savannah River, some fifteen miles below the little Georgia metropolis of the same name. Up the coast from British Florida labored another contingent commanded by General Augustine Prevost. A weak American force of less than 1,000, under General Robert Howe of North Carolina, maneuvered to get between the two bodies and their obvious objective, Savannah. Howe was brushed aside, his command badly scattered, and as 1779 came in, Sunbury and Augusta fell as well as Savannah, and all Georgia was under British control.

Through spring and summer Prevost made no important moves into the Carolinas, contenting himself with consolidating his position, gathering supplies, strengthening the ruinous fortifications of Savannah, and striving to win Georgian allegiance to the Crown. In this last he was so successful, at least on the surface, that the state legislature actually met under the authority of the British government.

Across the Savannah River in South Carolina, General Benjamin Lincoln of Massachusetts worked long and hard with patriots of that state, trying to build up a force of Continentals and militia strong enough to recapture Savannah. The task seemed hopeless, for there were no great reservoirs of manpower on which to draw as there had been in the Jerseys, Pennsylvania, or New England. And there was no chance of sealing Savannah off from seaborne supplies with the British fleet in control of coastal waters. Then someone thought of Admiral d'Estaing, lying off there in the French West Indies.

Communication was somehow established with the Admiral, who replied promptly. As soon as possible he would be off the mouth of the Savannah River with a strong fleet and transports carrying over 6,000 French regulars. In Charleston and in the camps about Purysburg on the north bank of the Savannah, men began to take heart. Now the great alliance between new America and ancient France would drive ahead under full sail.

It was no fault of either of the High Contracting Powers that this latest incursion of d'Estaing was marked for tragedy and failure from the start. The Admiral began unloading his troops on September 12, 1779. By the hundreds, his white-coated infantrymen and blue-coated gunners poured ashore and could probably have walked into Savannah, where Prevost was struggling desperately to repair the old earthworks. But the Admiral, his mind seemingly full of seventeenth-century warfare, halted his men and issued a formal summons to Prevost to surrender, issuing it not in the name of the allies nor with even a mild bow to the United States, but in the name of His Most Christian Majesty, Louis XVI.

General Benjamin Lincoln, arriving with a little American force, was most cavalierly treated by d'Estaing, as, indeed, nearly every officer, French or American, seemed to be. Not until September 23 did d'Estaing break ground for his more than adequate siege train, while every day the Savannah defenses loomed stronger and stronger. At last, on October 9, a joint attack was mounted, well planned on paper, poorly executed in the field. Prevost's men held, then counterattacked, and when the ghastly day was over Lincoln and d'Estaing counted up over 800 allied casualties out of a total strength of less than 5,000. Among the dead was the brilliant Pole, Casimir Pulaski. British losses in all categories were a little over 100.

Although Lincoln advocated resuming the assaults the Admiral would not hear of it. His ships were in unsheltered anchorages with the crews dying of scurvy; violent fall gales could be expected at any time, not to mention an enemy fleet. So d'Estaing re-embarked his troops and sailed away for Martinique while Lincoln wearily gathered up his men and took the sandy roads back to Charleston, wondering, as men had wondered after Newport, just what the alliance would really accomplish.

Up in Manhattan, Sir Henry Clinton learned of d'Estaing's departure, recalled to New York the 3,000 men who had been rotting at Newport, and then began to plan. Surely this was the proper time to put real pressure on the southern theater, to land near Charleston in formidable strength, and plow his way through the Carolinas into Virginia. The Thirteen States would seem even less formidable with their number reduced to nine and the Potomac as their southern boundary.

Heading well to the south of Charleston, the methodical Clinton landed his force on Johns Island and confined his fleet action to blockading the city from well offshore. Then he began a leisurely circling inland, and crossed the Ashley River on March 29, 1780.

View from the British lines during the siege of Charleston in 1780

General Benjamin Lincoln, instead of falling back into the interior where Clinton would have to fumble after him, shut himself behind the works of the city. In this Lincoln was not entirely to blame, since there was heavy Carolinian pressure on him to hold the capital at all costs. So the American army in the South, largely green and loosely organized, gave up its prime advantages of mobility and knowledge of the terrain in exchange for siege warfare against trained troops supported by a fleet. The outcome was reasonably predictable at the very start, as Clinton's solid 10,000 closed in about Lincoln's scant 5,000. Predictability became certainty when the one American retreat corridor to the back country was abruptly slammed. This exit had been held open hopefully by a force of some 500 mounted troops under General Isaac Huger, stationed about Monck's Corner some thirty miles from Charleston. Then Lieutenant Colonel Banastre Tarleton, who, as a very junior officer, had been instrumental in the capture of General Charles Lee in the Jerseys in '76, brought up his finely trained, well-equipped Tory Legion. On April 14, Tarleton led his command in a smashing attack on Huger that virtually wiped out the force at Monck's Corner. Tarleton, whose cavalry horses had died on the long voyage, forcing him to mount his men on horrible little beasts known locally as "tackies," seized nearly 100 fine dragoon-mounts. Now his Legion would be able to ride down any foreseeable opposition.

Clinton drew his lines tighter and tighter. His ships, avoiding Peter Parker's mistakes of 1776, skirted the harbor batteries and brought the city itself under fire. On May 12, 1780, Lincoln was forced into an unconditional surrender that turned his 5,000-odd Continentals and militia into prisoners of war. Huge quantities of supplies were lost, and nearly all the patriot leaders of South Carolina, political and military, were seized, leaving the whole Charleston Revolutionary movement headless, save for Governor John Rutledge and one or two others whom Lincoln had contrived to slip out of the city. The American cause had suffered the severest disaster of the entire conflict.

For the moment, this sudden, though not unexpected, victory turned the normally lethargic Clinton into a new, dynamic man. Now that Charleston was his, he set out to take the whole state, sending flying columns upcountry under the general direction of Lord Cornwallis, the man who had not known Breed's Hill, as Burgoyne and Clinton had. North to Camden along the

"To Charleston with fear,
The rebels repair;
D'Estaing scampers back
to his boats, sir;
Each blaming the other,
Each cursing his brother,
And—may they cut
each other's throats, sir."
—Loyalist Ballad, 1779

323

Wateree, west to oddly named Ninety-Six, northeast toward the North Carolina border went his compact, highly mobile forces, adding a new dimension to the southern conflict.

Benjamin Lincoln, by Sargent

On June 8, 1780, Clinton turned the Carolina command over to Cornwallis and sailed for New York with some 4,500 of his troops. Before leaving, he had sent a long report to Lord George Germain in London, stating: "I may venture to assert that there are few men in South Carolina who are not either our prisoners or in arms with us." There is little doubt that Clinton, writing in the cool elegance of the Brewton house in Charleston, believed these rather sweeping claims. Time was to show that his estimate was a little optimistic.

As Cornwallis, alert and active in the valley of the Wateree, began establishing a chain of forts to link British military progress with the sea, he was faced suddenly by another, more pressing problem. An American force was moving south out of North Carolina in the valiant hope of driving British, Hessians, and Tories down to the ghastly coastal swamps.

This American expedition had originally started out with the aim of relieving the pressure on Lincoln at Charleston. Qualitatively it was excellent, containing the always reliable Delaware and Maryland Continentals, backed by the infantry and cavalry commanded by the mysterious Frenchman, the Marquis de la Rouërie, who went under the simple sobriquet of Armand. Leading the whole force was huge Baron de Kalb, who had come to America with Lafayette in 1777 as an avowed soldier of fortune and had been transformed into a sincere, selfless patriot. With him were subordinates like General William Smallwood and Colonel Otho Holland Williams, Marylanders both. Quantitatively, it amounted to a few hundred men.

This command had made a killing march without transport, living off the thinly settled country. Then, when Charleston fell, it occurred to Congress that a foreigner should not be in chief command of the little column. So, ever hypnotized by Horatio Gates' rather dubious Freeman's Farm fame and by his own accounts of his mastery of the art of war, they ordered him south. Gates went down under no illusions concerning his problem, justly rating it as "an army without strength, a military chest without money, a department apparently deficient in public spirit and a climate that increases despondency . . ." Nonetheless, he took over the command from de Kalb in late July, 1780, at Hollinsworth's Farm on Deep River in North Carolina. Soon he was joined by Lieutenant Colonel Charles Porterfield with some Virginia militia, and by Major General Richard Caswell, remembered for his Moore's Creek campaign in '76, whose North Carolina levies raised the total to 3,000.

French cavalry leader Armand

En route toward Cornwallis, they met a shabby little troop of South Carolinians, "distinguished by small black leather caps and the wretchedness of their attire; their number did not exceed twenty men and boys, some white, some black, and all mounted, but most of them miserably equipped." One of their leaders was small and dark, and limped from a still-healing ankle fracture. The other was tall, lean, saturnine, and he recalled later that neither he nor his companion made a very spectacular appearance. They had made their way up the state through British and Tories, and their personal possessions consisted of "one rusty horse-fleam." Nevertheless, Gates took them on, and soon detached them to seize the Santee River crossings behind Camden, with the hope of cutting off British communications between there and Charleston. In this manner Lieutenant Colonel Francis Marion and Major Peter Horry took up once again their active partisan careers.

Cheerfully Gates pushed south, piling blunder onto blunder. Of the two possible routes to Camden, where Cornwallis lay, he chose the shorter but more barren one, against the advice of de Kalb and Williams. He also insisted that his command numbered a full 7,000. When shown returns that added up to a bare 3,000, he exclaimed dramatically, "Sir, there are enough for our purpose." He was also unmoved by de Kalb's warning that of his force only the Delawares, Marylanders, and Armand's men had been battle-tested. The rest were barely capable of marching in formation. His appreciation of his situation was at last expressed in astounding orders which were issued without consultation with any of his higher officers. With his green command, he decreed a night march and a surprise attack on the British.

Baron de Kalb

Through the night of August 15, the American army, already half-crippled by diarrhea induced by unwholesome and scanty rations, plodded wearily south, the main body over a road ankle-deep in sand, and the flankers floundering through underbrush and swamp, cut off from sight of the road by pine woods. About two in the morning, the advance of Armand's horsemen blundered into heavy British formations moving north along the same course. By uncanny coincidence, Cornwallis and Gates had mapped out identical moves. There was musketry in the unbearably humid night under the pines, Tarleton's Legion charged, and infantry on both sides became engaged. Then, as though by common dread of confused fighting in the dark, action was broken off, the two armies recoiled a little and halted.

Gates still had time to withdraw, a move which both de Kalb and Otho Williams fully expected after prisoners told them the strength of the British force. The American commander called a council of war, asked for opinions, and seemed to place most reliance on the rueful remarks of one officer that it was too late to retreat, a view that the more seasoned did not share. "We must fight, then," said Gates. "To your commands, gentlemen."

With those words he consigned his force to virtual destruction. The British attack came on at dawn, developed slowly as the leading skirmishers worked on through the thin growth of pines in the gray, misty light. Then it burst with full fury, its result as predictable as the fall of Charleston. The American left and center caved in, then broke in the utter, senseless panic of exhausted, raw men. Only on the right, where de Kalb was posted with the Marylanders and Delawares, was there real resistance.

For an hour and more, this bare 600 fought off all attacks, charged with the bayonet, re-formed, charged again, rallying about de Kalb's vast figure as about a standard. Cornwallis called off much of the pursuit of the broken militia, and threw the bulk of his force on the stubborn Continentals. Then de Kalb was down, out of action at last with his eleventh wound of the day. Tarleton's Legion charged again and the Delawares and the Marylanders were broken at last.

The death of de Kalb at Camden

With no rallying point designated in the case of defeat, men of all units streamed north through woods and swamps, harried and slashed and ridden down by Tarleton's horsemen until the latter from sheer weariness gave up, content with a record haul of prisoners and all the baggage and wagons of Gates' army.

Then, little by little, men began to find each other, grouping together for mutual protection, until a fairly steady flow of fugitives was on the road again, headed for the North Carolina border. A semblance of discipline appeared as officers like Otho Williams and William Smallwood and Armand made their influence felt. Charlotte in North Carolina was reached, and by now the column was accompanied by Whig men, women, and children. Friendly Catawba Indians joined the march, lugging with them badly wounded survivors of Tarleton's massacre of Buford's command in the Waxhaws. The first real halt was made at Salisbury, but it was a brief one. "From here," wrote William Seymour of the Delawares, "we marched on the 24th under the command of Genl. Smallwood, directing our route for Hillsborough, which we reached with much difficulty on the 6th of September, 200 miles from Campden."

There they found Major General Horatio Gates, who had left the field of Camden with the first waves of fugitives and had reached the town on August 19, three and one-half days after the battle. His army, which he had so glibly reckoned at 7,000 men in mid-August, now mustered less than 700, mostly without equipment, arms, blankets, artillery, ammunition, or food. The whole South lay at Cornwallis' feet.

A sudden tiny flicker of light appeared, a hopeful omen for the American cause, a warning to Cornwallis and his men had they been able to interpret it. On August 20, a mixed detachment of British and Tories, convoying a column of Camden prisoners to Charleston, was hit at daybreak by a strange mounted force that burst out of the swamps to strike hard. The prisoners were released, the detachment was captured, and its men were horribly chagrined to find that their assailants had numbered a bare seventeen, headed by a swarthy little man named Colonel Francis Marion.

Horatio Gates, from a pencil sketch by John Trumbull

Two months later, in October, 1780, an almost impromptu blow struck the British invasion forces. In an effort to clear his left flank, Cornwallis sent Major Patrick Ferguson (the same officer whose advance toward the Brandywine in '77 had frightened four little girls "close by Polly Buckwalter's Lane") into the western mountains with more than 1,000 Tories—both the trained, "imported" kind and the local bands. Out in the shaggy fringes of the state near the North Carolina border, Ferguson sent a warning to the "over-mountain men" in the so-called Watauga settlements of present Tennessee. They were to declare for the Crown on pain of invasion, destruction of their settlements, and the hanging of their leaders.

The reaction was instantaneous. The Watauga men, hardiest of hardy pioneers, had no intention of submitting to an invasion. In fact, if Ferguson wanted to fight, they would meet him rather more than halfway. Rallying about Colonels Isaac Shelby and "Nolichucky Jack" Sevier, they set out, each man self-sufficient with horse, Deckhard rifle, and a bag of parched corn. Colonel William Campbell of Virginia brought men to swell their ranks, Colonel Benjamin Cleveland of North Carolina came in, and other local leaders added still more men.

After some days of wilderness maneuvering, Ferguson was located at King's Mountain, a long, wooded hill which lay in both Carolinas. Some 900 of the best mounted frontiersmen were sent ahead, tethered their horses in the tree-thick lands at the base of the hill, and swarmed up to the attack. Using trees as cover, the over-mountain men worked up the steep slopes, keeping up a deadly fire until they reached the crest with slight loss. The end came quickly. Ferguson was shot down, panic struck the encircled survivors, and soon the entire Tory command was nothing but a mere battle statistic of killed, wounded, and prisoner. Annihilation was complete, except for some 200 who had been detached before the action for foraging, and who now stumbled east to safety. Inasmuch as Patrick Ferguson had been the only Englishman present, the

Patrick Ferguson, killed while trying to rally his men at King's Mountain

theory of "conquering America with Americans" was off to a very bad start.

Adding this staggering erasure of his left wing to the incessant wasp-borings of Marion, Sumter, and Pickens, Cornwallis began a quick revision of his plan for a pleasant, easy march north to the Potomac. Instead he settled down in winter quarters at Winnsboro, well to the west of Camden.

Other notions were being amended in distant quarters. Congress reluctantly decided that while it might still have full faith in Horatio Gates, the country and the army hardly shared it. A successor must be found and at once, if the southern theater were not to go by default. Suddenly unsure of its own military wisdom, Congress turned to the one man whose opinion it had consistently by-passed up to now, and almost begged George Washington to name a commander. Soon General Nathanael Greene, in charge of West Point and its area and expecting his Kitty to join him there for the winter, received a letter that bore the commander in chief's flowing signature. "It has been [Congress'] pleasure," Greene read, "to appoint an officer to command [the southern theater]. It is my wish to appoint You . . . I have only to add that I wish your earliest arrival, that there be no circumstances to retard your proceeding to the southward."

Greene seems to have been a little dubious concerning his fitness for such a command, but he need not have been. He had had extensive combat service as well as long months of duty as quartermaster, and thus knew a good deal about maintaining an army in the field as well as fighting. He was to take no troops with him, but merely to command the few hundred left over from the Camden wreckage. So, although Kitty was on the way, expecting several months with him above the Hudson, Greene followed his commander in chief's orders to the letter and set out at once, missing his wife by a matter of hours.

On December 2, 1780, Nathanael Greene took over command from Horatio Gates at Charlotte, North Carolina. Not wishing to add to Gates' discomfiture, Greene acted with the greatest tact and courtesy which, it must be said, was fully matched by the former. The amenities over, Gates rode off, and Greene's quick mind, trained by prewar study and wartime experience, leaped to a task which may be sketchily defined as the conquering of three states and the elimination of Cornwallis' army [*see* map, page 338].

Charlotte contained about thirty houses, dominated by a brick-pillared courthouse raised high above the red mud streets. Up the stairs leading to its second floor gallery clanked officer after officer to face searching volleys of questions as Nathanael Greene assayed his command. His subordinates were astounded, then delighted by the workings of his mind. Colonel William Polk of North Carolina burst out that Greene, "by the following morning understood [supply problems] better than Gates had done in the whole period of his command!"

These and other matters were enough to stagger any veteran general. There were about 800 men fit for duty out of 2,300, and only three days' rations for them. The military chest was empty, but even if it had not been, there would have been little to buy in the ravaged countryside. Clothes were in tatters, shoes deplorable. Morale was very low, the camps were filthy and badly sited; yet Greene sensed that something might be made of this command.

For one thing, his Continentals were the durable Delawares and Marylanders. Among his militia he noted many tough, self-reliant North Carolina and Georgia riflemen. For another, a point that Gates had studiously overlooked, the level of subordinate commanders was very high. There was the tested cavalry Colonel, William Washington, a distant cousin of the comman-

Nathanael Greene, after Peale

der in chief. Lieutenant Colonel Edward Carrington, the gunner, had fought on Greene's flank at Monmouth and shattered a British attack. Otho Williams had marched to Boston in '75 with Cresap's riflemen. Another Marylander, John Eager Howard, a man of extended service, caught Greene's eye, as did William Richardson Davie. When Greene appointed him commissary, Davie protested that he was a combat man, knew nothing of money and accounts. Greene soothed him: "Don't concern yourself. There is no money and hence no accounts."

John Eager Howard, by Peale

Then Greene warmly welcomed a newcomer to headquarters. Creaking and groaning with arthritis, a huge figure in fringed buckskin climbed the gallery steps, and men hailed the "Old Wagoner," Daniel Morgan. In retirement since 1779, due to continued overpassing by Congress, he had heeded this urgent call and, a Brigadier at last, had come out "to crack his whip once more." News reached Greene that he would also be joined by Lieutenant Colonel Henry Lee, to gain fame as "Light-Horse Harry" and, much later, to father another and still greater Virginian, Robert E. Lee. Lee was bringing his green-jacketed, helmeted Legion of some 300 men, a finely equipped and trained body.

Most of Greene's officers probably took it for granted that Lee's forces would be combined with those of his fellow Virginia cavalryman, William Washington. But Greene had other ideas. The day after his arrival he had heard about other men active in the Carolinas and had written a letter beginning, "I have not the honor of your acquaintance, but am no stranger to your character and merit . . ." He went on to outline his own ideas of how a guerrilla band could co-operate with a formal army, each keeping its own character. By devious ways the letter reached Snow's Island in the Great Pee Dee River in South Carolina, where it was read approvingly by Francis Marion in his secret lair that no British or Tory command was ever to find occupied. Then, in earnest of Greene's ideas and promises, Henry Lee's whole Legion was sent south to the Pee Dee to work with Marion, the "Swamp Fox," and his men. It turned out to be an ideal combination, in which guerrilla and Continental operated smoothly together, each gaining in knowledge from the other without losing any of his own peculiar virtues.

Greene considered his theater as a whole. Obviously he was too weak to attack Cornwallis. On the other hand, he very properly feared that his command would rot away if idle in winter quarters. Accordingly he coolly decided upon an outrageous military heresy—that of dividing a weaker command in the face of a stronger. Part of his force would move to what he called "a camp of repose" in the Cheraws, just across the South Carolina border on the Pee Dee. The rest, a bare 600 under Daniel Morgan, was to strike far to the west, making for the country between the Pacolet and the Broad. His hope was that Cornwallis, in turn, would split his army and send a detachment after Morgan which the latter would have a fair chance of beating. However, if the British moved in full strength for the Cheraws, the campaign and possibly the war would be over. It was a calculated risk that Greene and Morgan fully appreciated.

William Washington, by Peale

On December 21, 1780, Morgan headed west with a hard core of Delaware and Maryland Continentals, covered by William Washington's little cavalry corps. Word of his move reached Cornwallis, who had just been reinforced by the famous Brigade of Guards, bringing his total numbers to something over 4,000. Despite his far greater strength, the British commander hesitated, not from the sort of indecision that had so often struck Howe and Clinton, but because he was genuinely puzzled. As he saw it, if he struck with his whole force at the Cheraws, Morgan could strike down at Ninety-Six, then east down the Saluda and the Congaree to the Santee, wrecking the chain of British supply posts. If he went after Morgan, Greene could drive down the coast toward vital Charleston. So he did what Greene had hoped, and ordered out Tarleton and his Legion, backed by the 7th Royal Fusiliers, the 71st Highlanders, a detachment of the 17th Dragoons, and two light field-guns known as "grasshoppers."

Warned by Pickens and his roving men, the Old Wagoner estimated Tarleton's route and carefully chose the spot where the two bodies were to meet, a lightly wooded, level stretch in the very shadow of sinister King's Mountain. In peaceful times, this park-like tract had been used by drovers to rest and graze cattle being driven east to market. Its name and nature were repeated over and over in the state but this expanse alone is remembered as *the* Cowpens. On two low hills, one behind the other, Morgan posted his best troops, threw militia and riflemen south toward the Pacolet, and waited in the dawn of January 17, 1781.

From the southerly hill, Delaware men looked beyond the Pacolet and saw movement. Tarleton himself rode at the head of a small group of dragoons, their helmet-plumes tossing in the wind. Fire crackled out from the militia and riflemen, and the dragoons fell back. Then the fields beyond the Pacolet were suddenly thick with British and Tory infantry, and the dragoons formed up on either flank.

The militia fired, fired again, and fell back, a move that was interpreted both by the watching Continentals and the British as the start of panic. Actually it was a prearranged movement, planned and explained by Morgan to every militia officer and man. Almost casually they peeled off, retiring in good order behind the hill where the Continentals were posted. But the withdrawal made Tarleton so certain of rout that he swept his whole line forward, scattering the last of the militia and driving on up the hill where John Eager Howard commanded the Delawares and Marylanders. There was hard, desperate fighting on the slick, brown grass, and oily smoke welled up toward the thin sun. A misunderstood order caused a retirement of Howard's men, and Tarleton swept on for the kill, only to find himself brought up short beyond the crest by solidly re-formed lines of Continentals, plunging toward him with bayonets aslant. Out from the gap between the two hills Pickens' militiamen suddenly poured, and Kirkwood's Delaware command struck the British right and rear.

Instantly the picture changed, and British and Tories broke, throwing down their arms. Then the Americans smashed an attempted stand by the stubborn 71st, and Andrew Pickens quietly took the surrender of their Major, Archibald McArthur. In the rear, Tarleton, in a blind fury, tried to rally the dragoons for another charge, but Washington's troopers were among them, driving them farther and farther out of action in swirling, slashing defeat. At one moment Washington and Tarleton wheeled and circled about each other, cutting and parrying, then Washington's horse was wounded and at last American trumpets sounded the recall.

Among the trees by the Pacolet, Sergeant Major William Seymour of the Delawares panted as he leaned on his musket and surveyed the wreck of Tarleton's command, whose casualties and prisoners totaled about ninety per cent of the original force. Victory was due, Seymour thought, "to nothing else but Divine providence, they having 1,300 in the field of their best troops and we not 800 of standing [seasoned] troops." There was no doubt that "Divine providence" had helped, but the uncommon toughness and skill of Continentals and

Banastre Tarleton and his Legion

Otho Holland Williams, by Peale

militia, the excellent handling of men from squad-level upward, and Morgan's cool over-all direction had also been vital elements of the American victory.

Cornwallis was profoundly shocked when news of the debacle at the Cowpens finally reached him, but by no means shocked into inactivity. He started at once after Morgan, but he made the mistake of counting on his opponent to linger in the neighborhood of his victory over Tarleton. The British pursuing column moved swiftly, but it struck into thin air. Morgan had gone, slanting off toward the fords of the Catawba, 100 hard miles to the northeast.

Cheated of revenge, a Gage or a Howe would have fallen back to Winnsboro and Camden. Unlike them, Cornwallis decided on pursuit, despite the fact that he had twice lost his left wing, first at King's Mountain and now at the Cowpens. He further realized that he would have to move fast, and he had lost the cream of his light, mobile troops. Very well, he would cast precedent and regulations to the winds, strip down his army and start off. In two days he had burned or rendered useless all surplus wagons, supplies, and equipment, including his own. On January 28, 1781, he began his march. If he could not bring about open action he would strike for the fords of the Dan River, seeing clearly that those fords could be a deathtrap for all Greene's men if Cornwallis could reach them first.

Greene reacted to news of the Cowpens as quickly as Cornwallis had, and he seems to have foreseen, at least in part, the latter's plans. Striking across country almost alone to pick up Morgan's line of march, he ordered Isaac Huger to bring the rest of the Cheraw command north to the Dan at once. Carrington was to go on ahead and snap up all river boats for the crossing. Lee's highly mobile Legion, now working happily with Marion along the Congaree, was whistled up and told to join the great race for the Dan.

Through a February where rain turned into biting sleet and sleet clotted into wet, sticky snow, Greene's men and Cornwallis' labored on over roads made miserable by the weather. Greene's men were exceptionally tough and could have walked away from most British commands. But Cornwallis, like the Old Wagoner, could crack a whip, and his men answered every appeal for more speed, accepted cold camps and killing marches as grimly as did their quarry. There were obscure brushes at fords, fierce gallop-and-hack melees in sloppy fields and among the blackjack scrub.

This was a new kind of warfare for an American commander to face, with the British pursuit matching him stride for stride; but Greene was equal to it. He formed a small, highly mobile picked force of less than 700 men, composed of Washington's cavalry, Lee's troopers, and some Continental infantry and militia riflemen. He wanted Daniel Morgan to take command of this force, but ague and arthritis had finished the Old Wagoner's fighting days and the choice fell on Colonel Otho Williams of Maryland.

Williams' mission was simple to explain, hideously difficult to bring off. He trailed his men off to the west, let Cornwallis' advance see them, and then slanted away to the north. General O'Hara of the Guards was sent after Williams, and the two snapped and struck and parried through freezing nights and dripping days, O'Hara trying desperately to pin down the American screen, and Williams forever straining to keep his men between Greene on the east and Cornwallis on the west, while always refusing any major action. Rations ran out for both sides, men and horses died of exhaustion. Dried alligator, usually food for back-country hounds, became a delicacy.

On February 13, Williams had word that Greene's main force was about to cross the Dan. Still unable to shake off O'Hara's pursuit, the screening force turned, fought, disengaged, and strained on north. By midnight of the fourteenth, the last man of Lee's Legion, rear guard of the rear guard, was ferried over to the Virginia shore, just as the spearhead of the pursuit appeared to stare in bitter frustration at the bridgeless flood before them, for Greene had shifted all boats to the far side.

Cornwallis could make a formal report that as of that day, not a single American soldier was in arms against the Crown from Virginia down to Florida. Yet Greene's army, just across the Dan, was still in existence, as Washington's had always been in the north, while Marion, Pickens, and Sumter were very much alive in supposedly Crown-controlled South Carolina.

And what was Cornwallis to do now? He had lost over 200 men on the pursuit to the Dan, and had destroyed wagons and supplies in his attempt to overhaul Greene and Williams. His well-stocked base at Winnsboro was far, far to the south, so Cornwallis elected Hillsboro, North Carolina, as the best place to camp. Back his army tramped, its commander once again bemused by reports that the district swarmed with eager Tories. Installed in Hillsboro, Cornwallis issued proclamations so florid that Burgoyne might have envied them. He spoke of "His Majesty's most gracious wish to rescue his faithful and loyal subjects from the cruel tyranny under which they have groaned . . ." adding as an afterthought that if such oppressed souls came into Hillsboro with arms and perhaps ten days' rations, they would be more than welcome.

For a time Loyalists did come to him in surprising numbers; but across the Dan, Greene was stirring again. Henry Lee's horsemen swooped down to break up Tory formations heading for Hillsboro. Screens of Kirkwood's Delaware men broke up Tory meetings, snapped up supply parties, seized local leaders. Andrew Pickens' men filtered into the area. Tory Colonel Pyle's mounted command, pressing to join Cornwallis, was surprised near the Alamance by Lee and his troopers, and massacred with a ferocity that suggested Tarleton's exploits. Pickens, Lee, Kirkwood, and others clamped a sudden damper on Tory enthusiasm, and Cornwallis' flow of new allies dried to a mere trickle. He wrote sadly to Germain that his force was isolated "amongst timid friends and enjoining to inveterate rebels." Denied reinforcements, and finding that the Hillsboro area was stripped of supplies, Cornwallis had to plan some major step, particularly as his scouts brought him word that the supposedly beaten Greene was, in the face of all logic, moving his command south across the Dan again.

Once more Nathanael Greene was coolly assuming a calculated risk. Some added strength had been forwarded to him from Virginia by the indefatigable drillmaster, Baron von Steuben, and he now counted some 4,000 men under his command. But a bare 1,600 of these were Continentals, some of them utterly untested, and the Rhode Islander had only to look at a calendar to know that the time of much of his militia would soon run out. So south he went, William Washington and Henry Lee screening his advance, brushing aside Tory formations, clashing with Tarleton's always skillfully handled troopers. By March 14, 1781, Greene brought his force to a spot that he had carefully noted as a possible field of action during the retreat to the Dan.

It was just a dot on a map near the headwaters of Reedy Fork. There was a hill with a brick building known as Guilford Court House, with clearings about it and a little road which led south to Cornwallis' camps at New Garden. Greene hoped that Cornwallis would accept the challenge embodied in the American advance. If not, perhaps he could be lured out into the more open country about the courthouse of Greene's choice.

A cavalry charge on infantry

Greene was always willing to learn, and in studying his problem he thought deeply about Morgan's arrangements at the Cowpens. "You have a great number of militia," Morgan had written him. "If they fight, you beat Cornwallis, if not, he will beat you. Put the . . . militia in the center with some picked troops in their rear to shoot down the first man that runs." Accordingly, Greene made his dispositions: a heavy militia screen out in the flat woodland approaches to the courthouse hill, picked men behind them to keep them steady, and the cream of his troops on the slopes. With luck, Cornwallis' main onslaught would be well riddled by militia fire before reaching those slopes.

On the fifteenth, Greene sent Lee's cavalry south down the wood road, trying to draw out the main British force. He himself added another Morgan touch, riding among the exposed militia, telling them casually that all he asked of them was three volleys, after which they could fall back.

Lee's green-jacketed troopers broke in close to the British lines, completely upset Tarleton's dragoons in a stiff little fight, and then fell back toward Guilford Court House with the whole aroused British force after them. Men remembered the eerie hush of that bright March afternoon when the British advance sighted the militia-lined rail fence in the woods. The stillness was broken as North Carolinians coolly ripped out the three volleys that Greene had asked and then peeled off from the fence toward the second line. But the Cowpens fight was not to be repeated. Virginians in the second line became entangled in the woods and could offer little resistance as the fight swept north toward the brick courthouse. Disaster threatened, ebbed, threatened again. Washington's dragoons checked the course of the Guards, and down from the hill came John Howard with his Delawares and Marylanders.

Lee's Legion skirmishing at the Battle of Guilford Court House

There was wild fighting, with cocked hats, bearskins, bandaged heads, and silver helmets tangled in a whirl of bayonet lunges, gunfire, and swinging musket butts. The British line began to sag and fray dangerously. Cornwallis, seeing his own sudden peril, took the hard but militarily justifiable course of turning his artillery on the confused struggle, killing Briton and American with mechanical impartiality. Gradually, the two swaying masses drew apart.

A swift follow-up by Greene might have swept Cornwallis from the field; but the sun was sinking, and the last American reserves had been committed long ago. The Rhode Islander broke off the action, ordering a retreat under heavy fire, which his men carried out "with order and regularity" as a British observer noted. Cornwallis was left in possession of the field, but one-fourth of his men were casualties, including many irreplaceable officers. Worse, Greene's army, his true objective, was still in the field. The British General shook himself together and started east for Wilmington at the mouth of the Cape Fear River. Actually he was to go far beyond Wilmington, coming at last to the little village of Yorktown in Virginia.

Greene, to the surprise of many, turned away from pursuit. He had lost a paper battle at Guilford Court House, but he had won a campaign, and now his mission lay in the Carolinas. Making plans at once for an American move south, his first step was to rush a letter to Francis Marion, who at that moment was probably sitting undisturbed in the heart of some loathsome swamp, sipping vinegar. Messages also went out to Sumter and Pickens.

The theater into which Greene planned to move was at first glance bewildering, whether viewed on the spot or plotted on a map. Yet it was actually quite simple. The British hold on South Carolina was based on a chain of strong points, stamped on the face of the land like an inverted T. The T-bar reached west from Charleston on the coast to Ninety-Six in the far interior, lying roughly along the east-west rivers, the Santee, the Congaree, and the Saluda, which were virtually one stream whose name changed for no discernible reason from district to district. The T-upright followed the Wateree north from its union with the Santee to the base at Camden, beyond which the river was called the Catawba. Minor lines straggled off from the broad T-strokes, such as the route to Georgetown on Winyah Bay, well north of Charleston, and the one to Orangeburg, south of the Santee-Congaree line.

Along the bar and upright of the T moved the bulk of British traffic, bolstered by such little posts at strategic points as Forts Motte, Granby, and Watson. If this traffic flow could be broken somewhere in the center of the T-upright, the east-west T-bar might be rolled up and the British forced to fall clear back to the Charleston area. Greene lacked the strength to crush any major post by himself, but he counted on nullifying British military might by having Marion, Pickens, Sumter, and others deliver swift hit-and-run blows at various strong points, thus choking off reinforcements destined for the larger targets at which he himself wished to strike. As to his own main body, Greene laid down hard and fast rules. The army was to be carefully husbanded, never committed to such an extent that it could not be drawn off relatively intact. A drawn battle was far preferable to a victory whose losses might immobilize him.

Heroic engraving of Francis Marion

So the pattern was set. Irregulars were to tie up road and river traffic while the main body moved against troops temporarily isolated by such activity. The plans were kept secret from all save the highest brass. Trusted officers were sent to Marion, Pickens, and Sumter with messages. On April 9, 1781, Nathanael Greene, having sent Lee and his entire Legion plus a company of Marylanders to work with Marion, left North Carolina, and the real struggle for the South was under way.

The pattern of the campaign began at once, with the successes of one element canceling the failures of another. On the T-upright, Greene moved against Camden, now commanded by able, ugly Lord Rawdon. Rawdon swept out to meet him, found him posted on a low rise known as Hobkirk's Hill, and attacked. Greene had disposed his men in the familiar Cowpens-Guilford pattern, and for a while it seemed as though April 25, 1781, would go down as another American victory or, at least, a standoff. But there was mishandling of smaller units. Washington's cavalry had ridden clear around Rawdon's force, only to become immobilized by distance and by the weight of prisoners taken, and were out of action when most needed. The day ended with a sullen American retreat north toward Rugeley's Mills, near the site of Gates' defeat the year before, and Greene wrote to the Chevalier de La Luzerne in Philadelphia, "We fight, get beat, rise and fight again."

The main army had failed at Hobkirk's Hill, but the irregulars were faring better. Sumter skillfully harried Camden's supply lines, while Marion and Lee quietly captured Fort Watson. Reflecting dourly on all this and on the heavy losses that Hobkirk's Hill had cost him, Lord Rawdon abandoned Camden on May 10, burned a great quantity of military stores, and marched south to the T-bar. Even while his columns fell back down the Wateree, Lee and Marion popped out of their swamp-refuges to fall swiftly on Fort Motte, which covered the juncture of the Congaree, the Santee, and the Wateree, and captured it.

Lord Rawdon and a scene of the Hobkirk's Hill action, 1781

Greene had circled Rawdon's march with a small escort, and at Fort Motte he joined Lee and Marion. They must have struck him as an oddly assorted pair. Francis Marion—silent, swarthy, and wizened—wore a leather skullcap badly charred on one side, and a saber rusted into its scabbard. Henry Lee was handsome, florid, a little flamboyant, managing somehow to be a dandy in the deepest swamps with his plumed helmet, green jacket, white leather breeches, and knee boots. Yet Greene could sense the deep trust and liking between these disparate souls who complemented each other so well.

Now Greene had to break up this team for a while. Rawdon was coming fast down the Wateree, so Marion and his restless, leathery crew must go east and east again through the pine country, out into the cypress lands and into the palmettos by Winyah Bay, and make all the trouble they could in the Georgetown area. Lee's Legion and the Marylanders under Oldham were sent off to Fort Granby, a strong point west and north of Motte. Greene himself would take the main army west, off to the fort at Ninety-Six where his men would try siege operations against the New York Tory, Lieutenant Colonel John Cruger.

"Light-Horse Harry" Lee, by Peale

The campaign so far showed clearly the strength of the guerrilla-Continental pattern that Greene had evolved. Without Sumter and Marion, he would have been overwhelmed either at Hobkirk's Hill or afterwards. Without Greene, the guerrillas would have been hunted down and eliminated. While Greene immobilized the main British fighting strength, the others choked off the supply routes that carried lifeblood to British power.

Greene opened his formal siege of Ninety-Six on May 22, under the skilled guidance of the Pole Kosciuszko. Progress was slow, for Cruger's defense was superb, and the siege dragged on till mid-June. One night Greene's lookouts spotted beacon fires on the hilltops to the east, a warning that Rawdon was driving west hard and fast with a relief column. Greene patiently marked down another defeat in his record, broke camp, and melted away just before Rawdon marched onto the plains about Ninety-Six. Another defeat—but another objective gained, for Rawdon demolished the works and headed east, abandoning the post and bringing Cruger's heroic garrison with him.

When Greene had started out from North Carolina in April, British posts had stretched unbroken from Ninety-Six east to the sea, north from the Santee to Camden, and south to Augusta in Georgia. Now, in late June, the chain had melted and the British had certain control only in the Charleston area. The entire T was gone, save for a fragment of its east bar.

Summer began to burn down on Carolina swamp and plain, and in the ghastly heat and unbearable terrain, Greene and Rawdon's main forces sparred and maneuvered. A British officer later remembered "forced marches under the rage of a burning sun . . . sinking under the most excessive fatigue, not only destitute of every comfort, but almost of every necessary . . ." Most of these British had been brought up to formal warfare, but they staggered on, grimly meeting conditions that might have balked the toughest guerrilla.

At last the climate told on both armies and, weird as it sounds, they went into summer quarters. Rawdon withdrew his troops to Orangeburg, now abandoned by Sumter in accordance with guerrilla practice. Greene led his men out of the lowland swamps and bogs onto the fresh, emerald lift of the High Hills of Santee. This little range, never higher than 200 feet, began at the junction of the Congaree and Wateree and ran some twenty miles north.

Here the American command lay, recuperating among fresh, cool springs, under clean oak and chestnut growths, free of the drone of mosquitoes. Soon Greene had an army again, not a wavering column of staggering, fever-ridden invalids. But hill life was apparently too soft for the tough, restless men who followed Lee, Marion, Pickens, and Sumter. The last-named suddenly found himself willing to work in harness, and joining up with Marion and Lee, struck

A diagram of the siege of Ninety-Six

334

hard at British supply depots at Monck's Corner. The combined commands brought off 150 prisoners, 200 horses, and a long string of wagons. Then the trio scattered to watch a hundred river crossings for signs of British activity.

At Orangeburg, Lord Rawdon, shattered in health and disgusted with the progress of the campaign, tossed up his command and sailed for England, leaving the whole theater to Lieutenant Colonel Alexander Stuart of the 3rd East Kents, the famed Buffs. Summer rains drenched the whole state, rivers overflowed their banks, flooding the lowlands, and until the inundation ebbed, there could be no action in South Carolina.

Then the rains ceased, the floods began to recede, and in the third week of August, 1781, scouts brought word to the High Hills of Santee that Colonel Stuart was astir, moving along the south bank of the Santee some sixteen miles from the American base. Further intelligence told Greene that his opponent did not seem unduly concerned about American moves, probably because the floods still posed a military obstacle. The Rhode Islander sensed his opportunity, and began an agonizingly circuitous march around drowned lowlands, heading for Stuart. Making the excellent march-time of 38 miles in two days through swamp and flood and forest, he circled north, then dropped south again to the far banks of the Santee. There Kirkwood of the Delawares brought him word about a place called "Eutaw Springs where Lay Col. Stewart [sic] with the British Army Consisting of 2,000 men."

This was a stronger force than Greene had figured on; but at Laurens' plantation, not far from the Springs, Francis Marion and long strings of horsemen rode out of the forests to report to him. The command had just finished a 400-mile march through enemy territory, had rescued guerrilla leader William Harden from a British trap down on the Pon Pon without losing a man, and was now quite ready for such orders as General Greene might see fit to issue.

Most of Greene's trusted unit commanders, including the newly arrived Marquis de Malmédy, a veteran of long American service, were with him, but he still worried about his diminished numbers, caused by expired enlistments. With an abrupt switch from his usual policy he spoke to Marion about incorporating the rangy guerrillas into formal line of battle for the engagement that was coming. Marion accepted this sharp about-face and agreed that his men should take their places in the army along with Andrew Pickens' militia and some hasty levies that John Henderson and Jethro Sumner had brought up. For the moment, the swamp men were transformed into ordinary line troops.

Eutaw Springs derived its name from twin sources that well out of an underground river and flow north to the Santee via Eutaw Creek. In 1781 a fine two-story brick house stood close by the steep-sided creek, edged by a garden-sweep that ran on into a wide fenced clearing. This open space was split by an east-west road that forked off towards Monck's Corner and Charleston.

Alexander Stuart of the Buffs was an alert, energetic soldier in full control of the 2,000 camped in the fenced clearing. However, he had trouble in obtaining detailed information of Greene's approach. "Notwithstanding every exertion being made to gain intelligence of the enemy's situation, they rendered it impossible, by waylaying the bye-paths and passes through the different swamps," he reported later. As it was, he still felt so secure on September 8, 1781, that at dawn he sent out 100 unarmed men with a very small guard to fossick about a plantation for vegetables and potatoes.

While this group was grubbing away, two American deserters came into the palisade, reporting that Greene's whole force was on the move toward the brick house and the twin springs. Stuart did not quite believe this, but to be safe he

The Battle of Eutaw Springs, 1781

sent out the Boston Tory Major John Coffin with cavalry and infantry to investigate. Coffin's command very soon came on Major John Armstrong's mounted North Carolinians, and went into action at once, not knowing that Lee's green-coated troopers were riding close behind Armstrong. Lee sent his Legion into action and Coffin was driven back toward the springs in complete rout. Behind Lee, Greene's whole command was hurrying east. De Malmédy brought on the center with Marion and Pickens; Lee, Henderson, and Wade Hampton covered the flanks; while in the rear, Otho Williams, Jethro Sumner, William Washington, and Robert Kirkwood followed close.

Stuart reacted instantly at the first signs of Coffin's repulse and formed his men, but Greene's onset first dented, then crumpled Stuart's line.

His left collapsed, and soon Stuart's troops were pouring east down the Charleston road in unfeigned retreat. Only on the right, in the difficult, black-jack-covered terrain by the Eutaw house and the steep creek, was there solid resistance. There a tough, competent Major named Marjoribanks held firm with grenadiers and light infantry, beating off the best that Greene could send against him. William Washington whirled up with his plumed dragoons in an oblique charge only to have his men shot down among the blackjacks. Greene ordered infantry from his own right and center to join the attack, but unfortunately, the weary, hungry men had broken into the well-stocked British camp. Plunder and rum disorganized them, and the chance was gone.

Stuart, with admirable coolness, sensed a change in the situation and acted at once. Fugitives on the road were rounded up and brought back into formation, were rushed into the wild melee at the clearing. Somehow a sketchy line of battle, anchored on the immovable Marjoribanks, was established.

Greene, too, could readjust. Studying what lay before him under a stifling pall of dust and smoke, he realized that by massing for one more smash ahead he might well win a fine textbook victory. But that victory, like others he had consciously avoided in the past, might leave him with a skeleton army. And for all he knew, there was a fall campaign for which to prepare, and more operations that could last through 1782 and even 1783. As it was, he still had his army intact and had inflicted far more damage than he had suffered. So let Stuart keep the field of Eutaw Springs, as Cornwallis had kept that of Guilford Court House. Victory was something Nathanael Greene could not afford.

Like Cornwallis after Guilford, like Lord Rawdon after Hobkirk's Hill and Ninety-Six, Stuart lingered about the springs, buried his dead (including that magnificent fighter, Marjoribanks) and then took the long hot road back to Monck's Corner and Charleston, too badly mauled to stay where he was.

There was no way for either commander to know it, but Eutaw Springs was the Monmouth of the South. Never again would the two main armies of that theater meet in action. There was no thought of re-establishing the chain of posts from the coast to Ninety-Six. The whole T was gone for good. The British colors flew only at Charleston and Savannah, thanks to the Royal Navy.

The Rhode Islander had, between January and September, 1781, won a tremendous campaign, while never winning a battle. Always short of men, money, and supplies, he had calmly done what he could with what he had, utilizing resources to which many other generals would have been blind. The local forces of Marion and others had been developed to the utmost, in the knowledge that he could not have existed without them or they without him.

When Nathanael Greene's force finally closed in an arc about Charleston, it was an arc which was to be held until the last transport docked to take on board the last British soldier.

"General Washington wishes not only from his personal regard to General Greene, but from principles of generosity and justice to see him crowned with those laurels which from his unparalleled exertions he so richly deserves."
—Washington to Greene, 1781

Clinton Turns South

With the war in the North seemingly stalemated after Monmouth, Sir Henry Clinton received orders to begin in the South "operations which shall appear the most likely means of crushing the rebellion." In the thinly populated, swampy coastal lowlands of Georgia and the Carolinas—"a country as hot as the antechamber of Hell"—the British foresaw easy victory with the help of Tories supposedly eager to "flock to the King's standard." By all logic, the campaign should have succeeded, and indeed it was very nearly won, when Nathanael Greene assumed command of the southern department. Probably the ablest of Washington's lieutenants, Greene would conduct one of the war's most brilliant campaigns.

In December, 1778—long before Greene arrived—Clinton seized Savannah, gaining a foothold in Georgia. The next objective was Charleston, and, profiting from their errors in 1776, the British achieved their objective faultlessly. In May, 1780, they accepted the city's surrender, along with 5,500 troops and innumerable stores. The fall of Charleston opened the way for the British conquest of South Carolina.

Major General Nathanael Greene, by C. W. Peale

In 1779 a French-American force tried unsuccessfully to recapture Savannah. The allied investment of the town is shown above.

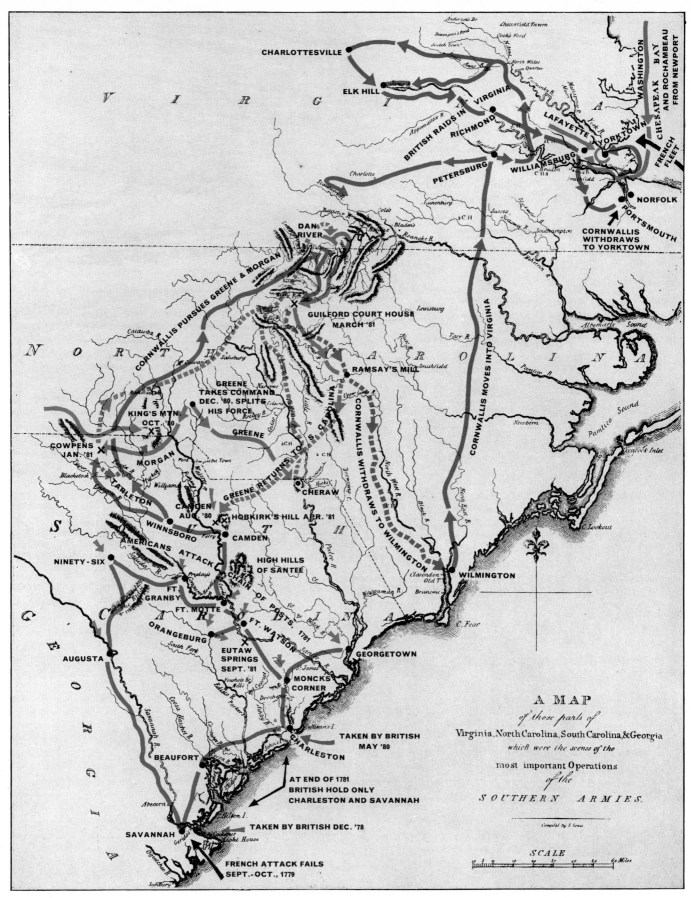

CHARLOTTESVILLE

ELK HILL

V I R G I N I A

BRITISH RAIDS IN VIRGINIA

RICHMOND

PETERSBURG

WILLIAMSBURG

LAFAYETTE

YORKTOWN

WASHINGTON

CHESAPEAK BAY AND ROCHAMBEAU FROM NEWPORT

FRENCH FLEET

NORFOLK

PORTSMOUTH

CORNWALLIS WITHDRAWS TO YORKTOWN

DAN RIVER

GUILFORD COURT HOUSE MARCH '81

N O R T H   C A R O L I N A

CORNWALLIS PURSUES GREENE & MORGAN

RAMSAY'S MILL

CORNWALLIS MOVES INTO VIRGINIA

Albemarle Sound

GREENE TAKES COMMAND DEC. '80, SPLITS HIS FORCE

KING'S MTN OCT. '80

GREENE

GREENE RETURNS TO S. CAROLINA

CORNWALLIS WITHDRAWS TO WILMINGTON

Pamlico Sound

COWPENS JAN. '81

MORGAN

TARLETON

CAMDEN AUG. '80

HOBKIRK'S HILL APR. '81

CHERAW

WINNSBORO

CAMDEN

S O U T H

AMERICANS ATTACK

CHAIN OF POSTS

HIGH HILLS OF SANTEE

C A R O L I N A

WILMINGTON

NINETY-SIX

FT. GRANBY

FT. MOTTE

FT. WATSON 1781

ORANGEBURG

EUTAW SPRINGS SEPT. '81

GEORGETOWN

AUGUSTA

MONCKS CORNER

G E O R G I A

BEAUFORT

CHARLESTON

TAKEN BY BRITISH MAY '80

AT END OF 1781 BRITISH HOLD ONLY CHARLESTON AND SAVANNAH

SAVANNAH

TAKEN BY BRITISH DEC. '78

FRENCH ATTACK FAILS SEPT.-OCT., 1779

A MAP
of those parts of
Virginia, North Carolina, South Carolina, & Georgia
which were the scenes of the
most important Operations
of the
SOUTHERN ARMIES.

Compiled by S. Lewis

SCALE

The locations of the major battles and movements of the armies during the war in the South are superimposed on this 1807 map. The routes of the British forces are shown in red, those of the Americans in blue.

Back-Country Victory

The "over-mountain men" from the Watauga settlements rendezvoused at Sycamore Flats (above) before marching on the Tory force at King's Mountain. The Tories fired too high at the attackers charging up the hillside (below) and were overwhelmed.

Charles Cornwallis, given command in the South, acted immediately to establish a chain of posts in South Carolina in the spring of 1780. Then, on August 16, he tightened his grip on the state at Camden by routing Horatio Gates and a makeshift army of Rebel militia, who "ran like a Torrent and bore all before them." Alexander Hamilton commented acidly that Gates' precipitous flight did "admirable credit to the activity of a man at his time of life."

Planning to expand his operations northward, Cornwallis sent his left wing, a Tory force under Patrick Ferguson, to sweep the interior of the Carolinas. On October 7 it was attacked at King's Mountain by what Ferguson called "back water men . . . a set of mongrels" under Isaac Shelby and John Sevier. The rugged pioneers killed Ferguson and knocked out eighty per cent of his command, a crushing defeat which disabused Cornwallis of any ideas of taking North Carolina in 1780.

The Southern Irregulars

If the British thought they had a stranglehold on South Carolina, they soon discovered that they were "in a d--d rebellious country," as one officer remarked. The patriots lacked organized armies, but guerrilla activities hurt the enemy badly. Rebel raiders drifted out of dismal swamps to strike isolated outposts, gobble up supply trains, and wreck Tory formations, and this constant hit-and-run warfare sapped the British strength by pinning down hundreds of regular troops.

Andrew Pickens, Thomas Sumter, and Francis Marion were the most prominent southern partisan leaders. Of the three, the famous "Swamp Fox" Marion understood best the role of a guerrilla force, and used his meager resources most effectively. On occasion these irregulars served with the main American army as raiders and scouts, but their outstanding contribution to ultimate American victory was in snapping up, one by one, the British posts which Cornwallis had so carefully established in South Carolina.

Legend has it that Marion once offered to share his "usual fare

Francis Marion's partisans cross the Pee Dee River to raid the enemy in South Carolina.
British Colonel Tarleton said that "the devil himself could not catch" the elusive Marion.

Andrew Pickens

Thomas Sumter

potatoes and water with an amazed British officer who was in his camp under a flag of truce.

The charming primitive painting at right depicts the exploit of one Peter Francisco (brandishing sword), a sort of southern Paul Bunyan, who is said to have taken on, singlehanded, nine British troopers of Tarleton's Legion and routed them. This gallant action supposedly occurred "in sight of a troop of four hundred" of the enemy, some of whom may be seen riding by in the background.

Greene's Hit-and-Run Tactics Succeed

This is Reynolds' portrait of Colonel Banastre Tarleton, a skilled, merciless cavalryman whom the Rebels called "Butcher." His slaughter of Colonel Abraham Buford's men after they had surrendered, in May, 1780, gave rise to the term "Tarleton's quarter."

In December, 1780, Nathanael Greene replaced Gates as commander of the southern army. Arriving at Charlotte, North Carolina, he found "but the shadow of an army in the midst of distress." Daringly, he assumed the offensive and split his army by sending Daniel Morgan to threaten Cornwallis' westernmost outposts. Banastre Tarleton was sent to head off this movement, but at the Cowpens on January 17 Morgan deployed his militia skillfully and wiped out Tarleton's 1,100-man force. A Carolinian recalled that "we made the proud Gineral Tarleton run doon the road helter-skelter." For the second time Cornwallis had lost the left wing of his army.

The angry British General pounded after the outnumbered Rebels, and Greene sought to get his army safely across the Dan River into Virginia. Burning his wagons and stripping his men to fighting trim, Cornwallis "made great expedition to get between Greene and the fords of the Dan." By a narrow margin he lost the race, and soon the audacious Greene returned to North Carolina, where the two armies met at Guilford Court House on March 15. The British won the field, but they were so badly mauled that Cornwallis had to retreat to his supply base at Wilmington. As Horace Walpole observed, "Lord Cornwallis has conquered his troops out of shoes and provisions and himself out of troops."

"Determined to carry the war immediately into South Carolina," Greene lost a battle to Lord Rawdon at Hobkirk's Hill on April 25, but kept up the pressure. Rawdon, seeing that the "whole interior country had revolted," began to withdraw, and all of the British posts were captured or evacuated in rapid succession. On September 8 the last bitter battle of the campaign was fought at Eutaw Springs. Greene said it was by far the most obstinate fight he ever witnessed, and although neither side gained a real victory, the British were so crippled that they had to withdraw. Greene had lost the battles but won the South, and on hearing that Washington had Cornwallis trapped in Yorktown, he wrote, "We have been beating the bush and the General has come to catch the bird."

Daniel Morgan (above) capped a fine war record with his victory at the Cowpens. The broadside at right informed Philadelphians of the retreat of the battered British army after the Guilford action.

Cornwallis Retreating!

PHILADELPHIA, April 7, 1781.

Extract of a Letter from Major-General *Greene*, dated CAMP, at *Buffelo Creek, March* 23, 1781.

"ON the 16th Inftant I wrote your Excellency, giving an Account of an Action which happened at Guilford Court-Houfe the Day before. I was then perfuaded that notwithftanding we were obliged to give up the Ground, we had reaped the Advantage of the Action. Circumftances fince confirm me in Opinion that the Enemy were too much gauled to improve their Succefs. We lay at the Iron-Works three Days, preparing ourfelves for another Action, and expecting the Enemy to advance: But of a fudden they took their Departure, leaving behind them evident Marks of Diftrefs. All our wounded at Guilford, which had fallen into their Hands, and 70 of their own, too bad to move, were left at New-Garden. Moft of their Officers fuffered-- Lord Cornwallis had his Horfe fhot under him--- Col. Steward, of the Guards was killed, General O Hara and Cols. Tarlton and Webfter, wounded. Only three Field-Officers efcaped, if Reports, which feem to be authentic, can be relied on.

Our Army are in good Spirits, notwithftanding our Sufferings, and are advancing towards the Enemy; they are retreating to Crofs-Creek.

In South-Carolina, Generals Sumpter and Marian have gained feveral little Advantages. In one the Enemy loft 60 Men, who had under their Care a large Quantity of Stores, which were taken, but by an unfortunate Miftake were afterwards re taken.

Publifhed by Order,

CHARLES THOMSON, Secretary.

§†§ Printed at N. WILLIS's Office.

William Washington's troopers (in blue) smash Tarleton's Legion at the Battle of Cowpens. Lines of infantry clash at the far right.

Washington, Lafayette, and aide Tench Tilghman at Yorktown, by Charles Willson Peale

THE WORLD TURNED UPSIDE DOWN

"The play, sir, is over."

Marquis de Lafayette—October, 1781

A 1780 drawing by Pierre Ozanne of Rochambeau's army embarking at Brest

OUT OF an afternoon fog that had rolled in from Beaver Tail in early July of 1780, emerged a string of cutters oaring General Comte Donatien de Rochambeau and his staff to the wharves of Newport, Rhode Island. The Count must have felt it a pity that the misty curtain hid the masts of the seven powerful ships of the line, four frigates, and thirty-odd transports which had dropped anchor out in the roads, some seventy days from Brest. The display would have made a spectacular backdrop for the warm welcome that their new American allies must surely be preparing. At least, Rochambeau and his party had a heartening report to deliver to their allies—one that would make up for the visual evidence which the fog had masked.

Nearly 5,000 first-rate French regulars were in the transports off there, assigned to the American theater "for the duration" and not to be whipped off to the West Indies at the whim of some minister in Paris. More than that, the veteran Count, whose military service dated back to his boyhood, was to place himself and his men under the orders of the American commander in chief, to serve in a subordinate capacity to George Washington, who had never known a day of European campaigning. All in all, Rochambeau had brought an unrestricted gift of immense proportions.

On shore it was apparent that something had gone very wrong. There was not the vaguest sign of any welcoming party, no senior American officer to whom the French General could report. He and his fellows wandered in a daze through the streets of handsome Newport, muttering *"Incroyable!"* or *"Tout à fait inouï!"* Rochambeau wrote that "There was no one about in the streets; only a few sad and frightened faces in the windows." Colonel Comte Guillaume de Deux-Ponts was struck by "A coldness and reserve [which] appear to me to be characteristic of the American nation; they seem to have little of that enthusiasm which one would suppose belongs to a people fighting for its liberties, and indeed they seem little suited to inspire enthusiasm in others." At last Rochambeau managed to rout out some local dignitaries and identify himself and his mission.

The French could hardly have arrived under conditions less likely to promote the alliance for which Franklin and others had fought so hard, and another international snarl, to match the bickerings that had attended d'Estaing and his convoy, seemed inevitable. Luckily, matters were righted in a remarkably short time. General William Heath of Roxbury, Massachusetts, who had been in the field since April 19, 1775, had been delayed on the way to Newport and now appeared to act as Washington's representative. Heath was everywhere, securing proper camp sites for the troops, locating water supplies, arranging for the purchase of provisions, and smoothing over the few rough spots that cropped up between the townsfolk and the newcomers.

He also saw to it that important civilians from adjoining states met the French high command. Over from Yale College in New Haven came President Ezra Stiles to dine with Rochambeau, bridging the language barrier with Latin, which he found "The Count spoke tolerably." William Channing came to town, a little standoffishly, and departed marveling. "The French Troops are a fine body of men . . . Neither Officers nor Men are the effeminate Beings we were heretofore taught to believe them. They are as large and as likely men as can be produced by any nation," he wrote later.

Newport in general was as impressed as Channing when the picked regiments of France disembarked, beautifully and efficiently equipped, mostly in white uniforms. The white broadcloth of the 41st Soissonnais bore vivid crimson facings, the 85th Saintonge, green, and the 13th Bourbonnais, black. The

A contemporary drawing of the French troops serving in America

Royal Deux-Ponts marched past the Redwood Library in blue coats set off by bright yellow facings and cuffs. But the American crowds gathered most eagerly about the cavalry, commanded by Armand Louis de Gontaut, Duc de Lauzun, an eye-filling unit from the tiniest kettledrummer to its rakehell Colonel. These horsemen clattered through town in black felt hussar busbies, white-plumed and gold-laced. Their sky-blue jackets were trimmed with yellow, white piping edged their yellow breeches, and blue pelisses trimmed with black fur were slung rakishly over their shoulders. The officers glittered in scarlet breeches, marten-fur busbies, crimson baldrics, and tiger-skin saddlecloths. Many of the 300 legionnaires were Poles who had been driven from their country by the latest partition and had taken root in France. These were equipped with long lances, a weapon new to America, while the rest, largely displaced Irishmen, had great curved sabers.

Such martial panache was a revelation to the people of Newport and Providence, but admiration might have turned into derision had these men appeared only as parade-ground soldiers. The most casual-minded observers noted an air of steady efficiency as the Frenchmen went about their work, while firm egalitarians conceded that, outside of Lauzun's Legion, there was little distinction in dress between officers and enlisted men.

The very day of his arrival, Rochambeau wrote to Washington, clearly defining his own status and that of his troops: "Sir: The commands of the King, my master, place me under the orders of Your Excellency. I come, wholly obedient and with the zeal and the veneration which I have for you and for the remarkable talents you have displayed in sustaining a war which will always be memorable." Rochambeau went on to explain in some detail that original plans called for two divisions of French troops, but that a shortage of transports had threatened to choke off the whole expedition. "So the King decided to send me off with the First Division, in which I have brought every man and all the provisions it was possible to embark at Brest." (It may be added that the 2nd Division, blocked by a British fleet, was still waiting to sail when the war ended.)

Washington replied, as of July 16, 1780, "I hasten to communicate to you with what happiness I have received the auspicious news of your safe arrival and in my name and in the name of the American Army I present to you the assurance of my deep appreciation and my lively gratitude to the Allies who have come so generously to our aid."

The appearance of the French at Newport was a highly dramatic event that unfortunately faded in anticlimax. It was as though a star performer had appeared with a great flourish on a stage only to find no scenery, no props, and the rest of the cast following different cues and a different script. Weeks slipped by, and the French high command became increasingly impatient that no role had been assigned its white-coated regiments. In mid-September Washington rode to Hartford to confer with Rochambeau, and the latter was disappointed that the commander in chief spoke only in generalities and extended no invitation to French officers to ride over to the Hudson and have a look at the American army.

Neither Washington nor Rochambeau was to blame for this impasse. The truth probably was that the American army was in very bad shape in terms of numbers and equipment, and Washington may have feared lest the professional French be so shocked by the draggled mass of Continentals and militia that they might well call for a fleet to take them back to France and out of this hopeless dilemma.

The landing of Rochambeau's force at Newport

"We seem to be verging so fast on destruction that I am filled with sensations to which I have been a stranger till within these three months."
—*George Washington, 1781*

347

The French settled down in Rhode Island, many of them chafing bitterly. Young Count Axel Fersen, Swedish aide to Rochambeau (and later to be caught up in the tragedy of Louis XVI and Marie Antoinette), wrote his father in Sweden: "Our position here is a very disagreeable one. We are vegetating at the very door of the enemy in a most disastrous state of idleness and uncertainty. . . . We are of no possible aid to our allies." Rochambeau himself, impatient like his fellows, seems to have understood now, as later, something of Washington's problems and to have deferred loyally to them. The Marquis de Ségur, a shrewd observer, wrote later that Rochambeau seemed "to have been purposely created to understand Washington and to be understood by him and to serve with Republicans . . . his example more even than his authority obliged us scrupulously to respect the rights, properties and customs of our allies."

This "example" must have been far-reaching, since there could have been bitter, violent trouble between the idle alien army and the Rhode Islanders. Somehow, mutual understanding, tolerance, and a willingness to cut corners on both sides combined to set up a remarkable record in the long months of waiting for action. There seem to have been few, if any, fights between troops and civilians. No spurious claims for damage were lodged against the French and, in return, Rochambeau's records hold no charges of Yankee profiteering.

Lauzun with his hussars and lancers was sent west into Connecticut and settled in the forest-clearing town of Lebanon. Here, even more than in sophisticated Newport, trouble could have developed out of contact between the inlanders and their exotic guests. But again the miracle of Newport was repeated. The Legion settled itself with an almost Yankee adaptability in the forest town. Lauzun became fascinated with the local sport of squirrel hunting and took visiting officers such as the Chevalier de Chastellux on woodland safaris. Old Governor Jonathan Trumbull often dined the French officers, and the same de Chastellux has left a vivid sketch of "this small, old man in the antique dress of the first settlers in the colony approaching a table surrounded by twenty hussar officers and without either disconcerting himself or losing anything of his formal stiffness," saying a long blessing before taking his chair.

The Legion is remembered in Lebanon to this day, and headquarters is still known as the "war office." Alden's Tavern was a favorite locale for the troopers who used to ride their mounts into the bar, and a good many foreign coins have been dug up on the old tavern site. The Legion field music played for the Lebanese, and apparently hussars and lancers staged musical rides for their hosts.

All this, whether in Newport or Providence or Lebanon, was small but important fare. Later French-American ventures might have bogged down or dragged futilely along had Rochambeau's men taken the long road to Yorktown with memories of bitter, quarrelsome days spent along Narragansett Bay or in the Lebanon clearings.

Comte de Rochambeau

Geographically, Virginia had been out of the war since a few nuisance-raids in the Tidewater country early in 1776. In all other ways, it had been as deeply immersed in it as any other state. The record of the Virginia Line in all theaters had been outstanding. Even more important, perhaps, the Old Dominion had been a vital economic cog in the combined machinery of the Thirteen States. Its exports of tobacco had been a powerful prop of Congressional credit at home and abroad. The army was dependent on it for large shipments of salt, so necessary in the preservation of rations.

None of these factors had been lost on the British high command. Lord Cornwallis, in particular, had bombarded Clinton with appeals to shift the main British base to the Chesapeake Bay area even at the cost of giving up Manhattan and its environs. Such a step, he and others felt, would bring a quick end to the war. Clinton was either unwilling or unable, due to shackling orders from London, 3,000 miles away, even to contemplate such a move, but his mind did turn toward possible neutralization of Virginia by other means.

In the spring of 1779 a strong amphibious force from New York appeared off the mouth of the James River, spilled its troops ashore at defenseless Portsmouth, flooded out through towns like Suffolk and Gosport, and finally re-embarked without the loss of a man. The naval commander, Vice Admiral Sir George Collier, and his military colleague Major General Edward Mathew, had an imposing score card to tally up on the voyage home. Ropewalks, shipyards, and naval stores had been destroyed, ships burned or captured to the number of 130, and 3,000 hogsheads of tobacco put to the torch. All in all, not counting loot from Tidewater plantations, they could count up some £2,000,000 damage inflicted on a state that was vital to the survival of the new nation.

Encouraged by such a successful hit-and-run coup, Clinton's rather slow thoughts turned to the possibility of basing a permanent raiding force on the James, and for its commander selected a man who would not be hampered by any nicety of feeling in dealing with arrant Rebels and their property. This, not too surprisingly, was Benedict Arnold, now a full-fledged British Brigadier General. To support him, and also perhaps to keep a sharp eye on him and his doings, Clinton nominated Colonel John Graves Simcoe, a fine soldier who had had much success in training Tory formations and who was later to play a big role in the founding of Upper Canada. With Simcoe was Colonel Thomas Dundas in a similar mentor-role, for Arnold's orders referred to the pair as officers "by whose advice he was to be guided in every important measure," a rather humiliating rider for a man who rated his own talents as highly as did Benedict Arnold.

In January, 1781, Arnold landed some 1,200 men near Westover, that lovely mansion whose brick walls still look out across smooth lawns toward the James. By the fifth he was at Richmond and pushing on to Westham, spreading havoc and destruction wherever he went, including an important munitions works at the latter place. Then he fell back along the south bank to Portsmouth and went into winter quarters.

Virginia could offer as little opposition to Arnold as it had been able to present to Collier and Mathew. Governor Thomas Jefferson has been bitterly criticized for tardiness in rallying his state, but a glance southward to the Carolinas where Greene was moving down the British T will show that much of the state's thinly populated energies had already been oriented in that direction. Help for Virginia must come from the outside.

Up in his winter quarters in the de Windt house at Tappan on the Hudson, Washington's eye took in Arnold's isolated position along the James. He thought he saw a chance to rid Virginia of the raiders and at the same time snap up the traitor Arnold, deeming the latter opportunity "an event particularly agreeable to this country." In February of 1781 he ordered Lafayette south with a picked force of some 1,200 New England and New Jersey troops who still bore the marks of von Steuben's training. As unit commanders, he named Colonel Joseph Vose of Massachusetts, Lieutenant Colonel de Gimat, a very able Frenchman who had arrived in America with Lafayette, and Lieutenant Colonel Francis Barber of New Jersey. This was a small command to

John Graves Simcoe

A broadside overstating the results of Destouches' expedition to Virginia undertake the defense of Virginia, but it was to be backed by the entire French Newport fleet, under Admiral Destouches, which would also be convoying 1,200 French troops.

At last France and America were moving together in an operation that had no limits in time or space, and, viewed from Tappan, Arnold's position was critical. However, bad weather and a strong British fleet under Admiral Marriott Arbuthnot intervened, and Destouches was forced to put back to Newport, having reached the very mouth of Chesapeake Bay. Lafayette kept doggedly on the march with his 1,200, seemingly undisturbed by the news that the redoubtable Major General William Phillips, Burgoyne's second-in-command in '77, had landed in Virginia with an added 2,600 men, superseding Arnold.

With each step of Lafayette's progress, enemy numbers seemed to pile up. In May, Cornwallis, having rested and refitted his men at Wilmington after the race for the Dan and Guilford Court House, appeared in Virginia with 1,500 men, while down from New York sailed still another 1,500 from Clinton's garrison, until the total British forces along the James came to some 7,200. The area about Petersburg was overrun, and British and Tory columns began stabbing north of the James, seemingly in complete control of the Tidewater section of the state.

While this British build-up was in progress, Lafayette had led his New Englanders and Jerseymen into Virginia and had pushed south as far as Richmond before he realized the strength that was massing against him. He managed to pick up Virginia militia and some Virginia Continentals from von Steuben's camps of instruction, men originally pointed for Greene's little force far south in the Carolinas, but even with these accretions he could count a bare 3,000. The young Marquis was on his first independent command, operating in strange country and with no one to whom to turn for advice. Panic, blunders, or false moves on his part could have been written down as the lamentable but inevitable results of giving so young a man such an operation to conduct; but Lafayette kept a clear head and clear vision. In late May, 1781, he wrote Washington, "Were I to fight a battle, I should be cut to pieces, the militia dispersed and the arms lost. Were I to decline fighting, the country would think itself given up. I am therefore determined to skirmish, but not to engage too far . . ." Then he added wryly, "Were I anyways equal to the enemy, I should be extremely happy in my present command, but I am not strong enough even to get beaten."

Cornwallis, now in over-all command due to the sudden death of William Phillips, seemed to feel that the young Marquis *was* quite strong enough to be beaten, and moved up from Petersburg. The little American force fell back north, covering ground that was to become tragically familiar less than a century later. The South Anna was crossed, and the North Anna, then Fredericksburg was reached, where the thin files saw many of the same buildings that were to quiver to the artillery of Lee and Burnside in 1862. Lafayette led his men on to Ely's Ford on the Rapidan, but Cornwallis gave up the chase at the North Anna and fell back to the James, where fresh troops and fresh orders could easily reach him under the aegis of the Royal Navy. Arnold had gone back to New York in no very pleasant frame of mind, due to his supersedence first by Phillips, then by Cornwallis. But Simcoe was still in the field and "Bloody Tarleton" had come up from Wilmington, full of valuable terroristic ideas learned in the Carolinas. These two leaders were sent far up the James,

British grenadier officer

deep into the west where, at Charlottesville, Tarleton's troopers nearly captured Thomas Jefferson. Stores of powder, clothing, and muskets were destroyed, some of them intended for Greene, some for the local theater. Lafayette still kept his men intact and out of reach, biding his time, waiting for reinforcements that he had reason to hope were on the way.

On June 10, 1781, the houses of little Fredericksburg echoed to the tramp of marching men, as they were to echo so often in the unguessed future. Down from the north came handsome Anthony Wayne with three regiments of the tried Pennsylvania Line under commanders like Richard Butler and Walter Stewart. Although the tall Marquis was Wayne's military superior, the Pennsylvanian was far more experienced, and an awkward situation might have developed. Luckily, Wayne subordinated himself completely to the young Frenchman and backed him loyally as long as their joint service lasted.

Now Lafayette felt strong enough to move. South he went from Fredericksburg, and new formations began to join him. Three brigades of Virginia militia under Generals Edward Stevens, Robert Lawson, and William Campbell reported. Out of von Steuben's camp came over 400 Virginia Continentals, led by the Dane, Febiger, who had served since Bunker's Hill. Continental artillery, commanded by Lieutenant Colonel Thomas Forrest, added nine good field guns. When sixty United States dragoons and a nearly equal number of mounted volunteers joined the force, the Marquis could tally up about 4,500 men.

New Englanders, Jerseymen, Pennsylvanians, and Virginians splashed through the familiar fords in the wake of Lafayette and Wayne—through the Rappahannock, the Rapidan, the North Anna, the South Anna, beating trails for future marches in a more tragic war. The Marquis handled this march cleverly, keeping his units on different roads, camping them well apart but always within supporting distance of each other, thus creating in the minds of Cornwallis' scouts and spies an illusion of numbers far beyond his scant 4,500.

Cornwallis was on the move down toward the York Peninsula and the American force hung in his rear, declining combat as long as possible. The first action came on June 26 when John Simcoe moved his green-coated Tories and supporting Hessian jägers to snap up an American supply dump on the Chickahominy, west of Williamsburg. A mixed detail of Pennsylvanians and Virginians, backed by cavalry, caught up with Simcoe at a tavern called Spencer's Ordinary. Simcoe, roughly handled at first, managed to break clear, thanks largely to the discipline of his busbied Queen's Rangers, and fell back toward Williamsburg, leaving all his wounded at the Ordinary. The encounter was unimportant, save for showing that while Lafayette's new command was composed of fine material, its units had not worked together long enough to become combat-wise as a group.

In his camps about Williamsburg and its mellow Georgian brick buildings, Cornwallis was apparently content to let time slip by. After all, he had very few worries. He had done great damage to Virginia, in addition to what Arnold and Phillips had accomplished. He had a great advantage in numbers over Lafayette and Wayne, and even if they should be miraculously reinforced to a dangerous strength he had only to whistle up the Royal Navy, embark for some other theater, and leave his enemies wasting away in empty terrain, their services lost to their country for an indefinite period. That, Cornwallis could tell himself complacently, was what having command of the sea meant to a soldier skillful enough to take advantage of it.

Marquis de Lafayette in Virginia, a sketch by Le Tour, *circa* 1783

Recruiting poster for the Queen's Rangers, printed in Philadelphia

Then orders came down from New York over those same sea lanes that he prized so much, orders that rather disturbed his equanimity. Sir Henry Clinton, alarmed by various signs and portents north of Manhattan Island, had sent a hurry call for a good 3,000 of Lord Cornwallis' men—almost the exact number that established his superiority over the Marquis. This was a severe blow, but, observing the activity of American scouts, it suddenly occurred to Cornwallis that he might be able to transform it into a glittering triumph right there in the Virginia theater, and at once. Through July 4 and 5 he moved his entire corps from Williamsburg to the north bank of the James and the Jamestown Ford, which the 3,000 must cross on their way to the embarkation point at Portsmouth, far down the south bank. As he hoped, both Lafayette and Wayne took this movement as a crossing en masse, and to further this belief Cornwallis made a great show of passing troops and supplies to the opposite shore. On July 6, the Marquis sent Wayne with Stewart's seasoned men of the Pennsylvania Line, supported by cavalry and riflemen, to Greenspring Farm, a scant half-mile from the spot where British outposts guarded the supposed passage of the James.

Down sloping green fields, across a wide swamp, Wayne's men pushed on toward the thick timber growth that masked the river, Armand's troopers covering one flank and John Mercer's Virginia horsemen the other. Green coats moved among the trees and the infantry of Tarleton's Legion opened fire on the American advance. Stubborn action developed, with everything that Wayne could see indicating a conventional rear-guard action at a river crossing, the trees between himself and the river masking the fact that the bulk of the British army was still on the north bank. A single, concerted sweep could have wiped out Wayne's force of 500 at any moment, but Cornwallis held off, not sure just where the rest of the American force might be. If it were nearby and about to support Wayne, the British commander would have a fine chance of bagging Lafayette along with Wayne, in which case the Virginia campaign would be over.

The supposed holding action at the ford snarled on, and smoke rolled over the meadows and down to the blue glint of the James. Shadows began to lengthen over the emerald grass as the sun dropped toward Malvern Hill and Richmond. At about five o'clock, Lafayette brought on the rest of his Continentals, surveyed the swaying fight south of him, and suddenly was seized with grave doubts that only a British rear guard remained on the north bank. Was he wise to commit his whole force?

He made his decision, held back most of his men, sending only the rest of the Pennsylvanians and a detachment of light infantry under veteran Major John Wyllys of Connecticut down over the wide swampy stretch to bolster Wayne. With this group went two of Forrest's Continental fieldpieces. The composition of these reinforcements convinced Cornwallis that his chance had come, that Lafayette was moving in. Out from behind the screening trees came a double line of scarlet, bayonets poised—veteran lines that had been tested over and over. There were the Guards, the 43rd Oxfords, the 23rd Welch, the 33rd West Ridings, the 71st Highlanders, and others. In overwhelming strength they bore down on the bare 900 now under Wayne. Wayne, surprisingly, ordered a counterattack which managed to check the onslaught for a short time, but soon his flanks were overlapped and a retreat began. Somehow his men managed to keep fair order under heavy pressure and were finally dragged out of action, though with the loss of the two fieldpieces. There was no British pursuit, Cornwallis very properly fearing action in the sudden dark that had fol-

This 1781 French map shows
Cornwallis' route to Yorktown

lowed a brilliant sunset, and Lafayette and Wayne limped back to Malvern Hill. The action known as Greenspring Farm was over.

Cornwallis gathered up his command, crossed the James, and pushed on to Suffolk and then Portsmouth, where the 3,000 were to embark for New York. But conflicting orders kept coming by sea from Clinton, eight days or more away. To make matters worse, such instructions were apt to be vague and almost always held an escape-clause for Clinton to the effect that if Cornwallis had other plans afoot, he could disregard Clinton's wishes. The tacit rider to such missives was that Cornwallis had better have a good reason for disregarding them. Since the two generals had radically conflicting ideas on how to conduct the war, this mist of uncertainty actually played into American hands. The immediate sufferers were the luckless 3,000 earmarked for New York, who were kept packing and unpacking, scrambling on and off ships as more instructions arrived from Manhattan. On July 8, 1781, two days after Greenspring Farm, their destination was changed to Philadelphia. On the twelfth, word was received that Clinton wanted them in New York after all. The twentieth brought a complete reversal for the bewildered men. They were to stay where they were.

Cornwallis also must have felt a little buffeted about. The same orders directed him to establish himself at Old Point Comfort, on the north shore of Hampton Roads where Fortress Monroe now stands. If possible, he was to occupy Yorktown as well. Surveying the Point, Cornwallis came to the conclusion that it would not do for a naval base, which was what Clinton had in mind. But Sir Henry had mentioned Yorktown, so there Cornwallis went, liked the site of the dying old tobacco port on the deepwater York River, and seized it, along with Gloucester Point on the opposite bank. Clinton made no objection to this move, at least in writing. So by chance the moribund little town was given a new lease on life, a lease which was to catapult it into immortality in the annals of the new nation.

View of the tobacco port of Yorktown, drawn before the Revolution

Through the June days of 1781, while Lafayette and Wayne and Cornwallis were chipping and sparring with each other in Virginia, while Nathanael Greene's little band was recuperating in South Carolina's High Hills of Santee, deep copper-sheathed drums and long cavalry trumpets were throbbing and blaring across the lower fringes of the New England states. Across Rhode Island, across Connecticut, the armies of France were on the march at last, heading for a rendezvous with Washington's men along the Hudson. There went the Bourbonnais and the blue-coated Royal Deux-Ponts, the Soissonnais and the Saintonge regiments, gaitered legs swinging in long, easy strides and varicolored pompons slanting up from little cocked hats. Out rode the lances and sabers of Lauzun's Legion from the clearings about Lebanon, and d'Aboville's endless artillery train rumbled and clanked over the highways.

They went on and on, through Plainfield and Windham, through Bolton and Hartford and Farmington, the little country towns echoing to the rataplan of French drums and the full-throated chorus of field music that played "The Huron March" or *"Malbrouk s'en va-t-en guerre, Mironton, mironton, mirontaine!"* As in the Newport area, French discipline on the march and in camp set American eyes bulging. Inhabitants were unmolested and the columns trailed no accumulation of damage claims in their wake. Then Connecticut was a memory, and North Castle in New York's Westchester County was reached.

At King's Bridge Lauzun's men saw fleeting action as they swung out of the line of march to back up General Benjamin Lincoln's men in an outpost scuffle,

Uniforms of the French navy and the Auxerrois Regiment

then rejoined the main body. At Dobbs Ferry many of the French officers had their first glimpse of George Washington. General de Chastellux had already met him and had hymned him to the skies on his return to Newport. Now General Cromot du Bourg saw the American commander welcome Rochambeau and was himself received "with the affability that is so natural to him. He is a very fine looking man. His bearing is noble in the highest degree . . ." General Mathieu Dumas thought that Washington's "dignified address . . . won every heart."

By no means a cosmopolitan, Washington had an instinctive flair for dealing with his allies. His formal address of welcome hit just the right notes, extending past the brass right down to the rawest poilu of 1781. "The regiment of Saintonge is entitled to particular acknowledgments, for the spirit with which the men continued and supported their march without one day's respite," he said, and this remark could have been extended to the entire column, whose march had been remarkable. Commissary Claude Blanchard reported to Admiral Barras that there had been no stragglers "except ten love-sick soldiers from the . . . Soissonnais who wanted to return to see their sweethearts in Newport." Anyone who has ever marched with troops can appreciate the achievement of moving nearly 5,000 men across 220 miles in eleven days with only ten stragglers to report.

Sizing up their American colleagues, the French were struck by the lack of a regulation uniform and by the great number of fringed hunting shirts, which they described as *casaques avec des franges.* They concluded that these "troops are intended for action and not for show." The paucity of American equipment shocked Abbé Claude Robin of the Soissonnais, who found in "tents, where three or four men live, not over forty pounds of baggage." The Abbé was also shrewd enough to take in Washington's method of shifting his men to conceal their true numbers. "Now with a few soldiers he forms a Spacious Camp and spreads a large number of tents. Then again with a large number of men he reduces his tentage and his force almost vanishes." At the time of Robin's observations there were probably less than 7,000 Americans in the area.

With their troops massed and waiting up the Hudson, Washington and Rochambeau spent long hours debating on their proper employment. It had been virtually specified in Rochambeau's orders that he was to co-operate with the commander in chief in driving Clinton out of New York, and Washington strongly favored such a course. Yet Rochambeau, while willing to follow any American lead, was dubious concerning the success of such a move.

Then on August 14, 1781, a courier swept up to Washington's quarters with news that completely changed the whole picture. Comte François Joseph Paul de Grasse had cleared the French West Indies with 28 ships of the line and a cloud of transports which carried the Agenais, Gâtinais, and Touraine regiments under General the Comte de St. Simon. Old plans were thrown away at once and a fresh campaign plotted out. Americans and French were to march overland and join Lafayette and Wayne in Virginia, where de Grasse would land the three West Indies regiments. Then the massed forces could be thrown against Cornwallis with a virtual certainty of success. There were two important "ifs," however. *If* de Grasse could not keep control of the waters about Chesapeake Bay, Cornwallis could either be reinforced or whisked out of reach by the Royal Navy. And *if* the long overland march could not be arranged and executed in time, the whole effort would go for naught, since de Grasse and St. Simon were under orders not to stay in North America after

A French officer's dress sword and its scabbard

Comte de Grasse

October 15, 1781. This was another reminder that France and England were engaged in a World War of which North America was just one more theater.

There were numerous problems connected with the joint move south, and the knottiest of all was finances. The American treasury was empty and could not be replenished until far too late. Luckily Rochambeau came generously to the rescue, offering Washington half of what was left in his own military chest. Sir Henry Clinton, who might have created serious difficulties, remained strangely passive and made no notable effort to break up the allied combination. When French and American details appeared on the Jersey shore and ostentatiously built a great system of ovens that could have baked bread for a massive attack force directed against Manhattan, he let the work go on and devoted more and more time to strengthening his defenses.

During the third week in August, the allies crossed to the west bank of the Hudson via King's Ferry, an endless shuttle of barges and longboats and rafts floating men and guns and wagons and horses, the very last load making the passage on the twenty-fifth. All during this time, the broad Hudson had been thick with small, helpless craft, and yet not a single British ship cleared from New York for action, no part of the land force tried to interfere. Colonel de Deux-Ponts wrote in profound relief and wonder: "An enemy, a little bold and able would have seized the moment . . . so favorable for him, so embarrassing for us, for an attack. His indifference and lethargy . . . is an enigma that cannot be solved by me."

Once on the west bank, the American contingent led the march south. Picked battalions of light troops had been drawn from many units. New England troops predominated, with a strong leavening from New York and New Jersey, but commanders from battalion-level up represented a startling melting of state and sectional lines. Alexander Hamilton led Connecticut men as well as New Yorkers. South Carolinian John Laurens brought on a mixed group of Massachusetts, Connecticut, and New Hampshire men. Henry Knox's guns bowled along behind John Lamb of New York and Ebenezer Stevens of Massachusetts, while the engineer train, drawn from New York and Connecticut, was under the Chevalier Louis Lebèque Duportail, whose American service went back to 1777.

There were weather-beaten faces on which the record of the whole war was written—from Breed's Hill to Long Island and the Hollow Way, from Trenton and Princeton to the Indian country, from the St. Lawrence to Freeman's Farm. Edward Hand was there, and Timothy Pickering, and Henry Dearborn. Benjamin Lincoln led a division, and Moses Hazen, James Clinton, and Elias Dayton headed brigades.

Through Trenton and Philadelphia, march tables were rigidly kept and there was little disorder or straggling in either army. But Washington and Rochambeau carried gnawing worries with them, for word had reached them that heavy British naval formations had cleared New York, heading south. Where was de Grasse and his north-bound flotilla? At last word came in, and witnesses commented on Washington's almost Gallic excitement as he passed the news on to Rochambeau. Admiral de Grasse was safe in Chesapeake Bay with 28 powerful ships. The 3,000 whitecoats under St. Simon were ashore, pressing on for a junction with Lafayette and Wayne. Cornwallis was sealed in from the sea by the French navy. Lafayette, Wayne, and St. Simon could contain him by land, and for the first time since 1775, a real American offensive victory loomed.

The tempo of the march was speeded up. The water routes were clear and

Chevalier Duportail, by Peale

Timothy Pickering, by Peale

The French fleet (left) stands out of Chesapeake Bay to meet Graves' attack

The Battle of the Virginia Capes: Graves attacks de Grasse's line

the combined forces could be shipped down Chesapeake Bay and thence up the James. There was an alarming shortage of boats, but busy agents raked up little schooners, open barges, and derelict ferries. In early September the leading columns reached Head of Elk in fine shape, with morale and spirits high, ready to embark. Boatload by boatload these men, who had made such a remarkable march down almost half a continent, worked across the bay and up the James to join their fellows under Lafayette and Wayne and St. Simon in the camps about Williamsburg. Slowly those camps swelled. First there were the original 9,800 French and Americans (3,000 or more of them militia). The total climbed to an impressive 11,000, to 14,000, and finally reached the 16,000 mark.

On September 14 the camps were astir, with French and Americans falling in at strict attention. Out of the east, through Virginia militia camps, a group of horsemen galloped furiously on. St. Simon's men, drawn up in superb order just west of the College of William and Mary, stared uncomprehendingly. The front ranks could see that the officer leading the newcomers was a very tall man in blue and buff, as immaculate as the blue and white of the American "Vayne" with whom these West Indies regiments had become familiar. Men in the Gâtinais ranks, in the Agenais, in the Touraine cocked their heads as the young Marquis de Lafayette in his American uniform went galloping out, accompanied by Monsieur le Gouverneur de la Virginie.

Outer sentries, amaranth or green or rose facings sharp against their white coats, saw the man in blue and buff drop from his horse, saw him embrace the young Marquis de Lafayette as though both had been proper Frenchmen. St. Simon was presented, introduced his regimental commanders, de Rostaing of the Gâtinais, Comte d'Autichamp of the Agenais, Vicomte de Poudeux of the Touraine. Rigid sentries and braced men in the regiments by the college did not need the cheering from the more distant American camps to tell them what was passing. This tall man could only be that fabulous "Vasinton" of whom they had heard, far off in Martinique or Haiti, and the big Frenchman with him must be their own Rochambeau. Throughout St. Simon's files, through the ranks of the regiments that had known Newport and the long march west and south, men raised cocked hats on their bayoneted muskets, lifted them high, cheering like the Americans.

This must have been a choking moment for Washington. He had spent a few quiet days at Mount Vernon, the first visit to his beloved estate since 1776, with his adored Martha and in the congenial company of Rochambeau, de Chastellux, and others. Then he had torn himself away and ridden hard for the camps that spread about Williamsburg near the neck of the Yorktown peninsula.

Yet there was little relaxing for him. Some days before, Admiral de Grasse had taken his combat ships out into the dim sea reaches beyond the mouth of the Chesapeake, and there were rumors that he had met the British under Admirals Thomas Graves and Samuel Hood. If the British had scattered the French fleet, then Cornwallis could laugh at the French-American land threat, and all the effort, all the treasure spent in the great southern movement had been in vain. And it would have been almost as bad, assuming that de Grasse had escaped unscathed, if the Royal Navy intercepted another fleet under Admiral Barras, some days out of Newport with the heavier French ordnance and tons of salt beef for the armies.

There was a formal dinner that night with St. Simon's massed bands playing for the guests, featuring passages from Grétry's *Lucille*. The senior guests could have been little distracted from their thoughts. Disaster to de Grasse and Barras would profoundly discourage the weary people of America and the French Court. Washington might reflect that although the laboriously prepared Articles of Confederation, which loosely bound the Thirteen States into a unit, had just been ratified, such acceptance could mean little without force of arms to back it up. What was happening out at sea in the rolling stretches beyond the Chesapeake capes?

The question was answered the very next day. Before dawn on September 15, word came from that phlegmatic Auvergnat, de Grasse, that he was back in Chesapeake Bay, that he had met Hood and Graves who had engaged and finally broken off action to scud north. Barras' highly important convoy was safe and making for James River anchorages. That one sea action, so tersely reported and so little noted save in detailed histories, unseen save by the relatively few participants, was actually the one decisive engagement of the war. It is ironic that not a single American soldier had taken part in the sudden climax of six years of bitter fighting. Yet there the record stands. The French had seized the one vital factor that America had lacked from the start, control of the seas, and were able to hold it just long enough [*see* map, page 284].

After a conference aboard the vast *Ville de Paris* with de Grasse, Washington and Rochambeau set to work in earnest. Cornwallis had dug in solidly at Yorktown and had also established works at Gloucester Point, on the north bank of the York. If he had enough small craft available, he might be able to ferry his 6,000-odd British, Tories, and Hessians across, drive up through Virginia and into Maryland and Pennsylvania, and rejoin Clinton. Rochambeau suggested that that would be a foolhardy move, since Cornwallis would be without base or supply lines, drifting north across a wild continent. Washington assured him that the British were very tough and that other armies in North America had moved farther and under worse conditions.

Gloucester Point was now watched by a far too flimsy force of Virginia militia under General "Joe Gourd" Weedon. Rochambeau would send Lauzun and his lancers and hussars across to join him, along with marines from de Grasse's ships. For over-all area command, Washington readily agreed to the selection of the Marquis de Choisy, who had been outstanding at the siege of Cracow in Poland some years ago. In the meantime, regular siege lines had been drawn about Yorktown and staffed with seasoned French and Americans. Up from the James rumbled the heavy guns of Henry Knox and François Marie d'Aboville, and were emplaced along with lighter fieldpieces and little coehorns, a weapon much like the trench-mortar of World War I.

Fire was opened from the allied lines, the advanced trenches pushed closer and closer until Cornwallis was forced to abandon his outer works, since he did not have enough troops to man them. That great gift, control of the sea, he might have reflected, could work both ways. However, he still had one supply route and possible escape-corridor through Gloucester Point. But on October 3, 1781, de Choisy pushed his lines right up to the British works, a move in which Banastre Tarleton and one of his convoys was badly mauled by a sudden charge of Lauzun's gaudy troopers, Tarleton narrowly missing death at the hands of Lauzun himself. The Gloucester door was slammed shut for good, and the British forces bottled up completely [*see* map, page 370].

From then on, the end was certain. On the night of October 14, the incessant allied cannonade was stilled for a moment, then the hush was broken

"*I caught sight of General Washington waving his hat at me with demonstrative gestures of the greatest joy. When I rode up to him, he explained that he had just received a dispatch . . . informing him that de Grasse had arrived.*"
—Comte de Rochambeau

Alexander Hamilton in the trenches about Yorktown

British plan of the Yorktown siege

by six cannon shots in rapid succession. Out from the allied left, picked companies of the Gâtinais and the Royal Deux-Ponts stormed forward under Count Guillaume of the latter regiment. On the right, lean companies of American light infantry were led out by Alexander Hamilton and Gimat. It was primarily bayonet work, like Wayne's night-rush at Stony Point, and the next day Cornwallis wrote dismally to Clinton, "the enemy carried two advanced redoubts by storm. . . . My situation now becomes very critical; we dare not show a gun to their old batteries, and I expect that their new ones will open to-morrow morning. . . . The safety of the place is, therefore, so precarious that I cannot recommend that the fleet and army should run great risque in endeavouring to save us." The last faint stars of hope were winking out in Yorktown's battered streets, and at Gloucester, John Graves Simcoe and Banastre Tarleton watched sadly while black-clad farrier sergeants knocked in the heads of horses rendered useless by starvation.

Knox and d'Aboville pushed their guns ahead to match every forward stride of the infantry. On the morning of the seventeenth, the fourth anniversary of Burgoyne's surrender, French and American 24-pounders and 18's and 16's, squat bulky mortars, and little coehorns were roaring at full blast. The haze of a soft Virginia fall day was thickened by welling cannon smoke, by geysers of loose red dirt thrown skyward. Dr. James Thacher, front-line surgeon since 1775, figured that at least 100 guns were at work. "The whole peninsula trembles under the incessant thunderings of our infernal machines," he wrote. He also found it worthy of note that there was almost no answering fire from the Yorktown works.

At about ten o'clock, the reeking haze that smothered the British lines lifted a little as gunners paused to shift their pieces onto new targets. Then, at the far left of the French emplacements, cannoneers and matrosses began to yell, pointing deep-cuffed hands at a great, curved mound known as the "Horn Work." There was movement through the thinning battle-fog off there, and men gripped rammer-staffs and carbines, shouted to nearby infantry supports. Scarlet showed vaguely against the sky, but it was not a desperate rush of hard-pressed men. One small figure, standing alone on the parapet, one little British drummer with gun smoke eddying about his spindly legs, valiantly hammered out a message from his taut drumhead. Fire slackened still more as the little scarlet figure, shabby bearskin cap erect, drummed on, and d'Aboville's men recognized the call, the request for a parley. Others farther to the right caught it, and Lieutenant Ebenezer Denny of the 4th Pennsylvania wrote that he had "never heard a drum equal to it—the most delightful music to us all."

British drummer boy

Now there was an officer on the parapet beside the diminutive drummer, waving a white cloth. Expected as this moment must have been, there was a stunned hush over the French-American lines. The French would have been justified in making the first contact with the parleying officer, but instead they held back, courteously sending word to the nearest American officer, who ran forward to meet the Englishman on the gnawed slope of the Horn Work.

George Washington, commander in chief of the allied forces, was busily writing letters back at Williamsburg, deaf for the moment to the Knox-d'Aboville bombardment and to its sudden stilling. An aide, red-faced with excitement, burst in on him with a sealed letter brought that very instant. The Virginian broke the seal, then froze as the writing swirled before his eyes: "I propose a cessation of hostilities for twenty four hours, and that two officers may be appointed by each side, to meet at Mr. Moore's house to settle terms for the surrender of the posts of York & Gloucester. I have the honor to be Sir Your most obedient and most humble Servant, Cornwallis."

Like his men, the commander in chief must have known the inevitability of this moment, so surely forecast by de Grasse's victory at sea and the closing of the Gloucester Point escape-route; yet its impact must have been staggering after the danger-fraught years that had passed before his eyes. He quickly rallied himself, called in John Trumbull of Connecticut and John Laurens of South Carolina, and carefully worked out his answer. "An Ardent Desire to spare the further Effusion of Blood, will readily incline me to listen to such Terms . . . as are admissible."

Down on the peninsula, gunfire stopped. French and American infantrymen crawled slowly to the tops of their parapets, French and American gunners worked out through their embrasures to stand in the sun and stare at the silent British lines, to loll almost incredulously in spots where a man could not have lived a few moments before. Throughout the day and into the night the hush continued, though some men, still battle-tense, were alarmed by an unusual shower of meteors across the soft, black sky, mistaking them for a fresh flight of explosive shells. The next day was unbroken by as much as a pistol-snap, and there was a shuttling back and forth between the lines as parleys went on and eager young aides dashed about. On the nineteenth, men in the French and American lines knew that Washington, Rochambeau, and Barras, the latter substituting for the ailing de Grasse, had met with the British, that a document had been signed, ending "Done in the trenches before Yorktown, in Virginia, October 19, 1781." The very first signature had read simply: "G. Washington."

By noon of that day the allied camps were stirring to the hard pecking of drums and the blare of French cavalry trumpets. The still air of a Virginia fall was rich with the smell of trampled grass and wood smoke, of oiled leather and the lingering tang of cooked rations. Roll was being called in the Saintonge Regiment, in Colonel Goose van Schaick's 1st New York, in the Soissonnais, in Nathan Rice's Massachusetts-Connecticut battalion. On the Yorktown road, Baron von Steuben chatted with General Benjamin Lincoln. Off to the left Baron de Vioménil and the Marquis de Chastellux, hands behind their backs, watched the gathering crowds of civilians, saw varnished coaches that had somehow escaped the depredations of Simcoe's and Tarleton's raids, commented on glossy carriage horses, on country carts and ungroomed dobbins, heard the grass swish under daintily slippered feet or crunch to the tread of home-cobbled shoes. Soldiers and civilians spoke, but their tones were hushed like those of an audience waiting for a theater curtain to rise.

Drums slammed out in a startling roar. Brasses and wood winds sent their notes throbbing into the soft blue of the sky as the French bands struck up the overture. Citizens and their wives and children cried out in delight, gasped at the toss and swirl of the drum majors' tasseled batons. Then the fields began to flow. On swung the blue and white of the Royal Deux-Ponts, the white slashed over with violet or black or green or crimson of other regiments which had come from so far to march out into a Virginia meadow. Under a frosting of bayonets they came, broke from column into line, then halted at the west edge of the Yorktown road in a crisp rattle of grounded arms.

To the east drab troops wheeled, headed by bands that, according to one listener, played "moderately well." There was a new tenseness in the crowds of onlookers as they turned to look at the bronzed, fringe-shirted men, staring in sudden comprehension that pages of their own history were being leafed

Cornwallis' letter to Washington asking for a cease-fire

Trumbull sketch of Moore house, in which surrender was signed

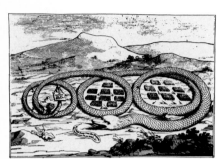

The "American Rattle Snake," having enveloped two British armies, has still a third "Apartment to Lett"

through before their eyes. Here came Lafayette with Vose and Wyllys and Laurens, bringing on the New Englanders. James Clinton led out New Yorkers under Goose van Schaick and Philip van Cortlandt, Jerseymen with Elias Dayton, Rhode Islanders with Jeremiah Olney. The trim panache of Anthony Wayne ushered in Walter Stewart's Pennsylvanians, and loose-striding Virginians swung by under Thomas Gaskins, followed by Mordecai Gist's Marylanders. Traces hissed, ironshod wheels thudded over sand, and here came fat Henry Knox heading the Continental artillery, with John Lamb of New York and Virginia's Edward Carrington, released by Nathanael Greene to serve on Virginia soil.

The passage was dazzling, hypnotic. People stood on tiptoe to pick out leaders who, up to now, had been largely names on a smeared newssheet. They looked for Parson Muhlenberg, so closely identified with their own troops, rigid Baron von Steuben, the Georgia Colonel Samuel Elbert, the devoted Chevalier Duportail, or Moses Hazen of the Canadian regiment. Now they saw them all, men of whom they had heard or read, under whom or with whom sons or husbands or brothers had served.

Tramp of foot, thud of hoof, and grind of wheel seemed to mutter out the whole story of these men and their absent fellows, of the American army in which they served, and the cause for which they, and their country with them, had endured so much and so long. There were sinister undercurrents that told of divided counsels, of selfishness local or widespread, of men who had made a profit from the sufferings and deaths of others—harder tones of plots, betrayal, and downright treason. But there were other, brighter chords telling of earlier days when men shouted that there must be no more Virginians or New Englanders or Carolinians, "but all of us Americans!" Repeated were the uneasy yet determined tones of Minutemen waiting on scores of village greens through an April night of '75. The rowlocks of the Marbleheaders could be heard, creaking as they saved a beaten army to fight again. Icy ruts crunched under gun wheels along a winter road to Trenton, and unseen forest trails crackled as men glided forward to close on Burgoyne. The voice of a British prisoner of war could be heard, telling of a wide, poverty-stricken district where whole families had but one blanket, having parted with the others "to supply their soldiers, yet you would be surprized with what cheerfulness they bend to [such sacrifices] to obtain that idol, Independency."

So harsh and ugly tones, bravely triumphant or eternally enduring tones told the story of a people and its army, that army whose men were always too few and were always just enough. Now that army was halting on the east side of the Yorktown road, facing the French. Drums beat again and the waiting ranks bristled to attention. Onto the field of Yorktown, at the head of his staff, rode the one man who was the living expression of those drab ranks to his right, and the people seen or unseen who stood behind them. On his big bay horse, George Washington rode out into the Virginia sunlight to meet his greatest glory, still calm, still ready to lead these men to meet whatever might lie before them when they left Yorktown.

Rochambeau came on, a little behind him, and the Virginian knew that without that quiet Frenchman's unfaltering support, the allied armies would not be drawn up before the silent works of Yorktown. And both men realized to the full that without the French fleet their campaign could have come to nothing. Washington turned to take his post at the American right, Rochambeau and Admiral Barras faced him on the French flank, and a hush fell over the whole rolling plain.

Detail from Trumbull's painting showing British General Charles O'Hara surrendering to Benjamin Lincoln

Then off by Yorktown and the river, sullen drums began to roll, as a scarlet-coated group rode out of the battered works, heading for the double line of troops along the highway. In the lead was a handsome man, General Charles O'Hara of the Guards, the same who had clung so close to Henry Lee and Otho Williams in the retreat to the Dan. O'Hara looked right and left as he came up, hesitated, then edged his horse toward Rochambeau. That General silently pointed to the opposite side, and O'Hara, confused by his own *gaffe*, presented himself to Washington.

The commander in chief was impassive, courteous. Where was Lord Cornwallis, the senior British officer? O'Hara explained that Cornwallis was ill and had deputized him to make the surrender. Still impassive, still courteous, Washington said that deputy should surrender to deputy, and with a characteristically generous gesture nominated General Benjamin Lincoln, who had undergone the humiliation of Charleston, to act for him. Lincoln, with a bow to his superior officer, rode forward, hoof-beats loud in the hush, touched O'Hara's sword in token acceptance, and then briefly told the Guardsman how the garrison was to march out and where it was to stack its arms before returning weaponless to Yorktown for further orders.

So the worn men marched out from the works, beaten because a French fleet had seized command of the sea from the Royal Navy and because the allied ground forces had utilized every possible advantage that that seizure had given them. Arms were stacked in a field guarded by Lauzun's lancers and hussars, and the prisoners of war started back for the works that they had defended so doggedly, the first stage on a long route that was to take them across Virginia, through Ashby's Gap in the Blue Ridge mountains, and on to Winchester in the Shenandoah or to Frederick in Maryland.

That night the commander in chief gave a dinner for General Charles O'Hara of the Guards, a bit of military courtesy that the Irishman accepted with a poise and dignity that won the admiration of young John Trumbull of Connecticut. But Trumbull, along with Washington's other secretary, Laurens, was spirited away from the table early by the host. The American army had just played its own part in a striking victory and Washington must report to that body which had first raised the army and placed it under his care.

He and his two secretaries worked late until finally a draft was made that satisfied him, a draft that reported on what the army, not its commander in chief, had done. "I have the Honor to inform Congress, that a Reduction of the British Army under the Command of Lord Cornwallis, is most happily effected. The unremitting Ardor which actuated every Officer and Soldier in the combined Army in this Occasion, has principally led to this Important Event, at an earlier period than my most sanguine Hope had induced me to expect." So far as Washington's own part in the campaign was concerned, he might have been reporting on some victory won by another general in a distant theater.

Important as Yorktown was, contemporary eyes saw it only as a great victory, not *the* great victory. Cornwallis had surrendered, like Burgoyne, but there still remained a potentially dangerous British force about Charleston, South Carolina, and the powerful main army was in the Manhattan area.

Through the rest of 1781 and during 1782, the belligerent powers remained poised, though relatively inert save in the West Indies. Clinton labored through plans for another stroke to be launched at the Middle States, centering on Philadelphia. Washington and Rochambeau assayed their own resources,

CONTINUED ON PAGE 364

Cornwallis' troops stacking arms: drawing by Johann Ramberg, 1784

Glorious Intelligence!

NORWICH, OCTOBER 26, 1781.
Friday Evening, Six o'Clock:
By a Gentleman this Moment from New-London we are favoured with the following Hand-Bill.

NEWPORT, OCTOBER 25.

YESTERDAY afternoon arrived in this harbour, Capt. Lovat, of the schooner Adventure, from York-River in Chesapeake-Bay, (which he left the 20th inst.) and brought us the glorious news of the surrender of Lord Cornwallis and his army prisoners of war to the allied army under the command of our illustrious General, and the French fleet under the command of his Excellency the Count de Graffe.

A cessation of arms took place on Thursday the 18th inst. in consequence of proposals from Lord Cornwallis for a capitulation.---His Lordship proposed a cessation of twenty-four hours, but two only were granted by his Excellency Gen. Washington. The articles were compleated the same day, and the next day the allied army took possession of York-Town.

By this glorious conquest Nine Thousand of the enemy, including seamen, fell into our hands, with an immense quantity of warlike stores, a forty gun ship, a frigate, an armed vessel, and about One Hundred Sail of Transports.

༄༄༄༄༄༄༄༄༄༄༄༄༄༄

NORWICH:
PRINTED BY JOHN TRUMBULL.

This broadside brought the news of Yorktown to Norwich, Connecticut

Overleaf: George III's personal copy of the John Mitchell map of North America, which he used during the peace negotiations

CONTINUED FROM PAGE 361

hoped for news of a French fleet up from the Indies that might again close the sea lanes long enough for a full-scale assault on New York, but nothing came of any of these projects.

Yet there were signs and omens for observant men to read, portents that pointed to a definite denouement. Late in 1782 the British, whose over-all command now lay in the hands of Sir Guy Carleton, Clinton's successor, gave up Charleston and Savannah. Surgeon James Thacher, now up the Hudson again with the main army, noted in August, 1782: "Flags are passing and repassing from this post to New York and back every day . . . By the intelligence which they bring . . . commissioners are sent from the court of London to Paris, where they are to meet French and American commissioners for the important purpose of negotiating a general peace."

Later it became known that peace would be concluded and that its basis would be American independence. But there were hitches and snarls. Armies were still in the field and there was never a time when men could say, "Now it's all over." The same pattern ran through 1783. News from abroad still pointed rather vaguely to some final windup, as it had in the past. In the American army enlistments ran out, as always, and numbers shrank steadily, for now there was no detectable emergency to rally men to the colors. The national economy, more precarious by the moment, could offer no inducement to bring troops into the ranks, while officers applied for, or merely took, leave of absence, fed up with looking after skeleton commands.

When in April the final treaty that acknowledged the complete independence of the United States of America was presented to Congress for ratification, there was national rejoicing, but the climax had come so gradually, fuzzed with so many "ifs" en route, that the keen edge of victory had been dulled to that of an old hoe blade in a New Hampshire cornpatch.

Events following ratification dragged on at the same springhalt gait. The seasons leaked away. In Manhattan, Carleton sat tight with his British and Hessians and Tories, not to mention the all-important Royal Navy, his tenure and forces looking very permanent. It was nearly December before the Crown troops were finally embarked in their transports and moved down the bay, ready to set a course for Nova Scotia or for England. At last New York, held by the British since 1776, could bid them a final farewell and greet the American army that General Henry Knox led triumphantly into town on the heels of their departure. Another farewell—sad, tense, and almost wordless—remained to be said on December 4, 1783.

Back in the golden, almost forgotten days of peace, in the year 1765, West India-born Samuel Fraunces had acquired, along with an enviable reputation as purveyor of fine food and wines, the old De Lancey mansion at the corner of Pearl and Broad streets in New York. Fraunces, the "Black Sam" of Philip Freneau's poem, had known stirring days in the dormered, gambrel-roofed mansion. Here, as times grew troubled, the leading Sons of Liberty met to talk and debate and plan, secure in their knowledge of their host's sympathies and discretion. Later, British officers replaced the Sons about the ever-famous table. The Englishmen seem to have been unaware of the fact that Fraunces' sympathies remained unchanged while his discretion must have increased many-fold, for after the war Congress and the New York legislature voted him cash grants for services to American prisoners of war and for "other acts," not specified but easily imagined.

Great days dawned for Fraunces as the war petered out. When General Sir

Trumbull's sketch for a proposed painting of the treaty signing

A GENERAL PEACE.

NEW-YORK, March 25, 1783.

LATE laſt Night, an EXPRESS from *New-Jerſey,* brought the following *Account.*

THAT on Sunday laſt, the Twenty-Third Inſtant, a Veſſel arrived at Philadelphia, in Thirty-five Days from Cadiz, with *Diſpatches* to the *Continental Congreſs,* informing them, that on Monday the Twentieth Day of January, the PRELIMINARIES to

A GENERAL PEACE,

Between *Great-Britain, France, Spain, Holland,* and the *United States* of *America,* were SIGNED at Paris, by all the Commiſſioners from thoſe Powers; in conſequence of which, Hoſtilities, by Sea and Land, were to *ceaſe* in Europe, on Wedneſday the Twentieth Day of February; and in America, on Thurſday the Twentieth Day of March, in the preſent Year One Thouſand Seven Hundred and Eighty-Three.

THIS very *important* Intelligence was laſt Night announced by the Firing of Cannon, and great Rejoicings at Elizabeth-Town.—Reſpecting the Particulars of this truly intereſting Event no more are yet received, but they are hourly expected.

Publiſhed by James Rivington, *Printer to the King's Moſt Excellent Majeſty.*

New York broadside announcing signing of the preliminary treaty

Guy Carleton went up the Hudson to confer with General George Washington at Tappan, the American commander in chief summoned Samuel Fraunces to act as headquarters caterer during Carleton's stay. When the British evacuation of New York was complete, American officers and civil dignitaries flocked through the fanlighted doors at Pearl and Broad streets.

But that fourth of December, 1783, brought Black Sam the greatest day that he had yet known. His windows were polished to make the most of the thin winter sun that filtered over the island, and his waxed floors glistened. In the main room waiters were setting out a great buffet lunch on linen-draped tables that held hot and cold joints and slices, platters of bread, golden mounds of butter, heaps of green "garden sauce." Along each of the big tables decanters of wine glistened beside stacks of polished glasses as Samuel Fraunces and his staff waited for the company to arrive.

One by one they came, spurs jingling and sabers clanking, flicking invisible bits of dust from worn blue sleeves, giving a furtive whisk of a handkerchief to mended boots. Fraunces knew most of them, like General Alexander Mac-Dougall, Son of Liberty a short decade ago, or the affably rigid Baron von Steuben with his glittering decoration nearly a palm's breadth across. Major Robert Burnet had commanded the rear guard of the little force that had marched into town on the heels of the departing British. The steps creaked as General Henry Knox edged his 280 pounds through the rather narrow door in the wake of General James Clinton of New York. There could have been quick, understanding glances between Samuel Fraunces and the strikingly handsome man from Connecticut, Major Benjamin Tallmadge, with his beautifully kept dragoon helmet, for the Major had been Washington's Chief of Intelligence, fully aware of those "other acts" for which the tavern keeper was later to be rewarded.

Map cartouche celebrating peace between England and America, 1783

Slowly the room filled up with faces known and unknown, but as Black Sam bustled about he missed the customary hum and buzz of old comrades-in-arms reunited. There were brief greetings, sketchy snatches of conversation that died quickly. Officers perched uneasily on the chairs set about the walls, glanced at each other, drummed on white knees with battle-scarred fingers.

Suddenly there was blue and buff in the corridor and Fraunces discreetly vanished as the guests snapped quickly to their feet, hats or helmets tucked correctly under their left arms. The commander in chief entered the room with a quick inclination of his powdered head, a few barely audible words of welcome. There was a muted rustle of response, then silence again, as though a group of strange children had been thrown together in an unfamiliar room. Washington made a hospitable gesture toward the tables but only a few officers edged up to them. As though to give the lead, the Virginian dabbed some food onto a plate, picked up a fork, set them both down. One officer remembered later that he had never seen men so hopelessly adrift, and he noted, when the commander in chief filled a glass, that the strong-fingered hand was shaky and the powdered head was bent. Other glasses were filled, but the officers who held them merely stared woodenly at the floor, as if avoiding each other's eyes and those of their chief.

Then the Virginian began to speak in an odd, tight voice, the words forming with difficulty, syllable by syllable. "With a heart full of love and gratitude, I now take leave of you." Slowly and carefully he added, "I most devoutly wish that your later days may be as prosperous and happy as your former ones have been glorious and honorable." He raised his glass. Here and there a man managed to stammer out some kind of a response. The commander in chief was speaking once more, struggling with each word while his cheeks glistened unashamedly, as did those of tough old von Steuben or of young Benjamin Tallmadge. "I cannot"—he stopped, and then went on with considerable effort—"I cannot come to each of you but shall feel obliged if each of you will come and take me by the hand."

The first to stir was vast Henry Knox, who moved blindly across the room, hand out. Washington started to take it, but memories of the old years together swept over him and he threw his arms about his Chief of Artillery, whom he had first met riding about the Boston lines back in '75.

One by one the others stumbled up to be greeted by the same accolade, simple, unaffected, immeasurably sad. Benjamin Tallmadge remembered, "Such a scene of sorrow and weeping I had never before witnessed, and hope I may never be called upon to witness again. . . . Not a word was uttered to break the solemn silence . . . or to interrupt the tenderness of the . . . scene. The simple thought that we were then about to part from the man who had conducted us through a long and bloody war, and under whose conduct the glory and independence of our country had been achieved, and that we should see his face no more in this world, seemed to me utterly insupportable. But the time of separation had come, and waving his hand to his grieving children around him, he left the room . . ."

Still the commander in chief's ordeal was not over. In the street he passed through a guard of honor and the vast crowds of New Yorkers who choked the lane leading to Whitehall Ferry. People along the way remembered as long as they lived his tense, set face, the convulsive throbbing of his jaw muscles, as he saw mothers holding up their children for a glimpse of that tall Virginia planter who had once stood before Congress and said, "I do not think myself equal to the command I am honored with."

He did not pass on alone. All the guests from Fraunces' Tavern had followed after him "in mournful silence to the wharf, where a prodigious crowd had assembled to witness the departure of the man who, under God, had been the great agent in establishing the glory and independence of these United States. As soon as he was seated, the barge put off into the river, and when out in the stream, our great and beloved General waved his hat and bid us a silent adieu." So Benjamin Tallmadge recalled that last affecting scene at Whitehall Ferry as the barge bore General George Washington across to Paulus Hook on the Jersey shore.

The handsome young Major of the 2nd United States Dragoons was wrong on one point. That restrained gesture of the commander in chief was not one of final parting. As in 1775 every state had turned to him for leadership, had sensed in him the embodiment of all that was best in national ideal and aim, so the country would turn to him again. Eight more grinding, wearing years were to be demanded of him as President. His was to be the task of calling forth the spiritual forces, the very essence of the new nation, of binding its parts together, of maintaining the fight against enemies within as well as without, of rallying it to hold fast the knowledge that freedom, however won, is never static, must always be fought for.

The War of the Revolution was over but the Revolution itself went on. The war had been only the curtain-raiser for the great, unending drama of the free man establishing himself in a free nation. What was the nature of this nation to be? In general, those who took part in its forming had keenly desired independence, but from that point men's ideas veered off on wild courses.

A decorative memorial to the victorious General Washington

There had to be some sort of a union and the Articles of Confederation showed the consciousness of that need. But how close a union was desirable? Too tight an organization could have throttled the life out of the very states that had brought it into being. Too loose a form might have turned the whole seaboard and interior into a collection of small, ever-divergent entities, pursuing narrow ends that could conflict to the point of outright war, and might have resulted in the creation of a dozen weak nations, always at war and ever dependent on the support of this or that European power.

The years ahead were to decide the final shape, but only after long, hot bickering that threatened at times to destroy the whole structure. The New England states, conditioned by their past to act as a unit, were in general the most receptive to a close federation. South Carolina, with its own unique and proud history, shied away violently, thus casting an ominous shadow of things to come in unborn years. Many Charleston leaders did not like even the flimsy Articles of Confederation, were to like the Constitution still less, and would claim in all sincerity that their delegates had far exceeded their powers in voting for independence in the first place. Like thinkers were to be found, in varying numbers, in all other states.

The Revolution had started as a political move underlying the various economic pressures of the times, and was bound to lead, eventually, to independence. During the war and afterward, the base of the Revolution had broadened to an extent undreamed of by most in the beginning, since such movements usually fall into the hands of men holding relatively radical views, more and more impatient of the old order.

Some changes in American life made their appearance almost at once, had, indeed, been underway before the outbreak of hostilities. Despite the Crown ban on trans-Allegheny settlement, a thin trickle of westbound emigrants had been working on through the Cumberland Gap, hacking out what was to be the Wilderness Road. War or no war, the trickle swelled to a stream, a flood, until by 1783 a good 25,000 souls were firmly lodged in the forbidden lands, were being joined daily by newcomers. Later, flatboats, keelboats, and broadhorns worked down the Ohio River in staggering numbers, bringing more and more settlers and their chattels.

Sketch, after Franklin's design, of a medal celebrating America's freedom

With the coming of peace, land was filling up in a less spectacular, less dramatic, but still important manner. Old Crown tracts, grants made to absentee landlords, and estates confiscated from Tories who had taken an active part in opposing the new order became national or state property and were generally sold in small parcels at very low prices. To pay off state and national troops, land warrants were issued, instruments which the holder could either convert into acres of his own or sell for spot cash. In most states, this redistribution of land made the status of "freeholder" available virtually to everyone.

In the course of a very few years, the whole picture of American land tenure, so important to a people then predominantly rural, changed to a degree barely imaginable a decade before. Probably few of these landholders, new or old, looked upon all this reshuffling as part of that Revolution on which they had so grimly embarked, but it put its stamp on them and on their heirs, whether the acres they took up lay along the route of Burgoyne's tragic march through New York state or on the terrain over which George Rogers Clark had struggled to victory with his gaunt men. They were independent people and would carry that characteristic with them in their long push across the continent to the Rocky Mountains and through the passes to the Pacific.

Men, as well as the land, underwent slower but equally vital changes. Through the easy acquisition of acres and the resultant qualification of the owner as a freeholder, the social status of thousands of people was improved, since the non-voter of the past became a voter. Before long the freehold qualification which obtained in many states was replaced by other standards until, by slow steps, universal white male suffrage was reached.

Rural though the nation was, commerce and industry began a lush flowering when they were freed from the old British restrictions. Able to trade where and with whom they pleased, American shipowners began nosing their prows far out into the seven seas, freighted with goods created by native ingenuity and skills. Manufacturing burgeoned, timidly at first and then more and more richly, ranging from household crafts to actual factories and plants. The Duc de La Rochefoucauld, traveling through Delaware after the war, was astounded to count more than sixty mills powered by the waters of little Brandywine Creek where his fellow countryman, Lafayette, had gone into action for the first time. Cities began to grow, spreading their influence deeper and deeper into the farmlands, foreshadowing the role urban communities would play in the years to come. Specie flowed in through ports, and less than a decade after Yorktown, the country could boast of its first three banks.

Men's thoughts could turn from the matter of mere growth to the question of channeling that growth, to bringing up a generation equipped to face ever-expanding problems and challenges. Back in 1775, the combined colonies could count no more than nine colleges, some of very recent origin—Harvard, William and Mary, Yale, Princeton, Columbia, the University of Pennsylvania, Brown, Dartmouth, and Rutgers, to give them all their modern names. By 1787 the list was swelled by Dickinson, Washington (in Maryland), St. John's, Georgetown, Abington, Washington (in Virginia), Hampden-Sydney, and Charleston. Graduates of all these institutions, new and old, joined in the push west, and founded or helped to found wilderness colleges which would swell in stature and importance.

Implicit in all this was a vista of unchecked expansion, embarked upon sometimes wisely, sometimes shortsightedly, often haphazardly by the founders of the new nation and those who flocked to join them in later years. That this expansion proceeded as it did was due in part to the nature of those men and the institutions that they devised, improvised, or stumbled upon. The pattern they had set in the formative days was to vary little as new areas were tapped, new settlers assimilated. The imprint of Virginia and New Jersey, Massachusetts and South Carolina, and their fellows was repeated as wilderness gave way to Territory and Territory to State. A Christopher Gadsden, a Patrick Henry, a John Adams, or a John Sullivan might have been bewildered by outward changes, but any of them would have been thoroughly at home in the founding days of Wisconsin, Iowa, or Colorado.

It was also the good fortune of the nation's founders, and of the nation itself, that history allowed them to shape their own destiny without important outside interference. The people and their representatives never had to stop and worry over how this or that step or innovation would be regarded by powerful, jealous close neighbors, as would have been the case in any European country.

So the future was America's, and into it marched Americans, laying step by step the foundations of a structure which, in time, was to be bulwark and beacon of the free world.

General George Washington

Gainsborough's portrait of Lieutenant General Charles Cornwallis was painted after Yorktown.

Opportunity Beckons in the South

After the Battle of Guilford Court House in March, 1781, Cornwallis, "quite tired of marching about the country," gave up chasing Greene. Turning to Virginia, a keystone of the Rebel war effort, he joined the traitor Arnold, now a British officer, in ravaging the state.

The summer months brought a dramatic quickening of events. Hoping for support from the French West Indies fleet, the French-American force in Newport moved south toward New York; and Clinton, envisioning a siege, ordered Cornwallis to pull back to a Chesapeake port and send him reinforcements. Actually, the over-cautious Clinton was quite secure, as Washington and the French commander, Rochambeau, soon perceived. When they received the heartening news that Admiral de Grasse's fleet had cleared the West Indies for Chesapeake Bay, the allied force set off at once for the little tobacco port of Yorktown, where Cornwallis lay. If de Grasse could reach the Chesapeake ahead of the Royal Navy, and hold the advantage, Cornwallis' entire army might be trapped.

The Siege of Yorktown

In Virginia Cornwallis dug in at Yorktown to await the Royal Navy. Early in September the allied army reached the head of Chesapeake Bay, where Rochambeau observed General Washington waving his hat at him in an attitude of elation mixed with relief. De Grasse's fleet had won the race and closed off the sea approaches to Yorktown. It was almost too much for the long-suffering Washington to believe.

Soon the allies, some 16,000 strong, were laying formal siege to Yorktown. The 1782 plan at left shows the opposing positions—British in red, French, brown, Americans, blue—before the town and on Gloucester Point across the York River. The besiegers tightened their death grip with the successful storming of two redoubts, and their guns soon enfiladed the British works. The "aweful music" of 52 allied guns continuously pounded Cornwallis' lines, causing a defender to write, "We could find no refuge in or out of the town."

On the night of October 14 two redoubts anchoring the left of the Yorktown lines were stormed, one by French, the other by Americans. Below, Rebels under Alexander Hamilton overrun the redcoats and raise the Stars and Stripes over the parapet.

Rochambeau (above) placed his French troops under Washington's command, and the two generals worked in close harmony during the campaign.

The Final Fruits
of the French Alliance

The painting above by Louis Van Blarenberghe, based on sketches by a French eyewitness, shows white-uniformed French troops marching into the siege lines around Yorktown while officers at center confer. On October 17, exactly four years after Burgoyne's surrender at Saratoga, Corn-

wallis wrote to Washington asking for a cease-fire, "to settle terms for the surrender of the posts of York & Gloucester." At 2 P.M. on October 19, 1781, as shown below by Van Blarenberghe, British bands struck up "The World Turned Upside Down," and the sullen redcoats quit their defenses.

Between ranks of French (rear) and Americans, they marched to the field at upper left to stack arms. That evening an American officer "noticed that the allied officers and soldiers could scarcely talk for laughing, and they could scarcely walk for jumping and dancing and singing as they went about."

Illumination.

COLONEL TILGHMAN, Aid
de Camp to his Excellency
General WASHINGTON, having
brought official acounts of the
SURRENDER of Lord Corn-
wallis, and the Garrifons of
York and Gloucefter, thofe Citizens who chufe to ILLUMI-
NATE on the GLORIOUS OC-
CASION, will do it this evening
at Six, and extinguifh their
lights at Nine o'clock.

Decorum and harmony are
earneftly recommended to every Citizen, and a general dif-
countenance to the leaft appearance of riot.

October 24, 1781.

*A Committee of Safety handbill (left) dated October 24, 1781, urged modera-
tion in celebrating the Yorktown victory. The Dutch print below, satirizing
Cornwallis' surrender, shows the Rebels (right background) as Indians. On the
near shore, Britain's emaciated cow of commerce is mocked by European enemies,
while an Englishman and a howling British lion mourn their empty war chest.*

England Accepts Defeat

The staggering news of Cornwallis' disaster reached England in late November, and Lord North received it "as he would have taken a ball in his breast." A war-weary nation called for peace, and Commons declared in March, 1782, that it "would consider as enemies to his Majesty and the Country all those who should advise or . . . attempt the further prosecution of offensive war on the Continent of North America." North's ministry fell, and peace commissioners were appointed by both sides.

Washington was not at all sure that Yorktown was the end. "My only apprehension," he wrote, "is lest the late important success, instead of exciting our exertions . . . should produce such a relaxation in the prosecution of the war, as will prolong the calamities of it." But Sir Guy Carleton, replacing Clinton as commanding general in America, proceeded to evacuate the cities of Savannah and Charleston "in consequence of an unsuccessful war."

Through the summer and fall of 1782 peace negotiators labored in Paris. On November 30 agreement was reached with the American commissioners, and when England came to terms with France and Spain, the formal treaty of peace was signed on September 3, 1783. Eight long, bitter years after a ragged volley was fired on Lexington Green, the war was officially over. America had won its independence.

In the delightful, distorted French view of Cornwallis' surrender at left, Yorktown appears as a medieval town, de Grasse's fleet is pointedly at water's edge, and the field of combat is dominated by the French, their officers on rearing mounts. Below, George III's proclamation called for a cessation of hostilities on February 14, 1783. The final peace treaty was signed some six months later.

By the KING.

A PROCLAMATION,

Declaring the Ceſſation of Arms, as well by Sea as Land, agreed upon between His Majeſty, the Moſt Chriſtian King, the King of *Spain*, the States General of the *United Provinces*, and the United States of *America*, and enjoining the Obſervance thereof.

GEORGE R.

HEREAS Proviſional Articles were ſigned at *Paris*, on the Thirtieth Day of *November* laſt, between Our Commiſſioner for treating of Peace with the Commiſſioners of the United States of *America* and the Commiſſioners of the ſaid States, to be inſerted in and to conſtitute the Treaty of Peace propoſed to be concluded between Us and the ſaid United States, when Terms of Peace ſhould be agreed upon between Us and His Moſt Chriſtian Majeſty: And whereas Preliminaries for reſtoring Peace between Us and His Moſt Chriſtian Majeſty were ſigned at *Verſailles* on the Twentieth Day of *January* laſt, by the Miniſters of Us and the Moſt Chriſtian King: And whereas Preliminaries for reſtoring Peace between Us and the King of *Spain*

Signing the Peace Treaty

When Benjamin West began painting the signing of the peace treaty, he started confidently with portraits (left to right) of John Jay, John Adams, Benjamin Franklin, Henry Laurens, and Franklin's grandson, William Temple Franklin, secretary to the American delegation. Unfortunately for West, the British commissioners refused to pose, and the picture was never finished.

ACKNOWLEDGMENTS AND INDEX

ACKNOWLEDGMENTS

The Editors are especially grateful to the following individuals and organizations for their generous assistance, and for their co-operation in making available pictorial materials in their collections:

The Abby Aldrich Rockefeller Folk Art Collection, Williamsburg, Va.—Mrs. Mary C. Black; The American Antiquarian Society, Worcester, Mass.—Clarence S. Brigham; The Archives of American Art, Detroit—Mrs. Miriam L. Lesley; The Bibliothèque Nationale, Paris—Mlle G. Antoine; The British Museum, London—B. P. C. Bridgewater; Mrs. John Nicholas Brown, Providence, R.I., and the Brown Collection librarian, Richard B. Harrington; The Chicago Historical Society—Mrs. Phyllis W. Healy, Mrs. Mary Frances Rhymer; Colonial Williamsburg, Inc., Williamsburg, Va.—Susan S. Armstrong; The Connecticut Historical Society, Hartford—Thompson R. Harlow; The Fort Ticonderoga (N.Y.) Museum—John H. G. Pell, Col. Edward P. Hamilton, Eleanor S. Murray; The Frick Art Reference Library, New York—Mrs. Henry W. Howell; The Henry E. Huntington Library and Art Gallery, San Marino, Calif.—Dorothy Bowen; The Henry Francis du Pont Winterthur (Del.) Museum—Dorothy W. Greer; The Historical Society of Pennsylvania, Philadelphia—R. N.

Williams, 2nd, J. Harcourt Givens, Sarah A. G. Smith; Frank T. Howard, Bryn Mawr, Pa.; Independence National Historical Park, Philadelphia—M. O. Anderson; The John Carter Brown Library, Providence—Marion W. Adams; The Library of Congress, Washington, D.C.—Virginia Daiker, Walter W. Ristow; *Life* Magazine—Dorothy L. Smith; The Mariners Museum, Warwick, Va.—Mrs. Agnes Brabrand, Mrs. Belinda Watkins; The Massachusetts Historical Society, Boston—Stephen T. Riley; The Metropolitan Museum of Art, New York—Janet Byrne, Mrs. Edward S. McGill; Morristown (N.J.) National Historical Park—Francis S. Ronalds; Musée National de la Coopération Franco-Américaine, Blérancourt, France—Max Terrier; The Museum of Fine Arts, Boston—Elizabeth P. Riegel; The National Archives, Washington, D.C.—Albert H. Leisinger, Jr.; The National Gallery of Art, Washington, D.C.—Huntington Cairns, Mrs. Elizabeth H. Ostertag; The National Gallery, London—M. F. Field; The National Maritime Museum, Greenwich, England—Michael S. Robinson, Miss P. Sichel; The National Portrait Gallery, London—Elizabeth Prevett; The New-York Historical Society—Carolyn Scoon, Arthur B. Carlson; The New York Public Library—Wilson G. Duprey,

Elizabeth E. Roth, Lewis M. Stark, Mrs. Maud D. Cole, John Gault; The New York State Historical Association, Cooperstown—Louis C. Jones; The Old Print Shop, New York—Harry Shaw Newman, Robert L. Harley; Harold L. Peterson, Arlington, Va.; The Philadelphia Museum of Art—Henry Clifford; The Pierpont Morgan Library, New York—Herbert Cahoon; The Public Archives of Canada, Ottawa—William Kaye Lamb; The Rhode Island Historical Society, Providence—Clifford P. Monahon; *Time* Magazine—Michael J. Phillips; The United States Naval Academy Museum, Annapolis, Md.—Captain Wade DeWeese; The Valley Forge (Pa.) Historical Society—R. R. Titus; The West Point (N.Y.) Museum—Frederick P. Todd; The William L. Clements Library, University of Michigan, Ann Arbor—Howard H. Peckham; The Yale University Art Gallery, New Haven, Conn.—Mrs. Elizabeth Burnham, Caroline Rollins, Mrs. Susan P. Collins.

Color photography of paintings: Herbert Loebel, Geoffrey Clements, New York; Charles P. Mills and Son, Philadelphia; George M. Cushing, Jr., Boston; Henry B. Beville, Washington, D.C.; Brian Seed (Black Star), London; Zoltan Wegner, London; Larry Burrows, London; Savitry (Rapho Guillumette), Paris.

PICTURE CREDITS

46 *The Wise Men of Gotham and their Goose:* William Humphrey, 1776; JCB Library **47** *Benjamin Franklin Before the Privy Council:* Christian Schussele, 1856; Huntington Library—*Magna Britannia: The Political Register,* 1767; JCB Library

THE EVE OF REVOLT: 48 Adams: Copley, *c.* 1770; City of Boston loan, Mus. of Fine Arts

Text Section: 50 Emmet Coll. NYPL **51** Patrick Campbell, *Travels,* 1793; Reserve Div. NYPL—J. Weld, *Travels,* 1799; Reserve Div. NYPL **52** Arents Coll. NYPL —Victor Collot, *Voyage,* 1826; Reserve Div. NYPL **53** Reserve Div. NYPL **54** LC **55** Print Div. NYPL **56** Pennsylvania *Journal,* 1765; Emmet Coll. NYPL **57** Pennsylvania *Journal,* 1765; Emmet Coll. NYPL—LC **58** Emmet Coll. NYPL **59** N-YHS—Hist. Soc. of Pa. **60** Metropolitan **61** Hist. Soc. of Pa. **62** Mass. Hist. Soc.—LC **63** Science Div. NYPL **64** Reserve Div. NYPL **65** Chamberlain Coll. Boston Public Library **66** AAS **67** *Royal American Magazine,* 1774; Spencer Coll. NYPL **68** Metropolitan—LC **69** Chicago Hist. Soc.—Metropolitan **70** N-YHS **71** Hist. Soc. of Pa.

Color Section: 73 *The Death of Wolfe* (detail): Benjamin West, 1770; National Gallery of Canada, Ottawa; courtesy *Life* **74** American settlement: after Thomas Pownall; *Scenographia Americana, c.* 1768; Spencer Coll. NYPL—Boone escorting pioneers: George Caleb Bingham, 1851; Washington University; courtesy *Time* **75** Travel on horseback: Benjamin Latrobe, *Journal;* NYPL—*The Residence of David Twining 1787:* Edward Hicks, *c.* 1845; Rockefeller Folk Art Coll.; courtesy *Ladies Home Journal* **76** Amory: Copley, *c.* 1768; Boston Mus. of Fine Arts—Portsmouth: Pierre Ozanne, 1778; Blérancourt **77** Salem: Joseph Orme, *c.* 1765; Essex Institute—Exchange table: Nathaniel Hurd, *c.* 1775; AAS **78** Rescinders bowl: Paul Revere, 1768; Boston Mus. of Fine Arts **78–79** Harvard: Revere, 1767; AAS **79** Revere: Copley, *c.* 1765; Boston Mus. of Fine Arts; courtesy *Time*—*Coasts of America,* 1766; Culver Service **80** Charleston: after T. Mellish; *Scenographia Americana, c.* 1768; Spencer Coll. NYPL—Indigo culture: after Henry Mouzon; Charleston Library Society—*The Old Plantation, c.* 1800; Rockefeller Folk Art. Coll.; courtesy *Ladies Home Journal* **81** Bruton Parish church: A. W. Thompson; Metropolitan—Tobacco wharf: Albert and Lotter map, 1784; Clements Library; courtesy CW **82** Trade card: James Smithers, *c.* 1770; Library Company of Philadelphia—Baltimore: after John Moale, 1752; Phelps Stokes Coll. NYPL **83** *Letters from a Farmer:* John Dickinson, 1768; Reserve Div. NYPL —Pennsylvania State House: after C. W. Peale; Hist. Soc. of Pa. **84–85** *Southeast Prospect of New York, c.* 1757; N-YHS **86** Henry: after Thomas Sully; CW—Paine: Bass Otis; Independence Hall—Hancock: Copley, 1765; City of Boston loan, Mus. of Fine Arts—Otis: Joseph Blackburn; Coll. of Mrs. Gertrude Hepp—Town meeting: John Trumbull, *M'Fingal,* 1795; LC **86–87** Williamsburg Capitol: Bodleian Plate, after John Bartram, *c.* 1740; CW—Snake and griffin: Revere, *Massachusetts Spy,* 1774; AAS **87** Colden: Matthew Pratt, 1772; Chamber of Commerce of the State of N.Y.—Hutchinson: attr. to Copley; Mass. Hist. Soc.—Dunmore: Reynolds; Coll. of Mrs. Elizabeth Murry loan, Scottish National Portrait Gallery **88** Halifax: Richard Short, 1777; OPS **89** Stamp collector effigy: Metropolitan—*Tory's Day of Judgement:* Elkanah Tisdale; Trumbull, *M'Fingal;* LC—Stamp: Emmet Coll. NYPL—*The Repeal:* Carrington Bowles, 1766; JCB Library **90** British troops landing in Boston: Revere, 1768; Winterthur; courtesy *Life* (Arnold Newman)—Boston Common: after Christian Remick, 1768; Phelps Stokes Coll. NYPL **91** Gage: Copley, *c.* 1768; Coll. of Colonel R. V. C. Bodley—Boston: J. B. Marston, 1801; Mass. Hist. Soc. **92** Boston Massacre: Revere, 1770; Metropolitan; courtesy *Life*—Coffins: Revere, 1770; LC **93** Whipple: Edward Savage; Naval Academy Mus.—Burning the *Gaspee:* C. D. W. Brownell, 1892; R.I. Hist. Soc. **94** Boston Tea Party; CW **94–95** Philadelphia: Thomas Birch, *c.* 1800; Hist. Soc. of Pa.

THE WAR BEGINS: 96 *Pulling Down the Statue of George III:* William Walcutt, 1854; Coll. of Gilbert Darlington

Text Section: 98 Hist. Soc. of Pa. **99** Benson J. Lossing, *The Pictorial Field-Book of the Revolution,* 1850—Emmet Coll. NYPL **100** AAS **101** Concord Antiquarian Soc.—Metropolitan **102** Conn. Hist. Soc.—Elroy M. Avery, *A History of the United States and its People,* 1908–9 **103** JCB Library **104** LC **105** Independence Hall—AAS **106** Chicago Hist. Soc.—Phelps Stokes Coll. NYPL **107** LC —Lexington Hist. Soc. **108** Boston Mus. of Fine Arts —Metropolitan **109** Conn. Hist. Soc. **110** NYPL **111** Mass. Hist. Soc.—Lossing, *op. cit.*

Color Section: 113 Pistols: Lexington Hist. Soc.—*A Plan of the Town and Harbour of Boston:* J. De Costa, 1775; JCB Library **114–115** Lexington and Concord: Amos Doolittle, 1775; Conn. Hist. Soc.; courtesy *Life* (114t & 115t)—Albany Institute of Hist. and Art; courtesy CW (114b & 115b) **116** Knox: Gilbert Stuart; City of Boston loan, Mus. of Fine Arts **116–117** Panorama of Boston: Lt. Williams, 1775; Mass. Hist. Soc. **117** Knox's artillery: Thomas Lovell; Joseph Dixon Crucible Co. **118** *The Battle of Bunker's Hill:* John Trumbull, 1786; Yale; courtesy *The World Book Encyclopedia* © Field Enterprises, Inc. **119** *An Exact View of The Late Battle at Charlestown:* Bernard Romans, 1775; JCB Library—*Bunkers Hill or America's Head Dress,* 1776; Winterthur—Evacuation of Boston: M. A. Wageman; N-YHS

FIRST CAMPAIGNS, NORTH AND SOUTH: 120 *The Death of General Montgomery in the Attack on Quebec* (detail): Trumbull, 1786; Yale

Text Section: 122 Manoir Richelieu Coll. of Canadiana **123** Independence Hall **124** Isaac Senter, *Journal;* Metropolitan—Public Archives of Canada **125** Phelps Stokes Coll. NYPL **126** Public Archives of Canada **127** N-YHS **128** OPS

Color Section: 129 *Arnold's March to Quebec:* N. C. Wyeth; Coll. of the Knoedler Galleries, N.Y.; courtesy Doubleday & Co.—Carleton: Coll. of Lieutenant Colonel Lord Dorchester **130** Quebec: Thomas Johnston, 1758; Phelps Stokes Coll. NYPL **131** Attack on Quebec: F. C. Yohn—Map: John Marshall, *The Life of George Washington,* Atlas, 1807; Map Div. NYPL—Death of Montgomery: E. F. Burney, 1789; Brown Coll. **132** Map: William Faden, 1776; Map Div. NYPL **132–133** *The Engagement on Lake Champlain:* H. Gilder, *c.* 1776; Cumberland Papers, Royal Coll. Windsor Castle, by Gracious Permission of H. M. the Queen **133** *God Bless our Armes, c.* 1776; Ft. Ticonderoga Mus. **134** Map; OPS **134–135** *Battle of Fort Moultrie:* John Blake White; The Capitol, Washington **135** Clinton: Thomas Day; Coll. of Vinton Freedley; courtesy Frick—Moultrie: Peale, 1782; Gibbes Art Gallery, Charleston—Parker: L. F. Abbott; NMM

THE DAY OF FREEDOM: 136 *The Declaration of Independence* (detail): Trumbull, *c.* 1786-96; Yale

Text Section: 138 Manuscript Div. NYPL **139** U.S. District Court, Philadelphia—Independence Hall **140** LC **141** Brown Coll. **142** From *Congress Voting Independence:* Pine and Savage; LC **143** N-YHS—Independence Hall **144** Yale—Independence Hall **145–148** LC **149** Independence Hall (both) **150** Metropolitan **151** Ft. Ticonderoga Mus.—Hist. Soc. of Pa. **152** Lossing, *op. cit.*

ARMS AND MEN: 153 *Surrender of Lord Cornwallis at Yorktown* (detail): Trumbull, *c.* 1786-96; Yale **154** Drill exercises: William Windham, *A Plan of Discipline,* 1759; NYPL—Drill positions: Timothy Pickering, *An Easy Plan of Discipline for a Militia,* 1775; Mass. Hist. Soc. **155** *Six-Pence a Day:* William Humphrey, 1775; Chicago Hist. Soc.—*Recruiting Serjeant:* William Humphrey, 1779; Brown Coll. **156–157** Small arms: Peterson Coll. (except Ferguson rifle, Smithsonian Institution); photographs, Henry B. Beville **158** Powder horn: Peterson Coll.—Cannon: C. W. Peale, *Diary,* 1778; American Philosophical Soc. **159** Gunner's calipers: Peterson Coll.—Examples of artillery: John Muller, *Treatise of Artillery,* 1768; Peterson Coll.—Ammunition wagon: Morristown National Hist. Park—Refining saltpeter: Revere, *Royal American Magazine,* 1774; Reserve Div. NYPL **160** Blockhouse: Thomas Anburey, *Travels,* 1789; Clements Library —Redoubt, 1776; Clinton Papers, Clements Library **160–161** *Military Architecture:* Bowles and Carver; Ft. Ticonderoga Mus. **162** Morristown camp; Morristown National Hist. Park—Newgate prison: Richard Brunton, *c.* 1799; Conn. Hist. Soc. **162–163** British camp: John Ward Dunsmore; N-YHS **163** Prisoners starving: Trumbull, *c.* 1780; Fordham University; courtesy Frick **164–165** Uniforms and equipment: West Point Mus.; Ft. Ticonderoga Mus.; Washington's Headquarters and Mus., Newburgh, N.Y.; Coll. of H. Charles McBarron; photograph, Arnold Newman **166–167** American soldiers and flag: Brown Coll.—Drum: Guilford Court House National Military Park **168–169** *Departure of Smallwood's Command from Annapolis:* A. W. Thompson; 175th Infantry, Maryland National Guard, Baltimore **169** Smallwood: Peale, 1782; Independence Hall—Flag: Gherardi Davis, *Regimental Colors in the War of the Revolution,* 1907; Reserve Div. NYPL **170** British flags: Davis, *op. cit.;* Reserve Div. NYPL—British soldier: Robert Sayer, 1786; Brown Coll. **170–171** *A Perspective View of an Encampment:* Bowles and Carver, 1780; Brown Coll. **172–173** German uniforms: J. H. Carl, *Hochfürst. Hessiches Corps, c.* 1784; Brown Coll. **173** Broadside, 1776; Hist. Soc. of Pa.—German helmet: Essex Institute—German flag: Davis, *op. cit.;* Reserve Div. NYPL **174** French flags: Davis, *op. cit.;* Reserve Div. NYPL—Rochambeau drilling troops: Thomas Colley, 1780; LC **174–175** French uniforms: studio of Nicolas Hoffman; Blérancourt

THE CRISIS: 176 Washington at Trenton: Sully; Union League of Philadelphia

Text Section: 178 Lossing, *op. cit.* **179** Phelps Stokes Coll. NYPL—JCB Library **180** Brown Coll. **181** Brown Coll. **182** Isaac Stuart, *Life of Captain Nathan Hale,* 1856 **183** Lossing, *op. cit.*—Phelps Stokes Coll. NYPL **184** Spencer Coll. NYPL—Brown Coll. **185** Phelps Stokes Coll. NYPL—Metropolitan **186** Lossing, *op. cit.* **187** West Point Mus. **188** Reserve Div. NYPL **189** N-YHS—Metropolitan **190** Lossing, *op. cit.*—Huntington Library **191** Princeton University Library **192** Princeton University Library

Color Section: 193 British squadron on the Hudson: attr. to C. T. Warren; Bailey Coll. Mariners Mus.; courtesy U.S. Naval Institute—Howe: C. Corbutt, 1777; Brown Coll. **194** *Howe War Plan:* William Faden, 1776; Phelps Stokes Coll. NYPL **195** British camp on Staten Island: Archibald Robertson, 1776; Spencer Coll. NYPL —Attack by fire ships: after James Wallace; *The Atlantic Neptune,* 1778; Mariners Mus. **196** *Battle of Long Island:* Alonzo Chappel; Coll. of William H. Duncan; courtesy CW **197** Putnam: Trumbull, 1790; Putnam Phalanx, Hartford; courtesy Wadsworth Atheneum—Stirling: Bass Otis; Independence Hall—Glover: after Trumbull; Francis S. Drake, *Life and Correspondence of Henry Knox,* 1873—Retreat from Long Island: M. A. Wageman; Emmet Coll. NYPL **198** Kip's Bay landing: Archibald Robertson, 1776; Spencer Coll. NYPL **198–199** Views of British occupation of New York: François X. Habermann, 1776; Morristown National Hist. Park **199** *Battle of Harlem Heights:* after Chappel; Emmet Coll. NYPL **200** *Forcing the Hudson River Passage:* Dominic Serres; Naval Academy Mus. **201** Attack on Fort Washington: Thomas Davies, 1776; Phelps Stokes Coll. NYPL; courtesy *Life*—Attack on Fort Lee; Thomas Davies, 1776; Emmet Coll. NYPL; courtesy *Life* **202** Map: William Faden, 1777; N-YHS—Retreat through New Jersey: John L. Thomson, *History . . . of the Revolution,* 1873 **203** Capture of Lee; Ft. Ticonderoga Mus.—Crossing the Delaware: Edward Hicks, *c.* 1834; Coll. of Nina Fletcher Little; courtesy *Life* **204** Battle of Trenton: after E. L. Henry; OPS; courtesy *Life*—Knox's headquarters: Drake, *op. cit.* **205** Captured Hessians: Johann Ramberg, *c.* 1784; Metropolitan—*Capture of the Hessians at Trenton:* Trumbull, *c.* 1786–96; Yale; courtesy *Time* **206–207** Nassau Hall: after H. Dawkins; Little Print Shop, Princeton, N.J.—*Battle of Princeton:* William Mercer; Hist. Soc. of Pa.

THE MAKING OF AN ARMY: 208 Washington at Valley Forge: W. Trego; Valley Forge Hist. Soc.

Text Section: 210 NYPL **211** Emmet Coll. NYPL **212** Emmet Coll. NYPL—Fordham University; courtesy Frick **213** Emmet Col. NYPL—JCB Library **214** Hist. Soc. of Pa. **215** George Weedon, *Orderly Book;* American Philosophical Soc.—NYPL **216** Phelps Stokes Coll. NYPL **217** Emmet Coll. NYPL **218** NYPL—Hist. Soc. of Pa. **219** Emmet Coll. NYPL **220** Independence Hall —Brown Coll. **221** LC **222** NYPL **223** Monmouth County Hist. Assoc.

Color Section: 225 *Battle of Paoli:* Xavier Della Gatta, 1782; Valley Forge Hist. Soc. **226** Wayne: Edward Savage; N-YHS **226–227** *Battle of Germantown:* Della Gatta, 1782; Valley Forge Hist. Soc. **228** *Mischianza:* J. F. Watson, *Annals of Philadelphia,* 1884—*State of the English*

INDEX